Glory Days

When horsepower and passion ruled Detroit

A Memoir by Jim Wangers

with Paul Zazarine

RB
ROBERT BENTLEY, INC.
AUTOMOTIVE PUBLISHERS

Glory Days

When horsepower and passion ruled Detroit

"Get one before you're too old to understand." *Page 175*

The Grand Prix emblem was the inspiration for the famous Royal Bobcat emblem. Page 77

Copies of this book may be purchased from selected booksellers, or directly from the publisher by mail. The publisher encourages comments from the reader of this book. Please write to Robert Bentley, Inc., Publishers at the address listed at the bottom of this page.

Since this page cannot legibly accommodate all the copyright notices, the Art Credits page at the back of this book listing the source of the photographs used constitutes an extension of the copyright page.

Library of Congress Cataloging-in-Publication Data

Wangers, Jim.
Glory days : when horsepower and passion ruled Detroit : a memoir / by Jim Wangers with Paul Zazarine.
p. cm.
Includes index.
ISBN 0-8376-0207-6 (alk. paper)
1. Wangers, Jim. 2. Automobile industry and trade--United States--Biography. 3. Pontiac automobile--Marketing--History.
I. Zazarine, Paul, 1952– II. Title
HD9710.U52W28 1998
338.7'6292'092--dc21
[B] 98-28711
CIP

Bentley Stock No. GGTO

00 99 98 8 7 6 5 4 3 2

The paper used in this publication is acid free and meets the requirements of the National Standard for Information Sciences-Permanence of Paper for Printed Library Materials. ∞

Glory Days: When Horsepower and Passion Ruled Detroit, by Jim Wangers, with Paul Zazarine

Manufactured in the United States of America

Cover Photo courtesy of Paul Zazarine.

RB ROBERT BENTLEY, INC. | AUTOMOTIVE PUBLISHERS

Information that makes the difference.®

1734 Massachusetts Avenue
Cambridge, MA 02138 USA
800-423-4595 / 617-547-4170
http://www.rb.com
e-mail: sales@rb.com

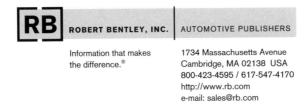

Introduction

It's Friday night and the traffic on Woodward Avenue for the Dream Cruise is already wall-to-wall. The crowd on both sides of the street is ten deep. My friend Eric Schiffer is driving my 1969 GTO Judge. The Michigan license plates read "Wangers." As we slowly creep along Woodward at 14 Mile, a teenage kid runs up to the Judge and pleads, "Do you guys know Jim Wangers?" Before I can answer, he asks again, "Did he really invent Woodward Avenue?"

WOODWARD AVENUE RUNS arrow-straight for 20 miles, connecting Detroit to the city of Pontiac. Along Woodward are suburban communities like Royal Oak, Ferndale and Birmingham. In the sixties, Woodward was the scene of the most incredible street action you could imagine. From 10 Mile Road in Royal Oak to Square Lake Road (about ten miles to the north) at the fringe of Pontiac, kids would bring their cars out to cruise. Every night Woodward would vibrate with excitement as cars cruised four abreast down Woodward's wide expanse.

I was there both as a spectator and a participant. Every morning I left my home in Royal Oak and drove north on Woodward to my office at MacManus John & Adams, Pontiac's ad agency. My office overlooked Woodward. When I drove home at night, chances were I'd get into at least one stoplight challenge. I knew Woodward, I knew the kids, and what it meant for them to win. I guess I was the biggest kid of all.

Over three decades ago, local communities and the police struggled to keep the racing under control. Eventually, Woodward was abandoned by the cruisers because of local pressure. Cruising on the wide boulevard became extinct.

Ironically, the same communities that worked so hard to end the cruising on Woodward in the sixties have banded together now in the nineties to enshrine the Golden Era. The event, known as the Woodward Dream Cruise, is a tribute to the days of musclecars and street performance. I am honored to be invited back regularly.

Over one million people and at least 30,000 cars, trucks and rods participate in these modern day Dream Cruise activities, making it the largest one-day automotive event in the world. Of course, the traffic is so jammed that it's impossible to average more than 10 miles per hour, but who cares? All of the American car makers are here with huge displays. Up and down the Avenue, there are car shows, parties, and dances.

On a typical Cruise weekend, I'll have the pleasure to meet and talk with many people who remember those wonderful days. I am often reminded just how much I had shaped their experiences and their enjoyment. I was fortunate enough to have been a part of John DeLorean's talented team at Pontiac, and was able to transmit to DeLorean the pulse of what was happening on the "avenue." DeLorean listened, and the result was a long line of Pontiac performance legends like the GTO, the Grand Prix, and the Trans Am.

I was passionate about my job, and that passion came easy.

My Judge is parked on a Birmingham street amidst a lineup of other musclecars. Through the crowd, a guy spots the "Wangers" license plates and walks up. "Is that Jim Wangers' car?" he asks. "Do you guys know him? I bet it's got a Ram Air V in there. When Wangers came out on Woodward, he was ready. I used to race him and his Royal Bobcats. No matter what you had, he had better!"

Dedicated to Duncan Michael and Ed Dufrene
Who have made the last half
Every bit as good as the first half

1

Early Fever

1 *First Crush on Cars*

FROM THE TIME I WAS A KID, I was nuts about cars.

I can remember when I used to go to school in the morning, whether there was two feet of snow on the ground or it was so hot outside you couldn't stand it, I would come out of my house, which was right in the city of Chicago, and get into my little imaginary car and start the engine by turning the key and stepping on the starter. That was how you started a car in those days. I even had what I thought was a pretty good imitation of an engine sound. On cold mornings, I stood there freezing my ass off while I was warming up my "car." Then I would put it in gear and drive away. I could even imitate the difference in engine sound between a Ford V-8 and the old Chevy stove-bolt six.

I used to collect *Saturday Evening Post* and *Life* magazines. They were my Bibles. I would go through every issue and cut out the automobile ads. Eventually I cut the cars out of the ads and put them on my bedroom wall. Most kids would think it was fun if you sat back and threw darts at them or something, but to me they were so sacred and so treasured that I wasn't about to do anything to desecrate them. Now that I think back about this, those ads first helped me to understand the exciting sales war that existed between Ford and Chevy and Plymouth. I would sometimes sit on my favorite street corner and watch the cars go by and count them. For example, if 53 Chevys passed, but only 49 Fords, I thought, "Chevys are more popular." From that early age, I decided that I had to be in the automobile business.

One of my very first experiences in the auto world happened at the 1938 Chicago Auto Show. I was not quite 12 at the time. The Chicago Auto show was the biggest in the U.S., where a lot of new models were introduced and a lot of money was spent on fantastic exhibits. Oldsmobile was presenting their new Hydra-matic transmission by showing a giant steering wheel and a

2

First "Ad Copy"

Left: (from left to right) My cousin Don Rappeport, my brother Bob age 7-1/2, and myself at age 5. Right: Leaning against the door of my dad's '37 Chevrolet in 1941. Notice the "hammered" front fender. My father was not a car guy, so washing the car or having body damage repaired was never a priority for him.

giant shift lever quadrant on the steering column. It was Friday night, the opening night of the show. A photographer from *The Chicago Daily News*, one of Chicago's major evening newspapers (big cities had many more "dailies" then than they do today), was looking to get a good picture of this exhibit. I was standing starry-eyed at the rotating circular exhibit, and I guess I must have given him a good impression. He said, "What's your name, kid?" I told him and he said, "Come on up here." Well, the steering wheel was bigger than I was. I had to reach out with both hands to grab it. He said, "Put one hand on one of the spokes of the steering wheel and put your other hand on the gear shift lever." He took the picture, and sure enough it showed up in the Saturday edition of *The Daily News*. The caption read, "11-year old Jimmy takes a turn on Oldsmobile's new Hydra-matic column shift lever." That was the first time I ever had my picture in the newspaper. Wow! Was I happy!

Looking back, I suppose I should have known I was destined to write ad copy, because a few years later I won a pretty significant contest. Hudson Motor Co. and its Chicago area dealers sponsored a contest open to all Chicago high school students. You had to describe in 150 words or less why you felt that Hudson was America's safest car. I went to a Hudson dealer, got the entry blank, wrote my 150 words and won the contest. I won a hundred bucks, which was big money in those days and, again, I got my picture in the local papers. Again...wow! But I wish I had won a new Hudson.

* * *

WHY HUDSON IS AMERICA'S SAFEST CAR.

SCREECH! BANG! CRASH!!!

"Honest Officer I couldn't help it, my brakes just wouldn't hold any tighter."

Crumpled fenders, broken windows and other serious damages can all be avoided by having brakes that will work and not falter when needed. What a feeling it is to have a set of brakes on your car that you can rely upon.

Believe it or not, the type on your car, Hydraulic, can fail as well as any other kind of brake because the vital fluid needed by them may evaporate and then they become totally ineffective. In a HUDSON it is a different story. If the Hydraulic fails the mechanical brakes controlled by the same pedal operate immediately to bring the car to a stop.

I am sure you must have turned a sharp corner or curve in your present make of car when the entire body and chassis tipped to one side throwing everybody awkwardly around.

But with HUDSON'S new "Auto Poise Control" every bit of possible swaying on a turn can be checked. Also with the new "Turn Indicator" possibilities of collisions from the rear are substantially reduced.

With these and many other exclusive features unquestionably HUDSON is "America's Safest Car," and again in 1941

"HUDSON'S THE CAR,
SAFEST BY FAR."

Submitted by: ____________

Senn High School,
5900 Glenwood Ave.,
Chicago, Ill.

This is a copy of my entry into the Hudson writing contest. I was 14 when I wrote why Hudson's features made it "Safest By Far." I won the contest and $100, which was a lot of money in 1941.

3

First "Ad Copy"

I WAS BORN AND RAISED ON THE NORTH side of Chicago, in a little community called Uptown, which in those days was still nice. I grew up in a middle class home. My father was in the map publishing business, and we got along okay.

We always had Chevys, but no one in my family shared my love for cars. My older brother Bob was passively interested in them, and my dad couldn't have cared less. As a matter of fact, he took abominable care of his gray 1927 Chevrolet two-door Coach (what we called a two-door sedan in those days). My mother had a matching gray '27 Chevy Coach that my grandfather won in a church raffle and had given to her. Our house had a small garage out back, and that's where my mother's car was always parked, while my dad's car stood outside. I made a career of keeping her car clean and shiny. All of that ended when my father's car was stolen and he took over use of my mother's car. We no longer had twin Chevys.

When I graduated from high school, the U.S. was already embroiled in World War II, so while I was still only seventeen, it was apparent that the

CV17 USS Bunker Hill was recovering from extensive Kamikaze damage at the Navy docks in Bremerton, Washington in 1944 when I was assigned to the ship as a radio operator. I was lucky enough to snap this picture of the Bunker Hill during her refittment. I ended up making lots of copies and selling them to my shipmates.

smart thing for me to do was to go into the service before the service came looking for me. I enlisted in the Navy. With no college I wasn't a serious candidate for any kind of special training. I ended up on the USS Bunker Hill, an Essex class aircraft carrier, as a radio operator. The War ended before I saw any action, and I spent the next two years going back and forth in the Pacific, bringing troops home.

Auto production had started back up late in 1945. Since I had lots of time on my hands on the Bunker Hill I wrote letters to all the automobile manufacturers to get their catalogs (there were no popular car magazines published then). It was my way of keeping informed. We'd get to port and I'd pick up my mail, which would consist of many boxes loaded with catalogs. I used to sit there and read those car catalogs like other guys read girlie magazines. Some of my shipmates used to ask if I was selling cars on the side. I was too dumb to realize that might have been a good idea. I came out of the Navy as a Radioman, 3rd Class, in the summer of 1946.

WHEN I CAME OUT OF THE SERVICE, I focussed on going to college, at the Illinois Institute of Technology, in Chicago, courtesy of the U.S. government. It turned out to be my first dose of reality.

In high school I had been totally committed to my own little private world of automobiles. I didn't want to be a salesman, and I didn't want to be a dealer. I wanted to go where they made cars. I wanted to get involved in designing cars, and that meant I needed to be an engineer. I had been a lousy engineering student in high school—I disliked mathematics and physics and could never really understand chemistry—but I did a pretty good job of faking it and getting good enough grades. At least I looked qualified when my record was examined.

But I was simply not prepared for college. I was just plain lousy in learning math, and I was even worse in understanding physics and chemistry—all the things you have to know if you want to be an engineer and design cars. Here I was enrolled in a first class engineering school, having to put in an incredible amount of time studying just to get a passing grade. I never flunked anything, but I sure came close. That turned out to be two of the worst years of my life: for the first time, I was actually involved in something I couldn't do very well.

Finally, at the point of throwing in the towel, I went to see my counselor. I explained that I wanted to be an engineer and that I wanted to be involved with the automobile industry. I was aware enough to know that the country was on the brink of a real boom. Everybody in the service had come home hungry for a new car. This pent-up demand would fuel the car market for many years, and I wanted to be in the thick of it. As I explained all this to him, he examined my pitiful engineering grades. He started chuckling. My counselor was probably in his early 30s and had been in the war. He looked at me and said something I will never forget. "Did you ever stop to think that somebody's got to sell all these cars? It may be a seller's market now, but there will come a time when there are more cars than there are buyers."

With that simple remark, he changed my life.

I realized that I could be involved in the automobile business without being an engineer. There was an awful lot of marketing and advertising and promoting and just plain selling that had to be done. My counselor suggested I struggle through engineering for the rest of that semester, then immediately transfer into the Liberal Arts or Business school. That fall I enrolled in the liberal arts school and discovered a whole new world. I had no trouble getting As and Bs, and worked toward a Bachelor's degree in English.

IT WAS WHILE I WAS IN SCHOOL THAT I put together my first real promotion. I was a good writer and worked for the college newspaper. Eventually I became the Managing Editor. Part of the responsibilities of that job was handling promotions, and one of my first projects was a home run.

Intramural sports at Illinois Tech was very popular, so I decided to build a contest around the intramural basketball championships. The tournament lasted about two weeks—something like the Final Four basketball tournament today. The contest was to pick the team that you thought was going to win the tournament and then write in 25 words or less why you thought they would win. This was in the spring of 1949. I had been reading about how the new 1949 Ford was totally redesigned and was the big news in the car business, so I decided to make a new 1949 Ford Custom model two-door the grand prize in our contest.

We contacted Ford's District Office in Chicago, explaining to them exactly what we had planned. Their new 1949 car was not out yet. In fact, as a mid-year model it would be introduced just about the same time that our tournament was over and we picked a winner. The Ford people were very cooperative. They agreed to provide a 1949 Custom model Ford for our winner. Imagine, a college newspaper giving away a car, especially a new car that was

The winner of the Illinois Tech contest, Tom Murray, carefully inspects his grand prize, a "new model" 1949 Ford. He good-naturedly went along with our spoof. Later on he received the use of a real '49 Ford for one month.

A 1949 *"Model Ford"*

making headlines. We didn't stop there. We contacted the local Coca-Cola distributor to have them provide many cases of Coke as runners-up prizes. We pushed the contest as hard as we could, and the excitement on campus was almost unbelievable.

The whole promotion would climax at the end of the final game on Saturday night, with the awards ceremony and a school dance. Interest built up fast and we ended up with more than 15 thousand entries. When we made the announcement in dramatic fashion there were probably five thousand people on hand. We darkened the gym as the winner's name was announced. This guy came running down out of the stands with the crowd roaring, expecting his car, as the Ford Custom model two-door drove into the gym on its own power—and that's just what it was, a model. I had a student from the electrical engineering school rig up the 1/25th scale Ford with a trailer that carried batteries, so the car could drive itself. The whole show was a huge spoof. The winner was down there in the spotlight. The gym doors opened up just wide enough to pass the model car, pulling the trailer. It was mayhem! Everyone realized at once they had been "had."

As you might expect, the paper received all kinds of angry mail and phone calls. We were accused of being cheaters, but from my point of view we had done nothing wrong. Nobody lost any money. We weren't in any serious trouble with the school administration, since they knew about the contest beforehand and had approved it. Actually, the guy who won did have free use of a new Ford for one month, just as the District Office had promised, and in those days a free car for one month was a big deal. Thus ended my first car promotion, and boy, did it work!

* * *

7

First Jobs

WHEN I GRADUATED IN 1949 I HAD no idea how to get into the car business. If I had stayed in engineering, I could have had my choice of jobs with any car company. Instead of going right into graduate work like I should have, I was somewhat pleased with my writing capabilities, and encouraged with my experience on the college newspaper, so I decided to look around Chicago for any kind of copywriting job.

After a fruitless period of searching, I successfully made contact with the *Chicago Daily News*. They offered me a job as a copyboy, at $27 per week. After all, this was my first job, and working for a big city newspaper sounded like a great opportunity. You didn't do anything glamorous as a copyboy, but you had a chance to meet important people and—if you kept your eyes and ears open and your big mouth closed—you could really learn about the business. The city editor of the paper was Mr. Clem Lane, and in his day he was quite a colorful character. He had white bushy hair and a stern, almost gruff presence. The city desk was his domain. When he wanted a copyboy he would holler, "Boy! Boy!" and you made sure you got over there fast. Clem Lane became a mentor and taught me a lot about the business.

I was there only four months when I got an opportunity to cover a high school basketball tournament for the sports department. At that time there were about 50 schools in Chicago participating in this holiday tournament. Covering this high school "stuff" was a "pain in the ass" to the guys in the sports department, so they were happy to give it to me. Frankly, because of Mr. Lane, I did a decent job and the next thing I knew I was getting more opportunities to cover high school sports, some even with a byline. The sports editor at the time was another of Chicago journalism's fabled characters, John P. Carmichael. He was a real pro and someone else who taught me a lot.

It was a big deal in those days, being a high school sports writer for a big daily newspaper—and also good experience. I was getting bylines once or twice a week and was feeling very good about myself. I got a tremendous raise, to $37 a week, and even though it was fun I soon realized that no one in the newspaper business was making serious money. Being a reporter was a labor of love, and I couldn't eat on just that. I had nearly a year of experience at the paper, so I started to look around the city for another writing job. I hadn't forgotten my devotion to the automobile, but in Chicago, there wasn't much I could find that combined my writing experience and the car business. There was one advertising agency in the city with a car account, Roche, Williams and Cleary, serving Studebaker. I knocked on their door at least ten times over the next year, but never got in far enough to even tell them my name.

Finally, I made a connection with the last national magazine publisher left in Chicago, Esquire. They even had their own building. I was hired as a circulation promotion copywriter on *Coronet*, a *Readers Digest* look-a-like magazine they were trying to make into a major success. My new salary of $55 a week was not bad money for a young guy only a year out of school. My job was writing cold subscription letters to potential new subscribers to *Coronet*.

I had saved a few dollars, and now that I had a decent job I started thinking about getting my own car. Ironically, for a guy who was that crazy about cars, all of the time I was in college and then working for $27 a week I hadn't owned my own car. In 1950, when I was 24 years old, I bought a 1947 Studebaker Commander Starlight Coupe with a flat-head six and a 3-speed stick, on the column, with overdrive. I chose it because it was new-looking and reasonably priced, but it wasn't very fast. The '47 lasted just long enough to get me interested in another Studebaker, a 1950 Commander Starlight Coupe that was cream-colored with a brown cloth interior. It was a gorgeous car, but what a slug! I hung onto that one just long enough for the '51 Studebakers to become affordable, which were now equipped with their first V-8 engine. I bought a demo with six thousand miles for $1700. This was a lot of money for me, but I just had to have that V-8!

In the late forties, the first car enthusiast magazines began hitting the newsstands, and like all gearheads I couldn't get enough of them. I started reading about how to hop-up a car, and it didn't take me long to start "screwin'" with my V-8 Studebaker. First it was a Weiand intake manifold with two dual-throat Stromberg carburetors; then came a new camshaft, the necessary heavy duty clutch assembly, and a dual exhaust system. I didn't really know what I was doing, but if *Hot Rod* Magazine said it worked, then I had to have it.

After finding my way around within the Esquire company, I learned I was to be placed in a special promotion group that met each month, before the next issue of *Coronet* was to go to press. We looked through every article and tried to figure out what promotional tie-in opportunities we could exploit. For example, the number one story in a particular issue might be a personal profile of Ed Sullivan, who was very popular at the time. Sullivan's TV show was sponsored by the Lincoln-Mercury dealers, so we would approach Lincoln-Mercury, tell them about this story and pitch all kinds of promotional tie-in opportunities. We would offer everything from posters for their showrooms to mailing inserts for their invoice billings. This was right up my alley and I loved it. It was really the highlight of my activity on *Coronet*, since most of my time was still spent writing those dumb subscription letters (I guess someone has to do it, because it works!).

I HAD BEEN WITH ESQUIRE ABOUT eight months and was beginning to master the "dark art" of writing subscription letters when management decided it was time to move their operation to New York City. They felt they could buy more creative talent there for less money. If you were making serious money, you weren't asked to move. Fortunately, I was low enough on the totempole that I was offered the opportunity to go.

Did I want to move to New York, or look for another job in Chicago? By now I had owned three Studebakers and had become somewhat of an expert on them. I thought that the only automotive opportunity for me in Chicago was at Studebaker or their ad agency, but both doors had been slammed in my face many times. My burning desire to get into the car industry hadn't waned, it had been moved temporarily to the back burner, so like so many young employees at Esquire, I chose the Big Apple. Some, however, refused the move. The guy who shared my office, writing subscription letters for *Esquire* magazine at the time, was one of them.

We had worked in the same small office with our desks crammed back-to-back for about six months. He was a scrawny guy, very morose, very quiet, and difficult to talk with. If you asked him to lunch he always had something else to do. It seemed like he was purposely aloof. When he did talk, it was mostly about his wife, and it was rarely positive. Frankly, he never had much nice to say about anything.

We were both invited to go to New York. Management made a big point out of calling us up to their office to tell us. On the way back down to our office this guy finally opens up. "Go to New York with these assholes? Are they nuts? And you shouldn't go either," he told me. "I'm gonna make you an offer that you can't turn down. Why don't you stay here in Chicago with me. I know what you can do," he went on. "I've read your stuff. I'm going to start another magazine and teach these guys how to reach young American men. *Esquire* is a piece of crap."

A Chance to Become a "Playboy"

Surprised as I listened to his ground floor offer, I decided to pass. As a result, I went to New York still writing those damned subscription letters, while Hugh Hefner stayed on in Chicago to start his own magazine. He called it *Playboy.* And he did in fact show them. So chalk that one up to one of the worst career choices I ever made. On the other hand, when I look back, I didn't like the guy and our working relationship probably wouldn't have lasted very long.

Hefner was very talented, though. While he was working next to me he published a book of cartoons, a series of pencil sketches about life in Chicago. The name of the book was "That Toddlin' Town," and they sold pretty well. I bet that book is an incredible collector's item today.

SHORTLY AFTER I MOVED TO NEW YORK I became acquainted with a young girl who was also working for Esquire. She was a lovely gal named Sylvia Horwitz. She was a very bright and attractive New York-bred girl. I started to have lunch with her, and it wasn't long before we were dating. We got to know each other very well, and the more time I spent with her the more I liked her. Now, I'm not sure I knew what it meant to be in love, but I was sure I was getting there fast. Finally, she took me home and introduced me to her father, who turned out to be the Chairman of the Board of the Barricini Candy Company, a very successful chocolate candy maker headquartered in Manhattan, with a chain of stores all over the area.

While I was getting deeply involved with Sylvia, I began to grow restless with my situation at Esquire. Every waking hour that I wasn't chained to my desk or spending some lovely hours with Sylvia, I was reading car magazines or the *Wall Street Journal* or the *New York Times* financial sections, all of which covered the auto industry in depth.

Finally I decided that it was time I really did what I wanted to do with my life. I had almost two years of successful creative writing under my belt, and although I didn't have much real automotive experience, I did have a damn good knowledge of automobiles and a driving passion to be in the business. So I decided, with Sylvia's support, that it was time to make an assault on the auto industry and try to get into the business I believed I was destined for.

I had become friendly with Esquire's national advertising manager, Joe Arnstein, and talked with him about what I wanted to do. "Look," he said, "I can help you. I know most of these guys personally. First, write a letter of self-introduction and include a resume. I'll give you our list of names and personal addresses. These will be all the important people, both at the auto companies and their ad agencies."

I took the list he gave me and wrote the letters. I was pretty naive. I described myself as a guy with a college degree who had been in the communications business for about two years. At that time I had just started to do some graduate work in journalism and marketing at Columbia University. I included my resume and sent out over 50 letters. I received four answers. One came from the Buick zone office in New York City advising me to make a phone appointment with a Mr. Frank Bridge, the Eastern Regional Sales Manager. Another came from Chevrolet, suggesting I come to Detroit (on my own) and get my name on their list. The third one was from the Detroit ad agency, Brooks, Smith, French and Dorrance. They handled Hudson Motor Co.'s advertising. They invited me, without offering to fly me, to come to Detroit to meet with them. If I wanted to wait until one of their executives would be in New York, they would be happy to interview me then, but couldn't promise me when that might happen.

The last letter was from Chuck Leonard, ad manager of Kaiser-Frazer. Kaiser-Frazer had recently undergone a major reorganization and had changed their ad agency, awarding the account to a New York shop, W. H. Weintraub & Co. As coincidence would have it, Bill Weintraub himself was one of the co-founders of *Esquire* magazine. Weintraub had left *Esquire* a few years back and had built a pretty successful ad agency. His biggest account was Revlon, the cosmetic giant, but at that point he was interested in staffing his new Kaiser account. Chuck Leonard at Kaiser was pretty gutsy and aggressive—plus he was the only one who offered to fly me to Detroit.

I'll never forget the day I flew into Detroit. We met at the K/F facility at Willow Run, near the airport. I had a good interview and seemed to impress Leonard, not with any knowledge of the car business but with my enthusiasm and knowledge of cars in general, especially with his new 1952 Kaiser Manhattan. At the end of my interview Leonard said, "I don't think I need you here in Detroit as much as I need you back in New York, with our new ad agency. Frankly, they don't know anything about our car, but they can do some nice advertising." Leonard felt I could help the most by using my product knowledge.

"I'm going to set up an interview for you back in New York with Bill Weintraub," Leonard said. "I want you to meet Bill himself, and a guy named John Morris." Morris was the account supervisor. "Do you know where Madison Avenue is in New York?" he asked me. "I work on that street," I replied.

"Do you know where 488 Madison Avenue is?" he then asked. I didn't tell him why I knew very well where 488 Madison Avenue was; it was actually the building where I worked!

I had succeeded in getting my foot in the door. I wasn't hired yet, but I was sure feeling good, and I still had another appointment. I jumped in a cab and went to downtown Detroit to meet the people at Brooks, Smith, French and Dorrance, the Hudson ad agency. I marched into Brooks, Smith's offices with a lot of confidence. I was met by a bright young account executive, Mr. Tom Lovelady. After my sensational meeting at K/F, I thought I was now an automotive marketing expert. I came on more aggressive and a little more outspoken than I should have. I criticized their ads for the recent introduction of their new small car, the Hudson Jet. The more I talked, the deeper I dug my hole. The last thing he needed was criticism from some smartass kid from New York who thought he was an expert because he had learned to spell Hudson. Obviously, I was not a big hit at Brooks, Smith, French and Dorrance. I never heard from them again.

Back in New York on the next Monday morning I walked out of my Esquire office at 488 Madison Avenue and took the elevator for my appointment at the Weintraub offices. It was almost unbelievable how they greeted me. They were literally waiting for me. Chuck Leonard had done his job. I first met John Morris, who then introduced me to Bill Weintraub. The only question now was, "How soon can you can start?" I thought I was really big time now. They were offering me close to $100 a week!

Sylvia was thrilled. I was happy, too, especially since I was now in the car business. I felt more responsible, and seriously started thinking about getting married. I really liked Sylvia's family, They were part of a different social set from what I had been used to. They were high level Jewish society. I felt confident that I had enough personal grace and charm and enough breeding to handle myself.

At that time my name was James Wangersheim. Nobody, including me, had ever heard of Jim Wangers. I've never talked much about this before because I never believed you should use an ethnic or religious background as an excuse for failure. But as I moved deeper into the automobile industry, I slowly learned about religious bias as it existed at that time. When I left Chicago and told everybody that I was ultimately hoping to work in Detroit, my family, my good friends, and even some colleagues at Esquire all told me the same thing: The automobile manufacturers had a reputation for not selecting Jewish people to participate in their management structure. My favorite uncle, who was in the retail tire business, said, "Look at the record, Jim. You don't have to be a genius to figure out that Henry Ford's an outright anti-Semite. There has never been any Jewish executives reach top management at any of the Detroit auto companies."

So I was warned, before I ever left Chicago in the very early 1950s, that you don't want to go to Detroit and try to get into the auto industry. "If you want to get in the car business," everyone told me, "sell cars here in Chicago and try to become a car dealer." Well, I didn't want to be a dealer. I didn't like selling cars. I was beginning to understand that marketing, advertising and promotion were my strengths. I wanted to work in Detroit. That's where I wanted to make my life and my career.

Leaving Esquire and going to Weintraub was an easy transition. I had been with Esquire long enough that almost everybody there knew how much I liked the car business. They liked me at Esquire, I think because I practiced one very good habit I learned from my father. "Keep your mouth shut," he would tell me. "Don't speak until it's the right time." I never forgot his advice (except, for my one interview at Brooks, Smith). Years later I found a little printed sign that I had framed and mounted on the wall behind my dcsk in every office I've ever occupied. It said, "Nothing replaces wisdom, but silence comes close."

12

From Chicago to New York

2

Learning the Ropes

When I joined Weintraub I was surprised to realize that I knew more about the Kaiser product than anybody else in the agency. Since I was new and a bit unsure, I was reserved in my first meetings, even though from my viewpoint they were making incredible mistakes in how they were selling their product.

For example, they thought they could just talk about how great their car was—how it appeared, how it made you feel to own it—without telling a more complete and compelling product story. Their ads featured no discussion about features, no product news, and no exclusive claims. They did, however, come up with a catchy new line to describe their styling, calling it "Anatomic Design." They just didn't exploit it fully.

After a week, I finally broke out of my shell and began to share with them what I thought. I expected some resentment, but was pleased to find that they welcomed my input. Ultimately, I think they thought it was helpful to have someone around who knew and cared about cars.

Well, my enthusiasm for the product turned around and bit me. I was with the agency in New York a little more than a month when Bill Weintraub himself came to me and said, "We like what you're doing. but we think you can do us more good in our Detroit office." They felt that I could impress the client more by having daily contact. They shoved me out the door with instructions to report to the Detroit office.

It was winter of 1952 when I moved and actually started working on the already introduced 1953 model line. Since I had joined the Weintraub agency as James Wangersheim, it meant I would have to go to Detroit with the same name—it would have been a little difficult to change my name at that point. I was unsure if that was going to be a problem or not.

I was ecstatic, however, about the move, and felt it was now time to propose marriage to Sylvia. I reminded her that I had accomplished my goal to be working in the auto industry, and what could be more perfect than for us to move to Detroit as man and wife, to start a new life together.

Her reaction floored me.

"I can't think of anything I'd rather do than to spend the rest of my life with you," she said, "but I don't want to move to Detroit. I have a wonderful home, a wonderful family and wonderful friends here in New York. We are very successful. I don't know why you can't join our world. I'd like you to talk to my father about your going to work for him."

She brought me to her home and arranged for her father to make a big pitch for me to join the family company. He said he had a lot of confidence in me, and felt I would fit very nicely into the company. This was another way of saying, "Jim, I want you to be my son-in-law."

I wasn't buying any of this. I wanted to work in the car business. The decision I then made was not easy. Whether Sylvia and I would have had a happy marriage is something I'll never know. That was the only time I slowed down long enough in my entire life to consider getting married. Once I decided not to and moved to Detroit, I threw myself into my work, and never again considered getting seriously involved in another relationship. From then on my work came first and anything else was secondary. Strangely, it took me a little longer than it should have to learn that, in Detroit, you had to show signs of stability and conformity. If there was anything that might have worked against me as I progressed over the years in the car business, it may have been the fact that I never married and had my own family. It's something I'll never know for sure.

About six months after I moved to Detroit, Sylvia changed her mind. But by then I had recovered from my disappointment, and had replaced her with my other love, cars.

Detroit was everything I had hoped it would be. It was like Chicago, but on a smaller scale. The city was vibrant and exciting back then, because the car industry was booming. Carmakers could sell everything they could build. Most manufacturers had recently released their first new cars since the end of World War II, and there was a tremendous pent-up demand. It was a carmaker's dream.

The Weintraub office was located in Dearborn, Michigan, and was managed by a great guy named Burt Durkee. Durkee was an institution in the auto industry. Before coming to Weintraub, he had been with J. Walter Thompson, where he had directed the entire Ford Division ad account. Weintraub thought enough of him to hire him away for a big salary just to run their modest office serving Kaiser. He had only one assistant, a media guy named Bob Clark. Bob was way ahead of his time in the media world. Back in those days we didn't have computer input on how to buy advertising, but Bob acted like he did! He taught me a lot about purchasing media.

Durkee was in the twilight of his career, and I was very lucky that he had chosen to be my mentor. He taught me lessons that I have never forgotten: how to deal with clients, and how to combine creative advertising and promotion into an entire marketing program. It was from him I learned that advertising was only one part of the marketing picture. He saw that I was good at keeping my mouth shut, and soon I was working right alongside him, doing things that guys in this business wouldn't get to do for maybe five or ten years after they started. That's the normal way you grew in the business in those days. You started by getting a chance to do a little production work then perhaps a little writing. You paid your dues and slowly worked your way up. Burt would talk to me about some of the top-level management decisions made by Kaiser, even though many of these decisions didn't always seem to be the best for the product or the company. He explained the economics and politics of the decisions, too. He didn't always know about the product, but he knew how to market it. As I said, I was lucky to find a boss like him, and I've never forgotten that.

Testing Kaiser Engines

BY 1953, MOST OF KAISER'S COMPETITORS in the mid-priced segment were offering new V-8 engines. Oldsmobile was first in 1949 with their overhead valve, high compression "Rocket." Chrysler, Desoto, Dodge, Studebaker, and Buick soon followed suit. Mercury still used their flathead, but it, too, was a V-8. Kaiser had no V-8 in development and was facing a tough market without a competitive engine.

To counter this, Kaiser engineers put together a highly secret "ride and drive" at their proving grounds in May of 1953. They set up four 1953 4-door Kaiser Manhattans with different V-8 engines: one had an Olds, one a Buick, one a Chrysler, and the fourth a Studebaker. A fifth car was equipped with Kaiser's existing Continental "Red Seal" flathead six-cylinder engine, which had been upgraded with a Paxton supercharger.

As part of the ad agency staff, I was invited to drive all these cars. All we were told about each car is what engine was in it. We were to choose which of the cars we liked the best and why. We then drove the cars for several hours. I thought I was in heaven! I couldn't believe you actually got paid for doing this. Here I was, the newest guy on the team, rubbing elbows with the top engineering and management people at Kaiser. All this after less than six months in the business.

The upshot, of course, was that all of the V-8 equipped cars were absolutely delightful. A Kaiser car had never felt like that before. It was clear that the V-8s made the Manhattan a much more sophisticated vehicle.

Still, you could build a case for the supercharged six. It performed almost as well as the V-8s, particularly at low rpm, where it produced a delightful increase in torque. Predictably, Kaiser chose to abandon plans to develop their own V-8 and went ahead with the supercharged Red Seal six. The argument was that they could give their car the competitive performance it needed, without having to go through the expense of developing or buying a V-8, at least for the short term.

So we were faced with the challenge of finding a way to make the supercharged six-cylinder appealing to buyers who were already attracted to the new V-8s. One of the writers in New York came up with the phrase, "Two Engines in One." The idea was that the new Kaiser Manhattan offered a proven, dependable and highly economical six that got good gas mileage, along with a supercharger that gave the engine exciting performance.

I went to work on a way to dramatize this line. I knew what a supercharger was all about, but how could we explain these benefits to the public? The trick was to find a venue where a supercharged engine could do what a naturally-aspirated V-8 engine could not. One of the things I knew about superchargers was that they manufacture their own atmospheric pressure. That meant they could perform at high altitude as well as they did at sea level, so we needed some sort of trial at a high altitude. There were no races that I could think of, but there were hill climbs, and the most famous hill climb in the world was at Pikes Peak. When I did a little investigating and found what the record was, I realized we could break it going up backwards.

I quickly put together the idea that we dramatize the "Two Engines in One" theme and prove the power of the supercharger by breaking the Pikes Peak hillclimb record. The New York guys liked it, so we prepared a major presentation for the top Kaiser people. Kaiser gave it serious consideration, but in the end turned it down because it would have cost too much money, about $150,000, which was a pretty hefty shot in 1953. This was bad news for me. For the first time, reality had broken in on my fantasy world. Maybe my opportunities at Kaiser were limited. As things turned out, I was right, but not for the reasons I thought at the time.

IN THE FALL OF 1953, WE WERE TOLD that 1955 was going be the last year for Kaiser passenger cars. There would be no 1956 models. In fact, they were in the process of buying Willys Motor Co., which was located in Toledo, Ohio, manufacturing the famous Jeep. Ward Canaday was both President and Chairman of the Board at Willys. He also owned their advertising agency, U. S. Advertising. Even though Kaiser was buying Willys, U.S. Advertising was a fixture and would continue to handle all Willys and Jeep advertising.

Kaiser then decided to close their Willow Run facility. They moved to Toledo and took the Weintraub agency with them to continue servicing what was left of the Kaiser account. "There's no way I'm going to Toledo," Burt Durkee declared to me. It wasn't long after, that he announced he was going to join The Maxon Agency, handling the Packard Motor Co. account. Packard had been in serious trouble since they had reorganized right after World War II. When Durkee told me he was taking that job I told him I'd love to go with him, hoping he would feel the same way.

Durkee looked at me in a fatherly way. "Don't be a fool. Not that I don't want you," he said, "but they're not going to replace me here at Weintraub. You're probably not going to get the money or the title, but you will get to do my job down in Toledo."

Burt went on to tell me he didn't think Kaiser was going to last much longer in the car business. In fact, because of the rising cost of labor and the need to constantly bring new products to market, survival would continue to

In July of 1954 I joined Campbell-Ewald as a writer in the sales promotion department. Back then I was younger and didn't have as much hair as today.

be difficult for all the smaller companies like Studebaker, Nash, Packard, Hudson, and Kaiser. Burt's counsel was to move to Toledo and take advantage of this incredible opportunity, to act as Account Supervisor for however short a period of time. At the very least, it would look good on my resume someday.

That's what I did. From October, 1953 until I left, I was Weintraub's Toledo office. I'd go to client meetings in Toledo and then immediately fly to New York to talk with management about what the client expected. It was a tremendous opportunity until The Weintraub Agency was discharged and Kaiser cars finally died. Even though I was given the chance to join U.S. Advertising, I'd really had enough with Toledo and Kaiser and Willys.

Looking back on working for Weintraub, one of my proudest achievements had been a catalog I produced for the introduction of their new sports car, the Kaiser Darrin. The layout was done by the New York creatives and I was asked to follow-up on the production. I had the photos taken at a brand-new studio just starting in Detroit called Boulevard Photographic. It was to be a black and white catalog, but it used some very different tonal variations. This was okay for this car because all of them were to be painted white. The catalog went on to win several awards, including the first for Boulevard Photographic, and I got an art director's award, too, which I always considered to have been a stroke of very good luck.

I SPREAD MY RESUME' AROUND TOWN and got on the phone. I got some interest from Campbell-Ewald, Chevrolet's advertising agency. They hired me as a copywriter in the agency's sales promotion and merchandising department. My immediate supervisor was a neat guy by the name of Milt Sandling. His immediate supervisor was Walter McCarthy, another nice guy, who reported to Colin Campbell (no relation), the Chevrolet account supervisor. Between Sandling, McCarthy and Campbell, I felt like I was traveling in some pretty sophisticated company.

When I joined Campbell-Ewald in March of 1954 I once again thought about shortening my name. This would be the perfect time to do it, before starting a new job at a new agency with a new client. Yet, in spite of the warnings I had received from my family and others before moving to Detroit I can honestly say that nothing ever happened to me personally—then or since—that suggested any Anti-Semitic bias in the industry. Nevertheless, at that time, shortening my name seemed like a good idea. Legally, I became James Wangers, and the "James" very quickly turned into "Jim."

3

Early Successes...and Failures

A Lost Opportunity for Chevy

I HAVE OFTEN JOKED THAT WHEN I resigned from Weintraub/Kaiser and went to Campbell-Ewald/Chevrolet, I moved from the bottom to the top. I had left Kaiser, the poorest selling vehicle in the market, and moved to Chevrolet, who had the best selling vehicle in the market.

In the spring of 1954, Campbell-Ewald was wrapping up their work on the introduction of the all-new 1955 "Motoramic" Chevrolet. While I was excited about working on the new model, I didn't think much of their advertising. The announcement ad read, "Introducing the new 1955 Motoramic Chevrolet, an all-new concept of low-cost motoring." Anyone interested in the car had to read all the way to the bottom of the ad, almost as if it was a secret, to learn about Chevrolet's all-new V-8 engine, called the Turbo-Fire V-8.

While at 265 cubic inches and only 162 horsepower with a 2-barrel carburetor it may not have looked like a performance engine, it did introduce some new ideas in valve-train design, including a stamped, lighter weight rocker arm and no rocker shaft. Anyone who knew about performance was quick to recognize that this was a significant development. Actually, the concept came out of Pontiac, developed by an engineer named Clayton Leach. Chevrolet just borrowed it.

It certainly was not my place to tell Campbell-Ewald that they were underpromoting this fabulous new engine. My job was to write showroom posters and sales training manuals for the dealers and their salespeople. Writing these required product knowledge, which was why I had been hired in the first place. Although I was upset at Chevy's failure to capitalize on its new engine in advertising, I did what I was told, watching the new car go through its announcement period and first quarter follow-up. Everybody had been so proud of the new '55 model, especially the Ferrari-styled eggcrate grille. This was a tremendous departure from any previous Chevrolet, and the traditional Chevy buyer was a little slow to warm-up. Suddenly, there was some sec-

Chevrolet Bel Air Convertible with Body by Fisher.
Blue-ribbon beauty
that's stealing the thunder from the high-priced cars!
Wherever outstanding cars are judged a surprising thing is happening. The spotlight is focusing on the new Chevrolets!
Surprising—because Chevrolet offers one of America's lowest-priced lines of cars. But not really astonishing when you consider that its designers had just one goal—to shatter all previous ideas about what a low-priced car could be and do.
The unparalleled manufacturing efficiency of Chevrolet and General Motors provided the means—and that's why you have a low-priced car that looks like a custom creation. That's why you get the thistledown softness of Glide-Ride front suspension, the choice of a hyper-efficient 162-h.p. V8 engine or two brilliant new 6's. That's why Chevrolet's extra-cost options included every luxury you might want. And that's why you should try a Chevrolet for the biggest surprise of your motoring life! . . . Chevrolet Division of General Motors, Detroit 2, Mich.
Motoramic
CHEVROLET
Drive it at your Chevrolet dealer's

Chevrolet had a new car and a new engine in 1955 when I joined Campbell-Ewald. I was astounded that Chevrolet ad writers didn't appreciate the incredible new small block V-8. The new Chevy looked so good, however, that I traded in my Studebaker for a Coral and Gray Bel Air convertible just like the one shown in this ad.

ond-guessing at the agency, and I felt stifled at not being able to respond.

My chance for some input came not long after, when we were told about a new engine power package. It consisted of a dual exhaust system and a 4-barrel carburetor, increasing horsepower to 180. The sales department was asked to develop a mailing to all the dealers announcing this new option, in

"Twin Pipes That Play Sweet Music." To promote the new 180-horsepower 4-barrel "Power Pack" Chevrolet with dual exhausts, we were asked to come up with a teaser to let the dealers know the package was coming. Remembering the Cracker Jack whistles I had as a child, I thought this inexpensive dual-chamber whistle was a perfect tie-in to highlight the new sound of Chevrolet performance. More than 5,000 whistles were distributed.

the hope that it would spark some new enthusiasm. Since I was in sales promotion, this was my assignment.

At that particular time, one of the crazes with kids was a little two-chambered whistle, similar to a coach's whistle. If you were lucky, you could get them as a prize in a box of Cracker Jack. Because of the two chambers, it had a distinct dual tone. I thought it was a perfect way to demonstrate dual exhausts, so I proposed that we get a bunch of these whistles, write a letter promoting the new Power Pack, and mail them out to the dealers. One of the more creative copywriters then came up with the line, "Twin Pipes That Play Sweet Music," which absolutely "made" the mailing. I wish I had thought of it. Chevy's marketing people liked the idea too, so we bought several thousand whistles and did the mailing. Everybody liked the line so much that it was used as the headline in the new engine announcement ad.

I KNEW FROM MY OWN EXPERIENCE that the 4-barrel carb, dual exhaust package would be just the thing Chevrolet needed to get people excited about their '55 model. I also realized that we needed a way to demonstrate just how capable this new "Power Pack Chevy," as they called it, really was.

For the past few years, NASCAR (National Association for Stock Car Auto Racing) had been conducting an event every February in Daytona Beach, Florida, called Speed Week. In those days, you could bring anything down to Daytona and "run" on the beach—seriously, all they cared about was that it had four wheels. You didn't need a roll bar or any other safety equipment. Obviously, you ran right after the tide went out, on the hard-packed sand. If your car was capable of going over a hundred miles per hour, you were eligible to join an organization called the Century Club. The big finale of Speed Week was the NASCAR-sponsored stock car race that was run partly on the beach and partly on a poorly paved black top road running parallel to the beach to complete the oval track.

There was no organized factory racing effort from Chevy in those days, however there was some communication between the interested Chevrolet engineers and a few experienced racers. These racers weren't professionals. They would travel to Daytona just for Speed Week, tape up their front ends, especially around the headlights, and try to go fast. About five thousand people usually gathered, and maybe a hundred fifty cars. Remarkably, there were very few cars that would run over 100 mph.

I knew about Speed Week. I had been there as a spectator the year before. In December of 1954 I went to my supervisor, Milt Sandling, and told him that I believed Chevrolet had an opportunity to make a great showing at Speed Week and could get some needed positive press about the new Power Pack option. I predicted that Chevrolet would clean house in its class against both Ford and Plymouth. I argued that, even though it was a small market segment, there were people out there who liked performance, and from Chevy it would be a huge surprise. Since Chevrolet was battling Ford and Plymouth for sales, I predicted that they would blow away the new Ford V-8 and Plymouth's new watered-down Hemi. (They called their engine design a "Polyspherical Combustion Chamber," but whatever they called it, it wasn't a real Hemi, and in most cases it didn't run.) I suggested to Sandling that the agency send me down to cover Speed Week firsthand to get information we could later use in Chevy advertising.

Sandling thought it was some kind of a boondoggle to get a free trip to Florida. He did take the concept up the ladder, however, all the way to Colin Campbell himself, whose response essentially was, "We don't want any part of this racing stuff, because Chevrolet is not in racing." It's hard to believe today, but in early 1955, NASCAR and Daytona were almost unheard of in America, except with the real racing enthusiast. Only Hudson, Oldsmobile, and Chrysler were currently involved with any factory support.

I still thought it was an opportunity we shouldn't miss, so I took earned vacation time, met some old friends from Chicago, and drove to Daytona Beach. It turned out to be exactly as I had predicted. There were 12 Chevrolets there, and all were equipped with the 180-horsepower Power Pack option. Every single one of the 12 Chevrolets ran faster than the best Ford or Plymouth. The fastest Chevrolet of all was a 210 two-door sedan (which was lighter than the Bel Air model) driven by Harold M. Tapscott, a Police Chief from Deland County, Florida. Chief Tapscott turned in a speed of over 112 mph, amazing for a Chevrolet (or any stock car) to run on the beach at that time. The only car that ran faster was a new Hemi-Powered Chrysler 300,

Don't argue with this baby!
All the low-priced cars
and most of the high-priced cars
tried it recently in official NASCAR* trials...
and took a licking!
Meet the champ! The new Chevrolet 180-h.p. "Super Turbo-Fire V8" – the most modern V8 on the road today.
You want facts, don't you? And not ours. Facts instead from an independent. outside source where the only thing that counts is who came in first, second, and so on. Here they are –
Daytona Beach. NASCAR Acceleration Tests Over Measured Mile From Standing Start. Chevrolet captured the 4 top positions in its class! 8 of the first 11! And on a time basis Chevrolet beat every high-priced car, too – but one!
Daytona Beach. NASCAR Straightaway Running open to cars delivered in Florida for $2,500 or less. Chevrolet captured the first two places, 7 out of the first 11 places!
Daytona Beach. NASCAR 2-Way Straightaway Running over measured mile. Open to cars from 250 to 299 cu. in. displacement. Chevrolet captured 3 of the first 5 places! None of its competition (What competition?) even finished "in the money"!
Columbia, S. C. NASCAR 100-Mile Race on half-mile track. Very tight turns. Chevrolet finished first! Way, way ahead – as in sales! With a new car, and no pit stops!
Fayetteville, N. C. NASCAR Late Model Event. After running the fastest qualifying round – (with a new car) – Chevrolet again finished first. Because of even tighter turns the driver chose to run the entire 150 laps in second gear! Yet no overheating or pit stops!
These facts you can't laugh off. Sales Leader, Road Leader, a crowning achievement of Chevrolet and General Motors. Try a Chevrolet and live in a land of going-away where you win all the arguments! Today, maybe? . . . Chevrolet Division of General Motors, Detroit 2, Mich.
*National Association for Stock Car Auto Racing
SPECIAL: Added power for the Chevrolet "Super Turbo-Fire V8" – the new 195-h.p. Special Power Kit now available at extra cost on special order.
CHEVROLET
SALES LEADER FOR 19 STRAIGHT YEARS

23

Chevrolet's Speed Week Success

Feeling cocky after their dominating wins in the NASCAR-certified 1955 Daytona Beach, Florida speed trials, Chevrolet boasts, "Don't argue with this baby!" in a June Motor Trend ad. After the February Daytona showing, Chevrolet's quickly organized factory racing program was already producing results. Chevrolet ads soon began to call out each new NASCAR win, with the equally confident line, "Watch this list grow." Note the box in the lower right of this ad announcing that the upgraded Corvette engine would now be available as a special order option on Chevy passenger cars.

which hit 115 mph. There was also a standing start event, and Chevrolet dominated that one too, beating everybody, including the Chrysler 300.

Back in Detroit I assembled a report that included names of all the participating cars, their drivers, and their recorded speeds and times. I was a new kid still trying to make the team, so I went a little overboard with details. I made sure copies were spread around the agency to all the important people. In my immature way, I was trying to say, "See, I told you so!" Reaction at the agency was underwhelming. They thought it was nothing more than some local outlaw racing, and believe it or not the report was not passed on to Chevrolet.

Thankfully, I wasn't the only one who recognized the significance of Chevrolet's performance at Daytona. The Associated Press put out a story on their wire service with a headline that read, "Chevy Sets Speed Mark At Daytona." The article went on to describe how Tapscott and his 1955 Chevrolet had set new records, and what an accomplishment it was for a low-priced car with no performance history. In a matter of days the story started popping up in newspapers everywhere with the same "Chevy Sets Speed Mark At Daytona" headline. Performance-oriented consumers read the story and went into Chevrolet dealerships all over the country, wanting to know what kind of Chevy had set the records.

Of course, the salespeople didn't know, so they went to their manager. The manager didn't know either, so the next step was to call the Zone Office. Zone offices all over the country were fielding calls, but they, too, didn't have any answers. This went on for about a week, when finally, several Zone Office people contacted Chevrolet's Central Office in Detroit. In response, Chevrolet turned to Campbell-Ewald to find out exactly what had happened at Speed Week. It was truly "divine intervention" for me.

In a matter of minutes, Milt Sandling was called in by his supervisor and told to "Get that report from Wangers and get it up to Chevrolet right away. Let's show them how efficient we are." Most everybody in the agency had probably filed their copy in their "circular file." I pulled my copy out, quickly ran off about ten more on the Xerox, and gave a couple to Sandling, who had it in the Chevrolet Sales Promotion Department that same day.

Sandling worked it into a major presentation, telling Chevrolet that they had sent one of their people to Daytona to observe the event and record the results. He wasn't invited to be at the first meeting, but I still had a friend there, Walter McCarthy, the Number Two guy on the Chevrolet account, who knew exactly what had happened. In my experience he was a more considerate person than Colin Campbell, and he had more authority than Milt Sandling. Sandling knew the score, but he couldn't do anything about it. McCarthy could. He came down from the meeting and headed right for my office, giving me about a ten-minute "atta boy." "We like this kind of thinking Jim," he said, "you have a future here." And, incidently, "Make damn sure we pay you for your trip to Florida."

Chevrolet was pleased with our work. The outcome resulted in their immediately asking the agency to put together a folder for all their dealerships. It was to be a small printed piece the salespeople could keep in their pockets to answer questions about Daytona. We were instructed to put it on nice stock and get it out fast. They also sent out posters for the dealership windows with the exact headline the AP had used, "Chevy Sets Speed Mark At Daytona." We were off! My credibility was now established with McCarthy. He told me to come in any time with ideas. I felt he was smart enough to see that this was just the beginning of the performance era for Chevrolet.

By late February a decision was made to change the entire creative approach in Chevrolet national advertising. The idea was to start building performance into the copy and to play down the Motoramic "Low-cost Motoring" theme. We were to focus on the new V-8 Chevrolet that had actually beat somebody. That's when an agency creative team first created the phrase, "The Hot One."

By this time, the racers had begun to notice what had happened at Daytona. They had been racing Fords, Hudsons, and Oldsmobiles, when out of the blue came these funny little "Shivolays," (as they were called in the South) and they were "kickin' ass." It didn't take long for some of these drivers to contact Chevrolet.

Factory Racing Contact

Unfortunately, the people at Chevrolet couldn't answer their questions about how to get a car or any heavy duty parts. Again, divine intervention. Chevrolet came to Campbell-Ewald, wanting to know if I could help field phone calls. At the very least they wanted me to make a list of the requests, since they simply weren't yet set up to do anything about them. All of a sudden, I was the official Chevrolet Racing Department.

I fielded calls from well-known racers like Herb Thomas and "Fonty" Flock, and from crew chiefs like Henry "Smokey" Yunick, all asking how they could get a "Shivolay." Most of them were interested in getting out of their Hudsons and into a Chevy. The Hudson Hornet had dominated stock car racing after it first came into the marketplace in 1951, but by 1955 it had become almost obsolete when compared to the new Olds "88" and the Chrysler 300.

I collected names, and told them I would turn in their requests to Chevrolet. Then I suggested that the smartest thing they could do was to go see a dealer. That's how naive I was: these guys weren't about to buy a car, they wanted Chevrolet to give them one! Some things in racing never change.

All of this excitement over Chevrolet performance was beginning to snowball, and McCarthy could see it was getting out of hand. He felt it was Campbell-Ewald's responsibility to develop a racing program for Chevrolet. He invited me to a special meeting he had set up with Tom Keating, the General Manager of Chevrolet, and Bill Power, the Sales Manager. Two members of the Sales Promotion Department, Bob Lund and Ted Hopkins, were also at the meeting (Lund later went on to become General Manager of Chevrolet; Hopkins eventually became the General Sales Manager of Cadillac). They were assigned the job of recommending what Chevrolet should do, after all the success at Daytona.

The outcome of the meeting was a decision to prepare a presentation to be made to the parent General Motors Corporation asking for a budget to establish a Chevrolet racing program. Because I had been the catalyst up to then, I was asked to develop the presentation. McCarthy gave me an office, assigned a great young writer named Henry Hager to the project, and gave us a month to put it together. He told us to ask for three million dollars, which today would be peanuts, but in 1955 was decent money.

"I've arrived!" I thought: not quite 30 years old and putting together Chevrolet's first factory racing program. The presentation would go up to the Corporation's legendary "14th floor" (where GM's top executives had their offices). If that wasn't enough, I was also moved over to join the Advertising group at Campbell-Ewald. If you were in the Advertising group, you were really "in." Where I'd come from, the Merchandising and Sales Promotion group, was considered a mere stepping stone.

THAT WAS MY WHIRLWIND ENTRY INTO the advertising world of Campbell-Ewald. All of a sudden I was the agency performance expert, and all of these important people were coming to see me—and I'd been with the agency less than a year. I even got the chance to meet Colin Campbell, the account supervisor. All I knew about him was that he had turned down my request to go to Speed Week. To his credit, however, he did tell me how much he appreciated what I had done, and how there would be some big things coming my way.

Meanwhile, we had completed the racing presentation, and it was approved by GM management on the spot. Chevrolet was now officially in racing. I still fielded calls from interested racers, but now I had an engineer assigned to help me. Finally, they announced plans to find some new people to head their fledgling racing program, and I was freed up to go out and cover some of the early races. Every weekend I was on a plane going south. Even as an unofficial Chevrolet "observer" it was tough to remain undercover. At first, everybody thought I was the official Chevrolet factory representative, because nobody else from Chevrolet wanted to get involved. As the teams got to know me, they hoped I would put in a good word for them back at the factory—of course I didn't have the authority to give away as much as a screwdriver.

About the time Chevrolet started winning races—primarily Herb Thomas, in a Smokey Yunick prepared car—the ads featuring the new "Hot One" theme were starting to break. After the fourth or fifth victory, the creative team at the agency (headed by a writer named Barney Clark) came up with the idea of placing little crossed checkered flags along the bottom of each ad, with the caption reading, "Watch this list grow," and as Chevy piled up more wins, the list did indeed grow.

For me, however, all was not right in "paradise." First, at McCarthy's direction I was given the responsibility of checking every performance or racing ad before it went to Chevrolet, to make certain the facts were correct. I became pretty well known in the creative department, and while I enjoyed the involvement, I always had the feeling that, to them, I was "that son of a bitch" who was responsible for killing all their good, early Motoramic ads, and now I was the guy who was tinkering with their new, good Hot One ads.

Second, I had a major set-back in May of 1955. Chevrolet announced their new racing director, a man with impeccable experience in the sport. He was Mauri Rose, three-time winner of the Indianapolis 500. Unfortunately, Rose had no experience in stock car racing, and seemed to have even less respect for stock car drivers.

The day I was introduced to Rose, I detected an unusually cool response. He asked no questions about the program, nor did he show any interest in what I knew about the teams using Chevys. Shortly after, Rose issued a memo formally confirming that Jim Wangers was not involved in any way in Chevrolet racing administration. The unfortunate part was that because of his open hostility to stock car racing and its drivers, he lasted less than one year. He had seen to it that I was completely out of the very program I had helped get off the ground. I had some comfort, however, from McCarthy. He knew Rose was a problem, and told me not to take it personally.

Pikes Peak Hill Climb Promotion

WHEN THE 1956 MODEL APPEARED WE were faced with a new challenge. While a few things had changed—such as the headlight brows, the grille, and the tail lights—it was mostly a styling improvement over the '55. Our task was to make it appear that they had improved the car, not just changed it. The standard automotive marketing philosophy at that time was to emphasize that newer was better. The styling of the '56 certainly was newer, but it was difficult to say exactly how this was better. Fortunately, someone came up with the obvious line, "The Hot One's even hotter," which got the campaign off to a great start.

Our performance advertising was working extraordinarily well. Chevrolet was winning races consistently, and the victory list was growing. Still, I thought we needed more to dramatize or prove our great new tag line. We needed a way to make an easy transition into promoting the '56 car.

Suddenly, the light went on: Pikes Peak. If it had been good enough for a desperate Kaiser, certainly it should work for a confident Chevrolet, and would prove, indeed, that the Hot One was even hotter. Remember, in 1955 Pikes Peak was still the most famous "hill" in the world, and it was a real challenge even to make it to the top. If we could break the record driving to the top with a new 1956 Chevy, even before the car was introduced, it would be a real coup.

I went to my files and pulled out the old Kaiser presentation, spending the better part of a day replacing the word "Kaiser" with "Chevrolet," and updating the marketing rationale to apply to our needs. I immediately took the finished pitch to Walter McCarthy. "I have something here I'd like you to read, " I said, laying it on his desk. "I think you'll find some potential in this."

Less than one hour later my phone rang. McCarthy's assessment was simple: "This is a winner. "

He bombarded me with questions. One of the first was, "Where did you come up with the idea?" I was bound and determined not to tell anybody that I had pitched the same concept to Kaiser only two years before. "You know

I'm a racing fan, " I answered, "and I think I understand how to market performance. There is a difference between performance and racing, you know. "

McCarthy said he couldn't find anything wrong with it. He immediately showed it to Colin Campbell, who called in his top creative guys. They wanted to see how it looked in ads before showing it to Chevrolet. They pitched it to Chevrolet management, who loved it. They decided to use it as a teaser for the '56 announcement, building a shroud to cover the entire car during the run, making it look very romantic...and very suspicious.

To drive the car up the mountain they tapped one of their young engineers, Zora Arkus-Duntov. Duntov was no stranger to speed and competition, having driven at Le Mans and Daytona in a Corvette. He practiced on the course and soon found he didn't have to go ridiculously fast to break the record.

All during the project I never had a chance to meet Zora, which even today, I regret. He seemed to think I was just another "pain in the ass" from the agency, and I never got a chance to change that impression.

The Pikes Peak run was a huge success. Duntov destroyed the record. Television was just coming into its own then, and along with radio it turned out to be the perfect media to promote our program. Chevrolet spent millions. They commissioned a young country singer named Burl Ives to write an original ballad about how "Man and machine conquered the mountain." Burl would say, "This is Burl Ives for your Chevrolet dealer," then go into his song. The Pikes Peak program proved dramatically that the Hot One really *was* even hotter.

Pikes Peak Hill Climb Promotion

IT WAS ABOUT THIS TIME THAT I BEGAN "reading my own press clippings." Since I had come up with two strong marketing ideas that had a positive effect on Chevrolet, I felt I deserved more recognition.

I made the mistake of telling McCarthy that I had been getting offers from some of our competition. It was the same silly line that everybody in the Ad business pulled, claiming "I don't want to leave, but...." McCarthy was a veteran. He knew Campbell-Ewald's policy was to recognize you when they got good and ready, and trying to force that recognition didn't work. Problem was, I was young and full of myself. McCarthy, as I requested, talked to Colin Campbell. Campbell had replied, "Maybe he ought to accept some of those other offers."

Truth was, I didn't have any offers. I learned my first hard lesson in the tough automotive world.

I quickly moved to get the word out that I was looking. I let it be known that I was the guy who had conceived the Pikes Peak promotion, which by now had become famous in ad circles. One of the first responses I got came from Jack Minor, the General Sales Manager of Dodge. He had been impressed with that promotion, and wanted to talk seriously with me.

I was pretty familiar with Dodge, and of course I liked their Hemi engine. Everybody knew of its great racing potential. This was what Jack Minor really wanted to talk about. "How do we make our racing victories work hard-

Engineer's Report:
1956 CHEVROLET

Behind Chevrolet's record-shattering Pikes Peak climb are important engineering changes

by ED COLE, *Chevrolet Chief Engineer*

Since Chevrolet's record-breaking run up Pikes Peak, people have asked me just what we've done to this new Chevrolet to make it the mountain-climbing champ.

Well, to begin with, our job was to produce a car that would out-perform last year's Chevy which, you'll recall, was the leading winner on the stock car tracks. That was a big order.

Our men started by making refinements in the "Super Turbo-Fire V8" engine. They raised the compression ratio to 9.25 to 1. Horsepower was boosted to 205. You can imagine what these changes did for performance!

Next we went to work on the "Blue-Flame" 6. The compression ratio went up to 8 to 1. Horsepower was increased to 140. The final result of these and other improvements is the most powerful, sweetest running 6 we've ever had in a Chevrolet passenger car!

Drivers who like a full-flow oil filter will be pleased to hear that we've made provision for one on our V8 engines. And *all* engines—both 6- and 8-cylinder—are now equipped with Hydraulic-Valve lifters. This eliminates the need for periodic valve adjustments.

Drop by and drive this record-breaking new Chevrolet at your Chevrolet dealer's. . . . Chevrolet Division of General Motors, Detroit 2, Michigan.

Chevrolet

1956 Chevrolet setting new record for Pikes Peak climb

Ed Cole, then Chief Engineer at Chevrolet, was often credited with being the father of the famed small-block V-8. Here Cole uses the "record-shattering" Pikes Peak hill climb win to boast about new improvements in the entire line of 1956 Chevrolet powerplants. Note the elaborate shrouds used to disguise the pre-announcement car used in the record run in August, 1955.

er?" he asked. He wanted me to join his Sales Promotion department and develop a racing promotion program to help Dodge build a new image. He felt—as I did then, and still do now—that a program built around a "Race on Sunday, sell on Monday" philosophy didn't always work. There needed to be additional support for such a program.

So far in my career I had been with two ad agencies. The thought of working for a client for a change appealed to me. It would give me some real factory experience.

When I left Campbell-Ewald. Walter McCarthy was sincerely sorry to see me go, and told me to stay in touch. Colin Campbell never knew I was gone.

4

Temporary Insider

I JOINED DODGE IN EARLY 1956, as an Assistant Sales Promotion Manager. My full responsibility, however, was to promote Dodge racing. At the time, Chrysler Corporation had a contract with Karl Kiekhaefer, who was president of Mercury Marine Outboard Engines, to field a team of Chrysler 300s and Dodge D-500s in stock car racing. A real tough Prussian engineer, Kiekhaefer knew exactly what he was doing, how he was going to do it, and when he was going to do it. Nobody disagreed with him. When he thought his cars needed a part, like a new exhaust manifold or a camshaft, he'd design it and make it himself. Chrysler would then buy it and assign a part number to it.

I had nothing to do with creating the car, but I was now charged with the responsibility of marketing the racing wins of the Dodge D-500. It took me almost four months to get to know Kiekhaefer, and I never did get to know him well. He was doing a sensational job for Chrysler, but he was his own man. For example, all Kiekhaefer Chrysler race cars were plastered with the name Mercury Marine along both sides. The fans sitting in the grandstands who couldn't identify cars very well saw this big car out there winning the race and probably thought they were looking at a Mercury. Kiekhaefer's Dodges were dressed out the same way. I tried to convince him that he should be promoting Chrysler and Dodge and not only his Mercury Outboard Motors. I learned very quickly that you didn't disagree with Karl Kiekhaefer.

The corporation was already enjoying some sales success with their specially packaged Chrysler 300, which bowed in 1955. That success was now shared with the other Divisions, as each introduced a special "packaged" car of their own. They were named the Plymouth Fury, the Dodge D-500, and the Desoto Adventurer. The most interesting thing about each of these cars was that, taking horsepower and weight into consideration, Chrysler was actually marketing the first true musclecars, almost ten years ahead of their time.

Although not recognized at the time, Chrysler produced the first "packaged" musclecar in 1955 with the introduction of the sporty C-300 coupe. Powered by their 331 cubic inch Hemi engine, the C-300 was rated at 300 horsepower, making it the most powerful production car offered at the time.

After the success of the C-300, the formula was copied by all Chrysler Divisions for 1956. Plymouth introduced the Fury, available only as a two-door hardtop in Eggshell White with an anodized gold aluminum side spear. Under the hood was a 301 cubic inch single quad engine rated at 240 horsepower. Sales soared in 1957 when the Fury was completely restyled. The Eggshell White exterior and gold anodized trim were carried over from 1956.

To preserve division identity, each of these cars featured different styling and different engines. In June 1956, Jack Minor was promoted to General Marketing Manager of the Plymouth Division. Chrysler management had decided once again to make a major commitment to Plymouth. Until that time, it had been sold through all Chrysler, Dodge, and DeSoto dealers as their low-priced alternative. While Plymouth had great distribution, it didn't have a good image. Plymouth was the "poor cousin." If you didn't like the Dodge, the dealer would try to put you into a lower-priced Plymouth. If a Desoto didn't fit your taste, or you couldn't afford a Chrysler, the dealer would try to keep you from walking by selling you the alternative Plymouth.

Now all that was going to change. They wanted Plymouth's new identity to confirm that it was no longer a stepchild at Chrysler. Corporate management felt that Jack Minor was the perfect guy to make this happen. Minor assembled a team of talented people while at Dodge, and offered all of us the chance to move over to Plymouth with him.

Some of the team chose to stay, like Ad Manager Arnie Thompson, and Dick Shugg, who ran a very competent Sales Promotion department. They weren't sure about this new Plymouth idea, and they liked it very well at Dodge. Lou Hagopian, who had been Dodge Marketing Director, moved over to Plymouth. (Lou later went on to become the President and, finally, Chairman of the Board of ad agency NW Ayer; they were the agency of record for Plymouth at the time.) I moved over under Lou as Sales Promotion Manager of the Plymouth Division.

Even though the change in jobs turned out to be more title than responsibility or salary, it actually made the press. I remember getting some nice letters and phone calls from some of my old friends at Campbell-Ewald, and even from some of the guys at *Esquire* magazine. The promotion brought a level of satisfaction to me that I could never have experienced at Campbell-Ewald on the Chevrolet account.

When I finally started at Plymouth, the sensationally styled new 1957 models were just beginning to arrive at the dealers. The award-winning "Suddenly it's 1960" ad campaign had already been launched, and Plymouth was really off to a good start on what would become one of its greatest sales years ever.

While I wasn't directly involved, I had a chance to be close to a remarkable advertising experience. Before Jack Minor took over at Plymouth he was given the opportunity to approve the new advertising campaign that would introduce the exciting 1957 cars to the public. When presented with the first campaign, he summarily rejected it and charged the ad agency to come up with a replacement campaign. It was already late Thursday, and he gave them the almost impossible deadline of having new ideas in his office by the following Monday morning.

The Plymouth account guys and their creative support team all went underground, quietly convening in a downtown Detroit hotel to work straight through the weekend. The following Monday morning, though bleary-eyed and exhausted, they presented one of the most creative and unique advertising ideas the auto industry had ever seen. They hit on the theme, "Suddenly it's 1960." This was an absolutely genius way of saying "This new car is three years ahead of its time." And the best part was that it actually looked like it was.

The 1957 cars had been scheduled to be 1958 models, appearing in midyear 1957. The 1956 cars were to be carried over as the 1957s. But in early 1956, when Chrysler management saw how badly their cars were selling, they moved the '58 cars up six months and introduced them at announcement time. Jumping a production model ahead one year was much easier to do in those days than it is today as there were no government emission certification or EPA mileage requirements to pose significant hurdles.

Unfortunately, some corners were cut in moving those cars up, and the

’57 models were somewhat compromised in build quality. For example, many side windows did not seal well, resulting in severe leaks. To counter this embarrassing situation, Plymouth prepared a demonstration for the press to show how they were fixing the problem. They set up a very elaborate water spray booth at the end of the assembly line. Once the spray was turned off, a team of inspectors would carefully examine each car for leaks. If there

Keep your eye on the D-500 . . .
IT’S A REAL BOMB!
These days, more and more of you guys who know and love cars are “talking up” the fabulous Dodge D-500. And no wonder! *This D-500 is a real bomb!*
In official NASCAR acceleration tests at Daytona Beach, the Dodge D-500 licked all cars—regardless of size, price or horsepower.
This D-500 gets out of the chute like a jackrabbit. Hugs the road like a dirt track special. Hits the turns without any squeal. Handles like a gem.
Though it performs like an expensive custom job, this D-500 is actually the slickest-looking *production car* to come up Main Street. Under the hood is a 260 hp. mill rarin’ to go (with big 12-inch center-plane brakes to stop it)!
You can buy a D-500 at any Dodge dealership in the country *in any body style* you like. (Costs only slightly more than $100.00 over standard models.) And it needs only *regular* Dodge service to keep it in razor-sharp condition.
So get behind the wheel and drive a D-500 today. See your Dodge dealer.
Most powerful engine in Dodge History!
260 hp. aircraft-type V-8 with 315 cubic inch displacement. 9.25 to 1 compression ratio. Bore 3.63 inches, stroke 3.80 inches. Also: 12-inch center-plane brakes with 15½ lbs. of car weight per sq. in. of lining area—a figure unequalled in American passenger cars—and one that approaches most sports cars and even racing cars.
Dodge D-500
AMERICA’S ACCELERATION CHAMPION
MOTOR LIFE, SEPTEMBER, 1956

This 1956 ad represents some of my early efforts to promote Dodge’s success in racing. The ad copy was a significant breakthrough because it used the “car talk ”of the new generation of enthusiasts. It wasn’t easy to persuade the agency’s copy writers to use these enthusiast terms.

were any leaks that car would be shuffled off to the "Hospital" for quick repair. Cars without leaks would be taken to the marshalling yard and put on a truck for delivery to a dealer. We had this show at the Plymouth plant on Mt. Elliot Road in Detroit, and brought in news people from all over the country to see this tremendous spray testing process, making sure there were no cars shipped with leaks.

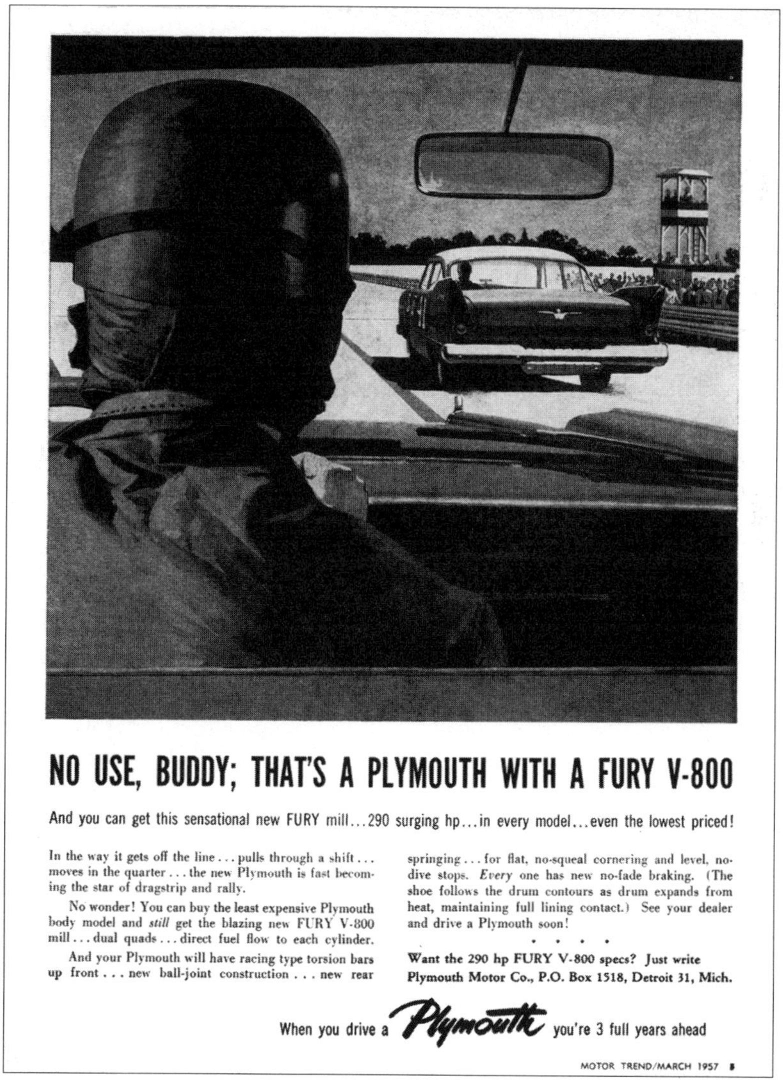
NO USE, BUDDY; THAT'S A PLYMOUTH WITH A FURY V-800
And you can get this sensational new FURY mill...290 surging hp...in every model...even the lowest priced!
In the way it gets off the line... pulls through a shift... moves in the quarter... the new Plymouth is fast becoming the star of dragstrip and rally.
No wonder! You can buy the least expensive Plymouth body model and still get the blazing new FURY V-800 mill... dual quads... direct fuel flow to each cylinder.
And your Plymouth will have racing type torsion bars up front... new ball-joint construction... new rear springing... for flat, no-squeal cornering and level, no-dive stops. Every one has new no-fade braking. (The shoe follows the drum contours as drum expands from heat, maintaining full lining contact.) See your dealer and drive a Plymouth soon!
Want the 290 hp FURY V-800 specs? Just write Plymouth Motor Co., P.O. Box 1518, Detroit 31, Mich.
When you drive a Plymouth you're 3 full years ahead
MOTOR TREND/MARCH 1957

I was moved over to Plymouth in 1957 and began working on the sensational new Fury. This ad was designed to promote the Fury as a performance car on both the street and the drag strip. Although Plymouth had no drag racing program, I wanted the average enthusiast to recognize that the Dual-Quad Fury V-800 was very competitive with the small block Chevy. Look closely and you can tell that the losing driver is at the wheel of a '57 Chevy.

What we didn't tell the press was that the cars that leaked actually went around the back of the plant and got on the same trucks to be shipped to the dealers. There was no "hospital." One out of every three cars leaked, and the factory relied on the dealers to fix them before they were sold.

FROM THE TIME I HAD MY FIRST V-8 Studebaker in 1951, I was fascinated by performance. When I arrived in Detroit in 1952, I had already modified the 232 cubic inch high compression overhead valve V-8. I added a set of Stromberg 2-barrel carburetors, dual exhausts, a performance camshaft, and a heavy duty clutch. With its 3.91:1 rear axle and a 3-speed overdrive stick, it had plenty of low-end response. It was a fun car, and reasonably competitive—for a Studebaker. In those days, the flat head Fords still pretty much dominated the street. There were a few new Olds Rocket 88s, and Chrysler was just coming in with their Hemi, but nobody took them seriously because they were only available with a semi-automatic transmission. Most of the cars that were competitive on the street at that time had 3-speed manual transmissions with the shifter mounted on the steering column. Most street racing was done from a rolling start, because no one had tires good enough to make a standing start.

It didn't take me long to discover a street racing group in Detroit. They called themselves "The High End Club." They met at Richard's Drive-In on the corner of Six Mile Road, James Couzens Highway, and Schaefer Road. It was one of those tri-cornered intersections, so common in Detroit. This was before street racing became so popular on Woodward Avenue.

The High End Club stood for exactly what the name suggested: their fondness for top speed. In the early fifties, James Couzens Highway extended past the city limits of Detroit at Eight Mile Road, and became a new four lane divided highway as it entered south Oakland County. There wasn't much activity out there in those days, and it was deserted at night. It was an absolutely ideal place to run. We'd start out at a 20-mph roll and run through the gears. Instead of stopping after the 1/4 mile, we would keep right on going, ending up in a flat-out, top speed contest. We'd run for two or maybe even three miles before we would have to slow down for a stop light.

I showed up a couple of times at Richard's with my Studebaker and was greeted with a few guffaws and snickers. I was finally given an opportunity to show it off against a couple of flat head Fords and a pretty straight Olds 88, and it performed well. I was invited to join the club. Their informal meetings at Richard's were usually on Friday or a Saturday night. Unfortunately, I had been in the habit of jumping in my car after work on Friday and making the six-hour drive to Chicago to spend the weekend with family and friends. When asked why I never came out on the weekends, I told them about my Chicago trips. Ironically, many of the other members also had weekend responsibilities, so we agreed to move our meetings to Thursday night. That Thursday night meeting became an institution, and even to this day there is a High End Club in Detroit that always meets on Thursday night. Today there's much more bench racing at their meetings than actual street racing, but the High End Club still is an important part of the heritage of organized street racing activity in the Detroit area. Back then, for me, it would become an important connection to a guy named Gil Kohn.

Gil was a 19-year-old kid who owned an old Fiat powered by a well set up small block Chevy. Back then it was common to take a light body and chassis like an Anglia or a Willys or a Fiat and stuff a V-8 in it. Those combinations were the best we had, even though they were primitive and not very reliable.

Gil was bright, enthusiastic, and a bit too rich. Shortly after I met him his father, who had a wholesale tobacco business in the Detroit area, passed away. Gil persuaded his mother to take some of the money they had received from the sale of the business and put it into a drag strip. He had been a High End Club participant and was so committed to the future of drag racing in the Detroit area that he was willing to put his money where his mouth was. There was another track, way out on the east side of town called Motor City Dragway, but it was crude, and figured to stay that way.

Discussions about the drag strip started in early 1957. I had disposed of my Studebaker while at Campbell-Ewald in early '55 and had acquired a '55 Chevy convertible. It had the 180-horsepower Power Pack engine with dual exhausts and a 3-speed manual transmission with overdrive on the column. That was a fairly sophisticated set up in that day.

Gil knew I worked in the auto industry and was aware of some of my promotional activities like the Chevrolet Pike's Peak program. For that reason, he approached me with his idea about building a drag strip. Unfortunately, I didn't have any money to invest, but Gil wasn't looking for money, he was looking for someone with promotion know-how and contacts in the racing and performance communities. He also wanted me to meet his mother and help sell her on the fact that the drag strip was a good investment. According to Gil, he wanted me to become a "big part" of the project.

Typical of the many naive mistakes I made early in my life, I took Gil Kohn at his word. I did not consult an attorney and draw up an agreement in writing, which I'm sure Gil would have signed at the time. Instead, I said I considered it a privilege to be involved. We "shook hands" over dinner at the Kohn home, where I met his mother, Mame, for the first time. My impression of her was that she was quiet.

Gil and I scoured the Detroit area. What we wanted was a track close enough to the city, but far enough out that the encroaching suburbs wouldn't someday cause it to be closed. It was also very important that the community be supportive. We found that Woodhaven, located in Brownstown Township a little southwest of the city, exactly fit our criteria. In the mid-fifties it was no more than a twenty-five minute drive from the most populated area of Detroit.

Through my work in the industry I had become acquainted with Wally Parks, who at that time was the most important figure in the world of drag racing. He was building the NHRA almost single-handed. When I approached Wally with the news that there could be a first-class drag strip in the Detroit area, his response was incredibly supportive. He had so far been unsuccessful in getting the Big Three automakers interested in drag racing. One reason was that there was no way to show them firsthand the public's interest and support since the NHRA had been holding their big National event since 1955 far away from Detroit.

Parks told me that if we could get a satisfactory track open by the first of August, 1959, he could deliver the NHRA Nationals on Labor Day weekend.

We soon found that the NHRA drove a pretty hard bargain. They wanted a hefty share of the gate and concessions. They knew the Nationals would draw well, especially in Detroit, after all, it was home to the U.S. auto industry. To bring in the NHRA, you had to be able to seat at least 5,000 people. The Labor Day Weekend schedule would see the races beginning on Friday night and running through Monday. A track seating 5,000 could attract close to 20,000 people over the course of the four-day event. Neither Gil nor his mother Mame Kohn complained about the NHRA's demands. They knew the numbers, and concluded it would be well worth their effort.

Another interested party to this was Petersen Publishing. In the late forties, Wally Parks had become close friends with fledgling magazine publisher Bob Petersen. Consequently, the NHRA and the Petersen Publishing Company grew up together.This marriage turned out to be a real benefit for the performance industry. Parks was working as editor of Petersen's *Hot Rod* Magazine while he was building the NHRA. (Later, he would disassociate himself from Petersen as the NHRA became more and more successful.) Having the Nationals in Detroit was a great opportunity for Petersen and his magazines. He had been only modestly successful in selling the Big Three ad space, and the extra visibility of the Nationals combined with *Hot Rod* could only bring more manufacturer interest.

I ALREADY HAD SOME CONNECTION WITH Petersen through their Detroit ad manager, Bob Brown. In 1957 Bob literally walked into my office at Plymouth unannounced, introduced himself, and explained that he had just joined the Petersen Publishing Company.

"I know quite a bit about selling space," Bob told me. "I know about schedules, deadlines, and even demographics, but I don't know anything about the auto industry. I was told that you're the guy to come to see if you want to know what's happening. I understand you like our magazines, and I figured this was a good place to start." He was already schmoozing me even before we became friends.

He was a good student, and quickly learned the reality of what he was facing. Most of the media buyers in Detroit had a bad impression of the auto enthusiast publications. They felt that these active car enthusiasts had every dime they owned tied up in their hobby and didn't have enough money to even think about buying a new car. They also thought every car enthusiast had dirty fingernails and always wore a dirty leather jacket. In addition, they were bothered that most of these new publications were "outlaw" and didn't have ABC (Audit Bureau of Circulation) numbers to prove their readership.

The ad buyers had closed their minds and didn't want to learn. In those days we didn't have the highly sophisticated, focused research that exists today. Consequently, because of this built-in bias, the car magazines were finding it tough to get any serious consideration. It was Bob Brown who changed that, and opened up the market to a whole new kind of thinking. Bob was probably the most serious advertising professional the Petersen Publishing Company ever had representing them. He sold his magazines to a tough and sophisticated automotive marketing community. Bob wasn't the most popular guy around town, but he was a winner. He built *Motor Trend, Hot Rod* and *Car Craft* magazines into the real media giants they were destined to be. These magazines, as well as the Petersen Publishing Company itself, were given much more respect in Detroit than they were in the other leading advertising communities, such as New York, Chicago, or even their home base in Los Angeles. That was because of Bob Brown.

Brown foresaw the marketing implications of racing in Detroit's backyard, and how a magazine like *Motor Trend* could become the absolute catalyst in that environment. When the Michigan International Speedway opened about 100 miles west of Detroit, Brown was the first "space peddler" to buy 50 of the best seats in the house and make an event out of it for his auto industry clients. He'd pick them up in a bus, and be the ultimate host from start to finish. He did the same thing for both the Daytona 500 and the Indy 500. Today, auto executives are treated to this same level of hospitality at race tracks all over the world, but Bob Brown was the first to do it in Detroit.

Brown was also the driving force behind building the successful *Motor Trend* Car of the Year program into what it is today. This award program, which was absolutely the very first of its type, has been the subject of jealous criticism ever since it has been in existence. The reality is that everybody is critical of it until they win it.

Brown, too, realized that bringing the NHRA Nationals to Detroit was the break he needed at Petersen. He didn't miss an opportunity. He hosted an open house right at the track inviting everybody from every automaker. He even had a drag racing expert in the Petersen tent to explain what was happening in this exciting new type of racing. The Petersen Publishing Company was magnificently represented in Detroit by Bob Brown, and I am proud to say that he was a very good student and a very good friend.

GIL KOHN GOT THE TRACK BUILT ON TIME, in spite of the time crunch. Construction had started in early fall of 1958, but stopped quickly after the first typical Detroit freeze. Serious construction didn't resume until mid-March, 1959, and with herculean effort. On Friday night August 31st, Labor Day weekend, the NHRA Nationals opened at the Detroit Dragway.

In those days, the NHRA had only one national event, their finals, and it was always held over Labor Day. The Detroit press corps really turned out, and yes, there were plenty of executives from the Big Three in the stands. They enjoyed the action and came away with a new respect for this competitive sport, which really showcased their products.

Long after the NHRA Nationals, the Detroit Dragway proved to be a huge success. I had also been brainstorming other new ideas, and at one point seriously thought about going into the racing industry full time. Gil talked about building tracks in some other markets. It looked like we really got into this business at the right time.

The more successful the Detroit Dragway became, the more Gil's mother Mame got involved. She was a tough businesswoman and had assumed managing the money. There was no question, right from the start the track made money. We had a good year, and began talking seriously about our growth plans. Up to this point I had not asked for any serious compensation. Based on our early verbal agreement I assumed I was a partner, however small. I brought up the subject of compensation in what had been a successful venture, especially with the NHRA event, and knowing that they were coming back the next year.

"We've decided we really don't need you anymore," I was told. "We're willing to pay you for bringing the NHRA Nationals to Detroit, but we don't want to have anybody but the family involved in the future." I don't know if anybody ever got sacked any harder. I was naive, and I paid the price.

Shut Out of the Dragway

I thought of getting a lawyer, but I couldn't prove the existence of an agreement. I had nothing in writing, only conversation. So the Kohn family and I agreed to disagree, less than one year after the opening of the track. I walked away with little more than the $1000 I accepted as payment for bringing the Nationals to Detroit. The Kohn family went on to become involved with several drag strips, one on Long Island, another in Indianapolis (which today is owned by the NHRA) and another in Houston, Texas.

In the end, I chose to be calm about the separation. By that time I was at Pontiac, and I had some big plans that involved drag racing. If I had fallen out with the Kohns I would not have been able to use the facility in the future. Still, it was a painful lesson in the realities of business.

AS SOON AS I BECAME SALES PROMOTION Manager at Plymouth, I began planning a marketing strategy for my favorite car, the stunning new 1957 Fury. I loved this car, with its special gold anodized trim, powerful dual-quad engine, and stunning looks. I saw all kinds of promotional opportunities, using it as a "halo" for the entire Plymouth line. I convinced the ad guys to buy a lot of space in the car magazines. In fact, I was responsible for *Motor Trend* and *Hot Rod* magazines getting their first automotive factory ad schedule, which was built around the Fury. We later followed up by buying the first full-color ad ever placed in these magazines by a Detroit automaker, also for the Fury.

Before the 1957 car, Plymouth was considered stodgy. The 1957 restyling made it look young and exciting, and now the Fury added the necessary performance.

Although changed very little in styling for 1958, the Fury got a new engine, a 350 cubic inch version of Chrysler's new B-engine program. This made a good car even better. Until then, all Furys were painted an eggshell white with a gold anodized stripe down the side. I had a special car painted in black with the same anodized gold trim. It was sensational! I called it the Black Fury, and had a special fender badge cast in gold featuring that name.

What I didn't know was that the people in product planning were not looking for input from marketing and sales. For example, they had already decided that for 1959 the Fury was going to become a full line of cars, including a Station Wagon and a four-door Sedan. Consequently, the Black Fury program died before it ever got off the ground. I was told to stop worrying about planning and stay in my marketing area.

It was at this time that the name Pontiac started to pop up all around town. The story was that a guy named Bunkie Knudsen had taken over the Pontiac Division in 1956 and had been given the responsibility of saving it from extinction. GM was considering dropping the entire car line because of several years of disappointing sales. The story went on that Knudsen was lighting a fire under Pontiac. He had already stripped the "Silver Streaks" off the car and was now planning to replace the traditional Indian Head emblem with a more contemporary looking symbol.

Automotive News, the industry's weekly newspaper, ran a story about him. It said he had issued a challenge to all of the people around him, including his ad agency: "We're going racing, and we're going to build some really exciting cars here at Pontiac, so you better get some new people on your staff who know and like cars." I was impressed. "Get some people who know and like cars!" This could be me, I thought. Here's a guy who likes cars, maybe as much as I do; I'd sure like to talk to him.

Pontiac's first modern V-8 lead the way in lightweight, stamped-steel valve train technology. Pontiac's conservative management underpromoted the excitement of the new engine, which led to a divisional house cleaning and set the stage for Bunkie Knudsen's appointment as General Manager.

Fortuitously, in an odd way, my setback at Plymouth was even more serious than I had thought. I had really antagonized some top level guys with my Black Fury idea and my penchant for sticking my nose into product planning, where they thought it didn't belong. It was over for me at Chrysler. It had been a great place to get some experience and learn what it was like to be a client, but it was time for me to look for a new job.

5

A Player on the "Hot" Team

Finally, Pontiac

REMEMBERING MY IMPRESSION OF what was going on at Pontiac, I thought that was a good place to start. I was unable to meet Mr. Knudsen directly, but I was successful in arranging an interview with Jim Graham, the Pontiac Account Supervisor at MacManus, John & Adams, Pontiac's advertising agency. The interview went great. We communicated very well. He could tell I knew quite a bit about cars and the car business. The fact that I was working was a plus, too; it seems as though the auto people in Detroit always liked to hire away from another car company. In this case they especially liked to be able to tell Knudsen that they "stole a car guy" from Chrysler!

In our first interview, Graham confessed to me that he had experienced some uncomfortable meetings with Knudsen. Graham liked cars, and had a good understanding about car marketing, but he was not an intense product guy, nor was he interested in racing or performance. Graham told me he wanted someone on his staff he could talk with to prepare for his meetings with Bunkie. He certainly didn't need help with Pontiac account business. He just wanted to be up-to-date with what was going on in the industry—particularly with the competition—to be able to tell Knudsen some things he might not already know.

So early in 1958, I joined the MacManus agency as an Assistant Account Executive. I came aboard just as the agency was creating their ad campaign to introduce the new 1959 Pontiac. I was thrown right into the middle of the activity, which provided an excellent opportunity to observe and learn a whole lot about the new car, and the men responsible for promoting it. This was an experience I had never been privileged to be involved with while at Chrysler or Chevrolet.

I was really impressed with Pontiac's aggressive desire to move away from their association with the "Indian." Chief Pontiac was a solid icon, but it immediately connected the car to that stodgy image. It really was grandpa's car: conservative, reliable, and dependable. While those certainly were all positive attributes, there was no excitement, no fun, no sex appeal, and that was not where Knudsen wanted his new Pontiac to be. Removing the Indian identification (including the familiar Chief Pontiac hood ornament, the one that lit up) was the right move.

What was even more significant about this car was its new stance, or tread width between the wheels. It gave the car a macho, muscular appearance with overtones of performance and handling.

I wasn't there to see it, but the story told is that the designers had mounted a new, wider 1959 prototype body on a carryover 1958 chassis. Needless to say, the body hung out over its wheels. Knudsen didn't like it, and neither did styling boss Harley Earl. It made this dramatically styled new body look ungainly. The car didn't even look safe, let alone attractive. Together Knudsen and Earl made the decision to move the wheels out further. Whether Knudsen actually uttered the infamous line, "This thing looks like a football player wearing ballet slippers!" has never been confirmed, but he did instruct the chassis engineers to move the wheels out so the car took a wider stance and didn't look like it was about to roll over. Thus was born the "Wide-Track Pontiac" for 1959. What's most interesting is that the Wide-Track concept was not a result of serious engineering, it was simply the answer to a bothersome styling problem.

The Origin of Wide-Track

How it got its name, however, is another story, and it reveals the dark side of our business.

The 1959 Pontiac was a sensational new car, and needed a new advertising theme. We concluded that the wider stance could be the foundation for that new theme.

Under the leadership of Milt Coulson, who was the Creative Director on

Jim Graham was the Pontiac account supervisor at MacManus from 1957 through 1962. Graham liked the work I had done at Chevrolet and Chrysler and hired me in 1958 in response to Knudsen's directive to find "people who like cars."

the Pontiac account, they conceived the term "Wide-Track." Everyone at the agency was blown away by the phrase. The theme was a natural. It accomplished something that every marketer tries to do, develop a nickname for their product, a name or a phrase that personifies it. If we could get Wide-Track associated quickly with the new 1959 Pontiac, it would not only separate it from previous Pontiacs, but would also make it stand out in an already overcrowded marketplace.

The agency team was very pleased with the presentation they had prepared for Knudsen and his staff, which included Frank Bridge, the General Sales Manager. Bridge had been transferred from Buick to provide Mr. Knudsen with an experienced sales arm.

Coulson's presentation was powerful. One of the highlights was the proposed newspaper announcement ad (TV was still in its infancy in those days), which was a double truck (two-page spread) with a simple line drawing of the new front end stretched across the entire two pages. The wheels were moved out as close as possible to the end of both sides of the car. This ad was to run with no Pontiac identification as a teaser the day before the actual new car announcement. The only copy was a line running across the bottom of the two pages, reading, "Who in the world builds this beauty?" The next day, announcement day, the same ad would run again, but this time the line across the bottom would read, "Introducing the new 1959 Pontiac. The only car with 'Wide-Track wheels.' " I thought it was great stuff. For some strange reason, Knudsen did not. He didn't reject it, but he didn't embrace it either. While he had no actual advertising experience, he knew what he liked, and he understood his own feelings. At the end of the meeting Knudsen simply said he was intrigued with the Wide-Track idea, but perhaps we ought to consider some alternatives. Everybody else on his staff was strangely very silent.

In those days it was normal for an ad agency to present two, or even three ideas for a new model announcement. The client would then select the one they liked best. MJ&A felt so strongly about the Wide-Track concept that they didn't present any alternatives. They came out with all guns firing behind Wide-Track. Naturally, it was with some dismay and concern that we left the meeting. Coulson was particularly upset, but he immediately went to work with his group on developing an alternative program. The people at MJ&A were pros, so it was no surprise when they came up with another idea, which in many ways was every bit as good as Wide-Track. I didn't like it, however, because it didn't come right out of the car, and didn't have the potential to become that desired nickname.

The new campaign was built around the term "Sports Stance," using a series of examples involving athletes. It showed how the long-ball hitter in baseball steps up to the plate, spreading his feet farther apart to take a wider, better balanced stance to hit that long home run. Another analogy was the football quarterback who spreads his feet further apart when setting up for that long touchdown pass. There were similar examples involving tennis and golf.

We went back to Pontiac where Milt Coulson made the second presentation. Coulson was very bright and very quick, and on occasion it was easy to misread him as appearing a bit too cute or sarcastic. He presented the new Sports Stance idea, and then immediately went back to reopen discussion on the Wide-Track program. Coulson made an impassioned plea for Wide-Track, pointing out that it not only introduced a totally new product, but also a new marketing era. Knudsen allowed that much of that was true, but then turned abruptly to his own people and said, "We'll excuse the agency now and review both of these ideas." He thanked us and said, "We'll let you know."

Nobody on the Pontiac account team that witnessed this experience was prepared for what happened next. Three days after Coulson's presentation, the President of the agency, Ernie Jones, and the top Pontiac account man, Jim Graham were invited to come back to Pontiac for a follow-up meeting.

"Well, you guys have sold me," Knudsen said matter-of-factly. He then proceeded to tell the MacManus management that he felt he had been insulted by Coulson during the presentation, and did not want to see him again at Pontiac. So while Knudsen bought the Wide-Track theme, he banished the creative genius who had invented it.

Interestingly enough, Wide-Track stayed with Pontiac all the way into the early seventies, when in fact they no longer had the widest tread in the industry. The Federal Trade Commission advised Pontiac that they had evidence to prove that the Wide-Track Pontiac concept was no longer true. But there were some very specific exceptions. Through the years, Pontiac had effectively varied the use of Wide-Track. For example, we called the Pontiac factory in Pontiac, Michigan, "Wide-Track Town." On many occasions the dealers were called "The Great Wide-Trackers," or "The Men of Wide-Track." All of these could remain in use, but in any reference to the car itself they could no longer describe it as the Wide-Track Pontiac.

WHO WAS SEMON E. "BUNKIE" KNUDSEN? Perhaps the best way to explain him is to understand that at General Motors today, the Division General Manager doesn't wield anywhere near the same clout he did forty years ago. A General Manager back then shaped the direction of his Division and literally called its every move. In 1956, when Bunkie Knudsen was charged by Harlow Curtice, then President of GM, to turn Pontiac around, he was given carte blanche to do whatever was necessary. There was a certain irony to that move, since Knudsen's father, "Big Bill" Knudsen, had been President of GM back in the thirties, and had tapped young Mr. Curtice to take over the floundering Buick Division, which was facing extinction much as Pontiac found itself in the mid-fifties. Twenty years later, Harlow Curtice, having successfully turned Buick around, was now GM's President, and remembering the opportunity Knudsen's father had offered him, he was now selecting Big Bill's son as the man to resurrect Pontiac.

To assist Knudsen, Curtice chose his long time friend, Frank Bridge, who had been an Assistant Sales Manager at Buick. Promoted to General

"MY WHAT WIDE TRACKS! - SUPPOSE IT COULD BE A PONTIAC ?"

The words "Wide-Track" and "Pontiac" became synonymous, proving that the term Wide-Track reached far beyond the Pontiac showroom. Every advertising man's dream is to have his product's slogan weave its way into the fabric of American culture, as it did in this cartoon.

Sales Manager at Pontiac, Bridge was brought in to assist Knudsen, who had little familiarity with marketing or sales. Bridge was an experienced sales manager, though he had only a small understanding of marketing. That wasn't important in the fifties, because the GM system itself didn't understand marketing, particularly the vast difference between sales and marketing. If you were a good sales manager, they thought you were just naturally a good marketer. The prevailing logic at the time was that anybody could understand advertising. The truth was that the ad agencies did most of the creative marketing, and the sales managers just approved it. The Public Relations folks, who should have been an important part of the marketing team, were off on their own, not reporting to the Sales Manager or even to the General Manager. Instead, they took their directions from the Corporate PR Manager. They put out good press releases on new models and on personnel promotions, but they certainly weren't part of the marketing, where they could have been a ton of help.

I felt that Knudsen never totally warmed up to Frank Bridge, but he was smart enough to recognize Bridge's strengths: good sales management, organized car distribution, and most important, dealer control. Pontiac dealers in the 1956–57 period were a dissatisfied and demoralized group. They had believed the 1955 product was going to completely solve all their problems, and it didn't. While the car was all-new, the marketing was not. By 1956, the "new" 1955 car had already faded into middle of the road "Silver Streak" mediocrity, and once again was overpowered by the exciting Olds Rocket on one side, and the new Hot One from Chevrolet on the other.

Another problem was their dealer age. They had been around for a long time and had made a lot of money. It was going to take some inspired leadership to get them jumping again. Bridge was good at that. He had a talent for motivating dealers, and he was also good at finding new dealers. Frank was the kind of guy who would socialize with his dealers and overnight become their buddy, their personal "in" at the factory. Frank was of the old school. He really knew how to "move iron." If the factory needed a few thousand more cars to make a quota for the month, he'd get on the phone and call Rudy in Minneapolis, Bob in Los Angeles, Lou down in St. Louis, and Eli over in New York City. He'd say, "Eli, I need another 50 cars from you, and I mean regular Catalinas, nothing special." In return, Bridge might slip a few hard-to-get Bonneville convertibles into the mix.

Knowing who to call was Bridge's strength. What he didn't understand however, was product image, and yet he was responsible for approving the advertising. Selling a new car to a prospect once in the Pontiac showroom was one thing, but bringing that prospect into the Pontiac showroom in the first place was the challenge. Why should a customer bother to look at a Pontiac when there was that "Hot Chevy" or a "swingin'" Olds Rocket or even a "sophisticated" Buick to see? Pontiac had no image to attract buyer interest. It was reliable and dependable, but so what? So was everything else. Was a Pontiac fun, or prestigious? If it was, no one knew it. Was it exciting? Hell no! At least nobody thought it was.

Sales vs. Marketing

So therein was the problem, and Frank Bridge didn't have the love, or the passion for the product to step up to it. Admittedly, image is not all that sells a car. Cars are still sold one at a time by a sales consultant in a showroom. But an exciting image sure brings a lot more eager and positive thinking customers into the showroom. If you don't get them in, you can't sell them—superstores, computers, websites notwithstanding.

Bunkie Knudsen was an engineer and a real "product guy" who simply loved cars. His primary responsibility was product. He had to get styling in line, get engineering aboard, and get manufacturing on the same team. But that was only the beginning.

When Knudsen got there Pontiac was a good car, but where did it go from there? The styling was awkward, the performance conservative, and the image...well, there wasn't one, or at least a good one. It was "Grandma's car." The advertising reflected this. Pontiac claimed it was a "General Motors Masterpiece." Ho-hum. They bragged that it was "Built to last 100,000 miles," and it usually did. Thus, their conservative owners were in no hurry to replace their old car, especially when the new one was no more exciting.

Pontiac offered two flat-head engines, an inline six and an inline eight. The eight was the highline package, and to show how middle-of-the-road it was, General Motors, in their proving grounds testing, used the Pontiac straight eight with a Hydra-matic transmission as the standard of acceptable performance for the entire Corporation! Any car in the GM lineup that couldn't run with the eight cylinder Pontiac was considered below average in performance. Conversely, a car that could beat the Pontiac straight eight was considered to be above average in performance.

The first thing Knudsen did when he arrived at Pontiac was to come to grips with this boring image problem, the problem that had the division headed for extinction. The famed Silver Streaks, a pair of chrome strips that went over the hood and down the rear deck, had decorated every Pontiac since the thirties. Removing them, as Knudsen did almost immediately after he arrived in 1956, was more symbolic than functional, but it served notice that this new guy understood: before you can change image, you've got to change product. By 1957, Pontiac had become a bit more handsome, and with its new 347 cubic inch engine it just might have been capable of "beating somebody."

Already underway, even before Knudsen got there, was a new Rochester fuel injection system. It was to bow on the 1957 Chevy and Pontiac. Unfortunately, Chevrolet was out in front because of their sporty Corvette. Knudsen knew that the Rochester system was exactly what Pontiac needed, but rather than offer this exciting new feature across the entire line, and let the Chevrolet Corvette steal the thunder, he decided to package it in a special model. That car, named Bonneville, was already in place, it too having been started before Bunkie arrived. As a limited production convertible, it was exactly what Knudsen had envisioned as the car to start changing Pontiac's stodgy image.

Named after a successful mid-fifties Pontiac dream car, and enhanced by a special record-breaking Pontiac speed run on the Bonneville Salt Flats in 1956, the Bonneville became the first public symbol of the rejuvenated Pontiac Division. When the car was introduced at the Daytona Beach Speed Week activities in early February 1957, it was an instant hit. It was just the image car Knudsen had envisioned. It was available only as a fuel injected convertible in very modest quantities (only 630). After all, a $5700 dollar Pontiac in 1957 wasn't meant for everybody, but it got great press and had people talking about Pontiac. Suddenly there was a new player in the game. In less than a year after taking over the Division, Knudsen had introduced a car that was ultimately to become one of the most sought-after Pontiacs of all time. Grandma was about to become a swinger.

ANOTHER MAN KNUDSEN RECRUITED for his new team was a very popular engineer from Oldsmobile, Elliot M. "Pete" Estes. Estes has been an Assistant Chief Engineer with Olds, and was joining Pontiac as their new Chief Engineer. While at Oldsmobile, Estes had been deeply involved with their successful Rocket engine program and the continuous improvement of their Hydra-matic transmission. Estes was known in the corporation as an engineer's engineer. He didn't have any particular experience in marketing, nor was he a racing enthusiast.

Knudsen and Estes worked well as a team. One of the smartest early moves they made was to hire a very talented young engineer who had become available after the collapse of the Studebaker-Packard organization. His name was John Zachary DeLorean, a name that would soon become indelibly imprinted in all the Pontiac history books. This trilogy of talent, Knudsen, Estes, and DeLorean, went on to build more than a decade of the most exciting and successful new cars the U.S. auto industry had ever seen, and all coming out of one manufacturer. I was lucky enough to be a part of it.

The introduction of the fuel injected Bonneville and the availability of the Tri-Power engine in 1957 began to chip away at the stodgy image. The '57 Pontiac was indeed a more youthful appearing car. Its front-end styling, while good looking, became very controversial and was the subject of many public jokes. Many thought the grille looked like an exploded view of a Remington electric shaver. The line, "I used my Pontiac to get a close shave this morning," was always good for a laugh. As a marketer, I didn't think that was all bad—at least people were thinking and talking about a Pontiac.

For 1958, Bonneville boasted an all-new body, featuring both a convertible and a hardtop coupe. Unfortunately, the entire U.S. auto industry suffered a huge sales tumble that year and Pontiac got caught in the middle. Only the new Bonneville enjoyed any kind of sales success, but in the end, 1958 turned out to be Pontiac's all-time modern low mark, when sales slipped to little more than 217, 000 units.

Since he had been given a five-year period in which to turn the Division around, Knudsen was again under some pressure, although GM management did understand that the 1958 sales setback was industry-wide. They also were aware of Knudsen's new 1959 car, and the fact that this was his first shot at bringing to market a complete program of his own. The fate of everybody connected with the division, even Mr. Knudsen himself, depended on the public acceptance of this new car. Well it didn't take long. 1959 was the turning point. The entire Pontiac line, from Bonneville to Star Chief to Catalina was the hit of all the early auto shows. The Indian continued to be downplayed. Catalina was no longer just a two-door hardtop, it was now a full line, as was the premium highline Bonneville. Only the Indian name Star Chief remained, as management didn't want to totally orphan all of the previous nameplates. We also knew we had to continue to use the Indian head emblem somewhere on the car, or we faced the chance of losing the trademark. Thus, the hi-beam headlight indicator in the center of the instrument cluster remained as the last symbolic silhouette of Chief Pontiac. Needless to say, Pontiac never again came close to matching those low 1958 sales numbers.

The new 1959 car introduced a whole new era, I like to call it the "Wide-Track Era." Not only the car, but the entire Division took on a new personality that would lead to an extended period of phenomenal sales growth, not matched in the industry before or since: From that low point of just over 200,000 sales in 1958 to more than 900,000 sales in 1969. Match that! The concept of "The Wide-Track Pontiac" became the umbrella for this whole new era. It wasn't just about styling or about engineering or about performance. It wasn't just about an old man's car suddenly becoming a teenager's

Right: Pontiac employees knew things would forever be changed when Knudsen ripped the "suspenders" off the 1957 model. It was a grandstand play that drove the message home: Pontiac was no longer connected to its old staid and conservative image. The move wasn't a total success, as the grille's appearance was jokingly compared to an electric shaver.

Above: The auto industry took it on the chin in 1958. A recession and styling excesses that turned off customers put a dent in Detroit's sales. Pontiac also suffered, selling only slightly more than 217,000 units, the division's all-time modern low. My first Pontiac was a 1958 Tri-Power Bonneville coupe painted in "Coffee and Cream."

delight. This was about bringing the right car into the right marketplace at the right time, and with the right promotion.

Amid this success a quirky controversy developed that made news headlines. Soon after the first owners got their new Wide-Track cars, they tried to get them washed at the automatic carwash and discovered that their new Wide-Track Pontiac was too wide to fit in the existing tracks. The car wash owners feared that this "wide stuff" was going to become a new trend throughout the industry, so they launched a formal plea, asking Pontiac to stop building these "foolish wide cars." They even threatened a lawsuit, and of course, that made the newspapers.

All that news became a positive, as public opinion was starting to believe that Pontiac had literally re-invented their car, and it was the newest of all the new cars on the road. Our Wide-Track advertising reinforced that image.

Another advantage the 1959 Pontiac enjoyed was its engine, featuring 389 cubic inches, with over 300 horsepower and over 400 lbs/ft of torque. For the first time, Pontiac was viewed as a big step up from Chevrolet. The advertising was no longer puffery or pushing just another "General Motors Masterpiece." It was now a "Wide-Track Pontiac," and that meant it had

Pontiac's new Wide-Track look resulted in an almost immediate sales turn around. Buell Starr, Manufacturing Manager and Bob Longpre, Production Manager, note Pontiac's successful production milestone.

style, a big engine (the biggest Chevy had that year was only 348 cubic inches), and new prestige. This new image came right out of the car. Here was a car that reached out and grabbed you right on the street. People could recognize it because of its stance. The car was literally a traveling ad selling itself.

I can remember sitting in the grandstands at the Daytona International Speedway in February, 1960, watching the Daytona 500. Early in the race, six Pontiacs had stretched out on the rest of the field by almost a quarter lap. There were some folks sitting right behind me who didn't know me or that I worked with Pontiac. One guy, the self-appointed racing expert, was explaining to the others, "Watch those Pontiacs when they go into the turns. See how they don't lean, and how much more stable they are than the rest of the cars? That's because they got that Wide-Track. Their wheels are mounted further out than every other car out there. That's what gives them that better grip in the turns!" It was as if I had written a script for him. Incidentally, a Pontiac didn't win that day. Junior Johnson won, driving a Chevy, proving that the fastest car doesn't always win the race.

Even though the '59 was considered to be a great-looking car, there was some controversy within Pontiac about the split grille front-end design. While it added significantly to the wider look, and helped make the car look more muscular, there were enough dissenters even in the design studio to cause concern. Though Bunkie himself loved the split grille, he listened to the dissenters. Consequently the 1960 car bowed with a more conventional, albeit very tasteful, new front end design. The grille stretched from headlight to headlight, with a decided horizontal look, meeting in the center to

In recognition of the Division's dramatic Wide-Track concept, Motor Trend named Pontiac its 1959 Car Of The Year. Bunkie Knudsen accepts the coveted trophy from Editor Walt Woron.

form a modest, forward-protruding "nose." Some called it a "coffin nose," others likened it to a shark.

We had featured the split grille in 1959 advertising, and in 1960 some of the public remembered. "What happened to the split grille?" they asked. Knudsen reversed his preference, and a split grille reappeared on all 1961 Pontiacs, including the new intermediate Tempest. There have been some compromises, of course, but the split-grille theme has remained a very important part of Pontiac's styling and image for almost 40 years.

KNUDSEN WAS AN INVETERATE RACER. Through the years he had befriended racers and race-car builders like Mickey Thompson, Ray Nichels, and Smoky Yunick, all young and proficient in their field. Bunkie put them on as consultants. There were even occasional rumors that Knudsen was so committed to developing a performance image for his new Pontiacs that he was contributing some of his own personal funds, when it was difficult to justify those kinds of expenditures to the Corporation.

Pontiac actually had some racing activity underway in 1956, even before Knudsen arrived. It was, in fact, the first time any Pontiac had ever entered into organized racing competition. They had commissioned race car builder Lou Moore to develop two cars to run in the NASCAR Grand National Stock Car Race on the beach at Daytona in February, 1956. Pontiac engineering had released some special equipment, including a dual 4-barrel intake manifold and carburetor package and a new hi-performance solid lifter camshaft. This combination was rated at 285 horsepower. The cars were driven by Cot-

In 1960, the split grille front end was replaced by a horizontal bar design (often called the "coffin nose") stretching from headlamp to headlamp. Ads emphasized that while all Pontiacs had Wide-Track, it was the stance of the tread, not the intimidating width of the car, that set Pontiac apart.

The 1961 Pontiac was smaller and lighter than its predecessor, a trend that was popular throughout the industry. The split-grille theme was back and new multi-colored interiors were introduced, sparked by styling coordinator Herb Kadau.

ton Owens and Buddy Krebs. Owens was a veteran of NASCAR Stock Car Racing right from its inception, while Krebs had been a very successful motorcycle racer.

I was at the race, representing Chrysler at the time, never dreaming that only two years later I would be deeply involved with promoting Pontiac. A Chrysler 300, driven by NASCAR champion Tim Flock was the car to beat. Nothing in the field was expected to match that Chrysler on the beach.

The race started as expected, with Flock's Chrysler stretching out to a comfortable lead, when suddenly everybody realized that two Pontiacs were hanging right with him. By lap 20, Flock's Chrysler 300 with the two Pontiacs right on its tail were almost a half lap ahead of the rest of the field. The Pontiacs couldn't pass the Chrysler, nor could the Chrysler run away from the Pontiacs. These three cars continued to stretch their lead over the pack until lap 24, when both Pontiacs threw their fan belts (at least that was the official report) and were forced to retire. Certainly, the stock car racing world was served notice as to what was coming from Pontiac.

Four months later, Knudsen took over and quickly grabbed the reins of the racing program, setting up Ray Nichels to organize it. Knudsen wanted to be up and running at Daytona Beach in February of 1957. If the 1956 Daytona experience had been good, 1957 was even better, as names like John Zink Jr., John Littlejohn, and Cotton Owens all participated in Pontiac's absolute dominance of the mid-winter Florida race activity.

The program produced some very satisfying results, although most of the special parts they used were supplied by aftermarket manufacturers. They developed items like intake manifolds, rear axle gears, camshafts and carburetors. Pontiac provided the specifications and the aftermarket fabricated the parts. We then put them in the parts catalogue, enabling the dealer to either stock the part or know how to order it.

Super Duty Begins

In the meantime Knudsen, who wanted these parts to be designed in-house, created a special group within his Engineering Department. It was to be called the Super Duty Group, a name that stuck around for a long time in the Pontiac performance world. At the same time in 1957, the Automobile Manufacturer's Association (AMA), whose members included all the domestic automakers, announced that they had reached a "gentlemen's agreement" amongst themselves to back out of organized racing and stop supplying any special support. Knudsen, who had decided to build his new Pontiac image around youth and performance—and that included an absolute must involvement with racing—was heard to say, "If those guys want to be fools and withdraw from racing, let them. But I've got a car to save, and I haven't got time to be a gentleman. We're going racing." He charged his new Super Duty Group with the responsibility of building Pontiac into a consistent winner on the track with all Pontiac parts, and they had to do it within two years.

Early members of that group were engine design specialists Malcolm R. "Mac" McKellar and Russ Gee, along with a young chassis expert named Bill Collins. Coordinating the group was Bill Klinger, who was a good engineer and a tough administrator. Though he knew a lot about performance, Bill was not a racer or even a racing enthusiast. Once the Super Duty program got off the ground, the parts distribution fell into the hands of a very capable guy named Frank Barnard.

Nobody knew the Pontiac engine better than the engineering team who had created it. The aftermarket certainly didn't have the resources to match Pontiac Engineering. A good example was the failure of the Iskendarian E-2 camshaft (not to suggest that Isky built bad camshafts). The camshaft performed beautifully when operating in the higher rpm range, but the metallurgy could not stand up to Pontiac's severe valve action at lower rpm. Some of this wear could also be traced to Pontiac's marginal oiling system, but the result was that this solid-lifter camshaft did not stand up to daily street use.

The goal of the Super Duty group was to develop a package of Pontiac parts that would withstand the stress of "heavy duty service." Consequently camshafts, crankshafts, forged connecting rods, special main and rod bearings, high compression pistons, high flow intake manifolds, special valves and free flowing exhaust manifolds were just a few of the components that were part of this new engine package, to be known as "The Super Duty."

The new exhaust manifolds, for example, were incredibly efficient for production pieces. In the past, production exhaust manifolds were always inefficient, and up to this time, there hadn't been much research in exhaust header development. In spite of their efficient design, these new manifolds were made of cast iron, making them very heavy. That didn't make a whole lot of difference to the NASCAR guys, but when Pontiac chose to take the Super Duty package to the drag strip, they attempted to lighten the weight of these new manifolds by casting them in aluminum. That cut their weight by more than fifty percent, but presented another problem. You could start your engine, clean off your tires, pull up to the starting line and make a quarter mile pass. Then you had to immediately shut down the engine, because if the aluminum manifolds got too hot they would actually melt. You didn't dare drive back the return road to the pits for fear the manifolds would just disintegrate.

When the much awaited Super Duty package arrived early in the 1960 model year, it was the winner Knudsen had hoped for. Remember, all the other carmakers had been backing off. As Pontiac picked up one win after another, we began to work them into advertising copy to supplement our Wide-Track message. We inferred that these new Pontiacs were winning on the race track because they had Wide-Track Wheels, and that's why they were so comfortable, so safe and so smooth. It was a perfect way to make "racing" work for the consumer. Most importantly it gave real product meaning to what was fast becoming the phenomenal Wide-Track era.

When the new Super Duty Pontiacs first entered competition, it was apparent from the very first lap around the race track that Pontiac was the car to beat. It got to the point where the joke around NASCAR was, "It will be a good race if those !#$%#$! Pontiacs don't show up." Every race was Pontiac's race to lose, and if they didn't win it was because they hit the wall or blew an engine.

KNUDSEN'S NEW TEAM WAS ALSO QUICK to recognize the rapid growth of drag racing in the late fifties, and made sure their new Super Duty parts were both appropriate and available to the new generation of stock car drag racers.

The number one drag racing sanctioning body, the National Hot Rod Association (NHRA) also quickly saw the wisdom of including stock cars as a major part of their program. They knew this new generation of car enthusiasts wanted to drive their car to work or to school during the week, and on

Super Duty Engines and Drag Racing

The Super Duty engine was strictly for racing competition. The H.O. (high output) engine went into the best performing production cars. There was one very clear rule that Pontiac followed without compromise: Any engine that used a solid lifter camshaft, such as the Super Duty, carried no factory warranty. The problem was that the severe valve action made it virtually impossible to keep a camshaft in that engine if you were going to do any idling around town. Starting up on a cold morning could "scuff" the camshaft so quickly that it would begin to lose its coating.

All production engines, even the H.O.s, were equipped with hydraulic lifters and therefore qualified for warranty. In fact, Pontiac would only build a car on the assembly line if it were equipped with hydraulic valve lifters. The Super Duty engines were installed on special order in the Engineering garage, or by the customer (dealer) at their facility. There was a disclaimer provided with every solid-lifter engine package (Super Duty) that stated it was "for racing purposes only."

As drag racing became more popular, the Super Duty Pontiacs that had performed so beautifully in NASCAR were coming into their own. Thanks to our image building around these NASCAR wins, the Super Duty Pontiac was starting to be perceived as the hot new ticket at the drags, too.

Although the Super Duty had the image, it wasn't a production engine and was difficult to get. The H.O. was the ultimate production-line, hydraulic-camshaft engine. That was the engine the part-time drag racer could get at any Pontiac dealership. It was great for a street car that could be driven back and forth to work or school during the week, and then taken to the drag strip on weekends. It was truly a weekend warrior and that's what was making the NHRA grow at that time. It wasn't the professional world of "ground shaking fuelers" or "alcohol burners" that drag racing has turned into today. NHRA drag racing then was just a good, inexpensive, exclusively American way of having fun with your car on the weekend. Today that's somehow been lost as the NHRA has turned drag racing, perhaps inevitably, into a high-powered, professional spectator sport. Whatever happened to the little guy?

the weekends take it out to the drag strip, throw on a set of Atlas Bucron tires, drop the exhaust pipes and have some real fun. There were tracks opening up all over the country. The NHRA Nationals were to return to Detroit in 1960, and I felt it was very important that Pontiac make a good showing with the new Super Duty cars. There were a few '58s and '59s showing up in the lower stock classes, and they were pretty competitive, but we needed to dominate the Super Stock class to really "put on a show."

The drag racing program required some new hardware. In NASCAR only one 4-barrel carburetor was allowed, while in drag racing the Rochester Tri-Power system seemed to be more appropriate. As the Super Duty engine program matured, Pontiac Engineering developed a two-piece, dual 4-barrel intake manifold to feed the new 421 cubic inch engine. Mac McKellar designed several new camshaft profiles specifically for quarter-mile acceleration. Pontiac also released lower axle ratios and heavier duty clutches. With lightweight body parts and aggressive factory backing, Pontiacs were now wining races on the high speed ovals and on the nation's leading drag strips with regularity, gaining more attention and support from performance enthusiasts everywhere.

It was Knudsen's idea that performance was going to lead the change in Pontiac's image. Even he, however, could not have predicted the impact of the Wide-Track look, backed by the Super Duty racing wins. We were using racing as the stage to prove our promise of performance. While every Wide-Track Pontiac on the street literally "shouted out" by its very muscular appearance, it was truly "Race on Sunday, Build Image for Monday" that sup-

Fitz and Van

One unique aspect of Pontiac print advertising in the early sixties was the use of art rather than photography. This started in 1959, coincidentally with the appearance of Wide-Track. The agency recommended that with the dramatic new stance and muscular appearance of the car, it would be better if we used artwork since we could exaggerate a little, making the car look longer and wider.

Pontiac agreed, and the agency then proceeded to search for the best car artist in the business. They actually found two: Art Fitzpatrick, who painted cars, and Van Kaufman, who was a specialist in backgrounds. They sold themselves as a team, under the name "Fitz and Van." Their absolutely gorgeous cars in beautiful, dream-like backgrounds quickly became a very important part of Pontiac's new image-building effort.

When the Fitz and Van campaign first got started, the car was always the star. They never let the background overpower the car, and, yes, they exaggerated the hell out of both the length and width. Today, this technique would be laughed at as a spoof or a cartoon, but in those days the look was so distinctive you could instantly recognize a Pontiac ad.

By 1965, what started out as a great idea in 1961 had grown into a nightmare. Fitz and Van had built such a strong relationship with Pontiac that they had a contract guaranteeing them first right of refusal to provide artwork for every four-color ad Pontiac produced. They became independent, even arrogant, travelling on their own to Europe or the Caribbean or South America, painting beautiful background scenes, yet always leaving room to strip in a car. They maintained the proper perspective, and knew exactly how to position the car. You'd swear it was all painted at the same time. They would then tell us which car we should use with which background. When we would tell them that the message in the ad was going to feature a Station Wagon, they'd say, "Can't you see that these kind of people would not drive a Station Wagon? You should use a convertible, and a Bonneville at that." They didn't care what we were trying to accomplish with the ad.

After the GM racing ban in the mid-sixties, Pontiac could no longer just talk ported the claim. Of course, the Super Duty engine package was not what the average Pontiac buyer was choosing, but the association of their exciting Pontiac with these NASCAR and NHRA winners led to great owner satisfaction.

By now, many marketing people in Detroit were beginning to recognize the baby boomer generation. Soon these young people would become very influential in the selection of the new family car. Pontiac was at the leading edge of that vision. I could see that we really needed to learn how to communicate with this new group, and fast. Part of this communication had already been established by the enthusiast press. Now we needed to translate that "car talk" into advertising.

Shortly after I joined MacManus, I moved fast to get Pontiac advertising placed in the enthusiast magazines. Although I didn't have the authority at first, I got to the right people, both at the agency and at Pontiac, and convinced them how important it was for us to be talking to the car enthusiast in our advertising, as they would be the first ones to understand this sophisticated new product. We were already enjoying some progress in this area, thanks to the success of our cars on the racetrack. Frankly, I think some of our best enthusiast ads were some of our first. For example in one we didn't even show a picture of the car, but rather relied on the headline and the copy to tell the whole story. Headlines like, "There's a Tiger loose in the streets," or "Hands off the grab bar Charley, you're tearing out the dash," certainly got attention. These winners written by ace copywriter Roger Proulx are still favorites in Detroit's advertising history. They only existed because of Pontiac's early understanding and respect for the real car enthusiast. We were beginning to integrate the performance message into Pontiac advertising. Understanding the very subtle difference between "racing" and "performance" was crucial.

PONTIAC'S IMAGE WAS CHANGING so fast we were hardly able to keep up. The consistent racing wins were getting so much national press that suddenly the

about performance in ads since they didn't have any racing wins to back it up. So it became necessary to dramatize performance in our visuals, using action like spinning wheels and smoking tires to capture the feeling of excitement in driving. This called for photography. Fitz and Van's artwork was now inappropriate.

When we told Fitz and Van, their reaction was to remind us that they had a contract. We went to Pontiac to get some support, only to find that Fitz and Van, behind our backs, had convinced the Pontiac people that they were entirely capable of painting action artwork. As a compromise, we proposed that Fitz and Van continue to paint all the full size cars, like the Bonneville and Grand Prix, while we would use photography for the sportier intermediates. They fought it. I pleaded with John DeLorean, who by then was General Manager, until he finally saw the need to make the change. I had the feeling that Fitz and Van sincerely believed that their artwork was the sole reason for Pontiac's success. They certainly did play a crucial role, but eventually the market changed, and their style was no longer relevant.

new Wide-Track Pontiac was the car to beat, on or off the track. All of the new Super Duty parts were listed in the Pontiac parts book right along with things like a manual linkage for a Tri-Power assembly and Hurst 3- and 4-speed shifters. These over-the-counter pieces all had Pontiac part numbers. I developed a special enthusiast magazine ad showing all of these options and letting it be known that they were available across the parts counter of nearly every Pontiac dealer in the United States.

That was a start at educating the consumer. The next challenge was to educate the dealers. When our parts distribution program started in 1959, it became painfully apparent that the majority of the Pontiac dealers didn't know anything about performance. Worse, few of them cared. When this new knowledgable customer came into a Pontiac dealership for the first time, they were often disappointed, realizing that they already knew more about the product than either the dealer or his salespeople. Very little information about the new parts was drifting down to the dealer level. There had been some factory communications to service managers and parts managers, but most of the dealers didn't understand how much profit potential there was in selling and installing these high performance parts. Any effort we could make to help our dealers better understand this new generation of Wide-Track performance would make a huge difference.

Selling Performance At the Dealer

I could clearly see that selling performance parts through our dealerships could continue to elevate Pontiac's image and make our cars even more appealing to the emerging youth market. I suggested we put together a travelling seminar, including a performance service expert and a performance parts expert, to go out to the zone offices (the zone office was the center of factory communication to its dealers at that time) and hold week-long training sessions. Any dealer in the zone who wanted to, could send representatives to the meeting and get a free lesson in how to sell not only performance Pontiac cars, but also the performance parts and service that went with them. We hoped the interested dealers would quickly see the profit potential from selling performance "Pontiac style."

The First Aluminum Styled Wheel

Success bred innovation, and Knudsen was an innovator. For example, working with wheel manufacturer Kelsey-Hayes, Pontiac introduced the industry's first styled aluminum wheel in 1960, and it was an instant hit. I wouldn't dream of going anywhere without a set of those aluminum wheels on my car. That's what made a Pontiac look like a Pontiac. In addition to being beautiful, the wheels were also functional. They were cast integrally with the brake drum for better cooling.

With the addition of these unique aluminum wheels, plus the basic shape of the body stretched out to match its new wider stance, a new 1960 Pontiac was a spectacle all by itself. Every time you saw one on the street, you turned around and looked at it. It was a travelling ad. Naturally, sales went up accordingly.

I pitched my concept to my supervisor at the agency, who allowed me to make a presentation in early 1959 to Bunkie Knudsen, Pete Estes, and Frank Bridge. As I spoke, Knudsen kept nodding his head in approval. Though he didn't say anything, I was still grateful that for the first time in my entire career I was talking about marketing performance and someone was listening.

Estes didn't react either way. Bridge was totally negative. "The dealers have enough trouble learning how to sell our regular cars," he stated. "They don't need to get involved with anything special." Knudsen didn't comment as the meeting ended. It appeared my idea was going down in flames.

The 20-minute drive from Pontiac's office back to MacManus was especially long. When I arrived, I learned there had been a call for me from Knudsen. I could see that everyone was interested: I was still a minor league executive at that time, and not expected to receive calls from the General Manager of Pontiac.

I started to panic. All I could think about was what poor Milt Coulson had gone through after pitching the Wide-Track concept. My hands trembled as I returned Knudsen's call. "I want to apologize to you," he stated. "I think we were a little rough on you guys. Frankly, I think it's a damn good idea, but I can't second guess my sales manager." (It was common knowledge that because of Knudsen's inexperience, Bridge's responsibility was to keep an eye on him.) "I'll tell you what you do," Knudsen went on. "Go out and find a dealer who would like to become a performance specialist, like a guinea pig. I can't guarantee him any money, but you can tell him that the factory is interested. Tell him that if there's ever an opportunity for us to do him a favor, he can count on it."

With this promise I approached two Pontiac dealers in Detroit. I went first to Packer Pontiac, primarily because they were the biggest dealer in the area. They actually had three stores: one in Detroit, one in Flint, and one in Miami, Florida.

Royal Pontiac was ultimately chosen to be a "guinea pig" to test the concept of a dealer selling performance in order to promote Pontiac product.

While Bill Packer, Jr. was intrigued with the idea of being Pontiac's "back door" performance dealer, he wanted some time to think about it. The second dealer, Ace Wilson, Jr. of Royal Pontiac in suburban Royal Oak, was overwhelmed with the idea. Once I made the pitch he never gave me the chance to leave, making the decision to participate on the spot.

The legend of Royal Pontiac was about to begin.

6

The Royal Treatment

SELLING ROYAL ON BECOMING PONTIAC'S unofficial performance dealer meant a lot more than just making the sale. I also came along as part of the deal. I wanted this concept to work. I wanted Pontiac to embrace it and offer it to dealers all over the country. Needless to say, I got very involved.

I remember the first time I walked into Royal Pontiac. I had made an appointment to meet the dealer, a young man named Asa "Ace" Wilson, Jr. The Wilson name was well recognized in the Detroit area, thanks to the family dairy business. Since Ace Jr. didn't like the dairy business, his dad Asa Sr. decided to help him buy a new car dealership. They purchased a small Pontiac facility in suburban Royal Oak and called it Royal Pontiac. Once it began to gain prominence the name was changed to Ace Wilson's Royal Pontiac.

Ace was a bit of a playboy and a fun loving rogue. Today, we'd call him a screw-up. He had trouble finishing college, trouble with a few marriages, and trouble in the dairy business. He was an aggressive young man who enjoyed life. While I later learned that he had a serious drinking problem, the picture that Ace Jr. presented to me was of a young, active dealer who liked cars, loved the car business, and thought that getting into racing would be a "blast." I made it very clear to Ace Jr. right from the beginning that I had no official authority from Pontiac, though I did have a nice rapport with Bunkie Knudsen, and that everything we did would certainly get Knudsen's attention.

With the strong support of Ace Jr., we put the first modern dealership performance program together. This was September, 1959.

The first priority was to go through the parts catalogs and make sure Royal stocked the right performance parts. I would have the opportunity to sit down with the salesmen, if they wanted, and go over all the product combinations involving special options and special parts. This would enable them to put together some pretty sophisticated cars, cars that could not be found at other Pontiac dealerships.

DO-IT-YOURSELF
DELIGHT
(and all you need is a pencil)
How'd you like to design yourself a car that fits you like the proverbial glove? Nothing to it. (A) Figure out what kind of car you're after. All-out competition? A real luxury chariot? You name it. And then (B) get your hands on a Pontiac option list. Check off the items that appeal to you, from a list that looks a quarter-mile long. You've got 10 engines to choose from, ranging from the 215-hp standard powerplant up to the wild blue yonder. Ten transmission options: two 3-speed synchromeshes, two 4-speed sticks* and six performance geared Hydra-Matics*. Axle ratios, suspension options*, all kinds of performance, comfort and convenience accessories* . . . well, you take it from there.
One word, though: plan to spend some time working out your specs. You're going to be driving it and you might as well enjoy it to the utmost. But with the Catalina's solidly sensible price tag and that long, long list of goodies, enjoying yourself is the easiest part. Pontiac Motor Division, General Motors Corporation.
PONTIAC
CATALINA
*Optional at extra cost.

We wanted to make enthusiasts aware that Pontiac had the hardware necessary to make their cars top performers. Much of this hardware could be installed on factory-ordered cars or be ordered over the parts counter. For the most part, dealers were unaware of these high performance parts and didn't care to know. For those dealers that did, like Royal Pontiac, it opened up new opportunities for profits.

Dealers didn't carry the high inventories they do today, especially cars with unusual options. A customer could order out a car and expect delivery in about three weeks. For example, if you wanted to save weight it was easy to get a car with no extra insulation. In a Catalina that saved almost 90 pounds. The car certainly would be noisier, but it was faster, too! You simply wrote "delete insulation" in the proper place on the order form. Customers could come in and tell the trained Royal salesman what they thought they wanted. The Royal salesman would then tell the customer how to order the car with exactly the right combination of options. That kind of professional counsel, totally understanding the product, was to become Royal's trademark.

In the early going, Ace Jr. loved every minute of it. He made sure he had a couple of sharp mechanics who knew how to service the performance cars. Most of them were H.O., or "A-engine" cars as we used to call them, equipped with a manual transmission, Tri-Power, a longer duration hydraulic camshaft, and the good exhaust systems. Royal always had a demo equipped with just the right performance options to be able to show their customers exactly what they could expect.

One salesman who really understood was Dick Jesse. He was jokingly called the "Performance Sales Manager." He sat in the front office and in the early days was the only guy interested in spending time with special customers. At first, the rest of the salesman all laughed at the idea and snickered at Jesse's title. They quit laughing, however, when they saw customers literally standing in line waiting to talk only to Dick Jesse. Suddenly they all wanted a piece of the action, although they were ill-prepared.

The almost immediate success of the Royal program proved that it was a good idea, that there was indeed an opportunity for a dealer to make significant additional profit selling performance.

Training Royal Salesmen

Royal Pontiac's General Sales Manager, Tom McQueen, was the quintessential stereotype. He knew every trick in the book about how to sell a car, he knew how to motivate and manage his salesman, and he knew how to get the most profit out of every deal. The last thing he wanted was to get involved with this "racing crap." "I don't understand it," McQueen would say, "and I don't want to understand it." He really didn't like cars. In his opinion the only good car was one that had just "gone over the curb." As Royal began to sell more and more performance cars and the profits grew, McQueen grudgingly accepted the program, but at the same time he constantly complained that selling these special performance cars got in the way of selling the "bread and butter."

Royal had two Service Managers. The top guy was named Joe Collogi. Joe was good, but he, too, didn't like performance cars. His logic was that if he "don't know anything about it" he didn't want it going on in his shop. This created a problem for Dick Jesse, since most of his customers came back to him for service.

Luckily, the Assistant Service Manager, Joe Voytusch, liked performance cars and enjoyed dealing with those customers. He automatically became the Performance Service Manager, and fortunately he and Jesse really worked well together. The parts department was managed by Sam Frontera, who later became almost as famous around Detroit as Royal itself. He was smart enough to see that if he followed the formula and stocked the right parts, he was going to have a bonanza. Doing so made Sam money, and he loved it. There were many times when other Detroit area Pontiac dealers would need a performance replacement part and couldn't find it. Reluctantly, they would call Royal, where Sam Frontera would not only have the part, he'd have it with a smile and even a reasonable price. Sam was a very important cog in Royal's success.

Sam was married to Louise Frontera, Royal's Office Manager. This turned out to be a real plus because Louise knew that the performance program was paying off, and she never let Ace Jr. forget it.

As the other salesmen started to sell performance cars—much to Dick Jesse's dismay—there was more action on the floor. No longer were there five or six customers waiting patiently to see Jesse, while every other salesman just stood around and watched. The other salesman had revolted as a group and demanded part of the action. But there were ground rules. You had to attend "Dick Jesse's school of Pontiac performance" before you could greet the first performance customer. Although Dick was forced to unveil his bag of tricks, he never gave away any customers. He did a superb job of keeping a very active customer list, and in many cases they became personal friends. With very few exceptions the other salesmen never made it, and Jesse soon had the bulk of the business back in his camp.

Using Drag Racing for Promotion

OF COURSE ROYAL'S CUSTOMERS DIDN'T just magically appear. This all had to be promoted. One of the first ways to do that was to put a car in action at the drag strip. Royal first started racing with regular production cars. We would take one of our demos to the track, and many times they ran so good we would actually sell them right there.

The first Royal race car was a red 1959 Catalina Hardtop Coupe, with a 3-speed stick on the column. It was powered by the 389 cubic inch "A" engine, rated at 345 horsepower and 425 lbs/ft of torque. To this the available aftermarket parts were added. These included a solid lifter Isky E-2 camshaft. Pontiac did not offer a 4-speed manual transmission in 1959, nor did they make a floor-mounted shifter for their 3-speed. Did you ever try to power-shift a Pontiac column shifter? Ugh!

With the introduction of the 1960 car, Pontiac unveiled the first over-the-parts-counter Super Duty drag racing engine package. Royal purchased a Coronado Red Catalina equipped with a 348 horsepower "A" engine and Pontiac's first factory installed 4-speed manual transmission, complete with a floor shifter. It was a base Catalina with practically no equipment, yet even after we converted the front bumper to aluminum (an official Pontiac part), it still weighed more than 4000 pounds. We were so naive about weight reduction in those days, we even ran the factory eight-lug wheels. We were able to get the car built without insulation, but it did have a heater because we knew that some day we would have to sell it. As a matter of fact, after the racing season ended, we put the '60 on the used car lot at Royal. Everybody knew that it was our race car, the car that won the Nationals, and for that reason they ignored it. It sat on the lot as if it were glued to the ground. It took six weeks for it to finally sell, and when it finally went over the curb, we never heard about it or saw it again. What that car would be worth today!

Shift for Yourself

We made a huge mistake when we built the '59 Catalina as our first Super Stocker. The NHRA did not allow a 4-speed manual transmission if it wasn't offered right from the factory. We thought we could get around that by installing a Hurst 3-speed floor shifter and dispose of the "three on the tree" factory shifter. "No way," said the NHRA. "If it came with a column shifter from the factory, that's the way you run it."

The '59 was impossible to shift, particularly from 1 to 2, when you had to go across the "H." First gear was down, so you pulled towards yourself and down. For second, you'd push up, go back across the "H" gate and then up again. That was a very difficult shift. The linkage just wasn't up to it, unless you paused and let the synchros catch up. The 2–3 shift was a different story, you just pulled straight down. So after suffering with all kinds of missed shifts and overwound engines, we finally set the car up with a 4.88:1 rear-end gear, which allowed us to start out in second and make just one shift. That enabled the car to run consistently in the low 14-second range, with an occasional shot in the high 13s. I think the very best run it ever made was a 13.93, which at the time was enough to claim it to be the first stock car ever to break into the 13-second bracket at the Detroit Dragway. It was running about 100 mph, but it just wasn't consistent.

When the 4-speed came along in 1960, it also brought with it a floor mounted shifter. What handicapped that car in the early days was the lousy Inland shift linkage. Inland was the original equipment vendor supplying General Motors. Their linkage arms were cheap and flimsy, in fact we called them "spaghetti." They worked well only when they were in perfect adjustment. Fortunately, Frank Rediker and his team knew how to keep the Inland shifter in adjustment. In those days, power shifting hadn't yet come into its own. Most of us were speed shifting, which meant you did use your clutch, and you lifted your foot on the accelerator, just a bit. The Hurst 4-speed shifter did not become available until 1962.

Even going the lightest route possible, the '60 still weighed 4200 pounds. Pontiac knew that to be competitive in drag racing it was going to need more than just a powerful engine. They were going to have to shave weight from the car. In the next few years they started to offer aluminum body parts—bumpers, fenders, hoods and braces. It was an advantage we wouldn't hold for long, however, as the competition would also soon go the lightweight route.

Royal's number one driver was a young guy named Bill Sidwell. He knew how to shift and drive in a straight line. He was a little irresponsible, maybe, but sometimes that's what it took to make a winning driver. One unfortunate Sunday in May of 1960, an incident occurred at the Detroit Dragway that changed the entire Royal organization.

It was a very hot day, and we had finished our practice runs. At this time we were still running the '59 Catalina. Sidwell decided he wanted to go to

Depending on your point of view, a set of Royal license plate frames were either an eyesore on your new Bonneville or a confirmation that you had the "baddest" Pontiac on the street. Conventional customers took the frames off and threw them in the trash because they didn't want to provide free advertising for the dealership. Today, an original Royal frame is a valuable piece of memorabilia.

lunch with a couple of his friends before eliminations started. He asked if it was O.K. "Of course," I replied, "take the tow car."

"I'd like to take the race car, and show my friends how good it is," he countered. It had run 13.98 at 100 miles per hour in practice.

"Are you nuts?" I said. "This car's not a street driver!" Our race car was set up for racing, and "Royal Pontiac" was emblazoned on both sides.

I saw him and his friends walk over to the tow car, a blue '60 Bonneville Vista. I walked away and forgot about the incident

About 45 minutes later I heard my name on the track's P.A. system. I climbed the steps to the timing tower and was told that the Royal race car had been involved in a terrible accident...on the street.

"What car?" I asked incredulously. "How do you know it was our car?"

"It's your race car," was the reply. "Royal's written all over it."

I immediately whirled around to look out the tower window to where the '59 should have still been parked. It was gone. I first turned ashen white with fear, and then red with rage. I ran down from the tower and found the Bonneville tow car sitting where Sidwell had left it. I grabbed one of our crew members, jumped in the Bonneville and stormed out of the track.

I had driven only a few minutes when I saw a crowd gathered on the side of the road. I pulled over and got out of the car. What I saw both scared and angered me. In the bottom of the ditch, still sitting on all four wheels, was our precious '59 Catalina race car. There wasn't a straight panel on the car, yet none of the damage looked bad enough to indicate that the car had actu-

Contrary to popular belief, the first Royal Hot Chief race car was a bright red 1959 Catalina (like the one shown) 389 cubic inch Tri-Power coupe. Drag racing rules prevented use of a floor-mounted shifter if not installed by the factory, making it necessary to use the unworkable 3-speed column-mounted shifter. To be competitive with this restriction, Royal set the car up with a 4.88:1 rear gear, allowing me to start out in second and make only one shift, pulling straight down, into third to complete the quarter mile. On several occasions the car dropped into the high thirteens.

ally hit anything. There were scrapes, scratches and modest dents everywhere—on the deck, the roof, fenders, doors and even the hood. Up front, the grille was virtually gone.

There was nobody in the car. Sitting on the shoulder of the ditch was Sidwell and his buddies. They were as green as the grass they were sitting on. Sidwell had forgotten that the front tires were pumped up to 40 lbs. of air for drag racing. He hit something and blew the left front tire at over 80 mph. The car had gone first off the road to the right and into the ditch, scraping it up pretty badly. It then ricochetted back on the road and headed straight for the ditch on the other side where it finally came to rest. The police showed me the course the car had taken over the length of about half a mile. How Sidwell managed to miss oncoming traffic is something only he knows.

Neither Sidwell or any of his friends had a mark on them. They were just scared sick from the experience. The police arrested Sidwell and took him away to jail, charged with felonious driving. The drag strip was new in the area and the local police were hard on anybody driving irresponsibly on the street. The other three guys went to a local hospital for a check-up.

Royal had to spend some serious money to get Sidwell off the hook. Needless to say, he was fired. The car, while not a total loss, required some very extensive repair work. We did get it back together again in time to take it to the NHRA Nationals in September.

By then we had installed a set of 4.88:1 gears in the rear end and were making second gear starts, requiring only one shift from the column shifter. Not the best launch, but at least we could complete a run. While the '59 was getting repaired, Royal decided to acquire a new 1960 Super Duty race car.

With Sidwell off the program, we had to find another driver. I decided I would take a shot at it. I had done enough drag racing, and I had done pretty well. I proceeded to drive our new '60 for the rest of the year, so by the time the Nationals came up I was pretty damn good at launching the car and shifting it. We also had an unfair advantage in that we had developed a very good tire combination with the help of our local Goodyear re-treader. We asked him if he could put tires in the re-treading process and not totally "cook" them. By leaving them slightly unfinished they were gummy and soft. The traction was superior to any street tire we had experienced up to that time. Drag slicks had not yet hit the NHRA scene. The only tire you could buy that provided any kind of adhesion was the Atlas Bucron. It was a butyl rubber tire, the first to have a super-soft compound. This goes back to the very early sixties, when everybody ran Atlas Bucrons. They were available at every Standard Oil gas station.

To give you an idea how much better our "cooked" retreads were, consider this example. In the 4-speed Royal car, you could launch with Bucrons at 2000 rpm. The car had such a heavy rear overhang it actually enhanced any tire's traction. With our specially prepared Goodyear recaps, however, I could launch at 2500 rpm in the same car. And that advantage helped us win races. Of course, we never told anybody. Our tires looked just like any other re-capped street tire.

NHRA's safety rules were pretty loose back then. We did have to wear a seatbelt, but no helmet. I wore my lucky white baseball cap. Since Royal was located so close to Pontiac, we received one of the first factory lightweight aluminum front bumpers.

We campaigned the 1960 car locally the rest of that summer, running every weekend and an occasional week night. We kept improving the car by getting more familiar with it. By Labor Day weekend of 1960, I was about as good as I was going to get. I felt very confident launching the car with those "cooked" recap tires. The engine had been blueprinted and hand assembled by Frank Rediker.

Frank was known for his work with superchargers and turbochargers long before they became popular. He was fascinated with what was going on at Royal Pontiac and had approached me about getting involved. Try as I might, I could never persuade him to leave the Olds dealership where he had worked for many years and come to Royal full time. He would work all day at the Olds dealership, and then after dinner come over to Royal and build our race engines. Frank was a great family man, and I had a lot of confidence in him. He was also responsible for a lot of the tricks that would become part of our Royal Bobcat package. Frank had a very capable and loyal assistant, named Win Brown, an old friend from the High End Club Days, who also contributed significantly to our early success. We had built a pretty good team now at Royal, with everybody getting along well.

The 1960 NHRA Nationals, in Detroit for the second consecutive Labor Day weekend, drew hundreds of racers, many driving Super Duty Pontiacs. There were more than 25,000 fans for the long weekend, and there were 55 entries in the Super Stock class alone. The Dodges and Plymouths were strong runners, particularly in the automatic transmission classes. Ford had introduced their new 352 cubic inch, 360 horsepower engine earlier in the year, and by now there were several good ones, really capable of "getting with the program."

Being back at the Detroit Dragway for the 1960 Nationals was bittersweet for me. I had been involved in building the track and bringing the NHRA to Detroit only one year earlier, only to be jilted by the Kohn family. But now I was back in a very competitive car with a good shot at winning a title. I was even more thankful that I hadn't burned my bridge with the Kohns, which probably would have prevented me from having what was to become my greatest day in drag racing.

The first elimination runs on Friday night were sort of practice, but they brought out a lot of the most competitive cars. The Royal Pontiac ran strong and I cleaned house, winning with a best run of 13.92 seconds at 102.5 mph. Anything below 14.10 elapsed time (ET) was considered very good. At that time, drag racing didn't use the "Christmas tree" start. Instead, a flagman stood between the two cars with two flags, one in each hand. He'd first point to the driver on the left, and then to the driver on the right. Then he would cross the flags and point them toward the ground. When he felt like it, he pulled the flag and the drivers would launch their cars.

I had developed a little trick to manipulate those flag starts. Many times the flagman, after going through his pointing procedure, held the flags a little longer than he should have. He was obviously trying to psyche out the drivers. After it got to a certain point, (usually about three seconds, which felt like three hours) I discovered that if you quickly revved up your engine and actually launched, his natural reaction would be to pull the flag. He couldn't charge you with a foul because he had actually pulled the flag at the same time you launched. It worked...some of the time.

The actual Super Stock eliminations were run on Saturday night, and all of the 55 cars entered showed up. There was some good competition, mostly from the other Pontiacs, but our Royal Pontiac Hot Chief #1 was the quickest. I had to make six runs, and finally won the class, with a low ET of 13.89 secs. at 102.67 mph, just a little bit quicker than I had run the previous night.

Incidentally, Clarence Walters in Hot Chief #3, the '59 Catalina, did pretty well too. He went all the way to the quarterfinals before getting eliminated. Dick Jesse in Hot Chief #2, our white automatic car, made it to the final run in the Super Stock Automatic Class, losing out to one of those good running Mopars, a 1960 Plymouth Fury, driven by famous Chrysler racer Al Eckstrand, who later became known as "The Lawman."

After we won on Saturday night, the NHRA, in an unusual move, impounded the top five cars in every class and instructed us to meet early Sunday morning at a garage they had selected close to the track. When we arrived, they wanted each team to pull a cylinder head. We were scheduled to run for Top Stock Eliminator Monday afternoon, and the last thing we wanted to do was dismantle a good running engine before that race. The NHRA tech inspectors wanted to check the displacement, examine the valve train, look at the camshaft, and take other measurements. We spent all day Sunday tearing down, getting inspected and then reassembling our engine. It was a real pain in the ass!

All top Super Stock cars were declared legal. The Top Stock Eliminator run-off, scheduled for Monday afternoon, Labor Day, was open to the 50 fastest cars, regardless of their class. They were selected by their established ETs during their class eliminations. Amazingly, many A-stock cars had run better than some of the Super Stock cars.

It was already hot when we arrived at the track early Monday morning. Crew chief Frank Rediker said, "I've got a long shot idea in mind. It's going to be real hot today, and that means the starting line will get soft, and that means you could get better traction than you had last Saturday night. I'd like to change the rear-end gears from 4.56:1 to a 4.88:1, to take advantage of that extra traction."

I trusted Rediker's knowledge, and we made the change. I had to adjust my shifting rhythm a little, as the shift points came up a lot faster now. Believe it or not, I used to shift by engine sound in those days, not by watching my tachometer. Fortunately, we had a couple of practice shots in the morning, which gave me the chance to experiment, and I found it did launch a little better with the 4.88:1 gears.

Rediker was absolutely correct. Everyone lost ET performance that day, but we didn't lose near as much. My best run on the cooler Saturday night had been 13.89 at over 102 mph, while my best run on the hot Monday afternoon was 14.15 seconds, at just a little over 100 mph.

The Hot Chief ran perfectly all afternoon. I ended up in the championship run against another Super Duty Pontiac owned by Pete Seaton, and driven by a real sharp young "shoe" named Jack Kay. Seaton was a popular Detroit racing figure, the son of GM Vice-President Louis Seaton, the Corporation's chief labor negotiator. Pete always had a good GM car, this time a Newport Blue 1960 Catalina coupe.

Although we had been serious competitors, Seaton offered to run his car at the Nationals with the Royal Pontiac name on the side, for money of course. We felt this would be a good move; the more Royal Pontiacs, the better. Incredibly, we ended up facing each other in the championship run-off, Royal vs. Royal.

As Kay and I went to the line for the big payoff run, I had a sudden surge of confidence, thinking about my 4.88:1 rear-end gearing and my "half-cooked" Goodyear re-caps. It was up to me to put it all together. I knew I could launch a little harder than Kay, and I was right. I popped out on him by

THE PONTIAC PRESS

TUESDAY, SEPTEMBER 20, 1960 — PONTIAC, MICHIGAN. — THIRTEEN

He Brags and Delivers With His Pontiac

KNOWS HIS PONTIACS — Jim Wangers is a natural for his job as a copywriter in the Pontiac Sales Aids and Literature Department of MacManus, John and Adams, Inc., Bloomfield Hills advertising agency. In his spare time he drag races his own 1960 Pontiac Catalina, and was the winner in this year's National Championship Drag Races.

HE'S THE CHAMP — Hardriding copywriter for MacManus, John & Adams, Inc., Bloomfield Hills advertising agency, Jim Wangers accepts the trophy for winning the super stock class race at this year's National Drag Races in his 1960 Pontiac Catalina. What does Wangers write about? Pontiac cars, naturally enough.

The Pontiac Press reported my 1960 Labor Day NHRA Top Stock Eliminator victory. The story also broke in the Detroit Free Press. The slant to the newspaper story was that I enjoyed racing Pontiacs as much as writing about them.

as much as a fender length, and held it all through first and second gear. I slowly inched ahead in third gear, and when I banged fourth, the ol' Hot Chief took one final leap, pulling out to a half-car length as we roared across the finish line. This was the first Pontiac to win an NHRA National event, and it was the first major drag racing win for the new Super Duty package.

What a day for Royal! Our pictures were taken at least a hundred times, and we were given this gorgeous four-foot trophy from the spark plug folks at Champion. In those days, a trophy was all you got for winning Top Stock Eliminator, but regardless of how tall the trophy might be, it still said "Top Stock Eliminator," and that's all we needed for Pontiac and for Royal.

It was a "local boy makes good" story in the Detroit newspapers. *The Pontiac Press* led the way with a four-column story on page two of their Tuesday morning sports section, about a Pontiac advertising copywriter who made his own news by winning a major racing event with his car and then writing ads about it.

I hadn't talked much about my racing with the folks at the ad agency. They knew I was interested in performance, but I certainly didn't tell them that I raced every weekend. For this big event I didn't want to get way out in front telling everybody to come out and watch, only to see me lose. And, as bad as this sounds, I was a bit of an intellectual snob. I thought drag racing might be a little too "redneck" for the advertising crowd. Boy, was I a jerk!

When I arrived at the office Tuesday morning, it was apparent that somebody had read the papers. In the main lobby, stretched all the way across one wall, was a banner reading, "Welcome, Champ!" I'll admit it, I thought the reaction at MacManus to my drag racing win might be adverse, so that hand-scrawled banner greeting me in the lobby really meant a lot. I was also very pleased that we had brought Royal to national prominence in less than one year, underscoring the legitimacy of my performance dealership idea. Of course, I didn't make Royal a winner by myself. I had been blessed to have some very talented people around me, many of whom I had first met while street racing.

There were handshakes and congratulations from everybody as I made my way to my office. The first call was from the guy who had hired me, Jim Graham. After the congratulations he said, "If you want anything, ask for it today. Today is your day. The first thing you're going to get is an opportunity to have lunch with Chief Engineer Pete Estes and a few of his engine guys who want to hear all about the car and the race. Lunch will be in Pontiac's Executive Dining Room, and I'll be there with you."

Pete was a very charming host and introduced me to everybody. He apologized that Bunkie wasn't available to join us, though I did have a nice meeting with Knudsen a couple of weeks later. John DeLorean, Bill Klinger, Bill Collins, and Mac McKellar were all at the lunch, and we talked at great length about the Super Duty engine. Think about it: Here I was, a guy who failed engineering school, talking one-on-one with professional Pontiac engineers about camshafts, head design and valve trains. I might have been in over my head, but everybody was nice, after all, it was my day, and the beginning of some good things to come.

This was also my first meeting with John DeLorean. He was now involved in all areas of the engineering department, although his first love was performance. We hit it off, and I didn't let that budding relationship get cold.

Back at MacManus, I was given the added responsibility of producing the Pontiac consumer catalogs in addition to the dealer sales album. Naturally, I wanted to get as much product information as possible in these catalogs and DeLorean was very helpful in setting me up with the right people in Engineering to get this done. It was a great opportunity, and it wasn't long before Pontiac catalogs were setting the industry standard with very sophisticated and well presented product and engine specs.

Everything was coming together. This was the Wide-Track era, with new product, new positioning, and a new image. In the short span of four years Pontiac had changed from middle-of-the-road Silver Streak mediocrity to the hottest new dude on the road, The Wide-Track Pontiac.

7

Forging the Bonds

TO UNDERLINE HOW QUICKLY THE Royal race car program prospered, consider that we started in late 1959 and in less than one year we won Top Stock Eliminator at the 1960 NHRA Nationals. The exposure in the Detroit press was tremendous, and two or three months later it started showing up in all the national car magazines. Each of the articles specifically mentioned the Pontiac win and Royal Pontiac. It was an incredible windfall for Royal.

We began to run some small classified ads in the Detroit newspapers: "Want to make your Pontiac run? Get a super tune-up from Royal." Up to that time we had been relying on our appearances at the local track, and word of mouth.

In the meantime, I had become known as the product expert at the ad agency. Pontiac offered a courtesy discount to all the agency employees, so a lot of us drove new Pontiacs. We could choose any dealer we wanted to deliver the car. Many of the agency folks asked me how to equip their new car to get it just the way they wanted—the right engine, the right trans, the right suspension, etc. One day, Ace Jr. said he'd like to have all those extra cars delivered through Royal. "Okay," I replied, "but you're going to have to give them some incentive." The result was that Ace offered a kickback. Any car billed through Royal Pontiac would earn the buyer five percent of the overall price of their car. MacManus was a big ad agency and their employees were buying about 100 Pontiacs every year. This was a nice piece of business. The cars became known as "Wangers Cars," and after some early problems, Ace and his service guys agreed to treat these special customers like, well....like special customers.

Royal's success continued to compound. They were putting a lot of good cars on the street, and many of them were getting trick tune-ups. The word got around that Royal was the place to go if you were interested in a good running Pontiac.

While the performance program was just starting to take off, Ace Jr.'s interest began to wane. He would sometimes be absent from the dealership for two or three days at a time. Word was he went "up north." The Wilson family had a nice place up in Petoskey, Michigan. While Ace Jr. loved cars, he tired quickly of the car business. Ace Sr., on the other hand, had become somewhat of a dour, cantankerous old man. There were times in personal conversation when I detected a touch of anti-Semitism. That feeling, I was told,

These two views show the first Royal Bobcat, a 1961 Catalina, which was painted white, not red as some historians believe. It was modestly refined with distinct exterior trim and "Bobcat" lettering across the tail lamp panel.

had come from a bad experience he encountered in the dairy business. I never knew the facts, and I never wanted to, but in time I would feel the sting of Wilson's hostility. Fortunately, Ace Jr. was smart enough to know that I was the program, and if I left he didn't have much going. Consequently, when he was around he would try to pacify me.

It had also become painfully obvious that it was time to either pump more money into the program or drop it. We always wanted to have a good race car, and make sure we were well represented at the local drag strip. Much of our performance parts business was now coming by mail from out of state. Many of the car magazines were interested in writing stories about what was going on at Ace Wilson's Royal Pontiac. "Would there be a 1961 Super Duty car?" they asked. Our response was to expand the racing effort by having two Super Duty cars for 1961, one a 4-speed and the other an Automatic. However, I didn't feel that just having two Royal Race Cars was enough to keep promoting the Royal program.

The Pontiacs our customers were buying from Royal were only "virtual" race cars. Sure, there were a few guys who did want actual Super Duty cars, even knowing that they were not suitable for the street, but we could convince most of our customers that these were not the right cars for them. Most of Royal's performance business was coming from young adults buying Catalinas or Venturas or even Bonnevilles. To build on the performance visibility we already had, we needed to give these special street cars an identity that would be recognized instantly by enthusiasts. Thus was born the first Royal Bobcat, a 1961 Catalina Hardtop Coupe.

At that time, Pontiac was using block letters to spell out Catalina, Star Chief or Bonneville on their cars. They were placed strategically at the rear of each car. The block letters were all the same size and all standing alone. I played around with the letters Catalina and Bonneville to see if I could find a new, catchy name. It didn't take long to come up with the word "Bobcat." It fit nicely in the same place on the car, and it looked like it came right out of the factory. Honestly, that's how we chose the name.

The first Royal Bobcats were all Catalinas, powered by the 348 horsepower Tri-Power 389 cubic inch "A" engine. They were usually equipped with a 4-speed manual transmission (an automatic was available), eight-lug aluminum wheels (painted in matching body color), heavy duty suspension, a tachometer, and a performance rear axle ratio. To make them run a little bit better, we offered our Royal Bobcat tune-up package, which included a set of

The 1962 Grand Prix emblem was the inspiration for the famous Royal Bobcat emblem. Made of embossed aluminum, the sticker was affixed on the fender or the sail panel of every Pontiac that received the "Royal" tune-up treatment.

Race on Sunday, Sell on Monday

I lost my Royal Pontiac benefactor at the factory when Knudsen was promoted to Chevrolet in 1961, and Pete Estes became General Manager of Pontiac. Estes had not been involved in the Royal project; it was strictly an experiment that Knudsen wanted to explore. Unfortunately, we never did get around to offering the performance seminars, and now that Knudsen was gone there was no way that was going to happen. Still, as Royal continued to grow other dealers became interested in the program. They didn't have the chance to take advantage of Royal's experience, and consequently many made costly mistakes.

There were as many as 50 dealers across the country that wanted to get involved in racing. They didn't understand that the Royal operation really was a marketing program; racing was only part of the effort. Most dealers went racing first and forgot about the marketing. If you win a race, that's great, but unless you merchandise that win by promoting that your dealership had the talent, the knowledge, and the wherewithal to build that winning race car, and were ready to share that knowledge with your customers, it would all go for naught. You were not going to automatically have a windfall of people rushing in.

When the potential customer did come into your dealership the day following your win at the track, they wanted to admire your race car and learn a little more about it, but what they really wanted was to talk about their car, either the one they had or the one they wanted to have. Those dealers who won on Sunday but didn't follow up by hiring informed sales and service people were doomed to fail, and unfortunately, too many of them did. "Race on Sunday, sell on Monday" only worked when the dealer had all the pieces in place.

ultra-thin headgaskets (headwork was optional), progressive Tri-Power carburetor linkage, a special distributor advance curve, blocked intake heat riser gaskets, a set of richer carburetor jets, and special locknuts for more positive valve adjustment. This basic model remained through 1962. The engine was upgraded to Pontiac's new 421 cubic inch in 1963. We never made a Bobcat out of a Bonneville. The Bonneville had a distinctive look of its own, and the Bonneville buyer wasn't looking for such a flashy car. A lot of customers didn't want the trim package, so they ordered out a regular car and added the Royal Bobcat package, resulting in quite a "sleeper."

Both 1961 Royal race cars were Super Duty Catalina Coupes, painted white with red stripes over the hood, across the roof, and down over the rear deck. We lettered them with a big "Royal" on the door, and towed them with a pair of similar Catalinas, these painted red with white stripes. The tow cars were equipped with the 348 horsepower "A" engine, and were fully Bobcatted. The Super Duty race cars ran good in '61 and were very popular everywhere we raced them. We even did some match racing.

For 1961, Royal fielded cars in both the Super Stock manual and automatic transmission classes. Initially, the cars were equipped with 389s, but we converted to Pontiac's new 421 as soon as they became available. As the 1960 NHRA National champions, Royal engaged in a series of traveling exhibitions for the first time.

Knudsen was always looking for new innovative concepts. The Kelsey-Hayes aluminum hub eight-lug wheel provided less unsprung weight and better braking. Pontiac was the first car maker to offer a styled road wheel in 1960. Shown here is a 1963-vintage wheel.

Thanks to the continued popularity of Super Stock racing, the Royal program thrived. Our 1962 Super Duty was perhaps the best car we ever had, although it didn't start out that way. We chose a Catalina two-door sedan rather than a coupe, to save a few pounds of weight. It was one of the first Pontiac Super Duty cars to come equipped from the factory with the lightweight aluminum package, including front bumpers, fenders and hood, and powered by the new 421 Super Duty engine, including the new "127" cylinder heads. Everything went together perfectly in assembling the engine, including an experiment Frank Rediker wanted to try. I remembered the success we had at the 1960 Nationals with Frank's experiments, so I told him to go ahead.

Frank's idea was to leave the expanders out of the oil rings on the pistons. This, he hoped, would significantly reduce friction, even though it might pass a little oil. The first time we started the engine, it smoked like hell. The more I drove it, the more it smoked. Every time I made a pass down the drag strip, the car would pour smoke out the tailpipes like I was spraying for mosquitoes, and the track announcer would say, "Uh oh! It looks like Royal blew their engine again."

While I never actually blew the engine, I never actually beat anybody either. The more we tuned the car, the more it became apparent that we were losing horsepower as well as oil. All through March and April I couldn't get the car out of the 13-second bracket. Thanks to better tires and bigger engines, any Super Stocker that wasn't running in the high 12s at 111–113 mph couldn't be competitive. The best run I had made with the car was 13.09 at 109 mph, which obviously didn't cut it

Over the Memorial Day weekend, The Detroit Dragway held their annual spring Super Stock event, attracting big names from all over the country. This was our turf and we were expected to show these out-of-towners how we did it in Detroit. For my first round I drew a car out of Akron, Ohio, fielded by Bill Knafel Pontiac and driven by a very competent guy named Arlen Vanke. Bill was a very enthusiastic, outspoken dealer. He was one of the dealers who was upset about all the press Royal Pontiac was getting. He wanted to show the folks at the factory that Royal wasn't the only dealer who could build fast race cars.

"The Tin Indian," as it was called, jumped right out on me and kept on going. Old Smoky went lumbering down the track with smoke pouring out both sides. I was humbly eliminated in the first round. Some days you eat the bear, and some days the bear eats you!

If losing in the first round at our home track wasn't humbling enough, the next day Knafel sent telegrams to Pete Estes and John DeLorean, reminding them who now was their number-one drag racing team. The "Tin Indian" didn't win that Memorial Day event, but Knafel sure acted like it had. Fortunately, Pontiac was not interested in team rivalry. There was a se-

Pontiac and Hurst...and a Bad Idea

It was inevitable that Pontiac and George Hurst would become partners. In 1961 the NHRA had made an arrangement with Hurst to award a new car to their Top Stock Car points leader. When George selected a Pontiac for the award, I said "Great, but why not make it a very special Pontiac. Let's give the winner a ready-to-race, 1961 Super Duty Catalina Coupe hand-built by Royal. The name Royal was painted on the side of car, along with "Hurst-Campbell."

The Stock Car points winner was an arrogant young racer named Bruce Morgan, who won the title driving an "A" stock 1957 Chevrolet. His reaction to winning the car was very peculiar. He was cool to the fact that it was a Pontiac, let alone a blueprinted race car. He sold it almost immediately. I felt it was a real insult, both to Hurst and to Pontiac, and it taught us a lesson. A straight 2-barrel Catalina coupe would have been a better prize.

lect group of drag racers, just like there was a select group of NASCAR racers. When the factory released new parts, everybody got them.

After this humiliating loss, we realized that we had to keep our car competitive. The day after the Memorial Day debacle, Rediker's experiment ended. We pulled the engine to give it a serious inspection. To our utter surprise, we had created a magnificent short block. We had been bathing the block in hot oil every time we made a run. The cylinder walls were in incredible shape, with no scratches or carbon deposits. We didn't have to do any serious honing, nor did we have to replace the pistons. We did replace all the bearings and piston rings (with expanders this time). Other than handlapping the valves, we weren't allowed to do anything more to the heads. We did make sure there were no hot spots in the combustion chambers.

In less than a week we had the engine back together and running. We put just enough miles on it to seat the rings and were ready to run again. The very first run out of the box with this new engine was a 12.82 at almost 112 mph. Before long, we had the car down in the high 12.6s, which was faster than anybody had run at the Memorial Day event. From that point on, the car just got better. The best run I made all year was a 12.38 at 116.37 mph.

In late August, we were invited to come to Indianapolis for a match race against Chrysler's Ramchargers. The Ramchargers team included Tom Hoover, Jim Thornton, Dale Reeker, and a very enthusiastic group of young Chrysler engineers. These guys were sharp. They were now running their new 413 cubic inch "Wedge" engine, and their newly styled cars were light. Their SS/A car featured Chrysler's TorqueFlite Automatic Transmission, which was considered the best racing automatic available at that time.

As it turned out, our match race with them was the Sunday before the NHRA Nationals were to be held on the same track. The Royal Super Duty was running just awesome that day, and we beat them three straight. I was running in the low 12.5s (my best run was a 12.52). We would launch right together, but when their TorqueFlite shifted from 1 to 2, I could stretch out my first gear, enabling me to pull out a full car length on them before hitting 2nd gear, and that was all I needed.

After the final race, we were both pulled to the side by Ed Eaton, the NHRA tech inspector. "It's not going to have any effect on what happened here today," Eaton told us, "but we want to do a fuel check on you guys." Both cars had a fuel sample removed and after about a half hour he came back. Looking first at the Ramchargers, Eaton said sarcastically, "We have absolutely no idea what you've got in this car. It doesn't fit any of our specs. We're pretty damn sure it's not pump gas, and while it's not illegal, it's going to be illegal next week." No one had specified what kind of fuel we had to run for the match race; it seemed that the Ramchargers were using a specially prepared fuel developed by Chrysler Engineering.

Then Eaton turned to us. "What you've got is Michigan Blue Sunoco, and that's O.K.," he said. "But don't bring it down here next week. We're going to have Indiana Sunoco here, and whether it's any different or not isn't important, because everybody's going to be using it."

The following week, we knew we were going to have to go through a pre race tech inspection so we came back a day early. That would allow us to get several runs during time trials. As we got into line to go through tech, we were told we were under protest. It was easy to figure out who had protested us. The claim was that our engine was moved back from its stock mounting position. Moving the engine back would be a neat trick, since it changed the front-to-rear weight distribution in favor of the rear, allowing for greater traction. The protest was clever, since it would be difficult to prove or disprove.

The truth was we weren't smart enough to have moved the engine back, but there were no specs available for the NHRA inspectors to check. Nobody knew where the engine should be placed in a Super Duty Pontiac, other than the regular mounting bracket, which had three adjustment holes. Naturally our engine was mounted in the most favorable hole, just like every other Super Duty. Finally, a call to Pete Estes at Pontiac confirmed that there was no information available to actually determine Super Duty engine placement. Late Friday night we were told we could run eliminations on Saturday, but by then the protest had accomplished what it set out to do: upset our practice plans and get us off balance for the whole weekend.

My first practice run was also my first elimination run, and I was matched against Dave Strickler, a successful young racer out of York, Pennsylvania, driving a 1962 409 Chevrolet known as the "The Old Reliable."

While Pontiac never got behind the idea of developing a high performance program for its dealers, there were a few that recognized how successful Royal had been and tried to emulate us. Some, like Myrtle Motors in Queens, New York, Knafel Pontiac in Akron, Ohio, Gay Pontiac in Dickinson, Texas, Livingston Pontiac in southern California, and Packer Pontiac in Detroit were successful in selling high performance cars. Others tried by going racing and then waiting for the customers to show up. They couldn't understand why it worked for Royal and not for them.

Strickler was a damn good driver, and he had me psyched out. I didn't get a very good launch and he beat me with a car that ran in the 12.9s. Only one week earlier, I'd been running in the 12.5s on the same track under almost the same conditions. Our trip to the Nationals with our very best car turned out to be a disaster.

AT THE END OF THE 1962 MODEL YEAR, we decided it was now time to begin promoting Royal Pontiac on a national basis. We had already earned some nice press with our cars, but we wanted to promote Royal's parts and service capabilities to a wider audience.

One product we were selling in real volume was a mechanical linkage for the Tri-Power carburetors. The factory Tri-Power assembly used a vacuum linkage to operate the two end carburetors. Only the center carburetor was employed while driving on light or part throttle. It wasn't until you floored it that the vacuum linkage kicked in and immediately opened the two end carburetors all the way. There were really only two positions, all the way closed or all the way open. The mechanical linkage permitted the two end carburetors to "come in" gradually. This was called, appropriately, "progressive linkage." The factory ultimately adopted the manual linkage option as original equipment.

Another great product was the rocker arm lock-nut. The Pontiac production engine did not have a rocker arm lock-nut to prevent the hydraulic valve lifters from "pumping up" at higher rpm. On the dragstrip, for example, when you wound your engine up close to 6000 rpm and pulled a quick shift, the engine would free-wind briefly over 6000 rpm. When this happened, you pumped up your lifters, which separated the valve lifter from the camshaft. You banged second, popped the clutch...and....nothing. Your engine would "piss and moan, and pop and sputter," and so would you, as you just lost a race. The way to solve that problem was to install the lock-nut on top of the rocker arm.

Finally, we went into the mail order business, forming The Royal Racing Team. To join, you simply sent in $3.00. That entitled you to a membership card, a decal for your car window, a parts catalog, and the opportunity to buy parts at a discount.

A Case of Perfect Marketing

A great example of how we achieved positive results by working closely with the magazines took place in 1962. For their May issue, *Motor Trend* had scheduled coverage of the Daytona 500 and the NHRA Winternationals. Pontiac was fortunate to win both events. Afterward, the agency worked feverishly to prepare and place ads showing readers that the special parts that went into these winning cars were available to every owner. At the same time, we had worked with *Motor Trend* on a road test of a Super Duty Bobcat 421, which was also included in the issue. It turned into a perfect marketing combination one-two punch.

Space was always a problem at Royal. The first Royal Pontiac on Main Street in Royal Oak was a meager little facility, and was only meant to be temporary. In the early 1960s, Royal moved to a beautiful new modern facility that was too small the day it opened. There was room for only five cars in the showroom, which even in those days was not ample. The lot could store no more than 35 new cars, and when they wanted to display used cars on the front line, that number would be cut in half. Around the back, a few body shop "deadheads" could be stored, however, the service department never had enough space for their customers. There was no room for parking and precious room for growth.

Royal had now become a hangout, the popular place to meet before going out to cruise Woodward. In the spring of 1962 I decided it was time to host "The First Annual Royal Pontiac Performance Open House." We advertised in all the Detroit newspapers and distributed handbills everywhere. In

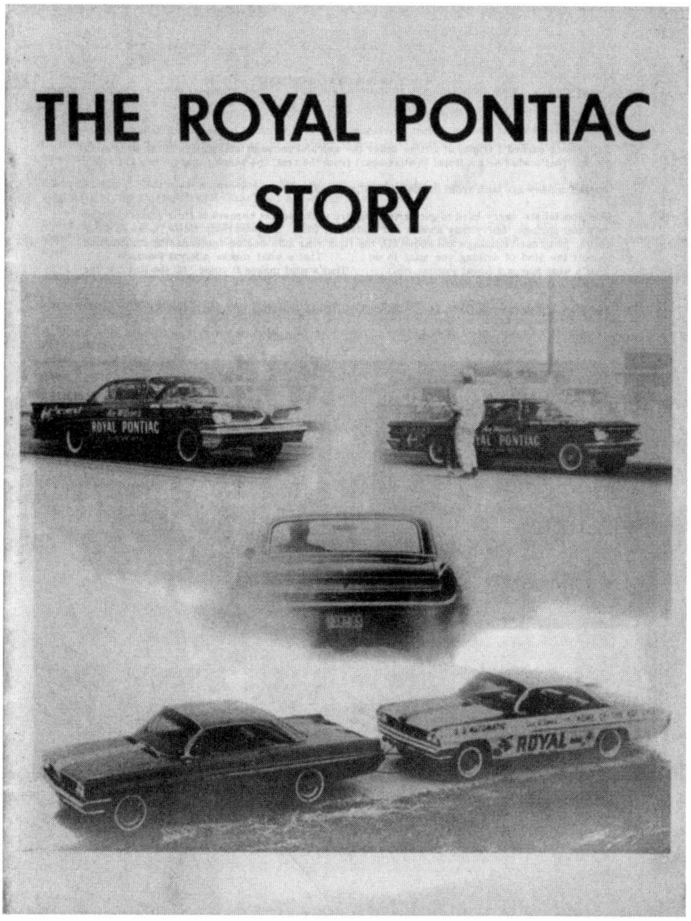

Royal produced a yearly publication that was given away at their annual open house. The publication included photos and stories about the Royal Bobcats, and later on a parts section.

those days, NASCAR Stock Car Racing was not televised, so unless you actually had the opportunity to have been at a race, you didn't have any idea what big-time stock car racing was all about. We procured films of the 1960 and 1961 Daytona 500 races and showed them in an impromptu theater set up in the service department.

We rolled out several very special Royal Bobcats, along with a large display of the Royal Bobcat Package, showing each of the components. The only cars on display were performance-oriented sporty Pontiacs. We had a variety of Catalinas, Grand Prixs, Bonnevilles, and some rare 4-barrel carbureted four-cylinder Tempests. We had more than 25 special new Pontiacs on display, perhaps more than all the rest of the Pontiac dealers in Detroit put

moving machine
either side of the line!
Pontiac Catalina
There's a good deal more to driving than a straight-line quarter-mile, and nobody knows that better than the performance-minded. Which is why Pontiac's Catalina shows up so often among you people.
One of the reasons for this popularity is the choice of engine/transmission teams. Standard equipment is a 215-hp Trophy V-8 hooked up to a three-speed stick, of course. But you can get a storming 405-horse engine and heavy-duty four-speed as extra-cost options. And other extra-cost options blanket the area in between, including automatics.
Wide-Track and Pontiac's own special handling precision come standard with the Catalina, naturally. So does a fat helping of pure luxury, without which you shouldn't allow yourself to be.
The great thing is that a new Catalina goes easy on your bankroll—this is Pontiac's lowest-priced full-sized series. Talk it over with your Pontiac dealer first chance you get. Plan to spend some time with him—you could use up a whole day just looking through that list of options, and a happier time you couldn't imagine.
(Oh, and if you'd like to check your Cat against the clocks, feel free. No fair making the Catalina do the pushing while the dragster has all the fun.) Pontiac Motor Division, General Motors Corporation.
APRIL 1962
13

This 1962 Catalina ad carried the message that no matter how you wanted to use your Pontiac, there was a drivetrain and a suspension that could fit your needs and your wallet. The ad also intimates that the Catalina was as much at home on the dragstrip as it was on the street. Just as in the Dodge D-500 and Plymouth Fury ads I had done in the late fifties, this Pontiac ad connected the car to the fun of grass roots drag racing.

together. We also invited some of our customers to display their special cars. The real hit of the show was our new 1962 Super Duty race car. This was the first time many people had ever had the chance to personally examine a factory drag race car. We also invited our sponsors—like Champion Spark Plugs, DA Oil, M&H Tires, and Hurst—to display their products.

We had just introduced the famous Royal Bobcat emblem (stolen from the Grand Prix) in time for this event. The original emblems were made of embossed aluminum, and we sold a ton of them for $1.50 apiece.

Of course admission was free. The event ran from Friday evening until Sunday afternoon and attracted over 15,000 people. The response was unbelievable. We knew we had a real winner, because the neighbors complained about the crowds, the noise, and the parking.

SINCE KNUDSEN HAD CHOSEN TO ignore the 1957 AMA "gentlemen's agreement" racing ban, Pontiac had a huge advantage in stock car competition. While Pontiac was racking up these wins, Ford, Chevrolet and Chrysler realized they'd been "had." They had gone to sleep, assuming everyone was playing by the rules. They awoke to the rude reality that Pontiacs were winning races and at the same time climbing into the number three sales position.

Pontiac Dominates Racing

From 1960 through 1962 and early into the '63 model year, Pontiac dominated professional stock car racing. They didn't always win, but they usually sat on the pole and at some point led every race. Superb professional drivers like Glenn "Fireball" Roberts, Joe Weatherly, Jack Smith, "Banjo" Mathews, Cotton Owens, Marvin Panch, Bobby Johns, Paul Goldsmith and Junior Johnson all were racing Pontiacs.

By 1961 Pontiac had wrapped up the NASCAR Manufacturer's Cup and repeated again in 1962. Pontiac won the Daytona 500 both those years, first with Marvin Panch, and then with "Fireball" Roberts. That win for Roberts was especially sweet since he had qualified his car no worse than third in both '60 and in '61, failing to win because of mechanical problems.

By the early 1960s, the premiere part of the show at every NHRA drag racing event was the stock car class. As competition really began to heat up, many of the car makers also began building special cars and offering special equipment. By the mid-sixties, it was out of hand, and Pontiac was partly to blame.

As the Super Duty drag racing program continued, we moved further to lighten the weight of our cars, or, as the pro racers would say, "add lightness." That led to the development of aluminum parts like bumpers, grilles, hoods, and fenders. In 1963, Pontiac tried a very serious weight-saving maneuver: they cut holes in the frame, creating the famous "Swiss Cheese" Catalina. Unfortunately, this experiment proved to be a failure, as nearly every frame broke and had to be repaired with heavy steel braces.

While it was a marvelous idea, we weren't naive enough to think we'd be the only one to do it. It took only a few months before every participating car maker had either aluminum or fiberglass front end parts on their cars. These cars were all considered limited-production, specially prepared vehicles with special engines, legal only to compete in drag racing's top stock car classes. Before this wave of crazy factory support ended, Chrysler was building altered wheelbase cars, while Ford was offering their intermediate sized new Fairlane with a full fiberglass package, a one-of-a kind Hemi engine, or even with an experimental overhead cam engine. Needless to say, the NHRA had created a "monster," one that would take a while to tame.

A Second Racing Ban

Pontiac, meanwhile, was outside the fray, because in 1963 they were hit with another racing ban, this time not from the AMA but from parent GM. The motivation for this internal ban was pressure on General Motors from the Federal government. This wasn't due to safety concerns or emission problems—they would come later in the decade. The heat was from the Justice department, who had determined that GM was getting too large a share of the U.S. car market. At the time GM was close to capturing 55 percent market share, and was dangerously close to getting 60 percent. Hard to believe these days! Sixty percent was the magic number that would trigger an anti-trust suit to eliminate any possibility of a General Motor's monopoly.

The Justice department made some veiled threats to the press that the government was considering the breakup of General Motors by spinning off the Chevrolet Division—at that point Chevrolet alone owned close to 30 percent of the market. Under the government's anti-trust move, Chevrolet would become a separate entity building passenger cars and trucks. General Motors would then consist of Pontiac, Oldsmobile, Buick, Cadillac, and

(Continued on 3rd page following)

Pontiac's Sales Gains

In 1961, Pontiac took over third place in the sales race, behind only Chevrolet and Ford. To snare number three, Pontiac knocked off the American Motors Rambler, which had become very popular in the late fifties when George Romney, AMC's President, built a whole ad campaign around their economical six-cylinder engine. At the time it was their only chance for survival because they didn't have a V-8. Sound familiar? He coined the phrase "gas guzzlers" when referring to his V-8 competitors, and it worked for a while. That campaign propelled Rambler past Plymouth into the number three slot early in 1959, but the early sixties performance race was about to begin, causing the six-cylinder Rambler to lose some of its appeal.

When Pontiac took over the coveted number three sales slot, we were already riding the Wide-Track success train. Wide-Track had become synonymous with Pontiac, almost as if it were a nickname. We changed first from Wide-Track Wheels to Wide-Track Ride, and then to Wide-Track Style. The city of Pontiac was called Wide-Track Town and some dealers were already calling themselves The Great Wide-Trackers. Finally, it all came together under the most appropriate use of the term, The Wide-Track Pontiac.

The 1962–63 Grand Prix: Right Place at the Right Time

The luxury/sport Grand Prix, one of the most significant cars born in the early days of the Wide-Track era, went on to become one of Pontiac's most treasured nameplates.

The history of the Grand Prix goes back to the introduction of the first four-passenger Ford Thunderbird in 1958. Ford dropped their sporty two-place car produced from 1955–57 and went to a higher-priced, more luxurious coupe. With this car, Ford invented the personal luxury/sport coupe segment.

Ford's success piqued interest at GM. They charged the Cadillac Division with preparing a car competitive to the new T-Bird and to have it ready for the marketplace as soon as possible. Cadillac presented their concept car, dubbed "LaSalle II," to GM management in 1960, but at the same time begged to be excluded from the project. Cadillac had been enjoying uncommonly good sales with their regular Coupe de Ville/Convertible models and didn't want another competitive car in their line. Those sure were the "good ol' days"! GM Management thus offered the program to their Buick, Olds, and Pontiac Divisions. Each was asked to present a marketing plan showing how they would image the car and how they would integrate it into their existing strategies.

Knudsen realized that Pontiac's emerging success with their Wide-Track cars put the Division at a disadvantage in gaining the nod from the Corporation. Consequently, he ordered his engineering department to begin developing a personal luxury/sport coupe of their own, while at the same time he went though the machinations of fashioning a presentation to the parent Corporation. Those familiar with the GTO's entry into the marketplace will recognize that maneuvers like this were necessary to stay competitive within the existing GM framework.

Pontiac engineers selected the newly styled, yet to be introduced 1962 Catalina Hardtop Coupe as a base for their luxury effort. They created a monochromatic styled interior (the first time this had been done in America), and introduced their new expanded vinyl (leather-like) seat covering. They removed all chrome trim from the exterior side panels, and used an exclusive new grille. A 4-barrel carburetor version of the famous 389 cubic inch V-8 was the standard engine, with dual exhausts, a modestly taut suspension lowering the body on the wheels, and the now-famous eight-lug aluminum wheels. The Pontiac Grand Prix package introduced to the public at the start of the 1962 model year beat the original Cadillac concept car (which was now a Buick called Riviera) into the marketplace by one full model year.

Originally thought of as only a first step into the new personal luxury/sport segment, Pontiac was overwhelmed with more than 30,000 sales. To meet new competition coming in 1963, the Grand Prix was totally restyled, introducing an exclusive new roofline that would separate it even further from the more con-

ventional Catalina or Bonneville sport coupes.

The 1963 car offered dramatic slab-sided styling, with no chrome or body side-sculpturing—a first on any domestic car. It was introduced in late 1962, featuring an exciting new color called Nocturne Blue. Everywhere the car was shown or advertised, it was wearing this new dark blue color. The first 5000 cars were all built in this color. The result was that all the early cars looked the same, giving the impression there were many more out there. This is an old marketing trick...and it still works.

1963 sales of more than 70,000 units set a record which stood until 1969, when another new generation of Grand Prix coupes were introduced. The 1963 slab-sided styling, though beautiful, actually became somewhat of a negative in the real world, as many of these cars picked up an inordinate amount of nicks and dings on their side panels, making it virtually mandatory that they be repainted, particularly when traded.

Along with existing nameplates like Bonneville and Le Mans, the Grand Prix fit magnificently into Pontiac's new Wide-Track performance image. Its head-start in the marketplace helped give it a clear sales edge over the Buick Riviera, an edge it has never relinquished.

GMC trucks, along with dozens of other subsidiaries like Delco, Frigidaire, and Rochester. General Motors management, intimidated somewhat by these threats, decided it would be wise to lower their profile. Withdrawing from aggressive participation in motorsports was certainly one way to do that. Ed Cole, now a corporate vice president, was put in charge.

Unlike the 1957 ban, Cole was determined to halt all of GM's racing activities, whether overt or clandestine. Cole had recently been General Manager of Chevrolet, so he knew all the tricks. He made it clear to each of the division General Managers that the corporation would not tolerate any "out the back door" or "under the table" dealings.

The internal edict banning GM participation in racing was announced in late 1962, just about the time the 1963 models were to be introduced. Many 1963 race cars had already been delivered to both NASCAR and NHRA teams, thus a racing ban would not result in these cars going away. To demonstrate an aggressive effort to promote their new racing ban, General Motors immediately stopped shipment of these specially prepared cars. The NHRA had no alternative but to remove the Super Duty Pontiacs and Z11 Chevrolets from their Stock classes. They created a special class called "F/X" (Factory Experimental). NASCAR was more liberal. They allowed both to continue to run, in their Grand National Series.

A Second Racing Ban

For Pontiac, the ban could not have come at a worse time. Their new performance image was starting to boost public recognition of its products. Although we never actually showed a Pontiac on a racetrack, Pontiac advertising used racing victories to prove the claims of better handling, better balance and a safer, more secure car. It was a back-up to reinforce the new Wide-Track image. But there was still a long way to go.

Mr. G. S. Stephens

ALL ZONE CAR DISTRIBUTORS

EFFECTIVE TODAY JANUARY 24, 1963 389 AND 421 SUPER DUTY ENGINES ARE CANCELLED AND NO FURTHER ORDERS WILL BE ACCEPTED. (421 HO ENGINES ARE STILL AVAILABLE.)

SUGGEST YOU ADVISE DEALERS WHO NORMALLY HANDLE THIS TYPE OF BUSINESS VERBALLY.

J. T. Wilson

J. T. WILSON - PONT. MTR. DIV.

JTW:WHM:et/C

GM lowered the boom on its Divisions on January 24, 1963 when it ordered a corporate ban on racing activities. Pontiac headquarters responded in turn with this terse announcement to its Zone Car Distributors that the Super Duty program was canceled and no further orders for engines or cars would be accepted.

FREE! Big, full-color reproduction of Fury painting! Write Plymouth Division, Chrysler Corp., Dept. DD, P.O. Box 1518, Detroit, Mich.
It's a rare car that rates a toast!
Fury owners . . . and all who have shared the great exhilaration of just handling a Fury . . . have an almost personal affection for this uncommonly spirited car.
Few automobiles in history have merited such regard. But Fury combines unusual, clean-limbed beauty with response and roadability very seldom found on wheels. A new Fury V-800 engine gives vigorous answer to your command—turning up a tremendous 290 horsepower, with 8-barrel carburetion for direct fuel flow to each cylinder.
Heavy-duty, racing-type torsion bars team with new ball-joint construction up front, and new asymmetrical rear springing, for level, no-sway cornering and no-dive, no-dip stops. New brakes virtually abolish fade; the shoe follows the drum as the drum expands under heat, maintaining full lining-to-drum contact.
And all this in a full-size car which still provides amazing car-and-driver intimacy. Try Fury. You'll be quite likely to propose a toast yourself!
For the man who really loves cars
Fury by PLYMOUTH

This was the first four-color automotive ad to be released as part of a schedule for Petersen car magazines. It was part of a four-ad schedule to run from March through June of 1957. I was pleased that the ad dramatized that there were people who cared this much for a production car. I had a hell of a time convincing the ad copy writers that such people existed. The painting of the actual car above the mantle was reproduced and offered free. We mailed out over 25,000 prints. Back in 1957 that was a remarkable response.

YOU GET THE SOLID QUALITY OF BODY BY FISHER.
Pontiac surrounds a man with beauty
and the solid security of wide-track wheels
We've been noticing something interesting about our men customers. When a man becomes the owner of a 1959 Pontiac he slices a few years off his age, becomes enthusiastic about driving almost anywhere any time, and holds his head a bit higher, a lot more proudly. It's not our imagination. It actually happens.
Unofficial psychology explains it this way: A man who works hard and gives his all to profession and family has earned the right to drive a great automobile. A Wide-Track Pontiac is a perfect reward.
Its trim, sleek lines gratify your sense of good taste and refinement. Yet they're well-defined lines, positive but uncluttered, consistent and clean. The unique grille is a good example: different but highly imaginative and pleasing.
Man is born to be a master and Pontiac gives you masterful control of this car with the security and stability of Wide-Track Wheels; wheels moved five inches farther apart. This widens the stance, not the car. You're balanced, with less lean and sway.
We assure all well-deserving men that this automobile will give you a vigorously fresh outlook on life, a feeling of youth, accomplishment and much, much pride. Show your wife this advertisement; she deserves a Pontiac, too.
PONTIAC MOTOR DIVISION · GENERAL MOTORS CORPORATION
THE ONLY CAR WITH WIDE-TRACK WHEELS
Dotted lines show conventional wheel positions. Pontiac's wheels are five inches farther apart. This widens the stance, not the car. Pontiac hugs tighter on curves and corners. Sway and lean are considerably reduced, ride is smoother, balanced, steadier.
PONTIAC! America's Number 1 Road Car!

The 1959 Pontiac was Bunkie Knudsen's first car, where he had total control. Artists Art Fitzpatrick and Van Kaufman captured Pontiac's new Wide-Track look in a series of paintings that were used in brochures and in print advertising. The artwork of Fitz and Van was a staple of Pontiac advertising for more than a decade, until it became too limiting for promotion of Pontiac's new performance image.

By 1960, Pontiac's aggressive racing program was beginning to pay off. Success in stock car racing resulted in hardware also being developed for drag racing. These Super Duty components contributed to a Pontiac winning the coveted Top Stock Eliminator title at the NHRA Nationals in Detroit on Labor Day weekend. (Painting is from a special series by Dana Forrester)

Tri-Power, three 2-barrel carburetors feeding eight cylinders, defined Pontiac performance for almost ten years, until 1967 when GM decreed (against Pontiac's wishes) that it would no longer be offered.

My luck ran out at the 1962 Summer Nationals. My only run was against Dave Strickler in the "Old Reliable" Z11 lightweight Chevy. I lost in the first round. GM's racing ban and the GTO were soon to follow.

To commemorate Pontiac's first win on the new high-banked oval track at Daytona in 1962, the Division commissioned artist Jack Smith to capture the moment in oil. I was honored to be chosen as technical adviser to Smith. The painting was used in 1963 for the annual Estes Award, which was given to dealers who equaled or bettered their previous year sales numbers. Many of these paintings still hang proudly in Pontiac dealer's offices.

The 1963 Royal race car was built on the famed "Swiss Cheese" chassis that bore a series of drilled holes to lighten the heavy frame. GM's withdrawal from competitive racing forced Royal to convert the car into the NHRA Factory Experimental class. In this run, I match raced with Ford favorite Dick Brannon in his fiberglass-equipped 1963-1/2 Galaxie. I lost.

There's a tiger loose in the streets.

It's late and your bedroom window is open. It's so quiet you can hear the frogs croaking out by the crossroads a good quarter mile away.

After a while a big-engined Something rumbles by in the night. It checks for a moment at the lights, then swings out onto the highway.

Suddenly a rising moan overrides the rumble as a bunch of extra throats get kicked wide open and start vacuuming air by the cubic acre. The moan gets drowned out in its turn by a booming exhaust note that someone ought to bottle and sell as pure essence of Car.

Three times the sound peaks, falls back, peaks again. The last shift into fourth, a throttling back to cruising speed, a dwindling grumble of thunder, and . . . gone. The frogs take up again where they left off.

Have you tried one of our 421s*? *370, 350, or 320 bhp available at extra cost.

the 421 makers—Pontiac

PONTIAC MOTOR DIVISION • GENERAL MOTORS CORPORATION

This ad (and the two following) were part of a 1964 series promoting full-sized Pontiac performance. What makes these ads unique is not only do they not show the product, but the copy in some cases becomes almost poetic as it describes the pure pleasure of driving a performance Pontiac. Written by MacManus copywriter Roger Proulx, the award-winning "There's a tiger loose in the streets" is still considered to be one of Pontiac's most popular ads.

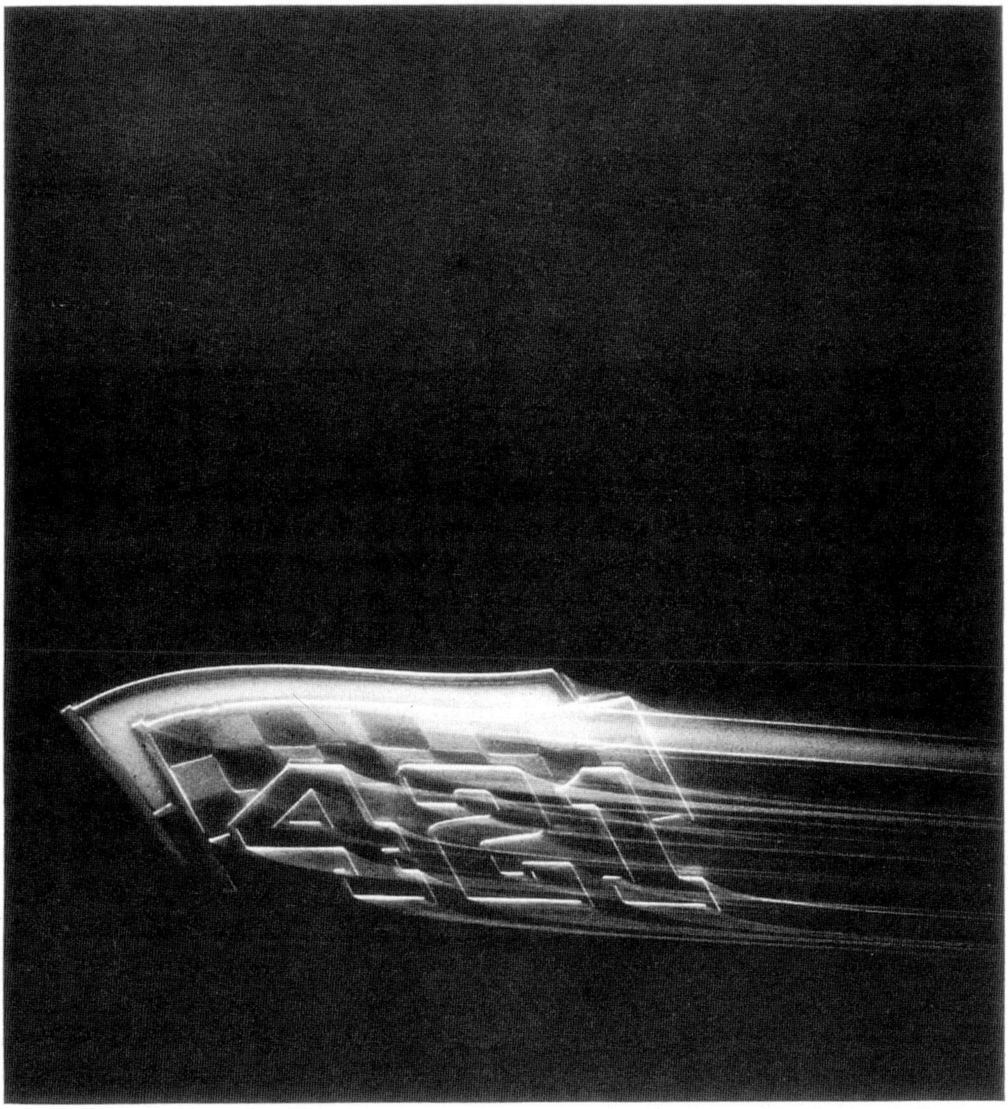

Hands off the grab bar, Charlie, you're tearing out the dash!

The faint *shoosh* of a seat being depressed. The metallic click of seat belts. A 12-volt starter rasps briefly, followed by a vast convulsion as things mechanical happen in a big way under the hood. The left front fender rises, then falls back again as torque prematurely shows its hand. A rumbling boom as of distant thunder. Dust sets to swirling suddenly in the path of a pair of downward pointing exhaust pipes. Someone has just prodded one of our 421's into fire-in-the-nostrils, show-me-a-road-any-road life. There are three such engines. Meet them:

Engine	Bhp @ rpm	Torque @ rpm	Displ., cu. in.	Carburetion	Compression Ratio
Trophy 421	320 @ 4400	455 @ 2800	421	1-4BBL	10.5:1
Trophy 421	350 @ 4600	454 @ 3200	421	3-2BBL	10.75:1
Trophy 421 HO	370 @ 5200	460 @ 3800	421	3-2BBL	10.75:1

the 421 makers—Pontiac

PONTIAC MOTOR DIVISION · GENERAL MOTORS CORPORATION

This was another classic performance ad that didn't show the product. Instead, it describes the exhilaration of acceleration that pins you against the seat. Unwary passengers would reach for the dash-mounted assist bar to hang on for dear life. The ad also describes in detail all of the high performance engine options offered by Pontiac.

Get in, turn on, leave abruptly.
This is where you aim a Catalina 2+2 from. Bucket seats, nylon-blend carpeting, custom steering wheel, the whole bit, all color-coordinated, in either sports coupe or convertible form.
The standard 389-cubic inch engine puts out 283 bhp when coupled to a 4-speed box*, 267 bhp with 3-speed Hydra-Matic*. (The 2+2 comes only with one of these two transmissions.) Both shifters are mounted in the standard console.
Much automobile.
If you want to make even more automobile of it, there's nothing to stop you from huddling with a Pontiac salesman and a list of performance options and doing wild things with an order form.
*Optional at extra cost
the 2+2 makers–Pontiac
PONTIAC MOTOR DIVISION • GENERAL MOTORS CORPORATION

To showcase the new 2+2 sport model, which was created to pump some excitement into the mundane Catalina lineup, this ad advises the reader to experience the thrill of driving a full-sized high performance Pontiac. Unfortunately, the base 2+2 came standard with a 389 cubic inch 2-barrel carburetor engine. More horsepower for the 2+2 was available at extra cost, pricing it dangerously close to the Grand Prix or Bonneville coupe.

When the Royal Racing Team mail order program really took off, we designed a special decal. A $3 fee entitled enthusiasts to discounts on performance parts, a membership card, and a Royal Racing Team decal. The first decal (left), designed in 1965, featured a growling "pussycat." That lasted only one year. The second emblem, released in early 1966 (bottom), introduced the now famous "Philoh" character carrying a Royal Bobcat emblem over his shoulder. We nicknamed him "Philoh the Fuck-up" because he graphically demonstrated that we were not always perfect and were capable of making mistakes (note how Philoh steps on the letter "C").

STOP
I wouldn't stand in the middle of the page if I were you...
It's a Pontiac GTO!
If you insist on reading at a time like this—that's a 6.5 litre Gran Turismo Omologato aimed right at you. 325 bhp @ 4800 rpm with 1-4BBL. It may have an optional 3-2BBL setup* with 348 bhp, look lively! As it goes by, notice the nylon red-circle tires and dual exhausts. Listen to the standard 3-speed transmission with Hurst shifter going through the motions. Or, the fully synchronized 4-speed* on the floor. Or, the automatic*—you can't tell from here. It may even have a console*. Like every GTO, it has heavy-duty springs, shocks and stabilizer. Quick, get off the page!
*Optional at extra cost.
the GTO makers—Pontiac
PONTIAC MOTOR DIVISION • GENERAL MOTORS CORPORATION

The key message in this early GTO ad was acceleration. I thought it was rather creative since we talked about our variety of engine and transmission combinations. It was always fun to brag in our ads about the GTO's 348 horsepower.

The GTO emblem was unique as it was the first time an American car maker had used "litres" instead of cubic inches to designate engine displacement. This was part of our effort to tie the GTO name into its European heritage. At the time, it was one of the most intricately stamped pieces of die-cast metal ever used by a car maker for an exterior emblem.

It was my idea for "Car and Driver" magazine to make a GTO comparison between the highly-revered Ferrari and the upstart Pontiac. The incredible article made the GTO legitimate, even in the eyes of the most critical sports car enthusiasts. For David E. Davis and "Car and Driver", it was the beginning of a whole new image for the magazine.

Two 1964 GTOs were made available to "Car and Driver," one a Nocturne Blue coupe (like the one shown above; the original car had the side view mirror on the front fender and a front mounted aerial on the right side) with a Tri-Power engine, wide-ratio 4-speed and 3.55:1 rear gears. This car was set up for the handling and cornering tests. The second GTO was painted Grenadier Red and was also equipped with a Tri-Power engine, but featured the optional close-ratio 4-speed and 3.90:1 rear gears. It had been set up as a Royal Bobcat, and was to be used for acceleration testing only.

Another significant image-building effort was the appearance of a Top 40 record named "GTO," recorded by a new group, Ronny and the Daytonas on the Amy-Mala label (top left). The record reached number four on the charts and lasted 17 weeks with over a million copies sold. Billboard magazine estimated that the record was played over seven million times on the nation's airwaves during that period. Later attempts at song promotions like the GeeTO Tiger song were not as successful.

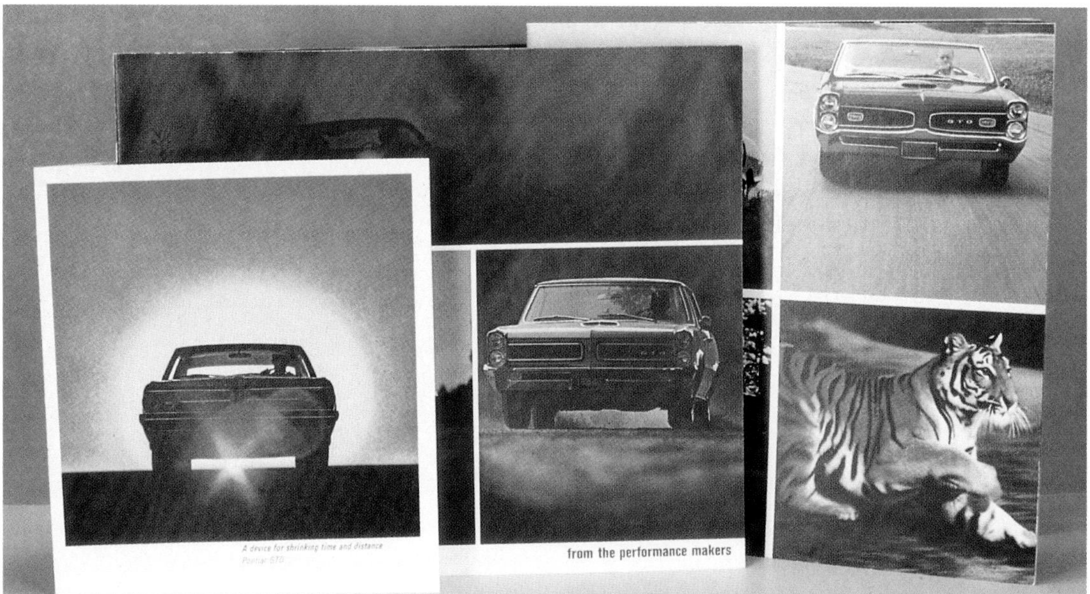

Beginning with the 1964 GTO, Pontiac began producing specific brochures for their high-performance models that set the standard for the industry. These brochures included specifications and technical information not listed in other manufacturer's catalogs. I insisted that we include as much technical information as we could to reinforce Pontiac's performance image, for example, cam specs, carburetor jet sizes, all available rear axle ratios, and specific model weights. DeLorean loved it.

Originally issued by Pontiac promoting the Tiger, metal license plates proved to be a huge success, especially in states requiring only one (rear) plate. A 1966 release for dealer promotions (shown) saw the GR-RRR! plate go to cardboard for showroom display.

The cliché "race on Sunday, sell on Monday" wasn't always true. Ford spent millions of dollars fielding specific drag race cars that competed in every NHRA class. Thousands of fans would watch these Fords win on the strip, and then head out to the parking lot and drive home in their Pontiac GTOs, perhaps beating a Mustang or humbling a Fairlane GT at a stoplight. Ford didn't understand the difference between racing and performance. One did not necessarily sell the other, especially as racing fans became more sophisticated and recognized these special-built cars were nothing like what was available in Ford showrooms. To their credit, Ford did turn things around in the eighties with the "5.0" Mustang. The Ford dealer Motorsports program of today is almost an exact copy of the Royal operation of the sixties.

GTO
15M·43
Pontiac Motor Division • General Motors Corporation
our Thing.
Standard equipment: Engine—389 cu. in., 335 bhp, 4BBL; dual exhausts, low-restriction mufflers, lightweight resonators; declutching fan; chromed low-restriction air cleaner, rocker covers, oil filler cap; 3-speed with Hurst shifter; heavy-duty springs, shocks, stabilizer bar; choice of premium 7.75 x 14 red-circle nylon tires or same-size rayon whitewall tires; 14 x 6JK wide-rim wheels; bucket seats; full carpeting; custom pinstriping.
Extra-cost performance equipment: Engine—389 cu. in., 360 bhp, 3-2BBL, with factory-installed mechanical linkage on stick shift jobs (Code 802); all-synchro 3-speed with Hurst shifter (Code 743); wide- and close-ratio 4-speeds with Hurst shifters (Code 744 and 778); Safe-T-Track limited-slip differential (Code 701); axle ratios—3.08, 3.23, 3.36, 3.55, and 3.90:1, factory installed; 4.11 and 4.33:1, dealer installed; metallic brake linings (Code 692); extra-stiff springs and shocks (Code 621); 20:1 quick steering (Code 612); 17.5:1 power steering (Code 501); tachometer, ammeter, oil pressure and water temp gauges (Code 504); high-performance transistorized ignition (Code 671); competition-type steel wheels (Code 691); exhaust splitters (Code 422); custom sports steering wheel (Code 524); heavy-duty radiator (Code 432); to be continued in our special GTO/2+2 performance catalog, free at any Pontiac dealer's.
Wide-Track Tiger—Pontiac GTO

An action shot of the very successful 1965 GTO carried the simple headline, "our Thing." In our ongoing effort at Pontiac to stay current, timely, and "hip" in our advertising this was a direct reference to popular public imagination of the time, which was focused on organized crime—known in some circles as "La Cosa Nostra," which means "Our Thing."

In 1966, the second year for Royal's traveling exhibition, the GeeTO Tigers were painted Tiger Gold, with one car having white flanks and the other black. Additional sponsors were brought in such as Hurst, Champion, M&H, and Thom McAn. The cars performed at 28 different drag strips, culminating with an appearance at the 1966 NHRA Summer Nationals at Indianapolis. (painting by Dana Forrester)

Re-imaging the 1967 GTO included a new theme line, "The Great One," which I did not like at first since I thought the play on GTO (turning it into TGO) would confuse our younger owners. Once I witnessed the willing acceptance of The Great One theme, I quickly became a supporter. These decals, which were part of a 1967 Pontiac poster offer available by mail, helped promote the new theme.

Ever since the 1964 Hot Rod road test debacle, I had made sure, thanks to John DeLorean's help, that I had a fleet of finely-tuned press cars available to the media. The three 1967 cars shown were all painted Tiger Gold and represented the three performance car lines Pontiac offered, the Firebird 400, the Ram Air GTO and a 428 H.O. 2+2. I particularly enjoyed driving the four-speed 2+2. As a Royal Bobcat, it was able to dip into the low 13s at 109 mph, despite its size.

Detroit's Woodward Avenue was the hotbed of street racing and cruising in the sixties. A night didn't go by without musclecars lining up for impromptu street races. Out front of drive-ins like Ted's or the Totem Pole, young drivers would be ready to race either from traffic light to traffic light or go out to the I-75 expressway for a top-speed battle with their street machines. (painting by Dana Forrester)

For example, one of the most popular phrases used to express acceleration performance back then was "pick up." As late as 1963, all our research showed that the public perceived an Oldsmobile to have better pick up than a Pontiac, even though Pontiac had "blown" Olds right off the racetrack. In those days it took a long time to change an image, especially without the impact of today's electronic media. You established a brand image slowly, and once you established that image it took an equally long time for it to decay. Oldsmobile had launched their Rocket 88 in the late forties. Even though they hadn't won many races and there were now faster cars on the road, the public's perception of that Rocket 88 still prevailed. For Pontiac, the promotion work started in 1957 was just beginning to pay off in the early sixties. Recognition of models like Bonneville and Catalina scored high, and the Wide-Track Pontiac name began to at least match Oldsmobile in the public's perception of performance cars.

It was also established early in 1962 that the four-cylinder transaxle Tempest was going to be discontinued. The transaxle and the "rope" driveshaft concept had been a marketing failure, and Pontiac recognized the need to quickly change that image. The new 1964 "A" body cars (Tempest/Le Mans) would be stronger and more reliable.

From a marketing perspective, these developments were both trouble and opportunity. I shared my concerns with John DeLorean, who by now was Chief Engineer. DeLorean had an innate passion for Pontiac, and that enthusiasm, combined with his engineering capability, was one of the reasons Pete Estes chose him to become Chief Engineer when he moved up to become Pontiac's General Manager. DeLorean's appointment to Chief Engineer was a surprise, since he was promoted over several veterans who had more seniority. It was Pete's insistence that secured John's appointment.

Over the brief time I had spent with John, I found him to be unusually interested in marketing, despite his lack of experience. Shortly after he became Chief Engineer he asked me to stop by his office. We discussed everything about the Division, including a lot about marketing and advertising. "I don't know too much about it," he told me, "but I figure you do, and maybe you can help me. You know, one of these days I'm going to be General Manager of this Division, and it's never too early to learn, I'd like to spend some time talking about our advertising. Tell me what we're doing and why?"

I began visiting him at least twice a week, sometimes even more, usually very early in the morning. Much to his credit, DeLorean wanted to be prepared when he went to staff meetings. I would show him some of our advertising ideas, how these developed into campaigns, and then some of the ads that were actually scheduled to run. He was quick to understand.

In one of my early morning meetings, we got around to talking about the marketing challenge we were facing. After the ban on racing took effect I remember asking John if there was something we could do to make our upcoming new Tempest more than just another nice new car. "Olds, Buick and Chevy all have similar nice cars too," I said. "We need to bring this new car into our Wide-Track world." I was becoming aware of the growing number of

(Continued on 3rd page following)

Failure of The Tempest

The Pontiac Tempest: Poor Quality Leads to Market Failure

In their second year of producing new small cars in this country, General Motors decided that every Division should offer some kind of a competitive small car. This meant that Buick, Olds, and Pontiac would follow Chevrolet (Chevy II and Corvair) with small entries of their own. They were to be called "intermediates."

In 1961, a year after the first Chevy Corvair, Ford Falcon and Plymouth Valiant appeared in the marketplace, Buick introduced their Special, Olds their F-85, and Pontiac their Tempest. GM even went to the expense of developing a lightweight 215 cubic inch all aluminum V-8 for these cars, an engine which delivered great mileage.

Even though the engine was a breakthrough development, it was still too small to be considered a performance powerplant. Bunkie Knudsen and his group at Pontiac, having laid out plans for the recovery of the Division, felt strongly that their new intermediate should not be just another "cookie cutter" car, nor a Pontiac version of the Buick and Olds. Knudsen and his team wanted a car that would be different enough to fit the new Pontiac image.

Although there was a modest amount of money available for development, Pontiac still had to work with parts from the Corporation. Pontiac engineers came up with an ingenious new powertrain. They took the existing 389 cubic inch V-8 Pontiac engine and cut it in half, longitudinally. Using only the right bank of the V-8, they created a 195 cubic inch inline four.

Pontiac now had their own four-cylinder engine, and it was a little powerhouse—195 cubic inches (3.2 liters) and loaded with torque. But there were problems. Cutting a smooth-running big bore V-8 in half created a serious balance problem. They knew they were going to have some vibration, but no one expected it to be as bad as it was, especially at idle.

There was little experience with electrostatic balancing or internal balance shaft procedures at that time. The flexible driveshaft, created by weaving strands of high tensile steel like a rope, was capable of absorbing a great deal of low rpm vibration, and as the engine accelerated into a higher rpm range, it smoothed out even more.

The engine had to be hooked-up first to the dampening driveshaft, and then to the transmission and differential. Thus, the need for a rear-mounted transaxle. By borrowing many parts from the existing Chevrolet Corvair, Pontiac found their answer. The result: One of the most original drivelines in the history of the industry. This was exactly what Knudsen wanted for his new intermediate-sized Pontiac. It would attract a tremendous amount of interest, not only for the car, but also for the Division.

The new car, named Pontiac Tempest, did exactly that. Not only did it create incredible worldwide attention, but in 1961 it also earned Pontiac their second *Motor Trend* Car Of The Year award in two years. The 1961 Tempest was originally introduced only as a four-door model. A very attractive coupe appeared in mid-year. In 1962 Pontiac introduced a deluxe version of what was now a four-car series (coupe, convertible, four-door, and wagon). The highline coupe and convertible were named Le Mans, a

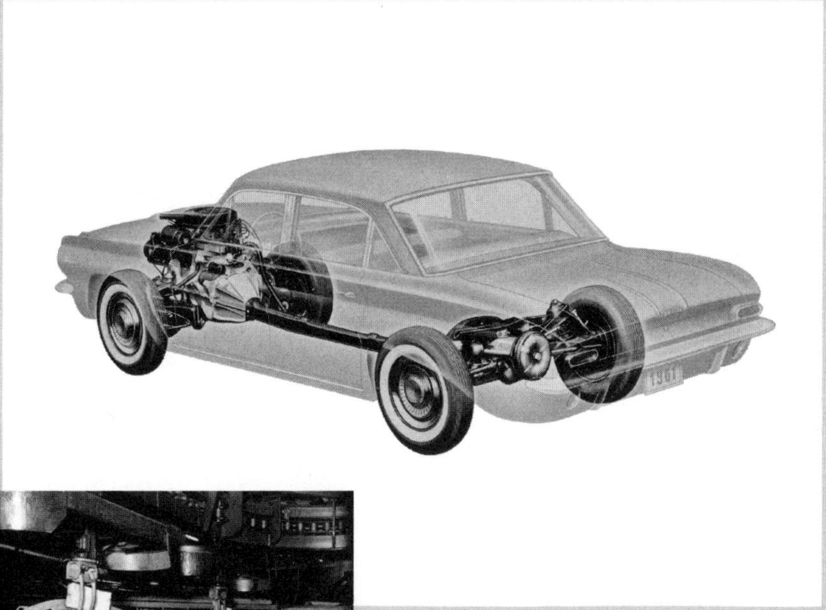

This shot from an engine plant shows that the 389 V-8 (foreground) and the slant 195 (background) were so similar that they could be assembled side-by-side.

name which went on to become a very important part of Pontiac history, serving as the basis for the 1964 GTO.

Many industry wags and self-appointed critics predicted that the driveline was foolhardy and would destroy itself in a very short time. Detractors were unanimous, in spite of the *Motor Trend* award. The critics were wrong. The woven steel driveshaft actually proved to be one of the most reliable parts of the new drivetrain. The problems were with the transaxle itself, as it simply was not strong enough, having been originally designed for the Chevy Corvair. Also, the inherent engine vibration was not only bothersome and noisy, it also caused premature stretching of the timing chain and uncommon wear on the standard Pontiac nylon timing gear. This produced bothersome valve noise, in spite of the normally self-adjusting hydraulic valve lifters. Many drivers who were not bothered by the noise ultimately let the car go long enough to have the timing chain snap, likely destroying the cylinder head.

Ultimately, the car failed in the marketplace. Today, these 1961–63 Tempest/Le Mans cars make great collector's items. But frankly, they are more fun to talk about than they are to drive.

The first time the word "tiger" ever appeared in Pontiac advertising was in early 1963 to identify the two optional Le Mans performance packages. The 4-barrel, four-cylinder 195-cubic inch version was referred to as a "Two-Tiger." The other package was the new 326-cubic inch V-8 that we called a "Three-Tiger."

young people coming of age in this country who would become qualified car buyers in the mid-sixties. They weren't called "baby boomers" yet, but they were coming, and Pontiac needed to be ready. What I didn't know was that DeLorean was already a step ahead of me in his thinking, that he had the idea for a car that would change everything.

I actually had very little to do with the development of this product, which eventually would be known as the Pontiac GTO. Through the years there have been many incredible misrepresentations of just how that famous car came about. In spite of my futile attempts to set the record straight that I came into the project only as a marketer, I have still been credited with having made too many contributions to the actual development of the car. I did not submit the idea of stuffing our 389 cubic inch engine into the new intermediate "A" body chassis. Chief Engineer John DeLorean and two of his favorite staff engineers, Bill Collins and Russ Gee were responsible for the creation of the car.

Here is how it happened.

DeLorean planned regular "What If?" sessions at the GM Proving grounds in Milford, Michigan, on Saturday mornings. He invited a select group from his engineering staff and a few other important people around the division to come to the grounds, dressed casually, and be prepared to have fun looking over new ideas. On rare occasions, I was lucky enough to be invited.

The birth of the GTO took place inside a proving grounds garage during one of these Saturday morning sessions. It was very early spring, 1963. A prototype 1964 Tempest Coupe equipped with a 326 cubic inch engine was up on a lift. DeLorean, Collins, and Gee were under the car, discussing the chassis. Collins casually mentioned, "You know John, with the engine mounts being the same, it would take us about twenty minutes to slip a 389 into this thing. We'll probably need some heavier springs in the front end, but the engine will fit right in."

John looked at him, caught an approving nod from Gee, and without uttering another word they were all in agreement.

One week later the group at the Saturday morning session was greeted by a prototype '64 Tempest coupe with a 389 engine in it. It had a 4-barrel carburetor and a 4-speed manual transmission. Needless to say, those lucky enough to drive it were overwhelmed. While it was never specifically mentioned, everybody "knew" that this was the car to put Pontiac's new "A" body in a class by itself, way above its Olds, Buick and Chevy sisters.

The 389 cubic inch engine was exactly what this new Tempest needed. It had plenty of low-end torque and lots of mid-range horsepower. With every new change, the prototype kept getting better. They added additional suspension tuning, a heavier clutch, and played with a different tire. DeLorean made it his personal driver. He had a habit of loaning it to some of his close friends, and on many occasions he had trouble getting it back.

As far as the name, that was also DeLorean's baby. Ferrari was using the term "GTO" on one of their new limited production cars. The FIA (Federation Internationale Automobile) owned the name, which in Italian meant "Gran Turismo Omologato" or "Grand Touring Homologated." Both the Ferrari and the Pontiac were indeed Grand Touring Cars, and both had been homologated, which meant that they were an end-product made out of different parts, all produced by the same manufacturer. In the case of the Pontiac GTO, it was very simple. We took a 389 cubic inch Bonneville engine that had been designed and built for our full-sized car, and "stuffed" it into our new intermediate sized Tempest/Le Mans.

It was the same at Ferrari. They had a very sophisticated dual overhead cam V-8 engine that they had been using strictly on the race track. They decided to install it in a street version of their race car. They called it a GTO, and it too, was a true homologation. Ferrari was using the name incorrectly however, because by FIA standards a manufacturer had to build at least 100 vehicles to qualify for use of the name. Ferrari never came close. Neither Pontiac nor Ferrari could copyright the name, nor could either one prevent the other from using it.

Building and naming it was one thing, getting the car approved for production by General Motors was another. This story has been told many times. DeLorean had shown the car to General Manager Pete Estes and Sales Manager Frank Bridge, explaining to them how timely it would be to use this car to kick-off the new 1964 Tempest/Le Mans line.

The biggest hurdle was an internal policy, stating very clearly that no car built by General Motors could have more than 10 lbs. of vehicle weight per cubic inch of engine displacement. You didn't have to be a brain surgeon to figure out that this car, weighing approximately 3500 lbs., and powered by the 389 cubic inch engine, wouldn't make the cut.

There was no way the Engineering Policy Committee, the corporate group that policed the Divisions, would ever approve the 389 Tempest as a model. It would be foolish to even submit it. Some kind of creative thinking was needed to find a way to slip the car through the system.

We learned that the Committee only had interest in new models, and did not get involved with approving options. Therefore, why not offer the 389 engine simply as an option, available only on the top-of-the-line Le Mans two-door models? Then it wouldn't have to be approved by the committee.

The GTO was born.

8

The Tiger Learns to Roar

Selling the GTO to the Corporation

HOW TO MARKET THE GTO WAS the subject of a very important meeting Pete Estes arranged between himself, John DeLorean, and Frank Bridge. When first shown the GTO, Bridge made it very clear that he didn't want it. "Frankly," he stated, "this thing is going to be a real pain in the ass." Frank was a good sales manager. Along with moving cars, his job was to maintain dealer relations. A good sales manager would almost always take his dealers' side whenever possible. In the case of the GTO, Frank didn't think the dealers needed a teenage hot rod in their showroom. Pontiac was doing fine, the 1963 full-size car had been one of the most successful cars we ever had, and the Division was a solid third in sales, behind only Chevrolet and Ford. But Bridge wasn't a marketer, and he didn't understand how vital it was for Pontiac to first overcome that shaky four-cylinder Tempest image.

I was in that meeting. I sat in the corner, watching DeLorean try patiently to deal with Bridge. Estes was silent, almost like a referee. DeLorean was pretty good at corporate politics, and after all this was his car. He wanted Bridge to commit to 5,000 so the car could be pre-sold to the dealers before the Corporation ever found out about it. The more Bridge protested, the angrier DeLorean got. Estes, who had a talent for handling these kinds of problems, finally turned to Bridge and said, masterfully, "Come on, Frank, you know you and your boys can sell 5,000 of anything."

Bridge smiled, almost as if he was embarrassed. Estes had hit him right in the middle of his ego.

"All right," Bridge said. "I'll put out a memo, and we'll turn it over to the Zones. We'll let the District Managers go out and see what kind of action they can drum up. If they can take 5,000 orders, I'll commit to it. But I don't want any more, and I bet you won't even sell 500."

Bridge's prediction turned out to be a joke. The dealers placed orders for the 5,000 cars in a matter of days. This was just what Estes and DeLorean needed to sell the GTO to GM management. When they confronted the Corporation, they knew it was already too late to cancel the car, as any interruption now would make Pontiac management look very irresponsible in front of their dealers.

In a way, it was easy for the Corporation to approve the initial order: Pontiac had sold 5,000 extra Le Mans Coupes that would not have normally been sold at this time. But the Corporation then added, "We don't want to see any more. Remember, just 5,000."

Certainly a great deal of credit must be given to Pete Estes, who put his GM career on the line. Had management taken a hard line and stuck to their rule, or had the GTO been an initial sales flop, it could have resulted in a black mark on Estes' record. That didn't happen; nevertheless, Pete Estes is, in a large part, responsible for the existence of the Pontiac GTO.

Because of the belated approval and the questionable early status of the GTO, it was intentionally omitted from Pontiac's 1964 full line catalog. After Pontiac started shipping cars to the dealers, we found it necessary to get more information into their hands. We hurriedly put a catalog together, with the marvelous line, "GTO: A device for shrinking time and distance" on the front cover. It talked about this special GTO option, and while it was very

In late summer 1963, Pontiac's factory reps started taking dealer orders for the new 1964 models. The big news was the drastically restyled Tempest/Le Mans series. After collecting volume orders for these cars, the factory reps then told the dealers about a special package available on Le Mans Coupes and Convertibles only, called the GTO. It was purposely downplayed, as the factory only wanted 5,000 orders, enough to guarantee that the Corporation would allow the car to be built. However, once the GTO-optioned Le Mans models arrived at the dealerships and were exposed to the public all hell broke loose. The result: Pontiac ended up with over 15,000 customer orders in less than six months.

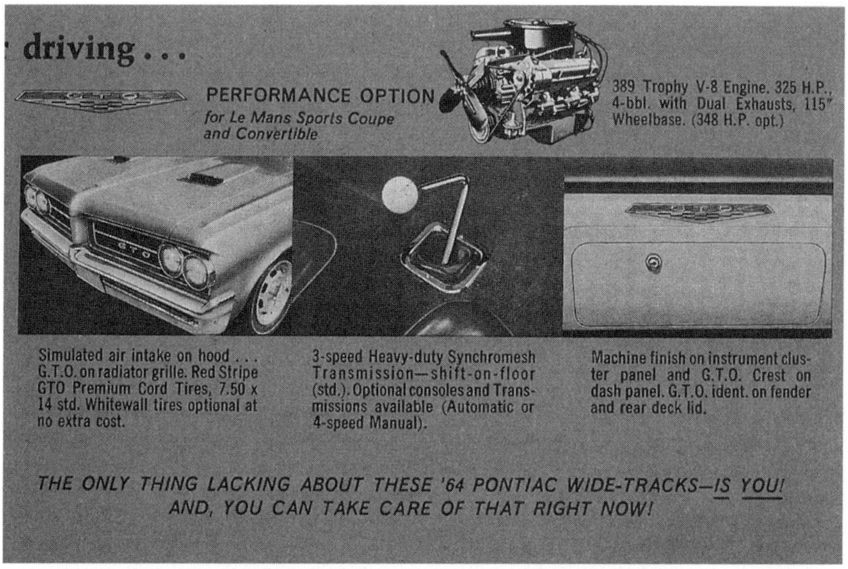

driving . . .
PERFORMANCE OPTION
for Le Mans Sports Coupe
and Convertible
389 Trophy V-8 Engine, 325 H.P., 4-bbl. with Dual Exhausts, 115" Wheelbase. (348 H.P. opt.)
Simulated air intake on hood . . . G.T.O. on radiator grille. Red Stripe GTO Premium Cord Tires, 7.50 x 14 std. Whitewall tires optional at no extra cost.
3-speed Heavy-duty Synchromesh Transmission—shift-on-floor (std.). Optional consoles and Transmissions available (Automatic or 4-speed Manual).
Machine finish on instrument cluster panel and G.T.O. Crest on dash panel. G.T.O. ident. on fender and rear deck lid.
THE ONLY THING LACKING ABOUT THESE '64 PONTIAC WIDE-TRACKS—IS YOU!
AND, YOU CAN TAKE CARE OF THAT RIGHT NOW!

Before the GTO brochure was released in March 1964, the only printed confirmation of the car and its performance engine was the back page of this folder the factory representatives used to obtain initial dealer orders.

Limited Early GTO Advertising

specific about features and specs, it didn't have our usual exciting, performance-oriented copy. In fact, it was purposely understated.

The decision not to over-promote the car during this critical announcement period was well founded. We continued to worry that somebody at GM might change their mind and pull the plug, and we weren't totally confident in how the public was going to react to the car. We scheduled no television commercials, and the only advertising we ran through 1964 were black-and-white insertions in the auto enthusiast magazines. I was so uncertain about the future of the GTO that I ordered a backup for my personal driver. It was a white Catalina Hardtop Coupe, with a red interior, a 421 cubic inch Tri-Power engine, and a close-ratio 4-speed with a 3.90:1 Safe-T-Track rear end. Needless to say, it never got built, once we knew for sure there was going to be a GTO.

What impressed me the most about driving the GTO was how good it felt right off the showroom floor. I was used to driving some pretty good running Pontiacs, as most of my recent cars had been Royal Bobcats. I could see the GTO as an incredible street machine, which was the goal. Truth was, we were taking Pontiac performance off the racetrack, like the Corporation wanted, and putting it on the street, like the Corporation didn't want.

The GTO delivered everything we had hoped for, although I was bothered by one serious shortcoming, its tires. Though good-looking on the car, with their trend-setting narrow red stripes, they were simply inadequate. Although the manufacturer, U.S. Royal, called them "tiger paws," I nicknamed them "infinity paws." You could launch the GTO from a standing start and burn rubber to infinity or until you backed off the gas pedal. Of course, this

GTO is for kicking up the kind of storm that others just talk up.
Standard Equipment: engine: 389-cu. in. Pontiac with 1-4BBL; bhp—325 @ 4800; torque—428 lb-ft @ 3200 rpm/dual-exhaust system/3-speed stick with Hurst shifter/heavy-duty clutch/ heavy-duty springs, shocks, stabilizer bar/special 7.50 x 14 red-line high-speed nylon cord tires (rayon cord whitewalls optional at no extra cost)/14 x 6JK wide-rim wheels/high-capacity radiator / declutching fan / high-capacity battery (66 plate, 61 amp. hr.)/chromed air cleaner, rocker covers, oil filler cap/bucket seats/standard axle ratio 3.23:1 (3.08, 3.36, 3.55 to 1 available on special order at no extra cost).
And some of our extra-cost Performance Options: engine: 389-cu. in. Pontiac with 3-2BBL (Code #809); bhp—348 @ 4900; torque—428 lb-ft @ 3600; 3.55:1 axle ratio standard with this engine option/4-speed with Hurst shifter (gear ratios 2.56:1, 1.91:1, 1.48:1, 1.00:1, and 2.64:1 reverse)/2-speed automatic with 2.20:1 torque converter/Safe-T-Track limited-slip differential (Code #701)/3.90:1 axle ratio available on special order with metallic brake linings, heavy-duty radiator and Safe-T-Track/handling kit—20:1 quick steering and extra-firm-control heavy-duty shocks (Code #612)/high-performance full transistor (breakerless) ignition (Code #671)/tachometer (Code #452)/custom sports steering wheel (Code #524)/exhaust splitters (Dealer installed)/wire wheel discs (Dealer installed)/ custom wheel discs, with spinner and brake cooling holes (Code #521)/console (Code #601).
the GTO makers—Pontiac
PONTIAC MOTOR DIVISION • GENERAL MOTORS CORPORATION

Once we felt confident that GM was going to let us keep the GTO in 1964, we created some advertising to help launch it. We were very careful not to use the general consumer media like network TV, or regular magazines and newspapers, for fear that a GM exec would see it and get upset. The entire 1964 GTO advertising campaign was a schedule of three B&W ads in the most popular auto magazines, to appeal to the heart of our market.

was a good way to make the car look like it had so much power it simply overpowered its tires, but most of the smoke was due to the inadequate traction of the tire itself.

Sales of the GTO took off modestly in October, while production was still limited, and really didn't produce any serious numbers until well into

When U.S. Royal approached us about using their new "tiger paw" tires on every new GTO, the opportunity for an advertising tie-in was a natural. We had already considered using the Tiger theme for the GTO, since it had been used in some 1963 Tempest/Le Mans advertising.

November and December. Initial public reaction to the car was good, and those dealers who had been successful in selling previous Pontiac performance cars jumped right on the GTO. The average dealer, however, was a little slow, even a bit reluctant to get behind the car, until customers started coming in asking about it. By now, both the Convertible and the Sports Coupe were in full production, and the Hardtop Coupe was about to come on-line. In addition, the 348 horsepower Tri-Power engine option had also been released.

The car really came alive when the March, 1964 issue of *Car and Driver* magazine appeared, with the controversial cover story featuring a perfor-

One of the most distinctive features of the first GTO was the sophisticated engine-turned dash surrounding the gauge cluster. This was an image building exclusive that set it apart from the rest of the Tempest/Le Mans line.

mance comparison between the world's two most famous GTOs: the new, upstart Pontiac against the legendary, world-class Ferrari.

The GTO brought to life in sheet-metal everything Pontiac had been trying to say in their advertising about the entire product line. As the GTO became the image leader of this newly created musclecar market segment, we set out to make sure that the Bonneville, the Grand Prix, and even the Star Chief and Catalina would become the "GTO" of their respective market segments.

ONE OF THE BEST PROMOTIONS WE ever put together was our first one, with *Car and Driver* magazine. David E. Davis was the Editor of *Car and Driver,* which recently had changed its name from *Sports Cars Illustrated.* Davis had previously spent some time in the sales and marketing department of *Road and Track* magazine, working for founders John and Elaine Bond. He then drifted over to *Car and Driver* as it was being reformatted with an announced intention of becoming a general interest car magazine with more emphasis on American cars. *Sports Cars Illustrated* had been written almost exclusively for foreign or import car owners, and in those days most of the interesting import cars were coming from Europe, more specifically from England. Those were the days of MGs, Morgans, Triumphs, and of course the mighty Jaguar.

I called Dave one day in early December, 1963 to tell him about this great new car, which we were calling GTO. I explained that we knew the name was not copyrighted and that it was being used by Ferrari. On the basis of the name overlap, I suggested that this could make for an interesting comparison test. As it turned out, even I didn't realize how timely an idea I had

The GTO Creative Team

We really began to get serious in the second half of the 1964 model year. DeLorean jokingly gave me the unofficial title of "GTO Sales Manager." I always thought that was his way of hitting back at Frank Bridge.

While I did not necessarily become the GTO Sales Manager, I certainly did become the GTO Advertising Manager. I didn't write the headlines or take any of the great photos, but I had a sensational creative group at the agency who did. They were a totally committed bunch who really loved the car. Through the years memorable contributors like Ron Monchak, Bob Wilkinson, Hal Bay, "Mickey" McGuire, Barry Lund, Don Gould, Art Morat, Bill Gilmore, Selby Cook, Clark Maddock and Gary Howell really made my life a pleasure. After I explained to them what I wanted, I usually got back better than I had asked for, which, needless to say, made selling it to Pontiac management as easy as "slicing a hot knife through butter."

And there was also the highly regarded TV production group, with Dick Pedecinni, Ann Ranta, Jerry Bruckheimer (of later Hollywood fame), and Bill Ostrow.

Two GTOs for the Test

proposed, not only for Pontiac, but also for the magazine. They were looking for a way to make a statement about their new direction, demonstrating how committed they had become to American performance iron. Apparently I had touched a very sensitive nerve with my GTO/GTO idea.

They said they'd like to schedule the test to take place between Christmas and New Years day. They arranged to rent the Daytona International Speedway and wanted a car as early as possible, so they could live with it for a week or so in New York City, and then drive it down to Florida. We agreed to that. They said they would get the Ferrari.

Regardless of the outcome, this was a "win-win" situation for Pontiac. Even if the Pontiac just sat on the same track with the Ferrari, that it was given some consideration by a well respected car magazine would certainly make an impression. For Ferrari, on the other hand, it was degrading and even ludicrous to be compared to a Pontiac. Legendary sports car racer Luigi Chinetti, head of Ferrari of North America at the time, was smart enough to see that this was a "lose-lose" situation for them. As it turned out, there would never be a Ferrari GTO made available to participate in the test.

We agreed to supply two Pontiac GTOs, one a stock Sports Coupe with standard suspension, a 348 horsepower Tri-Power engine, a wide-ratio 4-speed gearbox, and a limited-slip 3.55:1 rear end. We chose to use a pilot line car, thus it had no production VIN number. That car, known as "the blue car" since it was painted Nocturne Blue, was to be used for street driving and for road course and skid pad testing. The second GTO which became known as "the red car" since it was painted in Grenadier Red, also had the 348 Tri-Power engine, but used a close-ratio 4-speed, and a 3.90:1 limited-slip rear end. We built it as a Royal Bobcat specifically for the test, and provided *Car and Driver* with a complete information sheet detailing exactly what modifications had been made. The red car was set up exclusively for acceleration testing.

When it came time for *Car and Driver* to pick up the vehicles in Detroit, they only showed up with one driver, so they chose to take the blue car. They asked me to have the red car in Daytona Beach the day after Christmas.

On the 22nd of December I left Detroit for Florida in the red car with Bud Conrad, a young mechanic from Royal who was to maintain the GTOs during testing. We met Dave Davis, his wife, and *Car and Driver*'s Managing Editor, John Jerome, at the Daytona Speedway early on the morning of December 26. We had barely exchanged greetings when I began to hear about what a great car the Pontiac GTO was, how much fun they had with it in New York, and what a wonderful road car it had been coming down to Florida.

My first question was, "When is the Ferrari coming?"

At first I was sheepishly told, "Tomorrow, we hope. There had been some trouble getting the car released." I think they assumed I was smart enough to put two and two together. When the next day came and went and there was still no Ferrari, I quit asking.

In the meantime, they were doing a lot of photography with the two Pontiacs. First, they took them to the beach and got some shots on the sand. Most of the photography focused on the blue car, since they had become so fond of it. As a pre-production, hand-built pilot line car, it was exceptionally well assembled. I felt that the folks from *Car and Driver* were still foreign car snobs, and not up to date with what was going on in Detroit. Thus having them drive such a well-put-together sample certainly helped gain their respect for this new kind of American car.

The GTO was quick, it was strong, it made a great sound, and had tons of low-end response. But, there were a lot cars coming out of Detroit at that time, like Chevy's 409, the Chrysler Hemi, Ford's 390, and our own 421 Catalinas and Bonnevilles that also had similar performance. This was the first time they had spent any serious seat time in one of these new American performance cars, so living with the GTO just overwhelmed them. They would give it full throttle, and the Tri-Power would kick in with that intimidating intake howl coming from under the hood. The natural reaction would be to back off the throttle and start over, just to make sure you hadn't broken anything. They repeated that a couple of times and finally felt comfortable enough to make a shift into second gear. They were not power shifting, instead, they were shifting like a European road racer, slowly and precisely. Of course the gutsy Muncie 4-speed was capable of taking whatever punishment they might muster, but they didn't know that.

By the second day, it was finally confirmed that there would not be a Ferrari in Florida. They made light of it, reassuring me that they had already tested a GTO Ferrari and had acquired a stable-full of driving impressions and performance numbers. All they needed now was to get the numbers on the Pontiac.

One of the things that surprised me was that they had more photographic equipment than testing equipment. There was no fifth wheel, no accelerometer, and no sophisticated trap lights of any kind, though they did manage to produce a couple of stop watches. It became apparent that they weren't going to do any serious testing on the cars, but just go by "seat of the pants" feel. They threw together a makeshift skid pad, using orange cones they had borrowed from the Speedway, to run some evasive action and slalom maneuvers. As they began to generate numbers with their stopwatches, I became concerned. Their numbers were too good to be true. But I kept my mouth shut as I could hear both Davis and Jerome exclaim, "Boy, this thing does handle. I'm impressed!"

The third day, December 29, marked the beginning of the acceleration tests. This was the first time the *Car and Driver* people had spent any time in the red car, which was significantly stronger than the blue car. Their reaction was, "Is this possible?"

One of the first things they noticed was the sound, this time coming from the tailpipes. As part of the Bobcat kit the heat riser passages in the intake manifold were blocked, which resulted in a significant change in the exhaust note. We had to get under the car and prove that the exhaust systems were the same on both cars.

"Unbelievable" Acceleration

Once they got into the red car they would not get out of it. We spent the better part of the day making stop watch-timed runs. Quarter-mile, zero to 60 mph, zero to 70 mph, zero to 90 mph, and on up to well over 100 mph, over and over again. I was standing only five feet away from whoever was holding the stopwatch, and the numbers they were coming up with were unbelievable. The car was good, but not that good! The stock red line tires were skinny and had no real traction, so the car didn't launch particularly well. In addition, neither Davis or Jerome were experienced drag racers, so they didn't launch very well either. They weren't even burning rubber, yet the acceleration numbers were beyond anything I could do in a GTO. But I wasn't going to stop it, the numbers were all in our favor. When they came up with a zero to 60 in 4.6 seconds, and 0 to 100 in 11.8 seconds, I knew it was time for me to "shut up and watch." Our red GTO wouldn't have run from zero to 100 mph in 11.8 seconds even if it had been dropped off the top of the Empire State Building.

The acceleration tests continued until late in the day when the *Car and Driver* staff decided to take the red car through their impromptu handling course. Against my better judgement, I agreed. They pushed it too hard through the corners, and when it encountered too much oil sloshing in the pan during these severe directional changes it finally spun the number three rod bearing. That put an end to the day, and to the test.

We all gathered for a parting dinner, as everybody patted each other on the back about what a great test it had been. During dinner, they informed me that they had commissioned a special oil painting for the magazine cover, showing a Ferrari GTO and a Pontiac GTO engaged in fierce competition on a road course. This was final confirmation for me that there would never be a Ferrari put in an actual comparison test against our Pontiac.

As we finally left Daytona, the *Car and Driver* staff continued to be over-

PONTIAC TEMPEST GTO

Manufacturer: Pontiac Motor Division,
General Motors Corporation,
Pontiac, Michigan

Price as tested: $3377.91

ACCELERATION

Zero to	Seconds
30 mph	1.8
40 mph	2.4
50 mph	3.3
60 mph	4.6
70 mph	6.0
80 mph	7.5
90 mph	9.6
100 mph	11.8
Standing ¼ mile	115 mph in 13.1

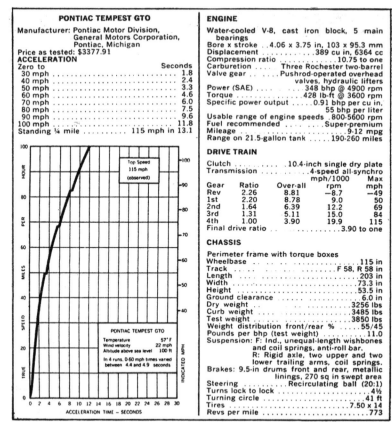

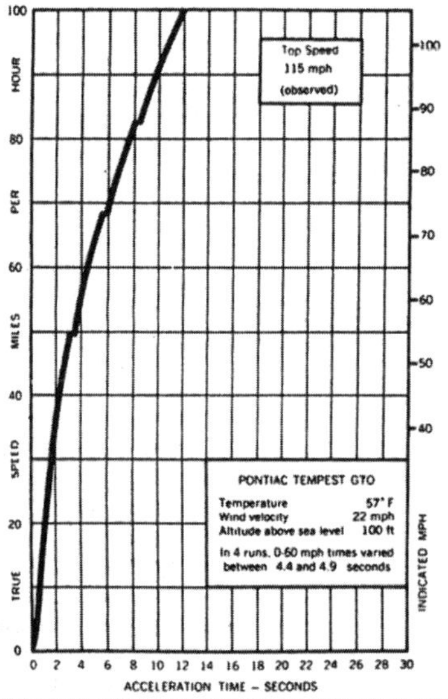

ENGINE

Water-cooled V-8, cast iron block, 5 main bearings

Bore x stroke	4.06 x 3.75 in, 103 x 95.3 mm
Displacement	389 cu in, 6364 cc
Compression ratio	10.75 to one
Carburetion	Three Rochester two-barrel
Valve gear	Pushrod-operated overhead valves, hydraulic lifters
Power (SAE)	348 bhp @ 4900 rpm
Torque	428 lb-ft @ 3600 rpm
Specific power output	0.91 bhp per cu in, 55 bhp per liter
Usable range of engine speeds	800-5600 rpm
Fuel recommended	Super-premium
Mileage	9-12 mpg
Range on 21.5-gallon tank	190-260 miles

DRIVE TRAIN

Clutch	10.4-inch single dry plate
Transmission	4-speed all-synchro

Gear	Ratio	Over-all	mph/1000 rpm	Max mph
Rev	2.26	8.81	−8.7	−49
1st	2.20	8.78	9.0	50
2nd	1.64	6.39	12.2	69
3rd	1.31	5.11	15.0	84
4th	1.00	3.90	19.9	115

Final drive ratio .... 3.90 to one

CHASSIS

Perimeter frame with torque boxes

Wheelbase	115 in
Track	F 58, R 58 in
Length	203 in
Width	73.3 in
Height	53.5 in
Ground clearance	6.0 in
Dry weight	3256 lbs
Curb weight	3485 lbs
Test weight	3850 lbs
Weight distribution front/rear %	55/45
Pounds per bhp (test weight)	11.0

Suspension: F: Ind., unequal-length wishbones and coil springs, anti-roll bar.
R: Rigid axle, two upper and two lower trailing arms, coil springs.

Brakes: 9.5-in drums front and rear, metallic linings, 270 sq in swept area

Steering	Recirculating ball (20:1)
Turns lock to lock	4½
Turning circle	41 ft
Tires	7.50 x 14
Revs per mile	773

During their first official road test of the GTO, Car and Driver magazine recorded acceleration numbers using a hand-held stop watch. I knew their numbers were not close to being accurate, but I sure as hell wasn't gong to stop them. This graph from the magazine shows the incredible 0–100 mph performance. Note how the line is almost straight.

whelmed by both GTOs. I had originally thought that the cars wouldn't shine in the handling tests, but would be competitive in acceleration. Their final observations were that the Pontiac was really quite close overall to the Ferrari, a lot closer than they had expected. They continued to talk about the unbelievable acceleration, and those wonderful sounds.

What they didn't know was that the red car was a *ringer.*

The car was built with a 389 cubic inch Tri-Power engine. However, I had it converted almost immediately to a 421cubic inch H.O. Tri-Power engine. Royal Pontiac then turned it into a Bobcat. With the engine in the car, once the "pyramid" casting was removed from the distributor boss and the casting numbers were updated, there was no visual way to tell the difference.

For years, rumors have persisted about the red car, and I have maintained that the car had a 389 under its hood. So why did I "massage" the truth? Because of the GTO's mystique. I liked the controversy that volleyed back and forth. Many historians have collected a path of paperwork proving that the red car moved around quite a bit before finally ending up at Royal Pontiac.

I'm here to admit, more than three decades after the fact, that yes, I did install a 421 H.O. Tri-Power engine in the red Royal Bobcat *Car and Driver* test car.

After the tests were over, I was faced with the task of either trying to have that engine replaced while in Florida, or bringing the car back to Detroit. We had planned to drive both cars back. Now I had to figure out what to do with a broken GTO, 1500 miles from home. I didn't want to take it to a local Pontiac dealer, as I certainly didn't want anybody looking under that hood. Finally, I decided to rent a bumper hitch and flat-tow the red car back to Detroit using the blue car. What irony!

Flat towing worked well until we ran into an incredible out-of-season snowstorm in Georgia. New Year's Day we were stranded in a motel watching bowl games because the roads were all closed, waiting to be plowed by snowplows that Georgia didn't have. I finally got back to Detroit on the 3rd of January 1964.

WHILE I WAS PREPARING FOR THE *Car and Driver* test, I was approached by an old friend who was now working for Young and Rubicam, Chrysler's advertising agency. Chrysler was aggressively moving back into racing, and they were looking for someone to show them how to turn their new-found racing success into new car sales.

They were preparing to make me an offer, he told me, and it would be substantial. As a matter of fact, it was twice what I was making at MacManus. While I wasn't looking to leave Pontiac, how could I run away from that? I told him I was going to be out of town for the holidays, and suggested we talk again, right after I returned.

The day before I left, he called me again, this time with a specific offer. "We want you on board before we go into our 1964 racing season. We've got a special spot for you, you'll be your own boss, reporting only to the top guy on the Chrysler account." Apparently they had tossed my name around at Chrysler and gotten a very good response—this from the company I was thrown out of just five years before. I finally learned that one of my friends at Chrysler, the then Chief Engineer at Plymouth, was now Plymouth's General Manager. His name was Bob Anderson, and when he heard that his ad agency was talking to me, he was pleased and told them to make sure it happened. I told Chrysler that they were making an attractive pitch, but I would have to wait until after the holidays before deciding.

While I was in Florida, one of those things happened that, well, just happen. Bob Anderson and John DeLorean were at the same holiday party. They had become good friends over the years. Anderson bragged to DeLorean, "We stole one of your guys. Did you know that Jim Wangers is coming to work for Chrysler?"

DeLorean didn't think it was very funny. Somehow he found me in Flor-

Snapped at the press preview for the 1965 Detroit Auto Show, this picture includes (from left) David E. Davis, then editor of Car and Driver magazine, me, Plymouth Division General Manager Bob Anderson (who later became CEO of North American Rockwell), and Pontiac General Manager John Z. DeLorean.

ida. His message read simply, "Please call ASAP." I had no idea why, other than he wanted to be brought up to date on the test.

When I finally reached him, his first words were, "What's this about your leaving?" DeLorean told me what Bob Anderson had told him, and continued that, "If Anderson knew about it, it must be a done deal. I want you to assure me," he continued, "that you won't leave until you come back and talk to Jones." He meant Ernie Jones, who was President of MJ&A. "I will have it all set up for you." What he was telling me, was that he was going to talk to my boss.

When I got back, not only did Ernie Jones want to see me, but Milt Coulson, the agency's top administrative executive, also had a call in for me—Milt was the guy who had annoyed Bunkie Knudsen with his too-aggressive presentation selling the Wide-Track theme back in 1959. I always felt comfortable with Milt, so his was the first call I returned. He asked me point blank, "What's it going to take to keep you from leaving?" Coulson told me that he knew the whole story, even as to how much I'd been offered.

"We aren't going to be able to match that money," he said, "but we aren't going to let you leave, either. So be smart, get what you want, and remember there's always a tomorrow. And," he added, "DeLorean wants you around for a while."

Armed with this information, I went in to see Ernie Jones. He proceeded

When I was elevated to a Senior Account Executive at MacManus, this photo was taken for the press release. While it has been used many times, what no one knows is that's not my '64 Goat (it belonged the Pontiac Creative Director Ron Monchak), that's not my trophy, and the helmet under my arm isn't mine, either. In fact, I didn't even own a helmet.

to tell me that he had been through this same kind of thing before, but that he was impressed with DeLorean's commitment to me. "I can't blame you for flexing your muscles," he added. What a friend John DeLorean turned out to be.

So, I started the new year with a good win for the GTO and a good adjustment for myself at the agency. The only thing left to do was to call Young and Rubicam and tell them that I was staying with MacManus. I wanted to make it clear that I wasn't playing both agencies against each other. I still hadn't forgotten my experience with Campbell-Ewald back in 1956.

WHEN THE *CAR AND DRIVER* STORY broke in March of 1964, everything changed. There had been other magazine road tests of the GTO, but nobody had come up with numbers like these. The spectacular cover line: "Zero to 100 mph in 11.8 seconds!" introduced not only a new kind of magazine, but also a new kind of car. Pontiac had created, and *Car and Driver* had discovered, the American musclecar.

There were many reactions to the story, not the least of which was that Chevrolet, Olds, and Buick realized they had been outsmarted by Pontiac. After protesting to the Corporation, they were finally told they, too, could have their own car, but their engineers knew that it wasn't going to be quite as easy or as quick to drop *their big* engines in *their little* cars. While they all had bigger engines in their system, they were actually different blocks, and required different chassis mounts. This was going to take some time, which is why when the first Chevelle SS, Olds 442, and Buick Gran-Sport bowed later in 1964, they were all forced to use high performance versions of their smaller engines. How prophetic was that statement made by Bill Collins as he stood under the car in the GM Proving Grounds garage.

Car and Driver received a number of letters praising them for their gutsy posture. But not all reaction was positive. They got a lot of mail from readers who were upset about their allowing this "Johnny-come-lately" Pontiac to compete on the same track with the legendary Ferrari. Of course, Dave Davis and his staff were smart enough to turn this into a positive. After all, they were trying to change their readers' perception of the magazine, and evidently they were being successful. They didn't care if they gave up two or three sports car subscribers, because they hoped they would pick up twice as many new subscribers interested in these new performance cars coming out of Detroit. *Car and Driver*'s arrogant editorial stance helped make the name Pontiac GTO stand for more than just another new car. One of our first ad headlines read, "I wouldn't stand in the middle of the page, if I were you. It's a Pontiac GTO!" And we didn't even have to explain what a GTO was; most everybody already knew. This magazine story had shaped the image of what the whole musclecar movement was going to become.

FROM THE BEGINNING, EVERY GTO BUILT with a manual transmission came equipped with a Hurst shifter. This was a real marketing plus, and we wanted to take advantage of it.

The Hurst shifter was already recognized as the finest shifter built in America. Most every car enthusiast quickly replaced their flimsy factory shifter with a Hurst, right after they acquired their new car. A number of me-too companies also tooled up floor shifters, but none were ever able to match the quality and durability of a Hurst. For a Pontiac to be equipped with a Hurst shifter from the factory said a great deal to enthusiast car buyers about Pontiac's commitment to their product.

To understand just how significant the Hurst floor-mounted shifter had become, consider that George Hurst had effectively negated in six months what it took Detroit twenty years to accomplish, which was to move the gear shift lever from the floor onto the steering column. Moving the floor shifter up to the steering column effectively converted a five-passenger car into a six-passenger car. With the shifter on the floor, a third passenger could not sit comfortably between the driver and the right front seat passenger. Nobody was thinking about consoles in those days, and bucket seats were still only available on limited production sports cars. Not only was the floor

Right from the beginning, manual transmission-equipped GTOs came with Hurst shifters installed at the factory. However, because of a GM corporate policy that prohibited using vendor's names, the shift lever was devoid of the word "Hurst." I convinced Pete Estes to overturn that policy by proving to him that it was a plus for Pontiac to be able to brag in their ads that the Hurst shifter was standard equipment. I knew that the first thing any serious enthusiast did when he got his new stick shift performance car was to trash the factory unit in favor of a Hurst. Beginning in 1965, every shifter had "Hurst" stamped on the lever and we promoted that in our advertising.

mounted shifter cheaper to build, but it also provided a more positive way of shifting, and had now become a marketing symbol for a new generation of sporty, high performance passenger cars. If you knew how to operate a floor shift quickly and smoothly, you were a true performance car driver.

Pontiac got the jump on the rest of the industry because of my personal relationship with George Hurst, which developed out of our mutual interest in drag racing. After having my race car converted, I said to George, "What a shame that every Pontiac owner can't enjoy this kind of shifting." I discussed it with DeLorean, and he invited me to bring George in for a talk. Together they worked out a profitable agreement that resulted in the Hurst shifter being offered as standard equipment on every Pontiac equipped with a manual transmission.

As a marketer, I wanted to use it in our advertising right away. The problem was that GM had a policy preventing any outside supplier from putting their name on a part or component (except tires) that was built into the car. I had to convince Pete Estes that it really meant more to Pontiac to be able say their cars came equipped right from the factory with a Hurst shifter by name, than it meant for Hurst to be able to say their shifter was original equipment on every Pontiac built with a manual transmission. Pete listened, and out of respect for my knowledge of the market allowed us to do it. Beginning with the 1965 models, every Pontiac floor shifter was clearly labeled "Hurst," and we saw to it that it was in our advertising.

George Hurst was a delightful man, totally in love with life, not particularly well educated, but very street-smart. George had a good feel and a good understanding, not only of the mechanics of his product, but also for the mechanics of the business. He was truly at the right place at the right time with the right product. He was also a natural marketer. He understood both personal and public relationships, and perhaps most importantly George was not afraid to spend a buck to make a buck.

It quickly became a plus when Hurst became part of the Pontiac family. Whenever Hurst/Campbell (which was the company name; Bill Campbell, a trained engineer, was George's partner) promoted their products or introduced a new product, they always selected a Pontiac to appear in their advertising and promotion.

AFTER THE *Car and Driver* TEST, *Hot Rod* magazine editor Ray Brock decided that he had better get more familiar with this new Pontiac. At the time, *Hot Rod* was the nation's number-one car enthusiast magazine. The GTO was still in short supply, so press vehicles weren't readily available. The staff at *Hot Rod* were already upset because Pontiac had not provided them with a GTO test car, and that became even more of a problem when they read about it in a competitive magazine. The Pontiac PR office in Los Angeles predictably didn't have a car to give to them. Angrily, Brock called the Zone Office, explaining who he was and demanding a GTO immediately. The Zone Manager explained that press cars were not normally handled by the Zone Office, but in trying to do his job for Pontiac he naively offered to loan them his company car, which had been built to his wife's specifications.

Negative Press

Her GTO was a Yellow convertible with a Pearl White interior, equipped with the base 4-barrel engine, a 2-speed automatic transmission, air conditioning, and a 3.08:1 open rear end. It was a gorgeous car, but not the car to give to *Hot Rod* for a test.

When it appeared, the story was promoted on the magazine's front cover. "We Test Pontiac's New GTO!" Remember this was 1964, and getting a good review in *Hot Rod* was like getting a good review for a Broadway play in the *New York Times*. As soon as I saw the story, with a picture of a convertible with wire wheel covers, I knew we were in trouble. The first line of the copy started out, "So what's the big deal?" Brock related how hard it was to get this Pontiac GTO in the first place, and then proceeded to damn it with faint praise. He noted that this new GTO didn't perform as well as the 327 cubic inch Chevy Impala convertible they had tested the previous month. Brock ended the story by chiding Pontiac for overhyping the car, which in his words was "good, but certainly nothing special."

With a copy of the magazine I burst into DeLorean's office and threw it down on his desk, charging, "For chrissake, John, we bust our ass building an image for this great car and then an article like this shows up, and especially in *Hot Rod* magazine."

DeLorean scanned the story and started to laugh. "What do you want me to do?" he asked. I told him I wanted a couple of cars that I could turn into Royal Bobcats and use solely for the press. I guaranteed him, "We'll never get press like this again."

Now, while I wasn't responsible for Pontiac's public relations (a very capable guy named Bob Emerick was), the PR guys didn't care a whole lot about performance and didn't know how to select the right cars for their fleet—I mean sophisticated things like the right rear-end ratio, the right transmission gears, heavy duty break linings, or even the right suspension options. Normally, the auto magazines were invited to what was called a "long lead" press preview, usually held in the summer of the previous year before the new models were announced. That meant that all the new 1964 cars were shown to the press in June of 1963. This allowed (as it still does today) the writers to test the new cars and write their stories for their fall issues, to appear simultaneously with the new car introductions. Since the GTO wasn't ready for the 1964 long lead it had received no press. This was no accident; that's the way Pontiac wanted it. After the car was finally approved, however, the PR department had been a little slow in getting them in front of the important enthusiast magazines.

DeLorean, still laughing at my passionate overreaction, agreed to my request for the two cars. He reached down in his desk drawer, pulled out a couple of new car order forms and said, "Order them out the way you want."

Royal Press Cars

I quickly put together a couple of hardtop coupes. Although both remained on the Pontiac Engineering books, they were kept at Royal. They were turned into Royal Bobcats almost immediately and promptly put to work. The writers enjoyed driving the faster, more capable Royal Bobcats, and we made sure that every writer knew exactly what had been done to the car they were testing.

We had a simple procedure every time an automotive writer came to town. We would pick them up at the airport with the car they were going to test, take them back to Royal, and then take them out to Woodward Ave. and let them "have at it." Occasionally we'd let a journalist take a car home for a long term test.

When the GTO was introduced, the Pontiac PR department sent out the usual pictures and press releases, and then walked away from the car. What we were trying to accomplish with our special Royal press cars was to keep them in front of their potential market throughout the entire model year. For example, we would make changes in tuning, gearing, suspension, brakes, even wheels, inviting individual magazines or writers to return for an "exclusive" story on these new modifications. In each case, it gave us an opportunity to make more news with our cars and keep them in front of the marketplace that really cared: the car enthusiasts.

By 1965, the GTO really came of age. The car magazines found that they would sell extra copies when they put a GTO on their cover, an honor that in the past had only been true for the revered Corvette. For some of the smaller magazines, that would mean a measurable boost in circulation. Even *Esquire* magazine did a story on Detroit's Woodward Avenue. Their writer, Dan Jedlicka, took a tour of Woodward in a Royal Bobcat. The story gave Pontiac exposure to an audience that didn't regularly read the car magazines, and I thought it was particularly ironic that here was *Esquire*, where I had started my career almost 20 years before, now doing a story about my favorite subject, Woodward Avenue, and the American musclecar culture.

Royal produced tremendous press for Pontiac, but it was a two-way street, as Pontiac provided significant support for Royal. For example, DeLorean had "hidden" the Royal press cars in his engineering budget. When DeLorean became General Manager in 1965, Steve Malone became Chief Engineer. The first time Malone discovered the Royal press cars in his budget, he cut them.

When I found out that Malone had cut my cars, I had no alternative but to call DeLorean. Somewhat piqued, DeLorean called Malone. To this day I don't know what he said, but we got our cars back, pronto! Even though Malone tried to drop them from his budget every year, DeLorean prevailed. I happened to be in his office one day when Malone called asking once again to "get rid of those damn Wangers cars!" DeLorean, usually even-tempered, let loose with a barrage of four-letter words that impressed even me.

Needless to say, that didn't do me any good with Steve Malone. He didn't like, nor did he understand how, this "outside bullshit," as he called it, was doing any good for Pontiac. And therein was the difference in leadership styles. DeLorean, even though he was an engineer, also understood marketing. He knew that through the Royal press car program Pontiac was communicating with their potential performance buyers, perhaps even more effectively than with advertising. The Pontiac PR guys didn't see the Royal Bobcat activity as being any different from what they were already doing, so they rejected any requests to add my cars to their fleet. DeLorean simply solved the problem by keeping the cars buried in the engineering budget.

ONE DAY SOON AFTER THE GTO had been introduced I received a phone call from John Wilkin, who was with a publishing company called Buckhorn Music out of Nashville, Tennessee. He had first called Bob Emerick to tell him about his idea for a rock'n'roll song about the GTO. Emerick wasn't interested, and passed Wilkin on to me—more in a show of disdain, I always felt.

I listened to Wilkin's presentation, making it very plain to him that there were limits to what Pontiac could do. I did tell them there could possibly be some action on the part of the individual dealers, who had a lot of contact with their local radio stations and bought a lot of commercial time.

Wilkin was just a kid, still in high school, but with a lot of moxie about the music business. His mother Marijohn Wilkin was already a successful country and western songwriter, and was a partner in Buckhorn. "Bucky," as young Wilkin liked to be called, had written the words and the music, and it was scheduled to be recorded on the Mala record label.

After listening to the song I thought it was "right on," but I suggested he try to build in a little more specific reference to the GTO. The line, "Three deuces and a four speed and a 389" were then written into the song. Wilkin was very cooperative. My contribution to the song was simply some timely advice and some direction on the lyrics. Somehow, over the years the story has emerged that Jim Wangers had more to do with that hit song. This is not true.

There was one word in the song that I could never understand, and that was the reference to the "Little Modified Ponton." Apparently, it was their nickname for Pontiac." I pointed out that some people called them "Ponchos," but I had never heard of a "Ponton." I've had a lot of trouble over the years explaining what Ponton really meant. Wilkin's nickname never did catch on. Also, the record was often referred to as "Little GTO," since that's the first line in the lyric. Actually, the name of the tune was just "GTO."

It was easier for a new record to get air time in those days. Many local stations programmed their own music in a format called "Top 40 Radio," which was aimed at the youth market, the very market we were trying so desperately to impress. Pontiac dealers were placing a lot of commercials on those stations. We felt that if we could get our dealers to tell their local stations about the record, it would certainly help to get more air time. As it turned out, the record was right on target. There already had been several releases about cars, most notably by the Beach Boys with tunes like "Little Deuce Coupe," "Shutdown," and "409."

A group was created to cut the record for Mala. They were named "Ronny and the Daytonas," and consisted of some talented session musicians, arrangers, and mixers working around Nashville. The record was released in late summer 1963, and quickly climbed to number four on the charts. The 45 rpm single sold more than one million copies and lasted on the Top 40 list for 17 consecutive weeks. An album was released very shortly after the single, and it, too, sold more than 500,000 copies. Sheet music was very popular then, and over 500,000 copies of that were also sold.

Billboard magazine estimated that the record "GTO" was played on the radio over seven million times while it was on the charts.What we had was a 2 minute and 29 second commercial for our new Pontiac.

After "GTO" became so popular there was a demand for personal appearances. So Ronny and the Daytonas had to be created all over again, this time with attractive teens to go along with Buck Wilkin. Even today, oldies radio stations play "GTO" when running through their list of the great hit records of the sixties.

It ended up as a great one-two marketing punch. The *Car and Driver* story, combined with the hit record "GTO," made the greatest new model announcement in all of Pontiac history. Yet the GTO still wasn't even a model, it was only an option. We ended the year selling over 32,000 cars because that was all we could build—that was all the 389 engines we could "steal" from Pontiac since the Division was having a good year with the full-size cars, too.

It was then we began to realize that this was more than just another new car. We had created a new kind of Pontiac. While we had initially thought of the GTO as only a "one shot" promotion to get the newly restyled intermediate Tempest/ Le Mans off the ground, suddenly we had much more going. We now had a car aimed perfectly at the exploding baby boomers.

SHORTLY AFTER THE START OF THE 1965 model year, Pete Estes was chosen to become the new General Manager of Chevrolet, following in Bunkie Knudsen's footsteps. John DeLorean, as he predicted, was promoted to General Manger of Pontiac, and at that time, became the youngest General Manager in the history of GM. Steve Malone took John's place as Pontiac's Chief Engineer.

For the GTO, all the things that should have been done to the 1964 car were done to the 1965. These included new front and rear end styling, full instrumentation, a new camshaft, better cylinder heads, a new intake manifold, and a little more sophistication in the suspension. We also introduced a new styled wheel just for the A-body cars, called the Rally Wheel. The GTO however, was still sold as an option, only available on the Le Mans.

It didn't take long for us to assume a posture of confidence, as some of the headlines we used on our early print ads certainly reflected. Consider the ad that simply showed the car with the headline "Our Thing," which was a direct play on the then famous "Cosa Nostra" concept. Another one read "There are a few great moments in life. This is one of them," or still another that read, "How to tell a real tiger from a pussycat. Drive it!"

We had formed a little group at the agency to work on the GTO. These folks loved the car, and had an understanding of what we were trying to achieve with it. It was a real experience to listen to them kick around ideas. They knew that no matter how zany the idea or how far out the copy, if I believed in it I'd sell it to Pontiac. One of the most difficult things creative advertising folks struggle with, even today, is to develop a good idea and then have to turn it over to somebody else to sell it. We were different. We knew how to talk to car enthusiasts because we were car enthusiasts. We knew from talking to these younger people that many of them were dragging their parents into Pontiac showrooms to look at the new GTO. How many of them would end up buying a new Catalina or a Bonneville, of course, we had no way of knowing. While we never used the corny line, we liked to think that "There was a little bit of GTO in every Pontiac."

When John DeLorean took over as General Manager, he said to me, "I'd like to see you run the Pontiac account at the agency." He made that same request to Ernie Jones. Jones resisted. He had his own plans on how to run the account. DeLorean's answer was, "Organize it however you want, but as far as I'm concerned, Wangers is running the account." He then proceeded to operate that way. Ernie knew, as did Colin John, who actually was doing a good job of running the account, that John and I had developed a close working relationship. They didn't feel threatened or compromised by the fact that John DeLorean used me as his confidante. They trusted me to keep them informed, and that's really the way it worked out.

My new position in the agency allowed me much more freedom. Finally, I began to get out from under the "gearhead" label I had been living with since my first day on the job.

One area where I did have some disagreements with the agency was in making Pontiac media choices, especially with the car enthusiast magazines.

Product Knowledge vs. Marketing Savvy

I'd like to talk a little bit about the subject of being a "gearhead" in a sales, marketing and advertising world. One of my strengths was always how well I knew the cars I worked on. While it's certainly good to know your product, especially one as sophisticated and complicated as an automobile, this can be a two-edged sword. It can stall a career as much as enhance it. It's easy to get typed, and that's one of the worst traps you can fall into. You become imaged as "that product guy" or as the product information "specialist" or as just a plain "gearhead." That's OK if it's a temporary stop on the way up. Everybody will have respect for you, and will seek you out to assure them that their product references and product specs are accurate and correct. But, that's where your input will stop. If you have a sales idea or a marketing suggestion or even a creative ad idea to offer, it will be too-often cast aside with a patronizing comment, "That's nice, but remember he's only a gearhead, what does he know about advertising or marketing?" Having good product knowledge is a real plus, but use it discretely and with calculated timing. It's too easy to get boxed in, with little chance to ever get out.

Ties with DeLorean

I wanted to place ads in magazines that didn't have verified circulation records, or an ABC (Audit Bureau of Circulation) rating. They spoke directly to our market, and their ad rates weren't very high. We really started a trend, and it wasn't long before everybody in town was doing the same thing. I'll never forget an experience I had with the magazine *Popular Hot Rodding*, which was a new title. Pontiac, in spite of our own sales success, was forced to accept a temporary cut in our advertising budget, because of a GM strike. We went through our magazine list and cut many publications. I received a frantic phone call from a young gentlemen named Bill Lloyd who was the ad manager of *Popular Hot Rodding*. "Jim" he pleaded, "Please don't cut us. We'll lose everybody else in Detroit too. What you don't realize is that the other advertisers in your town copy everything Pontiac does. If you cut us, they'll react, thinking you know something about us that they don't know." After I explained to him that this was only a temporary cut, because of production problems, he ran the ad free of charge, just to make sure Pontiac was in.

On some occasions, DeLorean would call me at home to let me know he had made a decision on an advertising buy. In those days it was not unusual for one advertiser to sponsor an entire TV show. I would ask him, "John, does your Advertising Manager know about this?" "No," he'd reply. "You tell him, and while you're at it, let those guys at the agency know too!" I could almost see him smiling through the telephone. He loved to create little situations like that, but he also knew he'd get what he wanted.

WITH THE SUCCESS OF THE GTO now virtually assured, Pontiac thought it might make sense to apply the same formula to their full-size car. The 2+2 had been introduced in 1964 as a low-priced, sporty package built off the

Our 1966 version of the double whammy.
The tiger scores again! Wide-Track Pontiac/'66

We tried to surround the entire Pontiac line with the fantastic performance aura of the GTO, all the way from the six-cylinder Sprint to the 421-equipped 2+2. Yet, no matter how hard we tried and how good the cars actually were, nothing ever came close to capturing the imagination of the buying public like the GTO.

Catalina. It featured bucket seats, a console, and a dressed-up interior. No performance or handling upgrades were part of the package.

Since the 389 engine had worked so well in a special Le Mans, they thought the 421 engine would be great in a special Catalina. Thus the all-new 1965 2+2 bowed with a 4-barrel carburetor version of the 421 engine as standard equipment. This was a significant effort, since neither the Grand Prix or Bonneville was ever offered with this engine as standard.

The 2+2 nameplate was also generic, like GTO, and could not be copyrighted. Who else had one? That's right, Ferrari. I suggested to *Car and Driver* that they do another Ferrari comparison test, and they jumped at the chance. They rented the famed Bridgehampton race track on the south shore of Long Island, New York, and invited us to bring along a 1965 Royal Bobcat 2+2 complete with a close-ratio 4-speed and a 3.90:1 rear axle. This time, they did procure a Ferrari 2+2, and commissioned experienced road race driver Walt Hansgen to wring out both cars. Hangsen fell in love with our Pontiac, and the rest was history. The Catalina 2+2 came very close to the comparable Ferrari in almost every part of the test.

The high point was an absolutely incredible 0–60 mph time Hangsen set with the Pontiac. Using a similar hand-held stopwatch technique like they had used at Daytona, Davis and Jerome recorded a 0–60 time of 3.9 seconds. I just shook my head in disbelief, but again kept quiet. When the magazine

The toughest kid on the block now has a big brother.

Pontiac Motor Division • General Motors Corporation

When we conjured up the GTO from our own private stockpile of sleek sheet metal and hairy machinery, we felt a lot like kids in a candy store. We couldn't stop at the bonbons or cherry-centered nougats. So we grabbed for the big-bodied Pontiac and started laying in things like heavy-duty shocks and springs and a 338-hp 421, and called it the 2+2. Once around the test track and our eyes bugged.

We rubbed our hands together and tossed in an all-synchro 3-speed with a Hurst floor shifter for moxie. Then we chrome-plated the rocker covers and air cleaner, and frosted the package with pinstriping, bucket seats and carpeting. (All this is standard equipment.) And we stood back and gloated.

Knowing full well that our customers like to visit the candy store on their own, we added a list of optional equipment that reads like an invoice for starting your own hot rod shop.

So do you buy the fabulous GTO or the incredible 2+2? That's your problem. We make 'em the way we see 'em.

Go get 'em, Tiger!

Wide-Track Pontiac Tigers: 2+2/GTO

119

*GTO
"Umbrella"*

The 1964 2+2 had been a "paper" Tiger, while all of our other Tigers had teeth. Just as we had glamorized the Le Mans with the GTO, I thought we could glamorize the 1965 Catalina with the 2+2, a lower-priced, full-sized high performance car. I convinced DeLorean and his product planning staff to put a package together with the 421 cubic inch engine, bucket seats, Hurst shifter, and heavy duty suspension. I expected the 1965 2+2 would follow the GTO's sales success. We built an ad that gave the 2+2 some of the GTO's aura with the title, "The toughest kid on the block now has a big brother." Its success seemed a sure thing, and even though it stuck around until 1967, the 2+2 never made it. Apparently it was priced and imaged a little too close to the Grand Prix and Bonneville Coupes.

While we were working to develop the GTO's image as our top performance car, we weren't neglecting our full-sized cars. We made sure they exuded an image of luxury with a performance attitude (sound familiar?). This 1964 Bonneville Brougham was built as part of a fleet of four for Teamster president Jimmy Hoffa and his top executives. Hoffa, a real car enthusiast, had these cars equipped with Tri-Power engines, dual exhausts, heavy duty suspension, eight-lug wheels, and even a Royal Bobcat emblem.

appeared on the newsstands, most readers just scoffed, thinking it was a misprint, or that the time actually referred to a 0–30 mph measurement.

As nice a car as this Catalina 2+2 was, it couldn't survive the competition coming from within the Pontiac showroom, losing sales to the GTO on one side and to the Bonneville and Grand Prix on the other. It was discontinued at the end of the 1967 model year, after only a little more than 27,000 had been built since its beginning in 1964.

ANOTHER GREAT MILESTONE IN PONTIAC marketing of the time was the Tiger theme. The early sixties proved to be the age of the Tiger. Esso (Eastern States Standard Oil) was screaming "Put a Tiger in your tank," while the United States Rubber Co. (U.S. Royal, later to become known as Uniroyal) had introduced a new tire they called the "tiger paw." Even Kellogg's, the breakfast cereal giant, had their character "Tony the Tiger" to promote their Sugar Frosted Flakes. We felt that the image of a Tiger and all the timely hipness it suggested would be perfect for our new GTO.

The Tiger had actually first entered Pontiac advertising in 1963, when we used it to distinguish the engine lineup in our Tempest. The ad referenced the "One-Tiger Tempest," which was the 1-barrel carburetor four-cylinder package, the "Two-Tiger Tempest," which was the 4-barrel carburetor 4-cylinder package, and the "Three Tiger Tempest," which was the 2-barrel carburetor 326 cubic inch V-8. This last combination was big news in 1963. Pontiac had been making a special engine for the GMC truck line at that time, and decided this would make a good engine for their new intermediate carline. The engine remained 336 cubic inches all through the 1963 model year, but because the Tempest/Le Mans only weighed 3200 lbs., it was promoted as a 326 engine to comply with GM regulations. By 1964, the engine actually was 326 cubic inches.

GTO
6.5 LITRE
GTO
For the man who wouldn't mind riding a tiger if someone'd only put wheels on it—Pontiac GTO
This piece of machinery is something our Engineering Department slipped a motherly big Pontiac 389-incher into and named the GTO.
It comes in hardtop, sports coupe and convertible form, based on the Le Mans—only sleekened down some and fitted with a special set of red-circle high-performance tires.
The looks you can see for yourself. The big deal is under the hood: 325 bhp at 4800 rpm and 428 lb-ft of torque at 3200 rpm. That's just the standard 4BBL engine. There's also a version with 348 bhp* at 4900 rpm and 428 lb-ft of torque at 3600 rpm.
*optional at extra cost.
This one does deep-breathing exercises through a 3-2BBL setup. Both make bad-tempered noises through dual pipes. As illustrated above, pairs of exhaust splitters on each flank, just behind the rear wheels, are available dealer installed*.
A 3-speed transmission is standard, stirred by a Hurst shifter on the floor. Extra-cost variations include an automatic with shift on the column . . . an all-synchro 4-speed on the floor . . . or a choice of any one of them sprouting out of a console.
Give yourself a blast of tonic. Sample one of these here big pussycats.
PONTIAC MOTOR DIVISON • GENERAL MOTORS CORPORATION
DECEMBER 1963

Our first GTO consumer advertising was restricted only to the automotive enthusiast magazines. We were afraid to attract the attention—and wrath—of corporate management by buying ad space in general media. These black-and-white photo-driven ads highlighted the Tiger theme we wanted to cultivate for the GTO.

We began to work the Tiger into our 1964 GTO ad copy very early. With our agreement to use their tiger paw tires on the new GTO, Uniroyal ran an ad in which they said, "What did you expect Pontiac to put on a tiger? Ordinary tires?"

The very first time Pontiac actually featured the Tiger for the GTO was in a car enthusiast magazine ad. It read, "For the man who wouldn't mind riding a Tiger if someone'd only put wheels on it—Pontiac GTO". The ad showed a 1964 GTO in action, with various features specific to the car surrounding it.

Based on the success of the first GTO record, we thought we could get lightning to strike twice by producing another. The idea was to find a nickname for the GTO and tie it into the Tiger. We called the record "The GeeTO Tiger." We even created a special group called "The Tigers," and got the record produced by the Colpix Record Co. We worked very hard at not making it a commercial, but the record sold only fair, never making the Top 40 charts. It did however, present a nice promotion opportunity for us.

We released a special version of "The GeeTO Tiger" record, with the flip side called "Big Sounds Of The GeeTO Tiger." The big sounds actually described a trip through the famous GM Proving Grounds, riding "shotgun" in a new 1965 Tri-Power GTO. The record was superbly produced, as the professional test driver put the car through a series of torturous testing procedures. The end product was great, but getting there was another story. When we approached the proving ground's management with our idea, they laughed. "No way," they responded, "we can't interrupt our schedule" Even John DeLorean couldn't change their thinking. Every GM Division valued their precious time at the "grounds," and nobody wanted to offend anybody out there. So, as it turned out, we never went near an actual proving grounds while recording. The exciting sounds of the car were captured at an old abandoned drag strip in the San Fernando Valley, in California. All voices, special sound effects and mixing was done inside a Capitol Records sound studio in their famous tower on Vine St., in downtown Hollywood.

Bound in a beautiful four-color jacket, complete with pictures of the car, the record was offered through a mail order program, tied into a national contest co-sponsored by Hurst. The contest required listening to the GeeTO Tiger record, counting the number of times the word "Tiger" was mentioned (the correct number was 42), and then writing in 50 words or less why you'd like to own a special GTO called the "GeeTO Tiger." The contest drew over 100,000 entries. The grand prize was indeed a one-of-a-kind, a 1965 Tri-Power hardtop, painted in special Hurst Gold with a black vinyl top. The car was fitted with a set of gold anodized Hurst wheels and a gold-plated Hurst floor shifter. The winner treasured the car, keeping it in beautiful shape. It's still around today, looking every bit as good as the day it was given away by George Hurst.

Hurst Gold paint was George Hurst's favorite car color. He developed it for use on a couple of his earlier Pontiac promotion cars. The Pontiac design staff liked the color well enough to introduce it into the market late in the 1965 model year. Pontiac called it Tiger Gold. The 1966 GTO announcement ad reading, "To all other cars from the Pontiac GTO, What's new pussycats?" featured a Tiger Gold hardtop with a black vinyl top and a set of plastic red fender liners. The car, the color, even the vinyl top went on to become very popular. The red plastic fender liners proved to be an option we couldn't give away.

Although the GTO would be nicknamed "The Goat" by its loving public, we tried to label it the "GeeTO Tiger." Pontiac worked with Hurst to promote the GeeTO Tiger name by staging a contest: participants had to count the number of times the word "Tiger" was in the song "GeeTO Tiger," and then write an essay of 50 words or less explaining why they wanted to win the real GeeTO Tiger, a very special GTO we gave away at the end of the contest. While the contest was popular, public opinion prevailed. The nickname GeeTO Tiger never caught on.

You don't know what a real tiger is
until you hear this GeeTO Tiger growl.
GeeTO TIGER!
Wide-Track Pontiac Tiger–GTO

"Big sounds of the GeeTO Tiger" was the flip side of 50,000 special copies of the GeeTO Tiger record. The sound effects featured an actual recording, from inside the car, of a Pontiac GTO in the garage and on the test track of the GM proving grounds in Milford, Michigan—at least the record sounded like it had all those sounds. In reality, the B-side was put together by a sound effects wizard in a studio at the Capitol Records building on Vine St. in Hollywood.

As the GTO grew, the Tiger grew as well. While GeeTO Tiger never caught on as a nickname, GeeTO Tiger promotions really opened the door for the Tiger to become a very successful symbol. Here we were, a bunch of slick, high-priced promoters trying to hang a nickname on this wonderful new car, when in reality, the kids who owned and loved it had already created

The tiger scores again!
It's dramatically fresh and new, but still very, very Pontiac. That's written all over it, from the no-doubt-about-it new front end to the trimly tailored rear. (Did you think for one minute that we'd leave out the unique Pontiac styling character you like so well? Never!) Another nice thing about the '66 Pontiacs is that there are more of them—3 new super-sumptuous Broughams and 4 Venturas. And of course for you other Pontiac lovers we've got a bright new Grand Prix, new Catalinas, new Star Chief Executives—all with new Wide-Track ride and improved cat-quick handling. But you'll discover those things when you turn one of our new '66 tigers loose. You'll find them where all the people are. Where else?
The formidable 2+2, also available as a hardtop.
66·103

By mid-1965, the Tiger had become an integral part of all GTO advertising. Pontiac management became increasingly aware of the Tiger's success and began allowing us to build the theme into other models such as the Le Mans and 2 + 2. By 1966, "The tiger scores again!" was our theme, and it referred to the entire Pontiac line.

the nickname we were looking for, they called it simply, "The Goat." After some research we concluded that the word "Goat" represented the closest English word the letters GTO spelled. Out of the mouths of the owners themselves came the name that has survived through the years.

By the middle of 1965 we were committed totally to the Tiger. We were shipping all kinds of merchandising and display items to the dealers for use in their showrooms: tiger skin rugs that could be draped over a hood; orange and black window trim featuring angry, growling tigers; wall plaques with protruding tiger heads; and thousands of Tiger tails, which could be used anywhere. As Pontiac continued to expand the number of performance models in their lineup, these cars became perfect candidates to be called "Tigers." The Catalina 2+2 and the 4-barrel six cylinder Sprint were good examples. It didn't take long before all of us were thinking the same thing: why not all Pontiacs? After all, even Bonnevilles were capable of behaving like Tigers. By 1966, one of the staunchest supporters of the Tiger theme was Frank Bridge, the very man who hated the whole Tiger idea when it was first proposed. Now, having seen it work for the GTO, Frank was ready to see it applied across the board. Thus, all 1966 Pontiacs were introduced as "The Wide-Track Tigers."

The Tiger Silenced

It all came to a screeching halt at the end of the 1966 model year, when GM Board Chairman James Roche shut down the campaign. Roche had issued a hint sometime earlier, expressing his dislike for the Tiger theme, but since it had been working so well, Division Manager DeLorean did not think this was sufficient reason to drop it. The end came in late summer of 1966. Roche was attending a Board meeting in the GM building on 57th St. in New York. Directly off the main lobby was a huge showroom, where each month a different GM Division had the opportunity to display their wares. The idea was to make this corporate showroom look exactly like a typical dealership. This month it was Pontiac's turn. As Roche walked in, he was overwhelmed by the incredible display of tigers. There were growling sound effects, jungle music, tiger tails, tiger rugs, tiger heads everywhere, demonstrating that all Pontiac's were "Wide-Track Tigers." Talk about being at the wrong place at the wrong time.

DeLorean got a call at home that night from his immediate boss, Ed Rollert, who was the GM Vice President in charge of all the car and truck divisions. He suggested, rather firmly, that Pontiac drop the Tiger theme. Apparently Roche, who had no marketing background, didn't think it was an appropriate symbol for a "responsible" GM Car Division. Naturally DeLorean, acting "responsibly," honored the request. Thus ended one of the most colorful, most aggressive and perhaps most effective ad campaigns Pontiac had ever embraced.

Still, 1966 was the year the GTO became a real car. No longer an option on the Le Mans, it was now its own model. Along with all the new GM A-body coupes, it featured a new roof styling package introducing the dramatic "tunneled" back window, or "backlite" as industry technicians called it. The tunnelling effect, along with the severely swept-back C-pillar, gave the car a

In 1966, "tunneled backlite styling" was introduced on the Le Mans and GTO, as well as all other intermediate size GM coupes. It was immediately accepted by the public. Tunnel-type roof slats lent themselves very well to the controversial vinyl roof. Vinyl top styling was very much in vogue in the sixties. Pontiac called theirs the Cordova top. I didn't think it made a good statement on a performance car, then or now.

The announcement ad for the 1966 GTO. The car reintroduced the Hurst Gold color with a new name, "Tiger Gold." The arrogant headline, "What's new, pussycats?" challenges all other muscle cars. Again, the copy was as timely as possible: "What's new pussycat?" was a Tom Jones song hit and the title of a popular movie. Stylish red plastic inner fender liners, introduced as an option in this ad, proved to be a disastrous market failure.

true fastback profile, while at the same time retaining the positive characteristics and luggage space convenience of a notchback. Interestingly, this tunneled styling had been given some consideration for the original 1964 A-body coupe. At that time, it was felt by many that it might be too severe. The 1964 A-body's conventional back window clearly established the car as a coupe. Now, facing the need for its first major facelift, this was a logical styling upgrade.

The GTO on TV

GTO stands for *Gran Turismo Omologato*. You've probably heard of it. A Pontiac in a saber-toothed tiger skin. The deceptively beautiful body comes in convertible, sports coupe, and hardtop configurations. With pinstriping. On a heavy-duty suspension system that thinks it's married to the ground. Bucket seats and carpeting. Wood-grained dash. Redlines or whitewalls at no extra cost. Chromed 335-hp 4 barrel under the hood. Fully-synchronized 3-speed on the column. Or order a heavy-duty all-synchro 3-speed or 4-speed with Hurst floor shifter. Or 2-speed auto. Or the 360-hp 3 2-BBL. There's a catalog full of options. See if you can get your Pontiac dealer to cough one up. That's the GTO/2+2 performance catalog. You'll recognize it. It vibrates.
Speak softly and carry a GTO
Pontiac Motor Division • General Motors Corporation

Pontiac's image-building cockiness of the time rears its head again, as a 1966 GTO hardtop in track test conditions is described with the line, "Speak softly and carry a GTO." The typically low-key arrogance in the copy was a well-planned advertising decision. It reflected the Division's confidence and helped Pontiac retain its image as the leader in the world of muscle cars. Note the eight-lug wheels on this pre-production test model. These wheels never made it to production, and no matter what anyone else may tell you, no cars were released with this wheel.

Right from the start it was apparent that we had another winner. Pontiac sold more than 97,000 GTOs in 1966, its best sales year ever. It seemed like we never could build enough cars to satisfy the demand.

WHEN IT CAME TO MARKETING the GTO on television, our initial approach was weak. While we wanted to get more aggressive with our advertising and depict the GTO for what it really was, we restricted that message to print only, and then only in the more sophisticated enthusiast magazines. We knew we'd barely been granted approval for the car, so when we did produce television commercials (there were none for the '64), we assumed GM management would be more likely to watch TV than read the car magazines so we were very conservative. We had women driving the car, and we even did one commercial where the voice over said that GTO stood for "Girls Take Over," with a young lady shifting the 4-speed and enjoying the pleasures of driving a convertible. It was not a "balls-out," aggressive kind of campaign, and we didn't spend much money.

You have to remember that at the time we were still thinking of the GTO as a way of promoting the Le Mans. We didn't think it would be a long-term model in the Pontiac lineup. We had such a nice story to tell about the GTO that we used it instead of the Le Mans on national television, although we still talked more about the Le Mans in the commercials.

All of that changed when the GTO took off in 1965. We realized it was going to be around for a while, and that we had created a new marketing segment as important—although different—as the Le Mans.

Our new approach first appeared with the 1965 *Motor Trend* Car of the Year commercial, which was a late spring release. The model year was more than half over and the GTO was flying out of showrooms, so Pontiac decided to let it all hang out. The *Motor Trend* award was given to Pontiac for its styling, engineering, and performance. The 1965 Pontiac line did in fact look like a fast, sporty, fun loving, devil-may-care car, and the commercial reflected that attitude.

Some of that action footage filmed for that commercial was outrageous, even by the loose standards of the sixties. In those days nobody had to wear a seatbelt or helmet, and the cars were driven to the ragged edge. Today, no one could air a commercial like that without the government and every safety watchdog in the country condemning the aggressive, high performance driving.

In 1966, we changed directions by committing the Tiger theme to the GTO on television. Tire squealing, revving engines, and flying dust were once again restricted to the enthusiast press. By now the GTO had become a symbol, and the Tiger tied in so beautifully to the car's image. We even had commercials of a tiger jumping in and out of an empty engine compartment.

One of the most exciting memories I have of filming tigers and GTOs occurred in the spring of '66. The idea was to show a tiger behind the wheel of a Tiger Gold '66 hardtop, with the tiger's paws on the steering wheel. The message we wanted to convey was, "This is the way to feel like a Tiger."

Motor Trend

"THE AUTOMOTIVE TESTING MAGAZINE"

5959 HOLLYWOOD BLVD., LOS ANGELES 28, CALIF. • HOLLYWOOD 6-2111

October 9, 1964

Mr. E. M. Estes
General Manager, Pontiac Motor Division and
Vice-President of General Motors Corp.
Pontiac Motors
Pontiac, Michigan

Dear Mr. Estes:

The editors of MOTOR TREND Magazine are very pleased to award the 1965 CAR OF THE YEAR to the entire line of Pontiac cars. Congratulations to your leadership under which your engineers and stylists have conceived a product worthy of this award.

The award for 1965 to Pontiac is "for styling and engineering leadership in the development of personalized passenger cars." Pontiac's leadership has certainly proven itself by the attempts of competitors to match your products. I would like to recall that this is the third time Pontiac has won this award and from the first in 1959, the second in 1961, and the current one in 1965 indicates most emphatically the trend of leadership necessary in this highly competitive field.

Again congratulations on your products that have earned this award.

Sincerely,

Charles E. Nerpel
Editor-Publisher

CEN:jmc

cc John DeLorean, Chief Engineer
Robert W. Emerick, Public Relations Director

Pontiac was on a roll in the sixties. It was no surprise when we won our third Motor Trend "Car of the Year" award in six years. This time, Motor Trend recognized our entire product lineup "for styling and engineering leadership in the development of personalized passenger cars."

An Angry Tiger

Working with wild animals is always risky, and tigers are among the most dangerous of all. They can change temper instantly and be hard to handle. When it came time to bring the tiger out of its cage and walk it over to the car, the handlers cautioned everybody to not turn their back on a tiger. When the tiger came out of the truck it stretched and roared a little. The car was ready, with the door open and some red meat on the floor. They took the tiger off its chain and coaxed it to jump inside the car. I didn't know how they were going to get it to sit up at the steering wheel, but the handlers knew what the shoot was about and they were very confident that this tiger would play along.

The tiger got in, but was not in the right position to begin filming. After about five minutes something began to bother the tiger. It roared a couple of

Pontiac's most successful use of their various Tiger promotional tie-ins came in 1966. This photo is from the filming of a TV commercial in the Mojave desert in southern California. In order to get the tiger to jump in and out of the car, we had to use 40 pounds of red meat to entice her into the required action. Working with a tiger on television shoots provided many exciting and scary moments.

times and pawed the instrument panel and the headliner. The longer the tiger stayed in there, the more unhappy it got. To use the terms of the handlers, the tiger got into "dis-temper," and it became apparent they weren't going to be able to control it.

By then, the handlers had warned us to back away, at least 200 feet, as they tried to get the tiger under control. The driver's door was still open, and since they had no leash on the tiger they wanted room in case it decided to bolt out of the car. The handlers got close enough to the car and chose to close the door—which, as they told us later, was the wrong thing to do. With the door shut the tiger apparently felt caged, and went into a real serious fit of dis-temper.

It began to devour the interior of the car, using its teeth and claws to grab the steering wheel and the instrument panel. It ripped the sun visors down and then went after the door panel and the tops of the seats. The handlers were apprehensive about getting close enough to fire a tranquilizer into the tiger, so they sat and watched as it destroyed the entire front half of the car's interior. There were long gashes in the seats, and the steering wheel had huge bite marks. The top of the instrument panel was virtually gone. The sun visors and headliner were ripped to shreds and the door panel on the right side was torn off.

Eventually the tiger wore itself out to the point where the handlers could tranquilize it and get it back to the truck. Needless to say, that ended the shoot for that day. In fact, we decided not to do that commercial again since the GTO appropriated for the shoot was virtually destroyed. Later on, there was some talk that the new car smell from the seats or the headliner had bothered the tiger. I prefer to believe what one of the most experienced handlers said: "It just got pissed."

AS GOOD AS 1966 WAS, THERE WERE some new challenges. Early in the year we learned of an edict from the corporation banning all advertising that even suggested speed or irresponsible driving. Detroit was getting heat from the government over advertising that promoted aggressive and competitive driving. GM, who lived in constant fear of the Feds threatening to break them up, played ball with the government on every front. Consequently Pontiac, as well as all other GM divisions, were directed to cease using illustrations that seemed to condone aggressive driving. Television or radio ads could no longer include roaring engines or screeching tires. In other words, all the good things that had been an important part of our GTO advertising were now forbidden. Now, we had to get creative all over again.

Thom McAn Promotion

One thing that occurred to me was the possibility of hitchhiking on somebody else's advertising using some kind of a tie-in promotion. I carefully researched the marketplace looking for products that had a strong appeal to young people. As is still true today, the one product category that kept showing up in my research was shoes. There was no Nike or Reebok in those days, but there was still some heated competition among the shoe manufacturers. One the most aggressive players was Thom McAn, which was a trademarked brand manufactured by The Melville Shoe Corporation of Providence, Rhode Island. Their biggest competitor was Kinney Shoes, owned then by dime store giant Woolworth. Thom McAn was a very successful organization in its own right. Although shopping malls were just coming into their own, they were quite proud of their many freestanding stores that stood by themselves, adjacent to conventional malls, providing a perfect place to display cars.

I also discovered that Thom McAn was the number-one buyer of airtime on America's Top 40 radio stations. After our experience with the record GTO we had learned to respect Top 40 radio's influence on young people. It seemed to me that Thom McAn offered the perfect promotional partner. We had developed a product that had great name recognition. If we could tie in with a manufacturer who had a compatible product with the same name recognition and who was interested in reaching the same market, perhaps we could put together a mutually beneficial promotion.

I went to DeLorean first and explained why I felt a tie-in with a leading youth oriented shoe manufacturer would work. He replied, "Do you like it?" That was his usual nod of preliminary approval. I then produced a formal proposal, detailing costs, goals, and benefits to Pontiac. DeLorean gave his

(Continued on 3rd page following)

Wide-Track Pontiac, TV and Movie Star

Strategically placing Pontiac cars in TV shows and Hollywood movies was an important part of our early image-building efforts, particularly during the start of the Wide-Track era. While product placement is a common practice today, 40 years ago it was a new marketing opportunity. Pontiac, as in so many other aspects, was at the forefront.

Pontiac's 1960s Advertising Manager John Malone was a real TV and movie fan. He became intrigued by the opportunities available to place the Division's products in starring roles on the many new major TV shows and movies of the time. The first big "break" was on the TV show "Naked City," one of the big hits of the early 1960s. The opening line of the show was, "There are eight million stories in the Naked City..." Well, Pontiac was one of them, as Catalinas and Bonnevilles starred as N.Y.C. police cars (and getaway cars), with actors Barry Fitzgerald and a young Paul Burke doing a lot of the driving. The handling qualities of Wide-Track were dramatically demonstrated as the cars whipped around the narrow streets of Manhattan.

Pontiacs again were in action scenes throughout a Miami, Florida-based thriller called "Surfside Six," starring teen heartthrob Troy Donahue as an undercover cop operating from a houseboat tied up at a Miami docksite. It was a particularly popular show with young people, and a perfect setting for the hot new Wide Tracks from Pontiac.

Ad Manager Malone moved Pontiac from Miami surf-bums to the heart of America as his next TV tie-in was on "My Three Sons," starring Hollywood great Fred MacMurray. Widower MacMurray tried to raise his young sons through many different situations, including teaching them how to drive. The GTO was now in the Pontiac lineup and already a huge success. Pontiac showed some of their special show cars on this show, which was a real first.

On "I Dream Of Jeannie," a young Larry Hagman played the part of a junior military officer who found genie Barbara Eden. Eden had all the requisite magic powers, including the ability to make Hagman's GTO convertible disappear whenever she wished.

Pontiac on the Screen

Perhaps Pontiac's best-known TV tie-in was with the incredibly popular pop group The Monkees and their TV show of the mid-sixties. We were given the opportunity to build a special GTO dubbed "The Monkeemobile," which, while provocative, did become an important part of the show.

We had the opportunity to get great exposure for an Orbit Orange 1970 GTO when it was selected to be one of the stars in the cult film "Two Lane Blacktop." Throughout the movie, actor Warren Oates (left) brags about the GTO's performance. Beach Boy Dennis Wilson (center), and singer James Taylor (right) also starred in the film.

Other TV placements were Robert Blake's GTO Judge hardtop in the opening of every episode of "Baretta," and James Garner's copper-colored Firebird (in the story-line, Rockford could not afford a Trans Am) in "The Rockford Files." And finally there was the talking Trans Am (named "Kit") driven by a young David Hasselhoff in "The Knight Rider" series.

Pontiac's break into the movies came after *Esquire* magazine published a short story, which then was made into a very successful cult film called "Two-Lane Blacktop." A 1970 Orbit Orange GTO hardtop (not a Judge) was driven by Warren Oates. His name in the film was "GTO," and his character was an arrogant, overconfident scoundrel who didn't have the capabilities to match his great car.

Other carmakers soon caught on to this image-building activity, but Pontiac seemed to have a knack for picking high profile shows and movies. For example, the car Gene Hackman drove under New York's El in "The French Connection," dodging pillars and pedestrians, was a four-door rust-colored Le Mans sedan. In "7 Ups" Roy Scheider drove a 1974 Ventura coupe while chasing bad guys in a Bonneville. In a spectacular crash, the Ventura runs under the back of a semi tractor-trailer to end the chase.

The grand-daddy car promotion film of all time, was, arguably, producer Hal Needham's "Smokey and the Bandit." While it featured Hollywood favorites Burt Reynolds, Sally Field and Jackie Gleason, the real star of the film was The Bandit, a black-and-gold trimmed Trans Am. To this day, Pontiac dealers report unusually high customer interest in black Trans Ams after a network rerun of one of the Bandit films.

Certainly, Pontiac didn't invent TV and movie product placement, but in the competitive world of automotive marketing they used it effectively to build and maintain a consistent image. Kudos to John Malone and his understanding love for the medium.

usual reply: "Okay, do it, and tell me about it after it's done. You know where to find the money." After all, I did control the special promotion budget.

So I approached Thom McAn with the idea of taking the image of our GTO and applying it to one of their shoes. The idea was to relate the image of the new shoe to the exciting image of the existing car. The Melville people were very receptive, and showed real interest in working out a program. We let them name the shoe "The GTO" and refer to it as "America's first high-performance shoe." I guess you could say it was like creating "Air GTOs"!

The shoe itself turned out to be provocative. It was offered only in black scotch-grained leather, and featured a severely pointed toe, which was very popular in the mid-sixties. It also had a rather high, beveled heel, which the ads logically pointed out "gave you a better opportunity to get a full throttle position on your accelerator pedal." The sole of the shoe formed the tread of a tire, and to complete the tie-in we let them sew a GTO emblem on the shoe's inner lining.

Melville's Advertising Manager Angelo Lavelli took the ball and ran with it. They agreed to expand their advertising effort, especially in Top 40 radio where they already dominated. They liked the idea of using roaring engines and squealing tires in their radio commercials as a way of building excitement. In fact their commercials were so good that we received many calls from the GM watchdogs, complaining that Pontiac was not cooperating with their new policy. Needless to say, it was great fun, telling them these were not Pontiac commercials, and we had no control over them.

Along with the radio commercials, the program also included a major contest. As our full contribution we agreed to provide 50 GTO hardtop

"America's first high-performance shoe." This mid-1966 tie-in between Pontiac and Thom McAn set a standard for tie-in promotions. The beauty of the project was that it worked hard to sell both GTO cars and Thom McAn shoes. The key was that the name GTO was so popular and had so much meaning for the young teen and preteen male American. These kids couldn't drive a GTO, but they could wear one. All 1,500 Thom McAn outlets featured front window displays with scale-model GTOs battling it out on a small drag strip...complete with operating Christmas Tree lights.

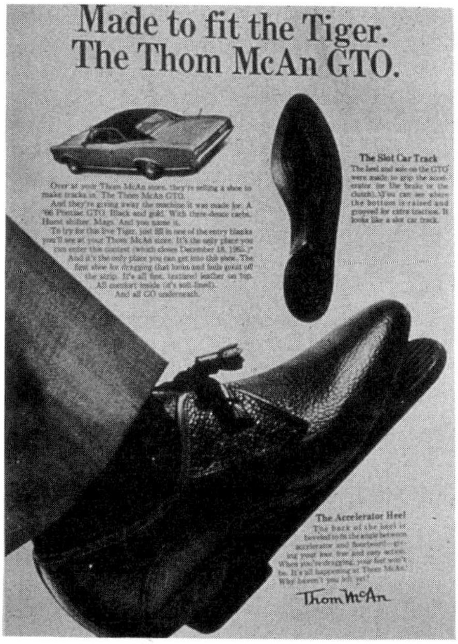

Building a Successful Tie-in Promotion

I have a philosophy about tie-in promotions that I've practiced during my entire career: Don't get into any kind of a tie-in promotion unless, in addition to the promised advertising, there is a guaranteed point-of-sale opportunity for your product. In other words, with the GTO shoe, if Thom McAn had not offered a guaranteed display program in their vast network of retail outlets I would have passed.

Just to have your highly imaged product given away as a prize in somebody's contest can sometimes turn around and bite you. The cynical public often reads that as, "I guess they can't sell them so they're giving them away." A good example of this was a 1988 McDonalds fast food tie-in program with Oldsmobile. The restyled new Cutlass Supreme was being given away in a huge sweepstakes contest, which required the entrant to visit the restaurant. Pictures of the car were prominently displayed, and a reference to the car was spelled out on the sweepstakes entry form. Now, I don't know about you, but I'm not thinking about my next new car when I'm trying to pick up a Big Mac for lunch. Oldsmobile had little reason for being there, and got only modest exposure in front of a market that really didn't care.

Many times, products with national retail distribution offer tie-in promotion programs where the point-of-sale opportunity depends on a disinterested third party, such as a department store or supermarket manager. If there is room, or if it's convenient, maybe they will allow a poster or a small display on the shelf or in a store window. That's not enough: If they can't guarantee point-of-sale display, forget it!

coupes (one contest prize for each state). The cars were all painted Tiger Gold with black vinyl tops, and the winner was given a choice of a 4-barrel or Tri-Power engine with either a 4-speed stick or an automatic transmission. They were all equipped with power steering, power brakes, AM radio, Rally I wheels, and a choice of a black or pearl white interior. These cars became known as the "Thom McAn GTOs," as a significant number of them were built for promotion and display.

Every bit of Thom McAn print advertising featured the Tiger Gold GTO. In addition to their massive radio blitz, they ran their normal print schedule in newspapers, and also expanded it to include the car enthusiast magazines. This was a real first.

Perhaps the biggest plus to Pontiac, in addition to the very timely radio advertising, was the Thom McAn store window displays. All 1500 Thom McAn stores had huge windows fronting the store.They were designed with vestibule-type entrances, allowing for display windows on both sides.

Their window display designer took full advantage of the personality of our car, creating entire miniature dragstrip worlds. First, they started with two 1/25 scale model GTO hardtops, painted Tiger Gold with a black top, red line Tiger Paws, and Rally I wheels. These sat on the starting line of a 1/25-scale dragstrip, with their front wheels up in the air and cotton mounted behind the rear wheels to simulate tire smoke. In between the two GTO models was a scale model drag racing "Christmas Tree," which operated 24 hours a day flashing yellow and green lights, as if actually starting a race. In every one of their 1500 stores, from one end of the country to the other, their store fronts all looked the same. In some stores, they had as many as four displays in the window, two on each side.

The contest was a simple sweepstakes. All you did was go into your Thom McAn showroom and fill out an entry form. The big plus was that you could go in as many times as you wanted and fill out as many entries as you wanted. Every contest entrant received a free set of decals featuring the famous 6.5 litre GTO emblem in various sizes. We had no way of knowing how many of those ended up on the bathroom mirror or on the old man's Buick, but it was a lot of promotion.

The program kicked off in August of 1965 to satisfy Thom McAn's back-to-school timing and Pontiac's scheduled 1966 new-model introduction. It was perfect for both participants. While we were particularly pleased with their extensive radio buy and their retail store window display, we also found that we had the opportunity to display the Thom McAn GTO in many good high-traffic areas.

The Thom McAn folks reported more than 500,000 sweepstakes entries, although some were duplicates. The bottom line was that we were ecstatic about the performance radio advertising, and Thom McAn was thrilled by the measurable increase in showroom traffic and sales volume. And not surprisingly, their sales increases did not come entirely from the GTO shoe.

As always, there were doubters. There were some people at Pontiac who had never been near a Thom McAn shoe store. It was, after all, a popularly priced shoe, and not the kind of store upscale auto executives patronized. There were some questions whether Pontiac should be tied-in with a Thom McAn at all. "Isn't that a little too teenaged," they asked. "Isn't the GTO a little too teenaged," I answered. The success both participants enjoyed in the promotion was the real answer.

THAT THE GTO CAME ON THE SCENE only eight months after the GM racing ban went into effect turned out to be a salvation for Royal Pontiac. After Pontiac pulled out of racing, Ace Jr. figured it would be a good time to drop the Royal Program. "If Pontiac is getting out of racing, why shouldn't we," he reasoned. One more time, I could see that even Ace didn't understand what he had in his operation, and couldn't understand the difference between racing and performance.

Fortunately, we didn't have to wait very long for our customers to provide the answer. With the appearance of the GTO, Pontiac had taken their performance story off the track and put it on the street. The surging youth market, already called the baby boomers, had fallen in love with the new GTO, and many of them were already looking for ways to make them faster.

In 1966, Pontiac, in keeping with their avant garde image, introduced a new single-overhead-cam (SOHC) in-line six-cylinder engine. Built off the 230 cubic inch Chevrolet six, the SOHC package made this engine a real Pontiac exclusive. Two versions were released, a 1-barrel carburetor for normal everyday use, while a 4-barrel carburetor version provided exciting performance for the special "Sprint" package. Even though this engine made a significant statement, in 1966 no one wanted a six-cylinder Pontiac, no matter how up to date it was. In 1967, the engine was expanded to 250 cubic inches and released for the new Firebird. It expired after the 1969 model due to lack of sales.

A Royal Pontiac-prepared 1966 Sprint with the 4-barrel carb version of the SOHC six-cylinder engine launches on the strip in a drag test conducted by Motor Trend magazine. A well set up 4-speed manual Royal Bobcat Sprint could turn a high 14-second quarter mile at 91 miles per hour.

As a result, in spite of Ace Wilson, Royal continued to grow.

Though the Super Duty engine was dead, and GM stopped production of their special parts, selling parts for the regular production performance cars, as long as they could be warranteed, was still OK. By now, Pontiac had some damn good running street engines, and all of the Bobcat kits were de-

The high-performance six-cylinder 4-barrel SOHC was called the "Sprint," and was introduced in 1966. We tried to marry every high performance Pontiac to our overwhelmingly successful GTO, dubbing this car in advertising "GTO Jr." In 1966, all Sprints were Tempest Custom models. But no matter how good a car this was, nobody wanted a six-cylinder Pontiac.

signed to serve these engines. At the same time, other Pontiac dealers were now more interested in selling performance parts. Many of them would buy their parts from Royal and sell them at a markup. Some of the dealers even copied Royal's parts, and that was OK too: while developed by Royal, they really were the result of a lot of help and support from the factory.

Royal Pontiac became the perfect front. Whenever there was a good performance story coming out of Pontiac, we would hide behind Royal. I would call a specific magazine editor, inviting him to get an inside story on a new Pontiac performance part, like the development of the new Ram Air pack-

The 1964 GTO breathed new life into the Royal Bobcat as the Super Duty era ended. We developed a Bobcat GTO that transformed an already quick street machine into a pavement pounder. Notice the Royal Bobcat emblem affixed to the sail panel.

age, or even a how-to story about installing progressive linkage on an old Tri-Power assembly. Every performance story that would keep Pontiac in the news would be generated through Royal.

As good as the GTO performed on the street, it was not particularly competitive in any of the top Stock Car classes. The best an early Tri-Power GTO could run in stock form was in the low 14-second bracket at about 98 mph. This made it a competitive B-Stocker. But add even the simplest Bobcat kit and that same GTO would now run in the mid 13s at around 102 mph. As tire technology got more sophisticated, that ET could be cut to the low 13s. By 1969, a Ram Air IV GTO with a Bobcat package could run in the high 12s. Give that car an NHRA blueprint, still with no cylinder head work and you could get it into the mid 12s at around 112 mph, which while good, would not be competitive in the NHRA Super Stock class.

Royal Pontiac sold over 2500 new Pontiacs in 1965. More than 1,000 of them were GTOs. To understand how significant that was, consider that total GTO sales in 1965 were only a little over 75,000. The Royal Bobcat had become almost as well known as the GTO itself.

Never did that become more evident to me than one summer night when I was out "foolin' around" on Woodward Avenue with my new 1968 Ram Air II GTO hardtop, which had just been Bobcatted. I spotted a nice looking Metallic Blue Plymouth Road Runner cruising around, so I naturally pulled up alongside, looking for a little action. The young guy and his girlfriend both noticed the Royal Bobcat emblem. It was obvious they wanted nothing to do with me or my Bobcat. After a few more engine blips, the driver finally rolled down his window and said, with a smile on his face, "No way, man! I'll be damned if I'm going let an old man driving his kid's car embarrass me in front of my girlfriend. Forget it!"

Royal was now taking up more of my time than I had planned. Every morning, on my way to the ad agency, I would stop there for a few minutes, a

Milt Schornack stands next to the GeeTO Tiger that appeared on the May 1966 cover of Car Craft magazine. Royal employees Dennis Frazho and Dave Warren explain the car to an unidentified customer.

GTO
DON'T GO???
They do if equipped by
ROYAL
All performance parts, service and information available to members of the ROYAL RACING TEAM only. Memberships now open, Annual dues $3.00. Information for all performance cars. Royal decal, club card and parts list sent with each membership.
If you are not a club member write to
ACE WILSON'S ROYAL PONTIAC
400 N. Main, Royal Oak, Mich.
Dept. 110

Royal placed ads in car enthusiast magazines promoting the Royal Racing Team. At its peak, membership in the Royal Racing Team exceeded 58,000 rabid fans, requiring additional help to keep up with the flood of mail.

few minutes would become a few hours, and soon a few hours became the whole morning. Sam Frontera, Royal's capable Parts Manager, tried to keep up with the growing mail order business, but it became too much. He hired two assistants just to process the mail.

In early 1965, Royal became very involved in the development of Pontiac's first Ram Air package. With some serious help from Pontiac engineering we created what was to become known as "the bathtub." It was a big plastic tub that fit around the carburetor, with foam rubber fitting snugly against the underside of the hood. We developed it for both the standard 4-barrel and the Tri-Power assembly. When the outside hood scoop was open, and the "bathtub" blocked out the hot air coming from the engine compartment, the carburetor could only breathe the cooler outside air.

When Royal tested this setup for Pontiac, they proved that at the end of a 1/4-mile run it effectively lowered the ambient air temperature inside the center carburetor of the Tri-Power assembly 55 degrees—although it produced no measurable ramming or forced air benefit. This meant we could richen the fuel/air mixture by installing larger carburetor jets. We also found we could advance engine timing proportionately. When the Ram Air package was released for dealer installation in 1965, it had some very specific tuning instructions. Royal was at the right place at the right time. By mid-year 1965 there were hundreds of GTOs running the Ram Air "bathtub" package, all supplied by Royal.

IN 1966 IT BECAME OBVIOUS TO ME THAT Pontiac had an image problem with the GTO on the drag strip. It was time to re-invent it. What we needed was a way to glamorize the car as a competitive drag racer, particularly for the part-time "weekend warrior." We needed a way to dramatize how quick a GTO could be made to run, while at the same time demonstrating its reliability. We came up with the idea of sending out a pair of well set up GTOs to appear in exhibitions. The show—and that's just what is was—would pit a "Tiger" driving one GTO, racing against a similar GTO with guest drivers. We found a guy who was a good drag racer, put him in an authentic Tiger suit, and called him the "Mystery Tiger." The two cars were named "The GeeTO Tigers" and were set up to run like absolute twins. They both featured blueprinted 421 H.O. engines, Tri-Power, a close-ratio 4-speed transmission, 3.90:1 Safe-T-Track rear ends, and "cheater slicks," as we used to call them. In 1966, they even looked like twins as they both were painted Tiger Gold, with one trimmed in white and the other in black.

The crowds loved the show, even though they never knew who actually was the Mystery Tiger. We changed him many times. His role was not only that of a good driver, but also as kind of goodwill ambassador. When he wasn't driving he'd be prowling around the dragstrip "scaring" little kids while at the same time entertaining them. He was armed with an unending supply of tiger tails, which he would hand out freely. It was a great PR statement for Pontiac, the GTO, and Royal.

The "Mystery Tiger"

When Pontiac pulled out of organized racing, Royal turned to putting together its own series of traveling exhibitions using GTOs. Coupled with the emerging GeeTO Tiger promotion, we also utilized other cues like tiger tails, tiger paws on the top of the cars, and the "Mystery Tiger" driver. In 1965, the GeeTO Tigers were Iris Mist and White Hardtops.

When every spectator and participant entered the track, they were given a numbered ticket. Through a drawing, ten winners were selected to get a chance to "beat the tiger." Each winner came down from the stands or out of the race pits, picked one of the GeeTO Tiger cars (the guest always had first choice), and proceeded to race against the Mystery Tiger. Of course they had to prove they had a valid driver's license and know how to shift a manual transmission. If they failed any of these requirements, we would give them a nice prize and select another winner.

Before each race the Mystery Tiger started his routine. No matter which car the contestant chose, the Mystery Tiger acted as if that was the better car and made a big fuss, as if he knew that car was faster...which it wasn't.

When they pulled up to the starting line, the Mystery Tiger would stop the action by jumping out of his car and grabbing the track broom. He'd start sweeping the track in front of his car and then, as if nobody was watching, he swept the dirt under the contestant's car. The crowd hooted and booed until he stopped and the track was properly cleaned. We made sure that at least three out of the ten contestants at each show beat the Tiger. Obviously, we did everything we could to make sure the cars were strong and dependable, knowing they would take a lot of abuse. One trick was to over-inflate the

We had a lot of fun on the GeeTO tour in 1966. The crowds loved the Mystery Tiger and his antics at the drag strip. For this publicity photo, Royal staff members Dennis Frazho (left) and John Kosmala take aim at the Mystery Tiger (this time John Politzer) as he tries to escape from the engine compartment.

tires. If one of the contestants tried to launch too hard, the tires would quickly "go up in smoke," and they would back off the throttle just as quickly. We also retarded the timing and built in a throttle stop.

There was only one time we hurt a car. We were having a special disc jockey promotion in Detroit, pitting the most popular DJs from the leading Top 40 radio stations against each other. One jock, preparing for his run, said confidently, "Oh sure, I know how to drive a 4-speed." He put the car in first gear, and then raced the entire quarter mile, in first gear! Needless to say, the hydraulic valve lifters protested. They "popped and moaned" all the way down the track, as the driver overwound the engine, sending short bursts of flames out the tail pipes. In the end he had bent every pushrod and even a few valves, enough to put the car out of action for the rest of that show.

To close its hugely successful season in 1966, the NHRA invited the GeeTO Tigers to the Nationals in Indianapolis, to be used as fill-ins between the big runoff races or when there was any unscheduled downtime on the starting line. During the season we had been running an effective tie-in promotion with the popular weekly racing newspaper *Drag News*. They had been a co-sponsor of the show, and were publishing a weekly column reporting on where it had been and where it was going to be. They would also glamorize the Tiger, listing the names of all the competing drivers and the results. *Drag News* was also running a contest for their readers, inviting them to guess who the Mystery Tiger really was, and in 50 words or less tell why they thought their choice was correct. We assembled hundreds of runner-up gifts, but the grand prize was an all-expense-paid trip to the NHRA Nationals in Indianapolis, where the Mystery Tiger would officially be unveiled.

We waited until close to the end of the season before deciding who actually would be the final Mystery Tiger. The drivers who had performed as the Tiger during the season were certainly good, but they were not famous. Ace Wilson was too old, John DeLorean was too busy, and I was too fat to fit into the tiger suit! But, let me tell you, the suit was so good that your closest friend could be standing in it right next to you and you would not know it was them. We finally found the perfect guy, my longtime friend George Hurst. George was fun-loving, certainly well-known, and was a good driver.

The final show was a success, but that's the way it was all year. The 1966 GeeTO Tigers were strong running cars and put on a hell of a show wherever they went. They were capable of running the 1/4 mile in 12.7 seconds at around 112 mph, well below the NHRA B-stock national record at the time.

After the crowd had watched them running around 13.50 seconds all afternoon, the Tiger would go into the tower, "borrow" the track microphone, and boast that he was the greatest and could beat any car at the track, running off their National Record. This would arouse some anger, but even

Hurst Wheels

In 1966, Pontiac made an attempt to fit their now famous eight-lug aluminum wheel to the GTO. They commissioned Kelsey- Hayes to have it ready for a mid-year introduction. When they finally got down to the short strokes of new tooling, they couldn't come anywhere near the price they were already delivering their similar wheel to Pontiac for the full-size car. They asked to be let out of the project and Pontiac reluctantly agreed. However, this was a disappointment. They did have the Rally I stamped steel wheel, which had been available since 1965, and were planning to release the new Rally II steel wheel in 1967. However, DeLorean wanted a more exotic, avant garde cast aluminum wheel.

After the decision to drop development on the eight lug, they looked at another aluminum wheel: a new Hurst effort. George really wanted his new wheel to be used as a factory installed item, along with his manual and automatic transmission shifters. Though his wheel was good looking, it was over-engineered and way too heavy. At that time, any product with the name Hurst on it had an image of unquestioned quality. George knew that and was not going to compromise with his wheel. In the aftermarket that was OK, because he could charge accordingly, but it was not practical to overbuild a product and try selling it competitively as an original equipment item.

Pontiac kept the door open and continued to plead with George to get his wheel down in price and weight, but there unfortunately was another problem. Wheels are classified as unsprung weight, and with the excessive weight of the Hurst wheel, the unsprung weight on the A-body car was above the corporate limit. Even though Pontiac was willing to bend, the Corporation stuck to their formula.

Close as it came, the Hurst wheel never made it into Pontiac production. Still, there were some sharp Pontiac Dealers who recognized a good opportunity and sold their customers a set of Hurst wheels more interest. We would then select one of the GeeTO Tigers, crank up the timing, drop the tire pressure, remove the throttle stop, and put in some fresh spark plugs. Very quickly we could get this car to run in the 12.70s. Back in 1966, when you ran off the NHRA National Record, if you ran too fast you didn't get eliminated. The Tigers were faster than their record, so as you might have guessed they beat off just about every challenger. Of course, the reason they were so much faster than their record was because they were cheaters—after all, this was only a show. It was drag racing burlesque, and it was fun. The big winner was the GTO. Pontiac loved it, and the dragstrip promoters loved it too.

ANOTHER GREAT TIE-IN PROMOTION WE were pleased to get involved with were the Autorama Custom Car Shows. These were car shows produced by a Detroit company known as Promotions, Inc. Promotions was run by Bob Larivee, who operated about 80% of the Custom Car Shows all over the country. These shows were very popular, featuring everything from personal customs to factory performance cars.

when they took delivery of their new Pontiac. The Rally II wheel, when introduced in 1967, was an immediate success. As it matured in the system it became available in a variety of offsets, widths, and wheel sizes, and soon became available on every car in the line.

The wheel that never was. A close-up of Pontiac's famed eight-lug aluminum wheel, which was integrally cast with the brake drum and ready for installation on all 1966 A-body cars. Shown here on a Sprint, the wheel never went into production because the final price from wheelmaker Kelsey-Hayes was too high. Without the wheel, A-body Pontiacs were left with only one styled wheel, the Rally I. Some consideration was given to using the very popular Hurst wheel, however, the wheel's pricing and its heavy weight made it prohibitive.

We wanted to come up with a combination promotion and display that could actually put our GTO in the hands of the young people who dreamed about owning one tomorrow, and might be instrumental in shaping their parent's car buying decisions. The idea was conceived by George Toteff of Model Products Corporation (MPC), and it was pure genius. George's idea was to build a 1/25:1 scale model dragstrip, complete even to a scale model Christmas Tree on the starting line.

On the track were a pair of 1/25:1 scale model GeeTO Tiger slot cars, painted exactly like the full-size GTOs participating in the GeeTO Tiger drag strip program. The track was approximately 60 ft. long. About 15 feet down the track from the starting line was a sign reading "Second Gear." As the car travelled another 15 feet there was another sign reading "Third Gear," and 15 feet further a final sign reading "Fourth Gear." The cars were hooked up electrically to an accelerator pedal in the two actual 1966 GTO cockpits, which sat right behind the starting line. The cockpit was complete with an instrument panel, a bucket seat, a steering wheel, an accelerator, and a Hurst floor shifter. We were giving the young pre-driver (the baby boomer) an opportunity to get into the seat of a full-size GTO, take the shifter in hand, stomp on the gas pedal, and fantasize as if making a real run down the dragstrip.

The whole idea was to keep the cars perfectly straight, because if the car veered a little either to the left or right, the tires would start to scrub off speed. If the driver kept the wheels straight, and shifted exactly when the car was right under each sign, they had a good chance to win the race. If they shifted too soon, they would temporarily break the electric circuit and the car would slow down. If they shifted too late, the circuit was again broken and it would take a little time for the car to regain its speed. This test proved

Model car kits of all kinds were extremely popular in the mid-sixties, and they directly reflected a car's popularity with young America. It's easy to see why the GTO was always at the top of model-makers sales charts. The 1968 Monkeemobile remains the second-best selling car model of all time behind the "General Lee," a 1969 Dodge Charger used on "The Dukes of Hazzard" TV show. AMT and MPC were the two most successful kit-building companies of the time.

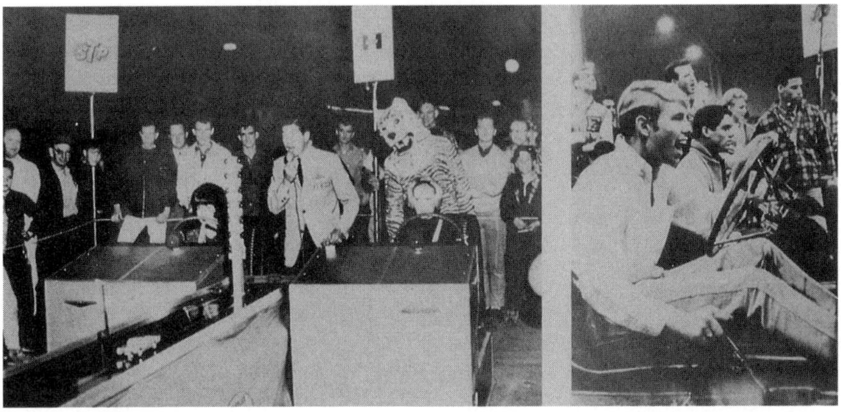

Sponsored by Pontiac, Hurst, and Thom McAn, an actual working scale-model drag strip traveled coast-to-coast, appearing at major custom car shows, attracting a new generation of high-performance car enthusiasts. Two contestants sat in a real GTO cockpit, and simulated a run through the 1/4 mile. Reaction time, depth perception, and coordination were all challenged. Inexperienced pre-teens often beat hard-nosed, sophisticated drag racers in a crowd-pleasing effort. Through the 1966 car show season more than 150,000 contestants were personally greeted by the host Tiger.

HOW TO COOK A TIGER

A Ford promotional piece from 1966, aimed at the enthusiast, when they were trying to take on the GTO with their Fairlane GTA. The car was nothing special, and went nowhere in the marketplace, but this is a good example of how pervasive—and successful—the Tiger theme was.

to be an incredibly good measure of both reaction time and depth perception, and provided a good race. Participants often stood in line for hours to take their turn. We finally had to restrict each contestant to five runs each.

Remember, this was 1966, so our famous Mystery Tiger was there armed with a loudspeaker, building excitement into every race. Naturally, all of our promotional tie-in sponsors were on hand, such as the NHRA, Hurst, Thom McAn, Champion Spark Plugs, even M&H Tires, who made drag slicks. We gave away thousands of Tiger tails and GTO decals, and every day we even awarded a couple pairs of Thom McAn GTO shoes. The Master of Ceremonies was Budd Anderson, a recognized leader in the model car and slot car world. Through the year 1966, the GTO Drag Strip travelled to 32 different cities and played in front of more than 150,000 fans.

Without a doubt, 1966 was our year. We had many successful tie-in promotions, our aggressive Tiger activity, our great advertising, and our new fastback roof styling. Was it any wonder the GTO set its all-time sales record that year, outselling all other musclecars combined?

A few of the sponsors of the time who made the GeeTO Tiger show possible.

9

Shifting Gears

Reshaping the GTO's Image

AS HIGH AS WE WERE FLYING IN 1966, we were confronted with some strong challenges as the model year drew to a close. Mr. Roche had killed the Tiger, which created problems beyond its impact on the GTO. Just as we were adjusting to the death of the Tiger, we were hit with a Corporate announcement that all multiple carburetion options on GM cars, i.e. Tri-Power, would be discontinued with the start of the 1967 model year. Only Chevrolet's Corvette would be exempt.

GM's motivation was self-serving. They could now boast to the government that they had again taken steps to downplay performance and the encouragement of aggressive driving. This really hit us where it hurt, as by now Pontiac and Tri-Power had almost become synonymous. Understanding image, and shaping product to meet that image, was perhaps one of the most significant contributions John DeLorean made to Pontiac. As Chief Engineer and then General Manager, John had enough control over the product and its marketing to keep the Division heading in the right direction. Some years later in the early 1970s, when I was consulting on the subject of image, I'll never forget a meeting I attended at Buick. The big Buicks were reeling under a serious sales slump. Due to the world oil embargo, fuel prices were climbing, and fuel supply was uncertain. Public tastes were changing, and Buick was worried. One important mid-aged sales executive made a comment that I think still speaks volumes about so many factory sales people not understanding the difference between marketing and sales. "You know," he observed, "I can't understand why people don't like our Electra 225, I sure like mine!"

I had to give a lot of credit to the product planners at Pontiac. In a sense, the personality of the GTO was forced to change. Fortunately, the car had matured significantly for 1967. Part of that maturation process was the addi-

Marketing the 1967 GTO presented a new challenge. We had lost multiple carburetion, our popular "Tiger" theme had been killed, and we were seriously restricted on how we could depict performance. We did, however, add a 3-speed automatic transmission, which opened up new marketing opportunities to appeal to a more diverse and sophisticated buyer. Sales of automatic transmission-equipped GTOs dramatically improved.

tion of GM's Turbo Hydra-matic, a new 3-speed automatic transmission offered on the GTO for the first time. It replaced the anemic 2-speed automatic we had suffered with since the beginning of the car.

Another engineering improvement introduced in 1967 was the Rochester 4-barrel Quadrajet carburetor. We had been using the old Carter AFB 4-barrel carburetor, which had been adequate for the base GTO engine as long as there was Tri-Power. The Quadrajet flowed more air than the Carter it replaced, and could actually provide performance equal to our top-of-the-line Tri-Power option. That's why the 1967 GTO H.O. and Ram Air engines with the new Q-Jet were rated at the same horsepower (360) as the 1966 Tri-Power engine. Displacement was also increased to 400 cubic inches thanks to a modest bore change. The flow characteristics of the new cylinder head were also improved.

The Q-Jet began proving right away that it was capable. The primary circuit was unusually small, so fuel economy and driveability actually improved (if anybody cared). The secondary circuit was significantly larger, and introduced a new method of richening or leaning out the jet sizes, simply by changing what they called the "metering rods." It was, in effect, quite similar to Tri-Power. Driving around town on the Quadrajet's lean primary circuit was like driving on the small 2-barrel center carb of the Tri-Power assembly. When you "kicked in" the richer Q-Jet secondary circuit, it was just like opening the two Tri-Power end carburetors.

Along with the new 3-speed Turbo Hydra-matic, Pontiac also added George Hurst's creative Dual Gate "His and Hers Shifter." Pontiac was the first manufacturer to use the Dual Gate, and it did add an element of real fun while driving an automatic transmission. Unfortunately, it was expensive. We never could get the unit price down low enough to make it possible to expand it to the entire line, especially to the Grand Prix and Bonneville. Thus the Dual Gate was never installed in any other car but the GTO, and then only on the 1967 and 1968 models.

Another innovation appearing for the first time in 1967 was a hood-mounted tachometer. Offering a tachometer as a factory option was not a new idea, but mounting it on the hood, right in the driver's line of sight was brilliant. Though in all honesty it was useless to a serious racer. Every time the hood was dropped, even normally, the shock would knock the tach out of calibration. What "made" the hood tach was its marketing opportunities. The fact that it sat out on the hood where everybody could see it gave it immediate impact: "Hey, this guy's got a tach, so that must be a fast car," envious observers would say. And it worked.

As we began the 1967 model year we all asked, "Had we compromised the GTO too much?" It took some of us a little too long to understand that it had changed for the better. Our marketing job was to keep the momentum going, even though we had to climb out from under our beloved Tri-Power and Tiger. Making introducing the 1967 model even more complicated was

Putting the tachometer on the hood was a great marketing idea but it wasn't practical. The tach's internal electronics could be scrambled by slamming the hood, plus it was subject to extreme heat, rain, condensation, and other external abuses. Still, the novelty of a hood-mounted tach on a GTO announced that the driver was a real knowledgable car enthusiast who understood the benefits of driving by engine rpm.

In conjunction with the introduction of the three-speed Turbo Hydramatic in the 1967 GTO, Hurst's Dual Gate shifter was added as standard equipment. Since Pontiac was already outfitting all of its manual-transmission models with a Hurst shifter, it was appropriate that the Dual Gate be used for automatic models (only when the optional console-mounted shifter was ordered). The Dual Gate (nicknamed the "His and Hers Shifter") offered the driver the choice of either leaving the transmission in drive or manually shifting through the gears.

that the styling was little changed from 1966. A new grille texture, restyled tail lights and a few new moldings were the only exterior changes. The 400 engine with the Quadrajet, while it was new, really looked like just another 4-barrel carb engine, even though we did offer a factory Ram Air package for it.

Another new problem was that the car was getting tougher to own. Some of the big insurance companies were beginning to single it out with stiff new surcharges, while the price of the car itself was creeping up. In addition there was also some new competition in the marketplace. 1966 and later advertising reflected this, with headlines like, "Others have caught on. But they haven't caught up," "Get one before you're too old to understand," and "Speak softly and carry a GTO."

The car magazines liked the new GTO, too. One actually called it. "King of the Supercars." Royal did some head-to-head testing for the car magazines right away with the new Q-Jet against the old Tri-Power, proving that the new 4-barrel could hold its own. Even with positive press, however, it was still a tough sell to the die-hard Tri-Power lover. A lot of our old customers were suspect, until they discovered that neither Olds, Buick, or Chevy offered multiple carburetion on passenger cars. Since word of the Tri-Power being dropped came out before the end of 1966 production, no 1967 models were ever assembled at the factory with Tri-Power.

1967 GTO Matures

There were new customers for the GTO in 1967, now in their late twenties and thirties. They wanted performance but not the "boy racer" look. The more mature GTO really appealed to them, especially with a good automatic transmission.

GTO had always been made available with an automatic transmission, but in its initial years it was offered only with bucket seats and floor-mounted shifters. In mid-year '67, an optional front bench seat was added to the line, forcing the shifter control to be mounted on the steering column. Honest...this really happened! In 1967, a low-compression economy version of the GTO was also offered with a 2-barrel carburetor.

Musclecar Competitors in 1967

By 1967, the GTO was starting to have some real competition in the musclecar marketplace. We always felt that Oldsmobile, with their 442, was our closest competitor. Their 400 cubic inch engine, which went into the car in 1965, was very capable. While we were at 389 cubic inches, they were 400, and while that wasn't a big difference, they had all the same options. They had Tri-Power and a functional Ram Air system even before Pontiac. Although a few GTO XS engine packages, including a factory Ram Air System, were built late in 1966, Pontiac's first factory-installed production Ram Air package didn't appear until 1967.

Buick, on the other hand, never really got into the market, always falling short on horsepower with their 401 cubic inch "vertical valve" engine. By the time they got it together in 1970 with their sensational 455 Gran Sport, the musclecar era was almost over. Somehow it seemed like Buick never should have built a musclecar in the first place—it just didn't fit their image. Even the 1986–87 turbocharged Grand National Coupe, with its tremendous performance, would have sold better as a Pontiac or a Chevy.

By mid-year 1966 Chevrolet finally had their big block 396 cubic inch engine pretty well developed, although it took them a little longer than it should to get it into the Chevelle. The SS 396 Chevelle offered a base 325 horsepower version, which was not a particularly good performer. The next step up, the 350 horsepower package, wasn't much better, but the top engine was the 375 horsepower 396, which was equipped with solid valve lifters allowing it to turn more rpm. Although it was plagued with the tuning

Our new theme, "The Great One," was certainly more suited for that kind of buyer. Some of our best ads came along in 1967. Probably the most significant was a full color two-page spread showing 24 different illustrations, each one promoting a different feature exclusive to the GTO. The headline on the spread read simply, "Now you know what makes The Great One great." Despite the loss of Tri-Power and the Tiger, The Great One rolled right along.

WITH THE CHANGES IN 1967 Royal, too, faced a new series of challenges. The death of the "Tiger" by corporate decree also meant that the GeeTO Tiger show was history. It didn't help that our insurance company informed us that they were no longer able to provide the liability coverage we needed for the show. It died a whole lot quicker than it was conceived! It seems like a lot of good ideas end up that way.

To cope with the damage to Pontiac's image due to the loss of Tri-Power, I had Royal prepare two early 1967 GTO press cars, both with the new Rochester Quadrajet 4-barrel carburetor and the 400 cubic inch engine. One car had a 4-speed manual and the other featured our new 3-speed Turbo Hydramatic automatic transmission. Both had the factory Ram Air "bathtub" options, and both were painted white with red interiors, a red pin stripe, and a black vinyl top (vinyl tops were really popular at that time). The 4-speed car received a full factory blueprint and was capable of running every bit as good problems inherent with a solid lifter engine, just like the Chrysler Street Hemi and Pontiac's Super Duty, when it was running right...look out!

Aside from the Street Hemi, Chrysler now had a big-wedge combustion chamber engine, with hydraulic lifters. They called it the "B" engine. They also had the best automatic transmission in the industry with their TorqueFlite. Although they were winning with their special race cars on the drag strip and in stock car racing, they had yet to understand how to package a true street performance car. This was a particular pleasure to me, since I remembered how ten years before Chrysler had literally invented the first musclecars and then proceeded to "blow it." They did get closer to understanding the market in 1967, however, when they released their packaged Plymouth GTX and Dodge R/T, but when they followed up in 1968 with the timely Plymouth Roadrunner and Dodge SuperBee, they got it right.

Ford was never really a competitor during the mid-sixties. Their high performance, or "Hi-Po" 289 cubic inch engine was the only true street performance powerplant they offered. It was a real screamer, but it had too few cubic inches and not enough torque—and it used solid valve lifters, resulting in the classic tuning problems. Ford had built some limited production special vehicles that performed very well on the race track, but this never translated into a good, high performance Ford you could buy right off the showroom floor. They had nothing, and nobody seemed to care.

as our similarly set up 1966 Tri-Power car. The Turbo Hydra-matic car, while not fully blueprinted, still received some good cylinder head work, extra thin head gaskets, rocker arm locknuts, a very fast distributor advance curve, and 3.90:1 rear gears.

We took both cars to the dragstrip to do a story for *Motor Trend* magazine demonstrating the different launch techniques for an automatic versus a manual transmission car. Part of that story clearly demonstrated that while the automatic would launch as good, maybe even better than the manual, when you ran the full quarter mile, four gears were better than three. We showed, however, that our automatic car was now very competitive and could run a low 13-second 1/4 mile.

Motor Trend took a bunch of good photos during the test, with one of the best showing the two white GTOs coming out of the hole side-by-side. The shot was taken from the direct rear, where the only visible difference between the cars was the last digit of the 1967 Michigan license plate number. It was a similarity that soon would play an unforgettable part in Royal history.

Shortly after we built the two white '67s, we were issued a challenge. Royal was always being challenged by local "hot shoes" who wanted to whip the big shot dealer. In this case, the challenger was an old Royal customer who had owned two Royal Bobcats, a '65 and a '66. When Chrysler's new Street Hemi appeared in the 1967 Dodge R/T and Plymouth GTX, he immediately traded his good-running '66 Bobcatted GTO for a '67 Plymouth

GTX. Then he got the word back to Royal that he was ready to show us what a fast car was really like. He wanted to run his Hemi automatic against our new automatic Royal Bobcat.

That was the kind of thing we loved. We always made it clear that Royal didn't run for money. If we were in fact the big shot dealership, we certainly shouldn't be taking money from our potential customers. The challenger lived on the east side of Detroit, so instead of going to Woodward, we set it up to meet at one of the popular gathering spots on Gratiot Avenue, the "Woodward" of the East Side.

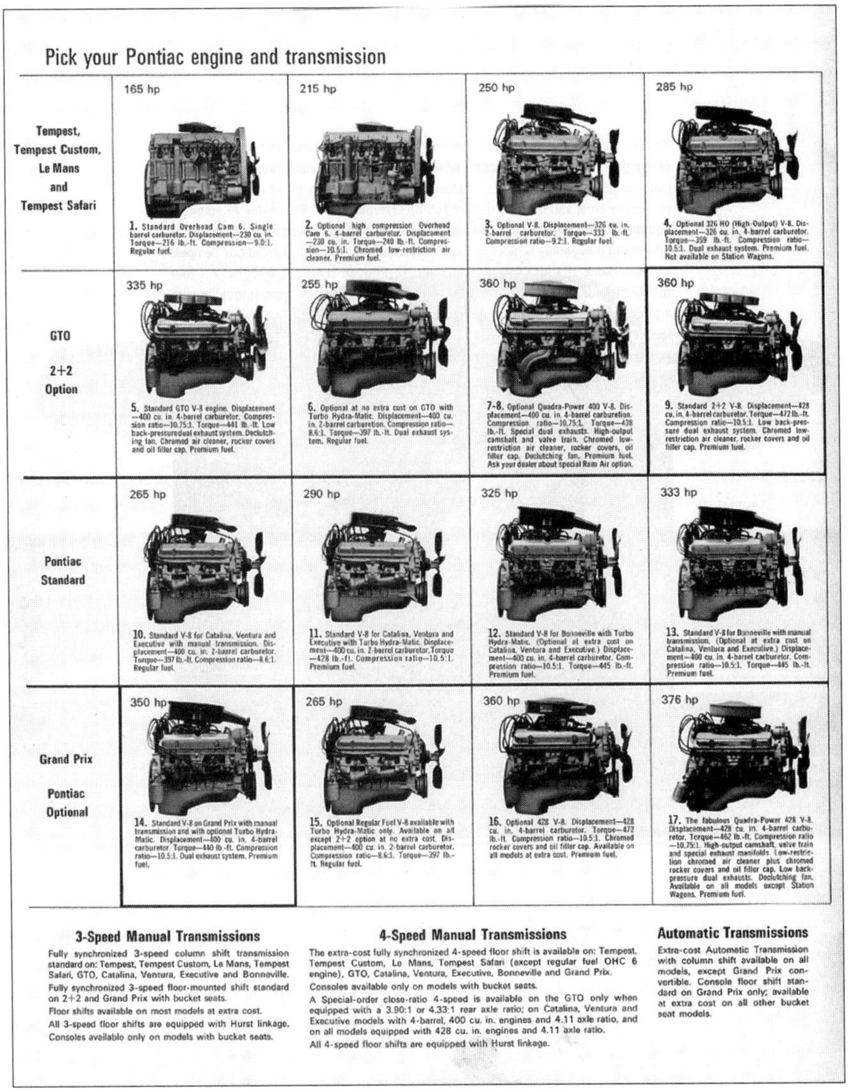

I always believed the Pontiac customer was sophisticated enough to appreciate detailed information about drivetrain specifications. I was able to convince Pontiac to put this kind of information in their catalogs and brochures beginning in 1962.

The night of the race a huge crowd had assembled, at least two hundred cars. The Hemi GTX was a jet-black coupe, and was parked right in the center of the crowd. We pulled in alongside of them with our white "Goat." From our experience, we knew that the Chrysler Hemi, unless it was really prepped, was not a good street machine. It had a bad habit of destroying its spark plugs when just cruising around. We had no reason to believe that there had been any serious work done to the challenger's car: he was so impressed by the fact that he had a Hemi that he probably never dreamed it would need work. In addition, he was a cheapskate. I remember we had trouble getting him to even Bobcat his GTO the year before. We predicted this Hemi to be a high 13-second car, running a little over a 100 mph. Our white automatic had run at the track in the low 13s at close to 106 mph, but as we had learned the hard way, never underestimate your competition!

We agreed to run out on I-94, also known as the Edsel Ford Freeway, which was about a five-mile drive from the meeting point. We headed north once on I-94, out of the city. The further out you got, the thinner the traffic, which made it easier to pull off the run. There were probably 25 cars following us.

Once out far enough, the GTO and the GTX lined up together at about 20 mph (neither car had the tires necessary to run from a standing start). Each car had a driver and a passenger, and the passenger in the right front seat of the car on the left would start the race by calling "Ready....Go!" Dave Warren, one of Royal's best wrenches and a former Mystery Tiger driver, was driving the Bobcat that night. He literally ran away from the Hemi, although we had a policy of trying not to win by more than two car lengths. I guess you could call it "sandbaggin'," as we often let the competition come back on us a bit, at the end of the race.

Dave did a superb job of putting the Plymouth Hemi down. But then, on the way back to the drive-in, a guy came up alongside of him driving a very nice yellow 1965 Corvette. I was riding in another car behind them, and could only helplessly watch what was about to happen. Another rule we practiced at Royal was that whenever we went out for a specific showdown race, we only lined up against the guy who challenged us. Never let another challenger coax you into another run.

As I feared, the guy in the yellow 'Vette did exactly that, he challenged Dave to another race. Dave was naturally excited over his first win, and he forgot the rules. Sure enough, he geared down and pulled even with the 'Vette, only to have the 'Vette pull out quickly to almost a car length lead—and hold it. I was furious!

When we got back to the drive-in meeting place, the fact that we had "blown away" the Street Hemi was lost in the uproar over our loss to the yellow Corvette. Our night had been significantly compromised. Racing was actually a sales promotion effort for the dealership, especially with these street prepared cars. It was totally different from going to the drag strip with a prepared Super Stocker. If you were interested in a good street machine, like our GTO, without racing tires and running through a full exhaust system, then

Royal Pontiac was the place to go. That's all we were trying to prove.

Naturally, there was tremendous interest in the Corvette. The guy driving it turned out to be your typical smartass. When asked if it had a big block, he replied, "You'll never know. I'm not opening this hood for nobody." In the end we had lost more than just a race. Our Royal Bobcat GTO was just another car there that night, as was the street Hemi.

I stewed about the situation for a few days, wondering how we could turn this thing around. Finally I hit on a plan. I told Dave Warren, who incidently was feeling very guilty, "Spread the word around that we found a broken valve spring in our GTO, and we would like to have another run against the yellow 'Vette." The word back from the owner was that he would run us, but only for $200. Though it was against our policy, we agreed. This was a special case and because the guy was such a jerk, it required a special plan.

Dave Warren lived between the drive-in meeting point and the Freeway where we raced. It was about a three-mile drive on Gratiot, a very busy street, to the Freeway from the drive-in, giving us plenty of time to "get lost." Dave had a garage behind his house, where we stashed the 4-speed GTO before the night of the race. When it came time to meet at the drive-in, we showed up in the automatic car, all ready to go. The place was even more mobbed. We gave the money to a neutral party, and arranged to meet at exactly the same spot on the Freeway. On the way, we ducked off Gratiot, stormed into Dave Warren's backyard, pulled out the stick shift car—an absolute twin to the automatic, although about 1/2 second quicker in the quarter mile—stored the automatic car in his garage, and using our prearranged short cut managed to be at the race site ahead of everyone else.

There were hundreds of street racers there to watch. We were totally confident that no one had picked up the car swap, and that no one got close enough to notice that this was a manual car. This was not too tough to do: remember, we started our races from a 20 mph roll. The Corvette was also a stick, and we figured the driver would be too preoccupied with his own shifting to count the number of shifts our car was making. Just to make certain, we hoped to pull out on him right from the start, so he would not get close enough to hear our car shift. The GTO jumped right out on the 'Vette, and we were careful not to run away from him. After all, there couldn't be too much improvement just by fixing a broken valve spring! Dave pulled out about two car lengths, and then backed off just enough to hold the 'Vette there. The guy just wouldn't quit, so Dave had to run a little more than a quarter mile.

When the race finally ended, Dave didn't make any attempt to stop, he kept right on going, as if headed back to the drive-in. He brought the 4-speed car back to his house, making the quick switch to the automatic, and ended up at the drive-in waiting for us all. He even had the hood up for everyone to see. Now we were the heroes! Nobody had been close enough to see or hear the car shift three times instead of two. Dave was good at shifting, and made sure he didn't chirp too much rubber shifting from first to second gear.

The neutral guy holding the money handed the $400 to Dave. As was planned, Dave kept our $200 and handed the other $200 back to the driver of the Corvette, saying, "Here, use this to bring your car over to Royal, maybe we can make it run a little better for you." We drove home triumphant. It was our night.

Everything was fine for about three months, until the *Motor Trend* article appeared. It didn't take long before the calls started. "Do you guys have two cars?" we were asked. "It says in *Motor Trend* that one GTO is a lot faster than the other. Which one beat the yellow Corvette?"

Our reply was simply, "You were there, you saw it, you had a chance to climb under the hood and even sit inside." Even our toughest critics were not able to come right out and say we had substituted a second car. It was probably one of the most fun times I have ever had in street racing.

Royal Pontiac became such an important part of the street scene that we even helped Pontiac sell a fleet of Catalinas with the Enforcer engine package to many of the Police departments responsible for patrolling Woodward Ave. Occasionally there would be a Police cruiser in the service department sitting side-by-side with a quick Bobcat that had been out cruising on the Avenue just the night before.

Royal Still Helps Promotions

Royal's Service Department was open on Saturday just to handle the huge volume of performance work. It was not unusual to get there as early as 7:30 in the morning and see a line of cars stretching from the dealership all the way around the block. Almost all of the cars wore out-of-town license plates. They'd make appointments for 15 cars and would end up doing work on maybe twice that many. Most wanted some form of a Bobcat tune-up, some wanted to buy parts, and some just wanted to see Royal Pontiac in person. Out-of-town customers would schedule appointments on Saturday mornings, hoping to get their work done in one day so they could cruise Woodward that night. The service bays were clogged as experienced performance "wrenches" like brothers Sid and Dave Warren, Milt Schornack, and Charlie Brumfield cranked out Bobcat installations as fast as they could.

For some it was like a religious pilgrimage, and we couldn't have been happier showing them the "Head Temple." Royal Pontiac had become sort of a tourist Mecca, and, not coincidentally, also a gold mine for Ace Wilson. Since I considered this as just another part of my work for Pontiac, I never really knew just how much money was made. Looking back, I should have asked for a piece of the action, but I was simply having too much fun! After all, I considered myself a factory marketing guy and Royal was an experiment, a form of market research. It was the perfect way to learn what your customers really thought about your product, and what changes and improvement they wanted in future models.

The attention I stirred up with our Royal Bobcats drew the interest of the pundits in the automotive press. Leon Mandel, today publisher of *Autoweek* magazine, wrote a story in the March, 1968 *Car and Driver* called "Svengali of the North," detailing my promotion activities for Pontiac, which had now become the "textbook" in Detroit on how to reach the burgeoning youth market.

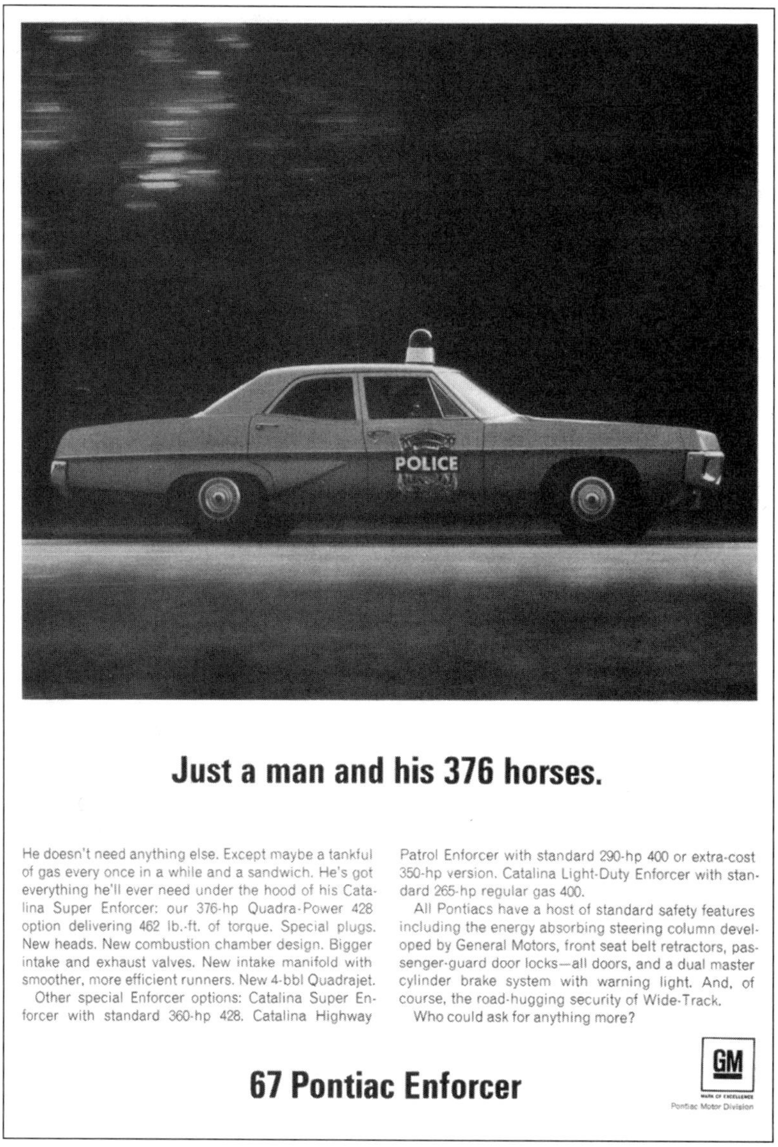

POLICE
Just a man and his 376 horses.
He doesn't need anything else. Except maybe a tankful of gas every once in a while and a sandwich. He's got everything he'll ever need under the hood of his Catalina Super Enforcer: our 376-hp Quadra-Power 428 option delivering 462 lb.-ft. of torque. Special plugs. New heads. New combustion chamber design. Bigger intake and exhaust valves. New intake manifold with smoother, more efficient runners. New 4-bbl Quadrajet.
Other special Enforcer options: Catalina Super Enforcer with standard 360-hp 428. Catalina Highway Patrol Enforcer with standard 290-hp 400 or extra-cost 350-hp version. Catalina Light-Duty Enforcer with standard 265-hp regular gas 400.
All Pontiacs have a host of standard safety features including the energy absorbing steering column developed by General Motors, front seat belt retractors, passenger-guard door locks—all doors, and a dual master cylinder brake system with warning light. And, of course, the road-hugging security of Wide-Track.
Who could ask for anything more?
67 Pontiac Enforcer
GM
Pontiac Motor Division

Royal's success did, however, prompt some complaints from other Pontiac dealers. Customers were walking into other dealerships all over the country, asking to see a Bobcat like the car they had read about in a magazine. Many dealers tried to duplicate them, while others just scoffed, writing the car off as a one-of-a-kind unreliable hot rod. The protests were not only about Royal Pontiac, however, but also about this guy, Jim Wangers, who was always being quoted. I was asked to step back and keep a lower profile.

* * *

We were still trying to coattail promotion of the full-size 428 cubic inch 2+2 and the Euro-oriented OHC Sprint to the highly successful GTO. It didn't work, as both models died soon after.

IN THE MID-SIXTIES, FORD'S FOUR-SEAT Mustang, which had become known as a "Pony Car," was becoming a hit in the marketplace. The GTO was never considered direct competition to the Mustang, since the two cars really appealed to two different market segments. The majority of early Mustangs were equipped with either a six-cylinder or small 2-barrel V-8 engine, neither of which would have attracted GTO customers. Ford's basic chassis design prevented them from installing a bigger V-8 engine, so their only performance package was the 289 cubic inch "Hi-Po" engine.

Still, GM couldn't ignore Ford's success, so in 1965 GM decided they had better develop a car to compete with the Mustang. The plan called for a GM pony car to be in the field by 1967. The vision was to build a unit construction car that was lightweight, agile, quick and responsive, both in performance and handling. The best unit construction platform in the GM system at that time was the Chevy Nova (X-body).

As the car (eventually code named the F-car) began to develop at Chevrolet, there were no plans to include Pontiac. That was fine with DeLorean.

He had always been anxious to bring a true Pontiac sports car into the marketplace, which by now in designs had become a four-seater powered by Pontiac's SOHC six-cylinder engine. It even had a name: Banshee. The Corporation had twice turned thumbs down on DeLorean's sports car proposal. They didn't think there was a need for a second GM division to compete in the sports car market segment already dominated by the Chevrolet Corvette. They were right. I never said to John that I disagreed with his plan, but then, I was never asked. He was still infatuated with his car.

In late 1965, GM management decided that Pontiac should share in the marketing of the new F-car. When the people at Oldsmobile found out about this decision to include Pontiac and not them, they threw a fit. Pontiac had outsmarted them in 1964 with the GTO, and now the Corporation had passed them over on the F-car program. GM wanted to release both the Chevrolet and the Pontiac models at the same time, in the fall of 1966, as 1967 models. That just wasn't possible, since Pontiac didn't have time to really create a "Pontiac." Bringing a re-badged Chevrolet into the market was not DeLorean's cup of tea. Pontiac asked for and received a six-month delay, and that delay turned out to be a blessing in disguise.

Chevrolet's roll-out of their version of the F-car, the Camaro, was lackluster to say the least, and the car did not get off to a very good start. One of

Throughout the early and mid-sixties, John DeLorean dreamed of a two-seat Pontiac sportscar. This prototype, named the Banshee, shared many off-the-shelf components with the Tempest, including the OHC six engine, front and rear suspension parts, and interior trim pieces. The corporation turned DeLorean down on his proposals as they didn't believe there was room for another entry in the two-seat sportscar market already dominated by the Chevrolet Corvette. I thought at the time GM made the right decision, and I still do. Why make competition for yourself?

Jack Humbert (left) was charged with taking the F-car platform already approved for Chevrolet as the Camaro, and designing a version that would have that unique Pontiac look. Humbert's design had a lower and wider look, even though the two cars shared the same basic sheetmetal. Chuck Jordan, (right) who would eventually head the GM's Design staff, was deeply involved in both the Camaro and Firebird projects.

the problems had to do with how the car was marketed. They had an RS (Rally Sport) version and an SS (Super Sport) version. The RS had specific styling cues such as covered headlamps, while the SS had specific performance cues. It was possible to order an SS and an RS package on the same car, which was confusing. In addition, many Camaros were being sold as base cars with six-cylinder engines, and that certainly was not the image they wanted to build. I remember one of the most damaging press comments about the car, reading, "If this is the best Chevrolet can do three years after the first Mustang, they better go back to the drawing boards."

The Camaro, frankly, was not an improved package over the Mustang. In many ways the styling was similar: a small passenger compartment, a long hood, and a short rear deck. Ford had already established the genre and Chevrolet had failed to break any new ground.

Pontiac watched with interest, with time to analyze Chevrolet's failures. The design studio did a superb job coming up with a split-grille front end that was distinctly Pontiac. The rear end featured slit type tail lamps reminiscent of the GTO and the Grand Prix. But it was DeLorean who deserved the credit for the personality and the panache of what was eventually named the 1967 Firebird. By that time he had given up on his idea for an exclusive Pontiac sports car.

For one thing, research on the name Banshee revealed that according to Irish mythology, it meant a wailing, howling sound hanging over the family home, predicting impending death of a family member—totally inappropriate for an automobile. For another, it would have been easy to bring to market a Camaro with a Pontiac front end and a Pontiac engine, but DeLorean would have none of that. Pontiac was always imaged to be a step up from Chevrolet, and the Firebird was going to prove that.

The first thing DeLorean did was change the stance. To his mind, the Camaro sat too high off its wheels and wore too narrow a tire, resulting in anything but a sporty look. DeLorean first insisted that all Pontiac Firebirds were going to be equipped right from the factory with the new 70-series Firestone Wide-Oval tire. When we put the Wide-Oval tire on the Firebird, already with its wide track configuration, the car took on the desired muscular look. All Firebirds were then lowered one inch. Unfortunately, the combination of the Wide-Oval tire and the lowered suspension resulted in an unusually hard ride—but it sure looked great!

DeLorean insisted from the start that he would not bring a Pontiac Pony Car into the world without including a big Pontiac engine. That one looked like a tough sell, since the Mustang didn't have a big engine, and neither did the Camaro. Perhaps Chevrolet was afraid of hurting the image of their Corvette, as they limited their engine options to a couple of standard sixes, a 327 cubic inch V-8, and a mild version of their 350 cubic inch V-8.

Pontiac instead offered an extensive array of engines in their new Firebird, starting with two versions of the marvelous new OHC six, two versions of the midsize 326 cubic inch V-8, and borrowed from the GTO, the fabulous 400 cubic inch V-8. Many of us were stunned when the Firebird 400 was approved, however the Corporation did insist on a horsepower limit. They had long since forgotten about their ten pounds per cubic inch of engine displacement rule, but now they were talking about rated horsepower versus car weight. The Firebird, 400 engine, even though it shared virtually all the same components as the engine in the GTO, had to be rated at a lower horsepower because of the Firebird's lower car weight.

If the Camaro seemed to lack a distinct personality, the Firebird had five, depending on engine selection. My team at the ad agency took one look and recognized a real opportunity. I like to think that we developed one of the best marketing ideas ever used to introduce a new car. We suggested that Pontiac package each of their five different Firebird models with its own personality. To my mind, the powertrain is really the heart of the car, which is a fact too many marketing people tend to forget.

More than just installing a big engine and releasing it as an extra cost option, Pontiac would seek out an image building name and package the powertrain around a Model. Order a 389 cubic inch engine in a 1964 Le Mans

Without doubt, the Firebird OHC six Sprint package was one of the best balanced performance cars Pontiac ever built. Nimble and quick, the Firebird Sprint was never truly appreciated by a market enamored by the V-8 engine. We introduced the OHC engine in the 1966 Tempest/Le Mans, a year before the Firebird was released. I've often wondered if the 1967 Firebird Sprint wouldn't have been more successful if the engine had been held back one year and released as an exclusive in this car.

and you got a GTO. Order the 421 cubic inch engine in the 1965 Catalina and you got a 2+2. Order a 4-barrel carburetor on the Tempest OHC six and you got a Sprint. Or, if you wanted a 428 cubic inch engine in the 1969 Grand Prix, you got an SJ. All of these cars had marketing personalities consistent with their powertrain.

The 1967 Firebird gave us the opportunity to really do this in spades. The agency prepared an absolutely dynamite presentation for DeLorean and his marketing staff. The idea was to introduce the new Firebirds as "The Magnificent Five:" a nice economical OHC six base Firebird, a smooth and docile Firebird V-8, a sophisticated, high winding OHC six Firebird Sprint, a fun-to-drive torquey Firebird H.O. V-8, and the fabulous Firebird 400, the car that nobody believed Pontiac would build. By creating five different models, each personified by its exclusive powertrain, Pontiac could establish their new pony car entry as a much more significant effort, not just another Chevrolet Camaro look-alike.

It worked. When the Firebird launched early in 1967, almost six months after the Camaro, the car was an immediate hit. The advertising line, "Pontiac introduces The Magnificent Five," put a spin on the car's image. The Pontiac program actually looked bigger than Chevrolet's effort. The press was highly complimentary to the Firebird, especially when it was compared side-by-side to the Camaro and Mustang. No wonder the cars marched out of showrooms almost as fast as they could be unloaded off the trucks—over 80,000 Pontiac Firebirds were sold in 1967, and that after a mid-year start.

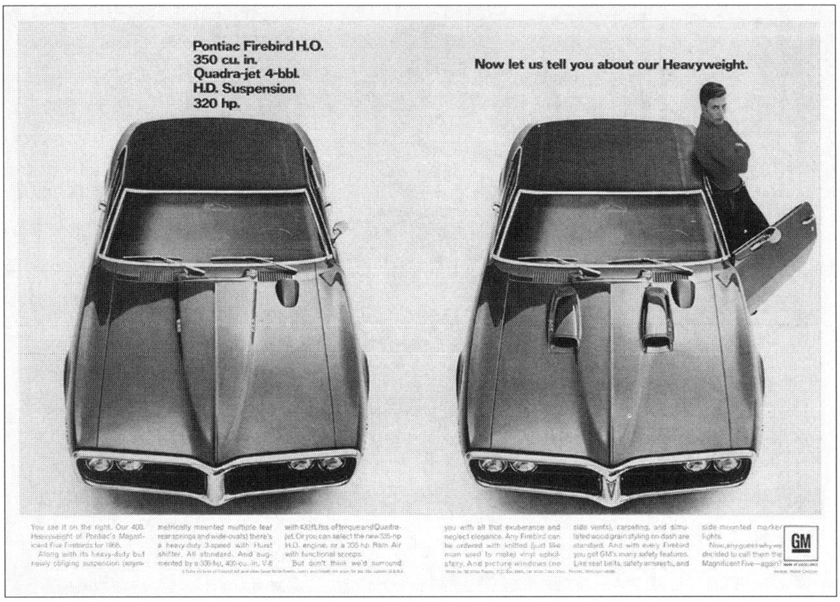

The 1968 introduction ad for the Firebird continued the use of the very effective "Magnificent Five" theme, where each car had a marketing personality based around the engine package.

Also introduced on the 1967 Firebird was a radical new color called Verdoro Green (a play on the word "verde" which is Spanish for green). Pontiac had created the color, and were given exclusive use of it. Verdoro Green wasn't the brainchild of any of the styling experts at GM. In fact, DeLorean's wife, Liz gets the credit. As the story goes, she saw an ashtray at a party and fell in love with the lush green color. She asked the hostess where it came from, and was informed that it had been purchased in Mexico. She suggested to John that it would make a beautiful color for one of Pontiac's new sporty cars. She borrowed the ashtray from the hostess and he, patronizingly, gave it to the people at Pittsburgh Paint, who at that time were one of GM's biggest paint sources. It took PPG a few months to develop the color, which actually ended up with a lot more going for it than the original ashtray.

The color looked good with both a black or a white vinyl top, matching the black or white interior. Later, Pontiac developed a green vinyl top to match a green interior.

Verdoro Green offered the Firebird yet another level of distinction over the Chevrolet Camaro, and certainly contributed to the immense popularity of the car. In 1968 Pontiac released Verdoro Green for all models, keeping it exclusive however to the Division. If Verdoro Green was a hit on the 1967 Firebird, it was an absolute "smash" on the 1968 GTO. We used it in the infamous "Woodward Avenue" ad, and it was the Endura nose of a Verdoro Green hardtop coupe that Pontiac's TV spokesman Paul Richards attacked with a crowbar. Verdoro Green became a real statement for Pontiac.

* * *

FOR SEVERAL YEARS, AS A SPIN-OFF of Speed Week in Daytona Beach in February, NASCAR and the Pure Oil Company had modestly promoted a series of what they called their "Safety and Performance Trials." This was Pure Oil's answer to the famed Mobil Gas Economy Run. They invited manufacturers to enter, providing classes for all different size vehicles and engines. The manufacturers had to guarantee the stock condition of the cars, and they had to provide the drivers.

The Pure Oil Trials, as the event was often known, was useful to manufacturers in advertising because it measured performance and handling. You couldn't mention the competition, but you could print the charts. In fact, as part of the program Pure Oil bought full-page newspaper and magazine ads and printed all the results.

In the past, Pontiac had done pretty well. In the early sixties, since we were so closely involved with NASCAR, we just sent the cars down and had them set up and driven by our NASCAR teams. I was involved as an emissary for Pontiac, and usually reported back on the results.

In 1967, Bob Emerick, Pontiac's PR manager, got interested in the Trials. Emerick had always been close to NASCAR, and that included a personal and business relationship with NASCAR chief Bill France, so it was logical that Emerick oversee the Pontiac entries this time.

At the Daytona International Speedway in February, 1966, Pontiac competed successfully in the NASCAR-supervised speed and performance trials sponsored by the Pure Oil Company (later to become Union Oil). The trials were held on the famed Daytona tri-oval. The photo shows a 1966 GTO preparing for an acceleration test against a 1966 Ford Fairlane GT.

The success and exposure of the Pure Oil Trials also attracted George Hurst. By now, Hurst was a large organization and was on the leading edge of the performance market. George wanted to become more aggressive in performance manufacturing and marketing, and he saw the trials as an opportunity to expand into that area. He sent his young assistant Jack Watson to negotiate a contract with Emerick to prepare and drive the 1967 Pontiacs in what were now being called the Union Safety and Performance Trials (Union Oil bought Pure Oil and merged the name).

I always believed that one of the reasons Emerick bought into Hurst's proposal was to cut me out of being involved in the Trials. What surprised me was that George Hurst seemed to want me out, too. I guess he was afraid of Royal Pontiac's involvement, which would have hurt Hurst's attempt to establish himself as the same kind of performance specialist as Royal Pontiac, but to a variety of carmakers. I was upset by this treatment, but I was too proud to say anything to George Hurst. I was still pretty close to George, but I made myself a promise that I wasn't going to talk about it to him.

Once the Trials were underway, it didn't take long before the Pontiacs started looking suspicious. The first event was the mileage test. The fuel tanks were topped off and the cars ran around the track at Daytona until they ran out of gas. Long after everyone else was on empty, two Catalinas were still out there running—in the end they got almost 30 miles to the gallon.

Apparently Hurst chose to get real "tricky" (a kind word) in the preparation of the cars, including installing auxiliary gas tanks between the inner and outer fenders. The Hurst people filled up the hidden tanks, then brought the cars to the NASCAR officials who filled up the normal tank. The problem was the Hurst people were stupid. Instead of getting 24 or 25 mpg, they achieved a mileage rate that no other car could come close to. The NASCAR officials discussed it, but initially did nothing. The Pontiacs were permitted to continue into the performance part of the trials.

This did not sit well with Jack Passino, head of Ford Motorsports. Passino carried a significant amount of weight with NASCAR because Ford was spending millions in stock car racing. Passino convinced the NASCAR officials that cheating was not to be tolerated, and lodged a formal complaint. NASCAR impounded the Pontiacs and called the Hurst team down at three in the morning for an inspection. They went through the cars from one end to another. Although no visible violations were discovered, because of the controversy and Ford's official complaint, NASCAR felt they had to disqualify the Pontiac team.

The story broke that the Pontiacs had been disqualified for undisclosed rules infractions. This was big news in Detroit. When I mentioned it to DeLorean, he just shrugged his shoulders and commented it was no big loss. The incident seemed to fade away.

About seven months later, the President of Union Oil and James Roche, Board Chairman of General Motors, sat together at a Detroit business function. In the course of the conversation, the President of Union Oil mentioned to Roche that he was surprised GM would allow a Vice-President and the head of a division to cheat in Union Oil's big event. Roche didn't know the first thing about it. He ordered a full report on what had happened with Pontiac and the Pure Oil Trials.

The Hurst people were brought in, but were quickly dismissed without having to admit culpability because they were a vendor. Whether or not the cheating was done with Emerick's or DeLorean's approval, I can't honestly say. DeLorean had certainly approved hiring Hurst under Emerick's supervision, but I was completely out of it and had no direct knowledge.

Emerick was called in and basically pointed the finger at DeLorean, who ended up taking the brunt of the punishment. DeLorean intimated to me he lost his bonus for 1967, which could have been a substantial amount, though he never took this as a serious setback in his career. He did say that as far as he was concerned, Bob Emerick did not work at Pontiac any more, and he wanted nothing more to do with him. Until DeLorean left for Chevrolet in 1969, he always relied on George Stevens, the number two man in the PR Department. Emerick and DeLorean would pass in the hall and not speak. They'd be at Pontiac events and wouldn't acknowledge each other's presence. DeLorean made sure Emerick had nothing to do.

Kellogg's and The Monkees Tie-in

AS I'VE TRIED TO DEMONSTRATE, one of the reasons for the success of the GTO was the string of good tie-in promotions we built around the car. George Toteff, from the model company MPC, came to me one day with another good idea for a tie-in with the pop singing group "The Monkees," who were about to star in their own TV show. George was close to Hollywood custom car builders like George Barris and Dean Jeffries, both of whom had built several cars for TV and feature films.

This really interested me, not so much for having the GTO appear on television, but for the opportunity to work out a promotion with The Monkee's sponsors, the giant breakfast cereal maker Kellogg's Co. of Battle Creek, Michigan. I couldn't help thinking of our experience with the Thom McAn GTO/shoe program. While it is good to get product TV exposure, it is always a "must" to wrap up good point-of-sale activity, whether in a retail store or in the home, as long as it produces personal contact with your product. This is a rule I have lived with since I first learned anything about marketing. The Thom McAn promotion was an absolute natural, because we not only got good advertising exposure, but we were absolutely guaranteed consistent point of sale display. Thom McAn owned their own stores, so we didn't have to beg for space.

In the case of The Monkees, we knew there wasn't any chance of getting a record from them, and anyway car songs were by then a tired subject. I quickly met with Kellogg's marketing people, who were proposing a big sweepstakes idea. "Not another contest giving away our popular car," I protested. No, they responded, the top prize in the sweepstakes would be an all expenses paid trip to Hollywood for two people, with an opportunity to actually appear with The Monkees on their own TV show. The winner would also get a new GTO convertible. They wanted the next 15 prizes to be GTO hardtop coupes. My first reaction was that this was outrageous, giving away our car as only the 2nd prize in their contest. What a put down!

But then they started throwing their numbers around, and things started to look a lot better. I didn't know much about the breakfast cereal business, that was obvious, so I was in for a real surprise. Their proposal was that they would put a four-color illustration of both a new GTO Convertible and a hardtop, plus a nice blurb about the cars on every box of the selected cereal during the time it would be involved in the promotion. In this case, they were talking about two cereals, Raisin Bran, which was a new product, and one of their old reliables, Rice Krispies. They were prepared to deliver a total of 42 million boxes of Raisin Bran and Rice Krispies over the period of the promotion. Their market research indicated that a standard size box of cereal would come off the pantry shelf and sit on the breakfast table six times before it was finally emptied. Of course, this was an average. Obviously, the cereal box would get attention while on the breakfast table, and each box would feature a picture and a pitch about our car. That's what I call "personal contact" with a product!

The promotion also involved creating a special vehicle for the TV show. It was to be called "The Monkeemobile." The Kellogg's people had selected a red 1967 GTO convertible for their main cereal box artwork, and promised that the special TV car would be the same color.

I had a little tougher time getting Pontiac approval on this project, but DeLorean liked it, and since the Thom McAn program had worked so well, I finally got the go-ahead in late June, 1966. I learned from George Toteff, who brought us the idea, that the Monkeemobile was going to be built by Dean Jeffries.

I acquired a Montero Red 1966 GTO convertible and had it delivered to Jeffries studio in California, along with renderings of how we would like the custom car to look. I then proceeded to wait. We learned that Jefferies did not like the renderings Pontiac had supplied, and since his deal was with the show's producers, and not with Pontiac, he would not acquiesce to Pontiac's designs. When I saw the final car I was pretty upset. The front end was OK—at least you could tell it started out as a GTO—but the body was hokey, if you wanted to be kind. Who ever heard of a four-door GTO convertible? The back end didn't look anything like a GTO. Finally, I was told to get out of the studio and let Jeffries perform. This car had to satisfy only The Monkees and their show producer. After all, why should Pontiac care, all they were doing was paying for it. I probably aged ten years during the project.

The car had started out as a 1966 model, but it didn't come out of Jeffries studio until early in 1967, and didn't get on the show until much later. The front end was so modified that it could easily pass for a 1966 or a 1967 or even a 1968. What started out to be a 1966 program ended up being a 1968 program. Jeffries took way too long to finish the car, and much as we didn't like it, we had to live with it. One solution was to ask Kellogg's to minimize the Monkeemobile on the cereal box, and they complied. It made the box art

The payoff for Pontiac in working with The Monkees was the tie-in promotion with Kellogg's. We were able to combine the excitement of appearing on The Monkee's television show with the chance of winning a new 1968 GTO. Along with this ad which, appeared heavily in general interest magazines and newspapers, we also got a good picture of our "Goat" on the back of 42 million boxes of cereal.

less busy, and made the stock 1968 Convertible illustration seem much more prominent.

There was incredible response to the contest. Kellogg's did some very good other advertising with our car, even on their own show. We also got great cooperation from the retail supermarkets prominently displaying posters and cereal boxes promoting pictures of the car, but it wasn't consistent, depending as it did on the enthusiasm of the individual store manager. The

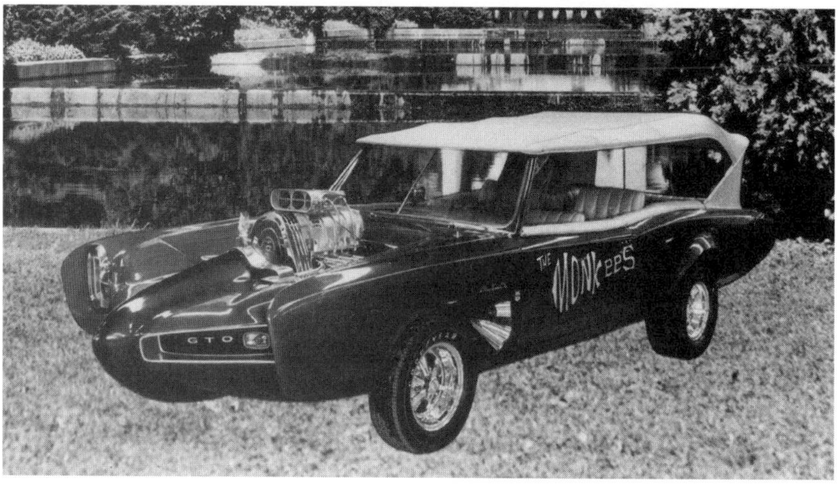

This rendering by Pontiac's Design Studio (top) shows how we wanted the Monkeemobile to look. It was submitted to custom car builder Dean Jeffries, who basically ignored it. Jeffries' final product (bottom) was not what we wanted.

real disappointment in the promotion was with Jeffries and the producers of the TV show. After approving the custom styled Monkeemobile, they decided they didn't like it and were reluctant to use it very often in the show. Needless to say, my critics at Pontiac just shook their heads. Fortunately, the promotion program with Kellogg's was so good that it more than made up for the disastrous car and the TV show.

As a side part of the deal, we agreed to provide the show's production team the use of new Pontiacs. We didn't actually give them the cars, we just gave them use of them. Each of The Monkees were provided a GTO convertible, and working with them was not the most pleasant part of the project. Davy Jones was a delightful young kid, but the rest had no respect for our car.

It was just a car, in fact somebody else's car, and they treated them just that way. We ended up having to exchange cars several times due to their careless treatment.

Here's a good example. The big, wrought iron main gate to the studio lot where the show was being produced was always closed, but not locked, during the day. It would swing open after a pretty good "nudge." As The Monkees approached the gate with their GTOs, they would blast their horn. If the attendant didn't get out to open the gate in time, they would open it for him—with the front bumper. After a few of these nudges, you can imagine how those front bumpers looked. Naturally they had to be replaced, often.

One night I got a call from our West Coast PR guy, frantically reporting that one of The Monkees had been picked up by the Los Angeles Police Department doing 125 mph on the Hollywood Freeway. He was not being held, but our GTO was in impound because they couldn't find any documentation proving who owned the car. Through a special leasing arrangement, the car actually belonged to the ad agency, and somehow the paper work had been separated from the car. After providing the proper information, I smelled a chance for some good press. "What's the chances of getting this in the L.A. Times," I asked. 125 mph was a pretty impressive speed, and it would have looked good in the paper that he was running that fast in a GTO. Well it was a good idea, but it didn't make the paper. It seems the show's producers squelched it.

The person who made out the best in this whole deal was George Toteff and his model company MPC. They released a kit of the Monkeemobile, which somehow looked better as a model than it did as a full-size car. The kit

One of the real winners in the whole Monkeemobile program was MPC, who sold over seven million model kits.

was well done and sold in excess of seven million, an all-time sales record that stood until a model kit of "General Lee," the 1969 Dodge Charger starring in the TV hit "Dukes of Hazard," outsold it.

In retrospect, we could have lived without building the Monkeemobile. It was at best a burlesque of the GTO, and dealing with The Monkees themselves required too much negative energy. Working with Kellogg's on the other hand, was a dream. What pros—and did they know their market. It would have been just as good a promotion without that lousy car.

TO REALLY APPRECIATE HOW important the GTO had become, consider the numbers. Pontiac sold over 475,000 Tempests and Le Mans in 1966 and 1967. The GTO added another 178,000 units, bringing, the total to over 650,000 mid-sized cars in just two years. In 1968, after the dramatic restyle, Pontiac sold over 340,000 cars, 87,000 of which were GTOs. But the most interesting number to consider during this three-year period was that over 75 percent of all these mid-sized Pontiac cars were two-door models—a Pillared Coupe, a Hardtop Coupe, or a Convertible—exactly the models that were available as a GTO. Pontiac was hounding Chevrolet's Chevelle for mid-sized sales leadership. We were clobbering the Olds Cutlass, burying the Buick Skylark, and actually outselling all the midsize entries from both Ford and Chrysler.

Introducing the 1968 GTO

There were two worries we had with the introduction of the 1968 models. The first was that the 1968 car was heavier, and offered more options. Pontiac was building more of them with air conditioning and automatic transmissions, and while the car was maturing, we didn't want the buyer to lose sight of the fact that it was still a high performance musclecar. Second, we were worried about acceptance of the new styling. It certainly was a departure from the previous lean and taut look. Some even referred to its more rounded design as a "pregnant" look. Shortly after the 1968 model got into the field, we did begin to hear complaints about its styling. It was apparent that most everyone who disliked the new car felt strongly about the linear lines of the previous car.

We decided that to deal with these two potential problems we needed to earn acceptance for the new car from our current owners and fans by emphasizing the GTO's heritage. We released a two-page color ad featuring a lineup of 1964–67 GTOs surrounding a husky new 1968 Solar Red hardtop, complete with the new optional hidden headlamps. The headline read, "There's only one great one. We've been proving it for five years." I don't know how much the ad contributed, but the styling resistance went away. It was a brand-marketing problem that we had anticipated, but it never really came to pass; in 1968 we had one of the best sales years in the GTO's history.

Perhaps the most significant change in the 1968 GTO was its body colored front bumper, marking the first time this dramatic new look was ever offered on any American car. Not only did this new colored bumper blend smartly into the new styling, it also provided a new level of bumper protection. It was made out of a rubber product called Endura, developed by Pon-

The GTO's Wide-Track look was totally restyled in 1968, with rounded body panels and smooth integration of the C-pillars into the rear quarter panels. The design was revolutionary, as was the front end, which introduced the new impact-resistant Endura bumper painted to match the exterior body color. Also, after three years of vertically-stacked headlamps, they were now placed horizontally. Hidden headlamps were offered as an option.

tiac (thanks to plastics wizard Josh Madden) in cooperation with the Dayton Rubber Co., and had the capability of absorbing an impact and then returning to its original shape. Needless to say this was a dramatic breakthrough, and it made the new GTO major news.

The highlight of our new model announcement was a TV commercial in which Pontiac spokesman Paul Richards walked around the new front end, slugging it seven times with a crowbar and doing no apparent damage.

Early into production, Pontiac encountered paint problems with the new Endura nose. The color match between the Endura and the sheetmetal became difficult to monitor. There also appeared to be some premature paint chipping and cracking on the Endura surface. In order to keep production moving, Pontiac temporarily released the Tempest/Le Mans chrome bumper on the GTO. As you might expect, it was not a very popular alternative, and very few were built. As soon as the problem was solved, the chrome bumper was discontinued. Because there were so few built, it is possible that a legitimate one, complete with verification, might today have some collector value.

The 1968 GTO used the same powertrain as the 1967, until late in the model year when Pontiac introduced a new engine called "Ram Air II." It was more than just another exciting engine with a fresh-air package. This new engine introduced the round exhaust port cylinder heads. The Ram Air system had become even more functional in 1968, because the newly designed twin air ducts were positioned higher on the hood, scooping up more air as it flowed over the front end.

Other 1968 GTO Features

GM
Others have caught on.
But they haven't caught up.
Imagine, for a moment, that you are in charge of designing an answer to the GTO. And that this has been your task since The Great One first rumbled into reality, sending shock waves through your offices.
Each year you've sent your answer into the streets. And, each year, seen it change into something merely mediocre alongside GTO's Hurst shifter, bulging hood scoops and Wide-Track. And, this year, humiliated by an incredible new kind of bumper.
And just when you're getting the hang of its extra-cost Ram Air (yours will surely out-GTO GTO next year), you find Pontiac has improved theirs. With a new high-lift cam, larger swirled exhaust valves, new freer breathing combustion chambers.
When the Car of the Year is improved even before the year is over, can your car ever catch up?
Pontiac Motor Division
The Great One by Pontiac
Anxious for 5 color pictures, specs and decals of the Great Wide-Tracks? Don't be. Send 30¢ (50¢ outside U.S.A.) to: '68 Wide-Tracks, P.O. Box 888E, 196 Wide-Track Blvd., Pontiac, Michigan 48056

The brashness of our advertising was founded on our confidence in the product and its continued mastery of the marketplace. Even by 1968, we knew our competitors were still struggling to equal the GTO's success. This ad was typical.

This performance potential, coupled with the innovative new Endura Bumper, made the 1968 "Goat" a very good candidate for the much cherished *Motor Trend* Car of the Year award. Competition that year was fierce. Also considered good candidates were the Plymouth Road Runner and the curvaceous Olds Cutlass. But the car with the inside track was the all new Dodge Charger, featuring a bold design not shared with any other car in the Chrysler lineup.

While the Endura front bumper was a tremendous breakthrough, it was also plagued with production problems that included fit and finish. These production difficulties required Pontiac to temporarily substitute a chrome bumper from the Le Mans. It was covertly characterized as the "Endura delete option" on the window sticker. It did not go over well with GTO buyers and was quietly dropped when the Endura bumper's production problems were solved.

Bob McCurry, the aggressive General Manager of Dodge was confident that the Charger was a "shoe in" to win the coveted industry award. Some of my friends inside Petersen Publishing Co. confirmed that, but at the same time gave me encouragement by telling me that our GTO had passed every one of their tests very well, and was also highly regarded.

I knew that if we were going to win the award, we were going to have to personally sell the *Motor Trend* staff on why the GTO was 1968's most significant new car. There was only one guy who could do that, John DeLorean. He was more than willing to cooperate. "What do you want me to do?" he asked, "and when?"

Within a day, DeLorean was on his way to the L.A office of *Motor Trend* to put on an impassioned plea for the GTO. I had a gut feeling that if a General Manager made a personal pitch to the *Motor Trend* staff, who never came in contact with someone on DeLorean's level, it could sway their decision. It did. We won, and DeLorean's last ditch effort played no small part in cementing that victory. Of course, we also had a very qualified product, and part of DeLorean's pitch was to make sure they knew just how much we respected their award and how we were going to "promote it."

Winning the *Motor Trend* Car Of The Year award for the fourth time in

GTO Spokesmen

By 1967, the GTO had sufficiently matured to justify exposing it to a more sophisticated market, which meant spending some money in television. To represent this new image of the GTO as "The Great One," we needed a new spokesman. William Conrad (star of the TV show Cannon) had been doing voice-overs for us; however, when he became identified with Ford Motor Company and the Lincoln Continental, we chose to look elsewhere.

We selected Paul Richards, who had enjoyed some success in TV and films, and with his good looks and deep voice was the embodiment of what Pontiac's spokesman should be. We felt that his self-confident attitude, with its overtones of performance and sophistication, would better match our print efforts.

His first ad for us introduced the 1967 GTO and the new slogan, "The Great One." The car was parked in a darkened soundstage as Richards, dressed in a well-tailored suit, walked around it describing it as "the ultimate driving machine" (long before it became BMW's tag line) and asking if the viewer was the kind of enthusiast who could appreciate what the car was all about. It was magic. Richards represented the image of the mid-life, 40-year-old executive who now was maturing to the point where he would like to have a sophisticated car with performance and excitement, but also with an automatic transmission.

With the introduction of the Endura front end in 1968, we became more aggressive in our television advertising and produced one of the most famous—and most awarded—commercials of the era. In it, Richards walks up to a 1968 GTO, crowbar in hand, and takes seven swings at the new color-keyed Endura bumper, which absorbs the punishment and still looks perfect. (In the real world, Pontiac was trying to solve paint match and paint adhesion problems.)

The commercial was a sensation. Along with the raves came the accusation that the crowbar in the commercial was made out of rubber. The claim was serious enough to warrant a response. We went back and re-filmed the ending so that Richards, after he finished beating the Endura bumper seven times, tossed the

nine years was not only very satisfying, but it quickly became an important part of our 1968 advertising effort. Our magazine introduction ad consisted of a special cover gatefold showing a beautiful 3/4 front shot of a GTO hardtop, featuring the new Endura bumper. The headline read simply, "Pontiac introduces its candidate for the 1968 Car Of The Year." It ran across the board in all the car magazines, not mentioning *Motor Trend*, just Car of the Year. In those days, there was only one car-of-the-year award.

Exactly one year later, when we introduced the all-new 1969 Grand Prix, we again bought a cover gatefold on many of the same magazines. This ad featured a similar view of a Pepper Green 1969 Grand Prix, while the copy read, "Last year we submitted our GTO as a candidate for The Car Of The Year. It won. Now we proudly submit our candidate for The 1969 Car Of The Year." Five wins in ten years was too much, even for *Motor Trend*, so though we really deserved it, we were forced to settle for second place behind the upstart Plymouth Road Runner.

crowbar down on the cement floor so it clanked just as any metal tool would. That effectively answered the critics.

If you watch the bumper commercial carefully, you'll notice that as he's swinging that crowbar Richards was rapidly running out of breath and almost struggles to say his lines. What no one knew was Richards, who was a heavy smoker, was already developing a fatal case of emphysema that would claim him within 18 months.

Richards did some voice-overs for Pontiac in 1969, always interpreting the copy perfectly and delivering it in the cocky and sure manner in which it was written. He was the spokesman we had hoped for and it was sad to see such talent cut down at such an early age.

Another "pitcher" for the GTO was Frank Sinatra. John DeLorean, because of Pontiac's uncommon success and his own good looks and sharp dressing habits, had become something of a magnate in the automotive world. He was soon rubbing shoulders with many well known celebrities, including Sinatra. When Sinatra acquired a new yacht and was looking for some new, more powerful Diesel engines for it, he asked DeLorean if they could work out an "arrangement," where Sinatra would get new GMC Diesels in exchange for "complimentary" work.

Having Frank Sinatra associated with both the GTO (and the Firebird) was right on target with our image. In one commercial Sinatra assumes the dual role of himself and a nightclub valet parking attendant. Frank as himself comes out of the club, amidst a group of screaming fans, jumps into his Verdoro Green GTO Convertible, and drives away. Frank as parking attendant says enviously, "Why didn't I learn to sing?" Paul Richards as the voice-over says confidently, "With this kind of a car, who needs to sing?" and then ends the commercial with an equally arrogant add on, "Tra La."

The most interesting reaction came from the auto industry. They all wondered how in the hell Pontiac could afford Sinatra—remember, this was 1969, and Frank was near the height of his career.

The GTO's revolutionary Endura front bumper, as well as its fabulous new styling, earned Pontiac its fourth Motor Trend Car Of The Year award in ten years (it didn't hurt that DeLorean made a personal appearance at the Motor Trend offices). Editor Walt Woron hands General Manager John DeLorean the last Motor Trend award Pontiac would receive.

Motor Trend's
Car of the Year Award
for the 4th time.
Third in sales
for the 8th straight year.
GM
Can there be more to this than just coincidence?

While reveling in our sales success throughout 1968, we never slowed down long enough to recognize this new competitor from across town, the Plymouth Road Runner. This new low priced musclecar racked up some pretty impressive sales figures in its first year, enough to pose a real threat to the beloved Goat. The 1968 Road Runner had been introduced with a first class tie-in promotion with Warner Bros., using a decal likeness of the famous Road Runner cartoon character as the actual nameplate on the car. I wish I had thought of that one. Even the horn duplicated the memorable "meep, meep" sound of the cartoon character.

The image they tried to convey was that, "Here is a new type of performance car at an attractive low price." The early production cars were noticeably de-contented. The two-door coupe had a front bench seat, rubber floor mats, hubcaps rather than styled wheels, and a 3-speed manual transmission. The big draw was that the car featured Plymouth's 383 cubic inch V-8 engine with a 4-barrel carburetor and dual exhausts. Frankly, to use a corny cliche, it provided tremendous "bang for the buck." The base car sold for as little as $2,800, while the GTO had by this time climbed into the $3,000-plus price range.

That "Woodward Ad"

The ad shows a tranquil scene: tucked beneath the trees in the crossover median of a quiet suburban boulevard sits a new Verdoro Green 1968 GTO with two young guys inside. Just above the car is a sign pointing to Detroit's Woodward Avenue, and across the bottom is the line, "The Great One by Pontiac. You know the rest of the story." It's hard to imagine that something as simple as this could create a firestorm of controversy, yet that's exactly what happened.

It began with GM's new corporate policy in 1967 that there be no evidence of or reference to aggressive driving in any advertising. This policy had not gone unnoticed at Pontiac, who had the most to lose in regard to the GTO's image of performance. Such was the corporation's power that all introduction ads for the new 1968 GTO showed this very exciting car only in static situations.

The original concept for what would become the infamous "Woodward Ad" had a 1968 GTO parked at a drive-in restaurant. Unfortunately, the background of the chosen drive-in proved to be unacceptable, so the car was moved to a grassy Woodward turnaround. The car was photographed standing still—as per corporate policy—but with the Woodward sign above, anyone who was tuned in at all to Pontiac knew that the two young men in their Goat were just waiting for a new Olds 442 or a big block Chevelle SS to pass by. "The rest of the story" was an easily imagined street race. The ad was sent "downtown" for review and it came back stamped "approved"—after all, it met all of the "no spinning tires" requirements.

Some months later Pontiac rented a billboard at literally the same spot where the photograph was taken. They used the same illustration, but with a new headline, "To Woodward Avenue with love from Pontiac." This turned out to be a huge mistake.

The billboard was up for only a short time when GM received a letter of complaint from the city council of Berkeley, Michigan, a small suburb bordering Woodward Ave. The council complained that Pontiac was "laughing" at the authorities while irresponsibly promoting street racing as a means of selling cars. GM's top management agreed and ordered Pontiac to remove the billboard and kill whatever remained of "those damned Woodward ads."

What was notable was that while the Road Runner was advertised with this low price, most of the buyers chose to upgrade, selecting the more popular options such as styled wheels, 4-speed transmission, bucket seats, and carpeting. Hence, while the final price was about the same as a GTO, the early low-price image of this Plymouth musclecar prevailed—remember what I said about how long it took to change an image in those days? Plymouth was to be congratulated for their marketing and promotion efforts on the car. Incidentally, the entire Road Runner concept was suggested to Plymouth by automotive journalist Brock Yates, who at the time was a successful columnist for *Car and Driver.*

You might say that Pontiac was asleep at the wheel. In 1967, Plymouth didn't even offer this car, yet by 1968 they were selling as many as 50,000. You can bet a lot of those sales were potential GTO customers. Plymouth's only musclecar until 1968 had been the GTX, which, while a good car, had never posed a serious threat in sales. But when that cocky little "bird" started running around screaming "meep, meep," suddenly this new Plymouth entry became a source for concern, one that Pontiac would need to address in the 1969 model year.

10

Judge...and Judgement

The Ad Hoc Committee

I WAS HONORED TO BE ASKED BY John DeLorean to work with a special product planning group inside Pontiac that was created to generate new product ideas. DeLorean wanted to maintain the Pontiac brand image of fun and youth-oriented excitement. That image came from some of the great earlier Wide-Track success cars like the Bonneville, Grand Prix, Le Mans, and GTO.

The group, which came to be known as "The Ad Hoc Committee," included Chairman Bill Collins and a highly select group of talented young Pontiac enthusiasts like Herb Adams, Jack Humbert, Dave Wood, Tom Nell, Herb Kadau and Ben Harrison. I considered it a great honor to be invited to work with this group, and while we didn't have a specific request from the division or from DeLorean to go after the Road Runner, it made sense to us to attack the problem. It's notable that this was the first time I could remember Pontiac reacting in the musclecar market. Up until then our role as leader of the segment had been unquestioned.

Our first thoughts were to go after Plymouth with a car every bit as low-priced but significantly more capable than the Road Runner, and to do it by compromising the GTO. We did away with the special GTO hood (though we kept the hood tachometer), and substituted the less expensive, more conventional Le Mans hood. We limited the car to only a pillared coupe, with only a bench front seat and a minimum of interior color choices. We stripped the styled Rallye II wheels of their trim rings and dropped the color-matching Endura front end in lieu of the chrome unit from the Le Mans.

To further reduce the price we limited transmission selection to either a floor-mounted 3-speed, a wide-ratio 4-speed, or the 3-speed automatic with a column shifter. The real "kicker" was the selection of our 350 cubic inch V-8 engine, fitted with high output cylinder heads right off the 400 cubic inch H.O. engine. A Quadrajet 4-barrel carb and dual exhausts were also part of the package. We then acquired a couple of absolutely stock 1968 Plymouth Road Runners and conducted a series of side-by-side tests, proving that with our new 350 cubic inch "GTO" engine we could confidently handle the 383 Road Runner from 0–60 mph and over a standing 1/4 mile. In fact, the more we ran the cars the better the 350 cubic inch GTO performed. None of the Road Runners ever beat our new price leader.

After acquiring this data we began preparing our formal presentation for DeLorean and his staff. We had affectionately named the car "E/T," which stood for "elapsed time," an appropriate name in the mid-sixties since it was a product of the very popular drag racing culture. We also wanted a new and exclusive color with which to introduce the car, but Pontiac was already using the one exclusive color allowed to each GM division—Verdoro Green. So we selected Carousel Red, a color already in the Pontiac system, but offered only on the F-body Firebird and Camaro (Chevrolet called it "Hugger Orange"). This bright orange color on the somewhat larger A-Body (Le Mans/GTO) made a very strong statement.

The "ET" vs. the Road Runner

Finally the presentation was ready to be shown to DeLorean. During our one hour delivery, he sat stone-faced, not saying a word and never changing expression. At the conclusion, he looked at us all and said, very coolly, "Over my dead body. Don't you guys know this is a 400 cubic inch world? As long as I have anything to say about it, there will never be a GTO with anything less than a 400 cubic inch engine. I recognize what you are trying to do, and I support the concept, but get that !@#!*% 350 out of that car!" He had our attention, to say the least. He concluded his statement: "Bring this car up to GTO standards and then we'll figure out how to cut the price."

So it was back to the drawing board. First, we redid "E/T" both as a hardtop and convertible, dropping the post coupe. We put back the bucket seats, the Endura front end, and the traditional GTO hood. What started out to be a new low priced GTO was rapidly becoming the highest priced GTO. The only feature that remained from the initial product were the Rallye II wheels, less trim rings.

One of the smartest moves we made in reconstructing what we were now thinking of as the "Ultimate GTO" was to include the Ram Air engines that were to be offered for the first time in 1969. The 366-horsepower Ram Air III was selected as the standard powerplant, while the underrated 370-horsepower Ram Air IV was listed as the only option. Now our new "GTO E/T" would not only handle the standard 383 cubic inch Road Runner, but it was also more than a match for their optional new 440 cubic inch "Six Pack."

This time we were really primed for our final presentation. It was scheduled to take place in the Engineering Garage, where DeLorean could actually drive the car. DeLorean was a little late, so the full group had assembled by the time he arrived. This time, after he saw the car, he was smiling like the "cat who just ate the canary." Clearly, he was more pleased with this new GTO concept. "All right guys, I'll buy your car." His smile broadened (as did ours). "But, let's forget about that silly name." Oh no, I thought, another DeLorean bombshell!

"Every time I turn on the TV these days," DeLorean continued, "I hear

The Plymouth Road Runner (top) prompted Pontiac to react. The initial proposal for a low-priced performance car to counter the Road Runner was called "ET" (for Elapsed Time). The proposal included a high output 350 cubic inch engine, and was instantly rejected by DeLorean, who responded by saying, "This is a 400 cubic-inch world. Over my dead body will a GTO ever have anything less."

this funny guy shouting 'Here comes da Judge, Here comes da Judge!' So, let's give them their damn Judge!" DeLorean, like many other people in late-sixties America, was a big fan of the popular NBC-TV show "Rowan and Martin's Laugh-In." That "funny guy" shouting "Here comes da Judge!" was a young "Flip" Wilson.

From that moment on, our new car was "The Judge." It became a case of "hype on our hype:" the original 1964 GTO was created to be an image-making "hype" for the more sedate Le Mans; now, The Judge was created to be a "hype" for the slumping GTO.

Royal Pontiac built the first Judge. Pontiac provided a Mist Green 1969 Ram Air IV hardtop along with some very specific instructions. We painted it Carousel Red, added a stand-up rear deck spoiler, a hood mounted tachometer, a Hurst T-handle shifter knob, and took the chrome trim rings off

Royal was commissioned to build the first prototype Judge, converting a Mist Green Ram Air IV hardtop from my press fleet. This picture shows the Bobcat's upper belt line stripe that would eventually evolve into the final three-colored pop-art Judge stripe. Note that "The Judge" decal on the front fender had already been approved.

the Rally II Wheels. The only thing that wasn't decided at this time was the striping and emblems. The car, with incomplete stripes and emblems, was photographed for early magazine stories and even made it all the way to the announcement ad and the new performance catalog.

It's ironic that the popular phrase, "Here comes da' Judge," was never used in any Pontiac advertisements for this car. An old-time vaudeville performer named Harold "Pigmeat" Markham had copyrighted the phrase. He had a very inflated idea of what it was worth, especially when he found out that General Motors wanted to buy the use of it for advertising. We never used that phrase in any communication from Pontiac, and I ought to know, I was the one charged with making sure we didn't.

But we did use just about every other Judge reference we could think of, such as "The Judge will rule," "All Rise for the Judge," and, "The Judge can be bought." The latter prompted an almost immediate outcry from the American Bar Association, resulting in our having to kill that particular ad.

Our ad campaign for 1969 used the theme "Breakaway in a Wide-Trackin' Pontiac." The memorable Breakaway music, written by Steve Karmen, a very talented New York-based songwriter and producer, was a big hit with the public. In fact, we sponsored a commercial record release of the tune. It was called simply "Breakaway," and told the story of a young man who, while maturing into adulthood, wanted to "Breakaway" from his trapped role in life and get out on his own.

The GTO Judge, however, was a different creature, and we felt obligated to advertise it differently. We took a tongue-in-cheek approach and said, "Yeah, it looks weird, but it runs like Hell!" When we decided to do a musical presentation of The Judge, we were a little ahead of our time. A very hip 60-second TV commercial featuring pop star Mark Lindsey and the group "Paul Revere and the Raiders" really helped launch our new baby on TV. Many mu-

Since we were restrained from using the term "Here Comes Da Judge," we used some familiar cliches like, "All rise for The Judge," or "The Judge can be bought." The latter resulted in howls of protest from the American Bar Association. This was the first time the matching Carousel Red Judge jacket was shown. The jacket was offered through the dealer's parts department.

Promoting the Judge

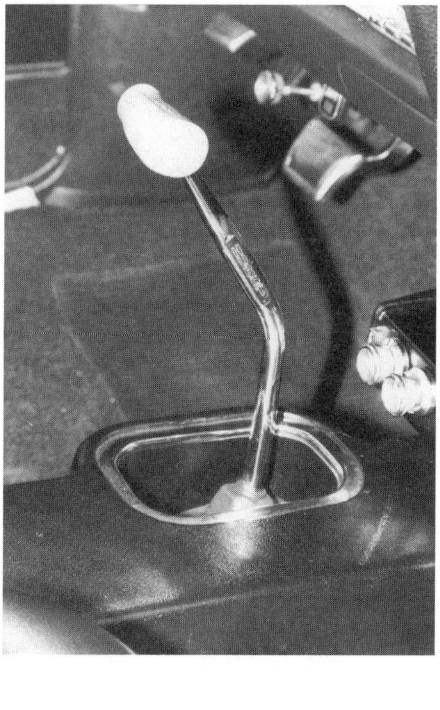

Standard equipment on the Judge was the epitome of the Hurst shifter family, the famous T- handle. It was supposed to be easier to grab and shift, however I found it to be clumsy and awkward. I took the T-handle off and used the traditional white shifter ball instead.

"Finance it, Clyde."

During 1968, the U.S was "captured" by the movie "Bonnie and Clyde," starring Warren Beatty and Faye Dunaway. They were portrayed as two romantic, Robin Hood-type bank robbers. We decided to do a spoof commercial using Bonnie and Clyde as a theme.

As usual, they were robbing a bank when their getaway car, an unidentified early thirties sedan, fails to start. They jump out of the getaway car and run to a nearby Pontiac dealership, (which just happens to be around the corner). Clyde asks, "You got something that moves?" The salesman responds "Sure, here's our new GTO, we call it 'The Great One.'" They take a Verdoro Green hardtop for a supposed demo ride. With the bank money, and the guns all in the backseat, the salesman goes into his regular sales pitch about the new GTO.

When the salesman asks how they're going to pay for it, Bonnie looks over at Clyde and says, "Finance it, Clyde." The commercial ends as they throw the unsuspecting salesman out of the GTO, along with a suitcase full of money. The car speeds off, money flying everywhere, with the salesman chasing them. "You paid too much! You got change coming!" he screams in vain.

That phrase, "Finance it, Clyde" got so popular that we produced a poster showing a GTO "speeding" down the road with the money flying around, and with the headline "Finance it, Clyde." We suggested the dealers put them up in their closing rooms. Again, that confident, almost arrogant display, plus the ability to poke fun at ourselves, had become an important part of our advertising posture.

sic fans agree that this 1969 commercial, for which Lindsey wrote the music, may have been one of the very first true music videos. The theme line of the commercial was, "Judge, the Special Great One from Pontiac." The entire soundtrack was captured on a 45-rpm record and distributed to our dealers to use as a giveaway. It was a unique looking record: the center of the Rally II wheel was used as the label so that the black part of the record looked exactly like a tire. The dealers gave away more than 50,000 copies.

The market timing of the Judge turned out to be a stroke of genius. The outrageous visual statement it made, with its wild orange color and psychedelic pop-art graphics, allowed it to become a darling of the protest generation. Its arrogant and outspoken posture literally shouted, "I know I may be a little funny-looking...but don't *@&% with me...or I'll blow your doors off!"—and with the Ram Air III or Ram Air IV engine, the driver usually could, no matter what the competition.

Today, The Judge looks tame, but when it first appeared in 1969 it was outrageous, especially the stand-up rear spoiler. Everybody laughed at it. I remember one enthusiast magazine did an early road test on the car and made the observation, "We have found a perfect car to take on picnics. This new rear deck spoiler makes a great cutting board to slice cheese." Many GTO loyalists even felt it was a little extreme. Some buyers wanted the orange color, but not the graphics. This was possible by writing in the appropriate box at the bottom of the order form, "Judge delete." This removed only the pop-art stripes and decals. The car still came with a Ram Air engine and spoiler.

As it turned out, The Judge had too much press exposure before it actually got into production. This angered the dealers. They had customers coming in to see it long before they ever received their first car. The 1969 Special Performance Catalog, released in January, included The Judge, which only

PERFORMANCE OPTIONS

"The Judge"—GTO only **(Code 554—UPC WT1)**

"The Judge"— (Code 554—UPC WT1)
Performance Features:

- Functional, Driver-controlled, Air-intake Scoops on Hood
- Quadra-jet Carb
- Hurst "T" Handle Stick Shift
- Chromed Rocker Arm Covers, Oil Filler Cap and Air Cleaner
- Free-flowing Dual Exhausts
- Full-width Rear Deck Airfoil
- Heavy-duty Springs and Shocks
- Heavy-rated Stabilizer Bar
- Variable-pitch, 5-blade Fan
- Dechromed Safety Rim Rally II Wheels
- G70—14 Wide-tread Fiber-glass-belted Tires (Black)
- Body Rally Stripes
- 400-Cu.-In. Ram Air V-8

Performance and Convenience Options Available:

- 4-speed Stick Shift
- Rally Sports Speed Shifter with Turbo Hydra-matic
- Ram Air IV Engine
- Rally Gauge Cluster with Rally Clock
- Rally Gauge Cluster with Instrument Panel Tach
- Hood-mounted Tach
- Custom Sports Steering Wheel
- Power Brakes—Front Disc
- G70—14 Redline or Whiteline Tires
- Power Bucket Seat for Driver
- Fast-ratio Power Steering

Identification: Ram Air Decal on Side of Hood Scoops; "The Judge" on Front Fenders; Airfoil and Instrument Panel; Three-color Vinyl Stripe on Upper Edge of Front Fender, Door and Quarter.

Standard Tire Size:
G70—14

Standard Engine:
400-Cu.-In., 366-HP, 4-BBL, Ram Air V-8

Available Engine:
400-Cu.-In., 370-HP, 4-BBL, Ram Air IV V-8

Standard Transmission:
Heavy-duty, 3-speed Manual—Stick Shift

Available Transmissions:
4-speed Manual—Stick Shift
Turbo Hydra-matic—Column Shift
Turbo Hydra-matic—Rally Sports Speed Shifter (with console only)

For "Judge" standard equipment and general specifications, see Page E-3 (GTO Section).

This page was sent to the dealers to be inserted in their 1969 sales album. All the features that were unique to The Judge were correctly pictured and listed. For the first three months of the model year this page was the only information dealers had for sales reference.

Though the 1969 Judge spoiler drew much criticism, it actually paled by comparison to the spoiler on the 1970 car. The original spoiler was replaced because it didn't work. It created no downforce, and may have been a detriment to the car's handling. The 1971 replacement (above) was far more effective.

exaggerated the shortage of the cars. By now, dealers had taken hundreds of orders and even their customers were getting impatient. This is not the way to successfully introduce a new car. Also, there were paint problems, stripe problems, even engine supply problems, all of which added up to late distribution, which upset the dealers even more.

One serious cause for the delay was a battle over the glovebox door emblem. The stylists first disagreed over whether there should be an emblem at all. They finally approved one, but when they saw the cheap looking little plastic emblem they immediately asked to have it removed. The emblem survived only the first month of production. DeLorean became concerned that this was the only interior ID on the car and ordered it reinstalled, where it remained for the rest of the model year. Years later, whether a Judge had a glovebox emblem or not became a real concern to collectors. Just because a Judge does not have a glovebox emblem, does not mean it's a fake.

The car shortage was now starting to cost the dealers money. Their attitude was very simple, if you haven't got a car, you can't sell it! Even though the Judge had been released in every Pontiac color, somehow the orange (Carousel Red) image had become a very important part of the car's personality. Most buyers didn't want any other color. By year end, over 80 percent of the Judge build was painted in Carousel Red.

Once the dealers started receiving cars, sales took off like gangbusters. Pontiac couldn't build them fast enough. Originally, they were all going to be built at the Pontiac assembly plant, however because of the crush of orders, they had to include the other A-body plants. By the end of the model year, Pontiac had sold more than 6,800 Judges in seven months, which was almost ten percent of all the GTOs they sold all year.

We felt that The Judge would also be a good opportunity to reinvent the GTO as a good class car for the part-time amateur drag racer. We put together a small drag racing program that worked through our dealers, who were encouraged to put a car in service themselves, or sell one to a customer who would agree to race it at the local drag strip. Every car had to be a Carousel Red Judge equipped with any powertrain we offered, so long as it qualified for an NHRA class (all GTOs competed in NHRA's "B" or "C" stock classes).

If a dealer wanted to participate, he bought the car at his regular discount. When the car was delivered, a duplicate drivetrain, including engine, transmission, driveshaft, and complete rear axle assembly was also included at no extra cost. The dealer was then required to keep a record of when the car went to the track, and how it was performing. If the dealer provided this information, all additional replacement parts would be supplied by Pontiac on an exchange basis, throughout the model year.

The program was a great success, as almost 100 dealers participated. The cars got great exposure, and since they all looked alike, it seemed like there many more cars in action (remember all those Nocturne Blue 1963 Grand Prixs?). We didn't care if the cars never made the lead story in the *National Dragster*, as long as they were out every weekend in front of a local crowd.

When it came to the question of the following model year, the Ad Hoc Committee recommended making the Judge a permanent model and continuing production into 1970. I disagreed strongly. I didn't feel we should build a "serious" car around an outrageous color, a pop-art decal, and a bi-

DeLorean aggressively supported Pontiac's re-entry into drag racing, but only on a grass roots level. Dealers were encouraged to sponsor a Carousel Red Judge (only) at their local drag strip in B/Stock competition. The goal was to catch the attention of the grass roots racer, proving how competitive a Judge could be in its class.

Against my urging, the 1970 Judge was brought back into the marketplace. This particular white paint scheme with black trim and new pop-art stripes didn't sell well. The 1970 Judge needed a color as exciting as Carousel Red to stimulate sales. Later in the model year Orbit Orange was released, resulting in an interesting turn around.

zarre spoiler. To me, The Judge was a promotion, a one hit wonder. A promotion like the Judge remains a serious car for only a short time. It did a great job of hyping both the GTO and Pontiac—in 1969—but in my opinion production should have stopped right there.

I didn't have anyone else agreeing with me. DeLorean had left Pontiac by that time, having been promoted to the post of General Manager at

Chevrolet shortly after the beginning of the 1969 model year. Pontiac's new management team looked at the success of the 1969 car and followed the committee's recommendation, releasing a 1970 model. It was featured in the new introductory GTO advertising campaign as "The Humbler," and was shown in the decidedly unexciting color of white with black accents. It died in the marketplace.

In a last minute attempt to save The Judge, a mid-year re-announcement was authorized, this time presenting the car in another outrageous color. A new shade of orange was selected, called "Orbit Orange," and it did help turn sales around. Of the more than 40,000 Goats sold in 1970, The Judge accounted for more than 3,800. Unfortunately, this was enough momentum to encourage management again to carry the car into the 1971 model year.

It was for 1971 that General Motors instructed their Divisions to drop the compression ratios of all their engines to accommodate the new low-lead fuel. This was just too much for even the mighty GTO to overcome. Sales dropped to little more than 10,000 units with only 374 of those built with The Judge option. After that, of course, The Judge finally disappeared. When a car is a failure in the marketplace, naturally very few of them are produced. Ironically, today the 1971 Judge is one of the most desirable of all collectible Pontiac musclecars, especially one of the only 17 convertibles.

In retrospect, The Judge was a great promotion for both the GTO and for Pontiac. It actually reinvented the "Goat," though it never really turned out to be the answer to the Plymouth Road Runner (which, remember, was our original goal). But the Road Runner grew up, too. With their 1969 model, the price was equal to or even higher than the GTO. Who knows where the original E/T concept would have gone? (Actually, Pontiac recreated it a few years later with their T-37 and GT-37 programs.)

Nevertheless, it was still a great promotion and a great car. But can you imagine trying to sell it today as we did in 1969? A bright-orange-colored car, complete with matching pop-art decal stripes and labels, built in Detroit with a "kick ass" engine that gets ten miles to the gallon, doesn't stop very well, and won't go around corners!

THE JUDGE WASN'T THE ONLY NEW MODEL introduced in 1969. The Firebird received a mild facelift for 1969, but not long after the introduction of the '69, word got around that the car was going to get a major restyling for 1970. Thus, the '69 became a "lame duck," and sales tumbled.

We tried to brainstorm some "hypes." Chevrolet, who was facing the same problem with the Camaro, got into promotions like the "Hugger," which was tied into the Indianapolis 500 Pace Car program. They also improved their Z/28 model with the addition of a 302 cubic inch high performance engine. Pontiac's solution was to introduce a sophisticated version of the Firebird 400, called the Trans Am.

Much of the Trans Am concept was the work of a dedicated enthusiast in Pontiac's engineering department named Herb Adams. Herb was a suspen-

3 individual color pictures of Pontiac performance cars, specs, book jackets and decals are yours for 40¢ (80¢ outside U.S.A.). Write to: '70 Wide-Tracks, P.O. Box 888, 196 Wide-Track Blvd., Pontiac, Mich. 48056.
(We take the fun of driving seriously.)
GM
GTO
Pontiac Motor Division
The quick way out of the little leagues.
Every year Pontiac's hard-nose gets tougher on upstarts.
Not that we go out of our way to humble amateur performers. We just take the fun of driving very seriously.
Like engines. GTO's standard is a 350-horse V-8. But this year there's a high-torque 455-cube V-8 to order, as well as two Ram Airs. So someone's bound to get his feelings hurt. Letting you order a new, low-restriction, exhaust should be the final blow.
Sorry, guys. But this is the big league. And it's time to make a cut.
The Humbler.

Purists generally consider the front-end of the 1970 Goat the best-looking of any GTO. The use of the Endura color-matched soft-nosed front-end, begun in 1968, was expanded to include the "frenched" (recessed) headlights. There was a new theme line for GTO this year. The Great One was now "The Humbler." DeLorean had left for Chevrolet by this time, and Jim McDonald was now Pontiac's General Manager. The tag (The Humbler) aroused concern from GM management and ire from newly-established Federal safety police because they thought it promoted dangerous, competitive street driving. The term disappeared very shortly into the model year. By the way, the critics of the term were, in my opinion, correct: we were trying to promote competitive performance!

sion guy and was way ahead of his time. He didn't have much patience for the teenage enthusiasts who embraced only the straight line muscle of the GTO. He saw the excitement and sophistication of these new Detroit cars in terms of handling and cornering. Herb led a team within Pontiac engineering that was an outgrowth of the original Super Duty group. They reported directly to DeLorean. They had developed a test car called the "PFST," which stood for "Pontiac Firebird Sprint Turismo." We laughed at its name, but it was a pretty capable road racing effort. More importantly, the PFST became the godfather of the Trans Am.

The Trans Am package included a tweaked suspension, special instrumentation, a special hood with functional leading edge air scoops, good-looking but non-functional brake cooling scoops, and a very nice stand-up rear deck spoiler. All T/As were fitted with Rally II wheels and the high performance Ram Air III or optional Ram Air IV engine. All were painted the same American racing colors, white with twin blue stripes, and were offered both as a coupe and a convertible. The name came from a new SCCA (Sports Car Club of America) racing series.

The Firebird Trans Am was introduced along with the GTO Judge, at a December 8th, 1967 press showing at Riverside Raceway in Riverside, Cali-

Firebird Becomes the Trans Am

In an attempt to inject some excitement into slumping 1969 Firebird sales, Pontiac introduced a "hype" in the form of a special model called the Trans Am. The name was borrowed from the Sports Car Club of America (SCCA) race series. The press gave us a hard time, since they thought we were going to race the car in the series, which had a 5.0 liter (300 cubic inch) engine size limit while the car came with a 6.5 liter (400 cubic inch) engine. Racing was never the intent. Still, a few '69 T/As were entered in the series that year, all powered by Chevrolet Z/28 engines. An overzealous racer had convinced the SCCA that Canadian Firebirds were built with the Chevy engine. Of course there were no "Canadian" Firebirds. All F-body cars were built in Ohio or California. The myth survives: even today you can race a Chevy powered '69 in SCCA competition.

fornia. We invited all the enthusiast magazines and leading west coast press to "wring out" these two new special high-performance Pontiacs. It seemed as though everyone in the press misunderstood both cars, but they were particularly hard on the Trans Am. They couldn't understand any reason for its existence, calling it no more than a "Firebird 400 with racing stripes."

Nobody took the car seriously, particularly the Pontiac dealer. As a result, the Trans Am died an early death, with only 697 of them having been built, including only eight convertibles. While the 1969 Trans Am was certainly a capable car, it just never got a chance. As a matter of fact, it was one of the first outright Pontiac failures since the start of the Wide-Track cra.

The 1969 Firebird ended up being carried over into early 1970, before the completely restyled new 1970-1/2 car appeared. The new Trans Am had a lot more panache and style than the first effort, reflecting Herb Adams' original intention of maturing it into a true American road car. The new Trans Am introduced the "Shaker" hood scoop and a small "Screaming Chicken" decal. As the 1970s wore on, the hood scoop and the decal would grow symbolically to lead the Pontiac Trans Am into becoming one of the most highly imaged cars in the world. In fact, in the model year 1979, more than 200,000 Firebirds were sold, and more than half of them were Trans Ams.

It took DeLorean longer than I would have liked to finally allow us to use the same type of exciting photography in full-size car advertising as we had so successfully used for the GTO and Firebird. Van Kaufman (left) and Art Fitzpatrick (far right) had charmed DeLorean, as they had Bunkie Knudsen and Pete Estes before him, making it difficult to get Pontiac's support to make the change.

Firebird corrals 345 horses into 400 cubic inches. That's a Break Away!
A Ram Air IV V-8 Break Away. Order it on any 1969 Firebird 400. And you'll have more horses per cube under rein than any other car in Firebird's class. 345 very healthy ponies. Which we develop with a 10.75:1 compression ratio, 4.12 x 3.75 bore and stroke, 4-barrel carburetor, high-output cam and springs, dual exhausts and oversize valves. And, of course, those functional hood scoops. Which, by the way, can be opened and closed from the driver's seat this year. A heavy-duty, 3-speed manual transmission is standard. But there's also a close-ratio, 4-speed manual and a 3-speed Turbo Hydra-matic, if you'd care to order same. By now, maybe you're thinking our Firebird 400 with Ram Air IV puts out something more than typical sporty performance. You're thinking. We told you, it's a Break Away.
GM
The Wide-Track Family for '69: Grand Prix, Bonneville, Brougham, Executive, Catalina, GTO, LeMans, Custom S, Tempest and Firebird. Pontiac Motor Division.
Break Away in a Wide-Track Firebird

197

Fitz and Van Revisited

To my mind, this was the ultimate example of what was wrong with using the Fitz and Van artwork to sell high performance. The product promoted is a Ram Air IV Firebird convertible—a high performance Pontiac aimed at young people who liked power. The way it is illustrated blurs that message by placing the car in a tranquil setting that certainly doesn't reinforce its performance image. This car could just as well have been a base six-cylinder Firebird.

1970 Trans Am Revives

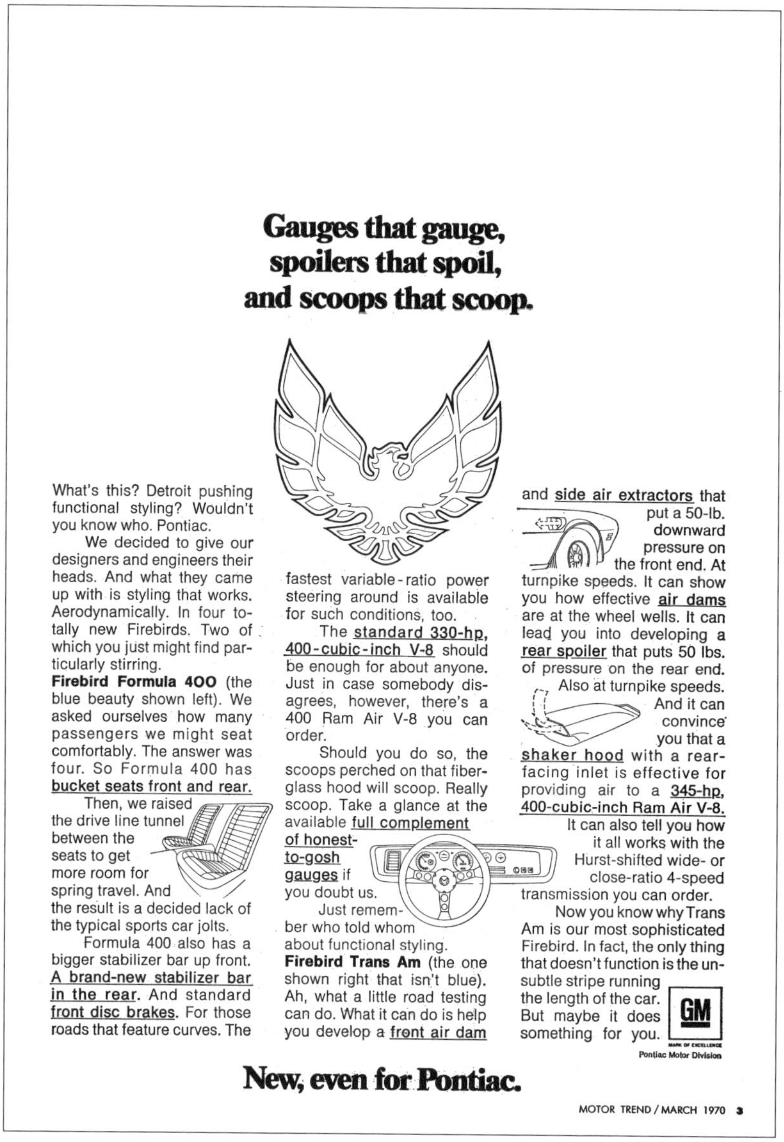

Gauges that gauge, spoilers that spoil, and scoops that scoop.

What's this? Detroit pushing functional styling? Wouldn't you know who. Pontiac.

We decided to give our designers and engineers their heads. And what they came up with is styling that works. Aerodynamically. In four totally new Firebirds. Two of which you just might find particularly stirring.

Firebird Formula 400 (the blue beauty shown left). We asked ourselves how many passengers we might seat comfortably. The answer was four. So Formula 400 has bucket seats front and rear.

Then, we raised the drive line tunnel between the seats to get more room for spring travel. And the result is a decided lack of the typical sports car jolts.

Formula 400 also has a bigger stabilizer bar up front. A brand-new stabilizer bar in the rear. And standard front disc brakes. For those roads that feature curves. The fastest variable-ratio power steering around is available for such conditions, too.

The standard 330-hp, 400-cubic-inch V-8 should be enough for about anyone. Just in case somebody disagrees, however, there's a 400 Ram Air V-8 you can order.

Should you do so, the scoops perched on that fiberglass hood will scoop. Really scoop. Take a glance at the available full complement of honest-to-gosh gauges if you doubt us.

Just remember who told whom about functional styling.

Firebird Trans Am (the one shown right that isn't blue). Ah, what a little road testing can do. What it can do is help you develop a front air dam and side air extractors that put a 50-lb. downward pressure on the front end. At turnpike speeds. It can show you how effective air dams are at the wheel wells. It can lead you into developing a rear spoiler that puts 50 lbs. of pressure on the rear end. Also at turnpike speeds.

And it can convince you that a shaker hood with a rear-facing inlet is effective for providing air to a 345-hp, 400-cubic-inch Ram Air V-8.

It can also tell you how it all works with the Hurst-shifted wide- or close-ratio 4-speed transmission you can order.

Now you know why Trans Am is our most sophisticated Firebird. In fact, the only thing that doesn't function is the unsubtle stripe running the length of the car. But maybe it does something for you.

GM
MARK OF EXCELLENCE
Pontiac Motor Division

New, even for Pontiac.

MOTOR TREND / MARCH 1970 3

It was a disappointing 1969 when both the press and the public rejected the Trans Am. The exciting new Trans Am, introduced as a 1970-1/2 model, was released in February of 1970, and won immediate acclaim. The car featured the appearance of the first "Shaker" hood scoop and a mini "Screaming Chicken" hood decal, along with a choice of Ram Air III or IV engines. Though sales were small (only about 2500), they did forecast what was ahead for Trans Am.

EVERY WINTER, I MADE ARRANGEMENTS to send a few of our press cars to Florida to do some timely magazine stories. Winter in Detroit put us out of business, and that meant no good performance press in the spring, when it was most important. We tested in Hollywood, Florida, renting the Miami Dragway for about a week. Testing cars in January meant good press in March and April.

In January of 1969, we brought our new '69 Ram Air IV Royal Bobcat to Florida. It was painted Crystal Turquoise with a special white accent, indicating a Royal Bobcat package. We wanted to remind people of the original 1962 Catalina Bobcat. This car would later appear in more magazine stories than any other car in Royal's history, fourteen in all. And it was fast. With a blueprinted Ram Air IV, a close-ratio 4-speed, and a 390:1 rear end, it ran the quarter mile in the low 12.7s at 113mph.

At this time, news about Pontiac's Ram Air V engine project was leaking out, and many of the magazines had asked about it. The new RA V was to be available in pieces over the parts counter, similar to the way the old Super Duty package had been distributed. Pontiac was showing some interest in getting back into stock car racing, and had become intrigued with Ford's tunnel-port wedge combustion chamber engine. They copied the tunnel-port head design, trying them on several different engines in their lineup. For example, they de-stroked the 400 cubic inch engine to create a 303 cubic inch package that would enable Pontiac to qualify for the new SCCA-sanctioned Trans Am racing series.

The tunnel port heads were no good on the 303 engine. They flowed way too much air for the small engine, killing most of the low-end torque. On the other hand, on the 428 engine the top end performance was disappointing because the larger-displacement engine couldn't run quite as high in the rpm range, where the tunnel port heads flowed the best. But when those magnificent tunnel port heads were bolted on the 400 engine, it worked bet-

The '69 Royal Bobcat was used as a test mule for a number of engine and drivetrain combinations. During a test in Miami, Florida in the winter of 1969, we experimented with a factory-built Ram Air V engine turning mid to high 12s before the engine spun a rod bearing.

ter. It made good horsepower and torque right across all the usable engine power bands. The 400 cubic inch Ram Air V was able to rev right up to 6,500 rpm, obviously requiring mechanical valve lifters, just like the Super Duty engine before it. Thus the RA V could never be offered as a production Pontiac engine, as it could not be warranteed.

We were asked by Pontiac Engineering to include the Ram Air V engine in our Florida testing. If it worked well, they agreed to let us get some very timely press, and satisfy the magazine writers. Our specific assignment was to install the Ram Air V engine in our Crystal Turquoise Royal Bobcat right after we had finished testing our blueprinted Ram Air IV. They specifically asked us not to "tune" their Ram Air V engine, just install it and run it as it came out of the crate. They wanted the same driver, on the same track, at the same time of day, and under the same weather conditions. We thought this would make a sensational story. So did both *Car Craft* and *High Performance Cars* magazines.

The Ram Air IV Bobcat ran predictably in the low 12.7s at a little over 113 mph. With the Ram Air V, the best run we made was a 12.82 at 114 mph before the engine spun a rod bearing. I think if we had been able to make more runs, we could have improved on those times. It was obviously more powerful than the blueprinted RA IV, but remember, it was a committed racing engine. Unfortunately, Pontiac decided not to pursue a return to NASCAR racing, thus the RA V engine project was allowed to die. No reports of our RA V experience in Florida were ever released to the press.

The 1969 GTO was virtually unchanged from the previous year. Under the hood it was a different story. A new generation of engines were introduced, capped by the magnificent 370-horsepower Ram Air IV.

Not everything we were doing at Royal was aimed at the GTO. We were also building some terrific Firebirds, and had developed an exciting package for the redesigned 1969 Grand Prix. In fact, the '69 Royal Bobcat Grand Prix featured a unique paint scheme that ultimately became the prototype for the 1970 Hurst SSJ Grand Prix.

We also continued with an active Royal press car program. Although many of the people at Pontiac never really understood the Royal program, it attracted significant attention both at Chrysler and Ford. They wanted to study the Royal Pontiac operation to understand how we made racing work so well in the showroom.

One of the top guys in the Motorsports operation at Ford, Jack Passino, asked if he could bring some of his people over to look at Royal's operation. He couldn't figure out how we were selling performance cars so successfully and Ford was not. After all, Ford was winning on the race track in nearly every venue, but they couldn't translate those wins into showroom sales.

Before extending an invitation to the "enemy," I checked with DeLorean. He approved. Ace Jr. promised to be available for the agreed upon visit but when the day actually arrived, Ace was "up north." As I expected, Passino was ready to talk to Ace about a franchise opportunity if he would agree to put together a Ford performance store. Poor Ace! Ford eventually did put together a deal in suburban Los Angeles for a West Coast Ford performance store, but they did exactly what everybody else before them had done, they built race cars. They sponsored plenty of fast Fords with one-of-a-kind special engines on the race track, but, so did a lot of other Ford dealers

The Ford problem was really not with their dealers, it was with their cars. They did not build a fast street car on their production line, or a street car that could easily be made to go fast like the Royal Bobcat. They certainly knew how to build one-of-a-kind race cars, like the Thunderbolt, or the Shelby Cobra, or the Boss 429, or the famed Tunnel Port, but that's exactly what they were, race cars that performed magnificently on the track. Their street counterparts were losers, especially when they lined up alongside a good street car like a Royal Bobcat GTO.

The first good high performance Ford street car to hit the market was the 1969 Mustang Cobra-Jet, powered by a 428 cubic inch wedge engine, using hydraulic valve lifters. This car was quick, yet streetable and reliable, and would respond to tuning. Unfortunately, it didn't stick around in the Ford system very long before it was modified to run with a solid lifter camshaft and became just another good race car. The ugly truth was that nobody at Ford really understood the difference between racing and performance.

SOON AFTER DELOREAN BECAME General Manager of Pontiac in 1965, I brought up the subject of his acquiring a serious marketing guy for the position of Marketing Manager. He was one of the few execs at GM who understood the difference between sales and marketing, and therefore could appreciate that Pontiac needed some marketing moxie inside the Division. There was some greed in my plea, too: *I wanted the job*. I thought

(We take the fun of driving seriously.)
Any licensed driver is eligible to participate.
In the beginning of tomorrow. Which is where it's at when you take your seat in the 1970 Firebird Trans Am.
The stick is from Hurst. And it controls a wide-ratio 4-speed transmission. Just right for making the 400 Ram Air V-8 do what you want it to.
You'll know exactly what it's doing, too. Thanks to the tach, speedometer, voltmeter and oil, water and fuel gauges set in that engine-turned aluminum instrument panel.
The thick wheel is our 14" Formula version. It goes directly to the extra-quick, variable-ratio power steering. You have to feel it to believe it.
Outside, the Trans Am is all function. An air dam under the Endura bumper and a spoiler at each wheel will help keep the car aerodynamically stable. Cooling air, that goes to the engine, is vented through two side air extractors. Preventing air buildup in the engine compartment. All these good things are standard. And combined with the rear spoiler, they create a downward pressure of 50 lbs., both front and rear. At turnpike speeds.
Trans Am. It's our ultimate Firebird.
The Firebird Formula 400 is enough to be anyone else's ultimate car. It develops 430 lb-ft of torque from the standard 400 V-8. Order Ram Air, and those twin fiberglass scoops allow cold air to be rammed into the four-barrel carburetor.
Like every Firebird, the Formula 400 has front bucket seats. Bucket-type seats in the rear. Front *and* rear stabilizer bars help give a flatter ride.
Trans Am or Formula 400. Only Pontiac could build them. So naturally they're only at your Pontiac dealer's. Better get over there. If you want in on the beginning of tomorrow.
GM
Firebird. New, even for Pontiac.

The Firebird and the Trans Am were totally restyled for 1970-1/2, featuring a dramatic new body. The Trans Am was a huge sales success in 1970, introducing new cues such the "Screaming Chicken" hood decal and the "Shaker" hood scoop, both of which would become icons of Firebird performance as the decade wore on. The new Trans Am borrowed the "engine-turned" dash applique first introduced on the 1964 GTO. Also making its debut was the new Formula model, which was a more attractively priced package for our high performance engines. I felt the very idea of the Formula concept was wrong, as it compromised the Trans Am image.

I was perfect for it—hell, it was basically what I was doing anyway. He agreed with the idea, but he also knew what a difficult task it would be to sell this concept to "the 14th floor." The idea died.

About a year later, out of nowhere, he came to me. "You know, Wangers, you were absolutely right, I really do need a marketing guy in here." This was good news, but there was also some bad news. "Only it's not going to be you. I've already got you and I know what you can do, working outside the system. So what I need is a guy inside the system, just like you. Then I'll have two guys just like you."

He asked me to get the ad agency involved, requesting that we do the screening and only send him the best. We made the usual inquires with the headhunters around town, but this had to be done very discreetly since DeLorean didn't want the Corporation to know about it. He established some tough criteria. He didn't want to talk to anybody from inside the Corporation, and he didn't want to talk to anybody highly placed at Ford or Chrysler. For more than a year we ran one candidate after another in front of him, and, for one reason after another, every one of them failed.

DeLorean's charade continued for another few months, until one day out of nowhere I got another call. This time it came at 6:30 in the morning at my home. "I've got something very important to talk to you about, could you be in my office in an hour?" He had a good sized, rather plush office on the top floor of the old Pontiac Administration building on Saginaw Street in downtown Pontiac. At 7:30am sharp I was in his office, even before his secretary. He closed the door, which was a little unusual. DeLorean never closed his office door.

"I've changed my mind," DeLorean started. "I want you to be my Marketing Manager. I've been talking to enough of these marketing guys over this past year to realize that I'm not going to find what I want. I guess I should quit while I'm ahead. You're the guy I want. I've already been downtown and got a budget approved, so I better deliver somebody pretty quick."

It was summer 1968, and DeLorean had been in office since 1965, so I figured he'd have at least another year at Pontiac. DeLorean continued, "I'd like to submit your name to the Corporation as fast as I can."

I said, "The first thing we'd better do is tell the agency and I'm not the guy to do that. It's got to come from you, otherwise Jones won't believe it." DeLorean agreed to speak with Ernie Jones, and then shared some more of his strategy with me. "We want to keep this low key. I don't want my own organization to know about it until it's approved, and I don't see that happening for another 60 days."

The next day I got a call from Jones. "I just heard about your good luck, and I want you to know how much I support it. I'm pleased that the agency is going to feed a guy to the division. That doesn't happen very often. Now that you are a client." Jones ended with the classic, "Why don't we have lunch?"

I met him at the Oakland Hills Country Club, not far from the office. It was one of the most exclusive clubs in the Detroit area. This alone was a real treat for me. Ernie Jones was a genuinely nice guy, who for the first time since I had known him let his hair down.

(Continued on 3rd page following)

Remaking the Grand Prix

John DeLorean was the consummate marketer. He understood trends, sensed shifting buyer's tastes, and reacted with the right product at the right time. He also knew how to listen to the talent he had surrounded himself with. They were nearly as astute at reading the market as DeLorean.

In the mid-sixties, it was apparent that Grand Prix sales were trending downward. Part of this could be blamed on the GTO, which was attracting customers away. The Grand Prix was also looking more like a Bonneville and had lost the unique styling cues and image it had enjoyed from 1962–65. By 1967, even though Pontiac had sunk a lot of money into it (even adding a convertible to the lineup), the Grand Prix was not going any where except downwards. The market for big sporty cars was shrinking

Since the 1968 model was already locked in, a decision had to be made whether to continue the Grand Prix on its current platform or radically revamp the car and breathe fresh life into what was still a dynamite nameplate. Pontiac's marketing group, lead by Ben Harrison, had an alternative idea. Why not move the Grand Prix over to the A-body (Tempest/ Le Mans sedan) platform from the larger B-body (Bonneville) and design a coupe body? Harrison put together a presentation to DeLorean, suggesting Pontiac totally restructure the Grand Prix for 1969 and position the car in the emerging personal luxury market.

Harrison made his pitch in the spring of 1967, which didn't leave much time to re-engineer the1969 model, but using the A-body chassis saved a lot of engineering time. The stylists proposed a long hood/

We had found gatefold covers to be highly effective in announcing our 1967 and 1968 performance models. To introduce the new 1969 Grand Prix, we purchased the October 1968 covers of every major automotive magazine. We facetiously tied the success of the 1968 GTO, which did win the Car Of The Year award, to the announcement of our new and equally exciting 1969 Grand Prix. It should have won.

short deck format. The interior boasted a "cockpit" look with a wrap-around instrument panel. Once all was approved, DeLorean called a meeting with the major departments of engineering, manufacturing, and sales to advise them the decision on building the car had been made. "Anyone who has a problem better speak up now," he said. The production people voiced some concern about vendors being able to deliver new parts in time. At that point, DeLorean halted the meeting and said, "We are going to do this car and we are going to deliver it in the fall of 1968."

The redesigned 1969 Grand Prix came to market on schedule and was a smash. We really didn't understand how magnificent the Grand Prix was until it was built. The long hood and short deck echoed the classic lines of the Duesenberg. No one else offered a car that looked like the Grand Prix, and the public accepted it in droves. Sales surpassed that of 1963, and the Grand Prix went on to be one of the best-selling cars of the decade for Pontiac.

The 1969 Grand Prix was truly John DeLorean's car, with a little help from market researcher Ben Harrison, who suggested converting the full-size Grand Prix to the smaller A-body sedan chassis. It was an immediate success and became the image leader for all personal luxury coupes. In an era of excess, the 1969 Grand Prix could brag about having the longest hood in the industry.

"You know," Jones confided, "I don't like DeLorean. He certainly is a hell of a car guy, and he's doing a beautiful job with Pontiac, but he gets into my business a little more than he should. But I know he has a lot of respect for you, so stick with him. There's no limit to where he can take you." Over that lunch, Jones and I worked out the agency's plan. He, too, didn't want the rest of the agency to know about the change until it was absolutely ready to happen. Finally we reviewed some candidates within the agency for my replacement, most of which were acceptable, since I had already trained them.

The next "sixty days" were uncomfortable. I couldn't tell anybody, and trying to deal with DeLorean was clumsy. It seemed like every other day he told me that the approval was coming and not to worry. "Your job isn't going to change, you're just going to be sitting on the other side of the desk."

Well, something did happen, and it didn't take 60 days. But the news from DeLorean brought about a change even I wasn't expecting.

"It didn't go through?" I asked, after his phoned request that I come right out to his office. "No, no, nothing like that," DeLorean replied. "Don't worry, nothing's going to change. It's only going to get better." I arrived at his office to find a beaming DeLorean sitting smugly behind his desk.

DeLorean Leaves Pontiac

"I just found out that I'm going to Chevrolet, as General Manager, and it's going to happen soon. I sure as a hell don't want you at Pontiac, while I'm at Chevrolet." He proceeded to tell me he was making plans for me to come with him to Chevrolet.

"You can get just as excited about a 396 Super Sport as you are about a GTO, can't you? I'll set it up with Tom Adams at their ad agency (you remember Campbell-Ewald—what comes around goes around) and you can step right in. You'll be doing just what you're doing now, and in one year you'll be running the account, I'll see to it."

I told DeLorean I thought the agency switch was a bad idea. They'd hire me because he told them to, but I'd never be anything more than "DeLorean's boy." Dropping me into Campbell-Ewald would be like dropping me into enemy territory. It was different at MacManus, I'd been there for almost ten years before DeLorean assumed command and they knew me, and they understood my relationship with DeLorean.

"I'll make it right," DeLorean retorted.

"What about me working directly for you at Chevrolet," I asked.

"That's a possibility, but I would prefer it go the other way, at least as a start," he concluded.

I walked out of that meeting with the following reactions, not necessarily in order: disappointed, confused, excited, anxious, and suspect. But if nothing else, it had interesting possibilities.

WHEN JOHN DELOREAN TOLD ME early in 1969 that he was being promoted to General Manager at Chevrolet and invited me to go with him, my immediate response was, "John, there's nothing I would rather do than stay on your team." I didn't see any future for myself at Pontiac without DeLorean, but leaving Pontiac also meant leaving Royal.

I told Ace about the possibility of moving with DeLorean. "You should start thinking about what you want to do with the mail order business," I suggested. "You've got something here that's worth some money."

"Jim," Ace replied, "I don't want to stay involved if you're not going to be here." I was a little disappointed at how quickly he wanted out, knowing how profitable it had become. He offered me the opportunity to buy it, but I didn't feel I could justify buying something I had virtually created. It probably was a dumb move on my part, but at that time I was already thinking Chevrolet, and of moving on to the next chapter in my life. Royal seemed in the past.

I at least agreed to assist Ace in selling the Royal Racing Team, to make sure it went to the right buyer and for the right dollar. A couple of superficial feelers went out to other Pontiac dealers, but none showed serious interest.

After talking to several potential buyers, one popped up out of the blue, George DeLorean, John's younger brother. George was a serious racer and a performance guy who was running a successful race shop in Detroit. He was very good at building race cars, but he didn't understand the street scene. Still, he was willing to buy the complete Royal Racing Team package, including keeping on Milt Schornack and some of the other personnel.

I was not necessarily pleased about the deal, but George's company, Leader Automotive, purchased The Royal Racing Team in late 1969. George did invite Dave Warren and Milt Schornack to join him, and agreed to keep the name Royal. Although he wasn't particularly fond of it, he was smart enough to respect the value of the Royal name.

Milt Schornack and Dave Warren clashed with George right from the start. He began to assert his racing experience, pushing more aggressive camshaft profiles, more compression, too much carburetion, and way too loud an exhaust rumble. Many potential customers found these cars disappointing. George DeLorean was on a collision course with them. He refused to listen to advice from either Schornack or Warren who together had literally built hundreds of Royal Bobcats and had a very good idea of what the street market wanted. Predictably, it didn't take long for both Schornack and Warren to serve notice.

By 1970 the musclecar craze was beginning to slow down. Although it would be more than four years before Federal emissions standards really began to choke off horsepower. For George DeLorean and Leader Automotive, his early 1960s Super Duty thinking turned out to be his demise. Most of his Royal customers lost interest. That marvelous mailing list that had taken so much effort to build just melted away. Leader Automotive never actually closed their doors, but they stumbled along, retaining only a small but loyal list of totally devoted customers.

Other people also took the change hard. Parts Manager Sam Frontera was upset because that extra performance business had been sold right out from under him. His wife Louise, the dealership Business Manager, knew it was going to show up dramatically on the monthly statement. Even master performance salesman Dick Jesse had enough, as he left to start his own small performance shop, hoping to relive his days of glory. He still wanted to be a racer, and acquired a 1965 GTO, put a big Pontiac engine in it, completely modified it, including an altered wheel base, and showed up with an exhibition car. Jesse named it "Mr. Un-Switchable" to capitalize on a popular cigarette advertising theme of the time, "I'd rather fight than switch." Even if Pontiac was totally out of racing, Jesse wasn't going to switch brands. It was a catchy theme and Jesse even used it for the name of his new shop. Unfortunately, neither the car or the shop were successful. Like George DeLorean, Jesse of all people forgot what Royal Pontiac had been all about, which was to service the true street machine owner. Jesse was the guy who drove his GTO daily, used it as a demo, and then took it out to the drag strip on weekends. Unfortunately Jesse wanted to go racing, and it lasted just long enough for him to lose all his money.

You don't kill an operation as good as The Royal Racing Team overnight, but George came close. He forgot about pursuing the magazines for good press. He didn't develop new items or new techniques for his eager members, and perhaps most importantly, he didn't stay close enough to Pontiac Engineering.

Some people at Royal got what they wanted as the program phased out. Ace Wilson, Sr. and Tom McQueen no longer had to see those "damned hot rod kids" hanging around the dealership. Ace Wilson Jr. was now almost permanently "up north." Years after Ace Jr.'s death, Ace Sr. became somewhat of a hero to Pontiac enthusiasts. He was asked to appear at some of their events, even graciously signing autographs. Just the name "Ace Wilson" would reignite the excitement of the Royal Pontiac decade. I think that in the end, Ace Sr. really believed that it was he, and not his son, that did all those wonderful things for Pontiac. God bless him!

In 1970, I talked to Pontiac's Detroit Zone Manager, John Johnson, about my buying Royal Pontiac. I had left the ad agency by that time (as detailed later) and was still trying to decide what was next for me. Johnson felt I might be a good candidate to prop up the franchise. When he approached Ace Sr. with the idea, Wilson supposedly responded, "I wouldn't sell my dealership to that Hebe if he was the last guy on earth." It didn't surprise me, and it was one of the few times I ever had religion thrown in my face, but his prejudiced attitude turned out to be a blessing in disguise. I didn't like what was happening at Pontiac under the direction of new General Manager McDonald, and it didn't take long for the car buying public to catch on too. A "new" Royal never would have worked.

The Denver, Colorado group that eventually bought Royal Pontiac was headed by an old friend and former member of The High End Club, Doug Spedding. After leaving Detroit in 1968, Spedding bought a Chevrolet store in Denver and had done extremely well with it. That same success, however, didn't repeat itself at Royal, now renamed Shaffo Pontiac (Bob Shaffo had been General Manager of Spedding Chevrolet in Denver). Long-time customers didn't like Shaffo's high-pressure sales tactics, and not too much later Pontiac "requested" that Spedding sell the dealership. There had been too many customer complaints.

This time it was sold locally, to Jim Fresard, who had been the used car manager at Mathews-Hargraves Chevrolet, also located in Royal Oak. Fresard was well-known in the community. It became known as Jim Fresard Pontiac, and almost from the day he took it over it started to turn around. Some years later Fresard bought the Buick franchise in Royal Oak, combining the two GM product lines in a beautiful Pontiac/Buick super store.

In 1985, the GTO Association of America held their national convention in Detroit. One of the scheduled activities was to be a tour of the old Royal Pontiac facility. Jim Fresard was kind enough to lead a surprisingly large group of GTO enthusiasts through the facility. The event was particularly disappointing for me because there was absolutely nothing remaining from the old Royal days, not even a decal. When Fresard was awarded the Buick franchise, he built a completely new showroom, changing the appearance of the entire facility. I got a surprising phone call a few days before the old Royal Pontiac showroom was to be torn down, inviting me to come over and watch. I responded to the invitation and walked away with a couple of the red bricks that had supported the showroom for all those years. Just a few years later, I had the distinct privilege of donating these two beautiful red bricks to a special charity raffle sponsored by the GTOAA at their National convention in Atlanta, Georgia. The benefactor of the raffle was the Atlanta Boys Club. Two proud GTO enthusiasts each have an original brick from the "Temple of Pontiac Performance" in Royal Oak, Michigan, and the Atlanta Boys Club has an extra couple of bucks in their coffers.

That pretty much wraps up the story of Royal Pontiac. All that remains today are the memories.

F. JAMES MCDONALD SUCCEEDED DeLorean as Pontiac General Manager. While certainly a nice guy, he did not possess the love for cars and that innate feel for product that both Knudsen and DeLorean had. While Pete Estes was not a car enthusiast, he was a good engineer, and he trained himself to understand marketing. Estes was also a very good listener. When Estes liked what he heard, he supported his people. A good example of that was John DeLorean, who as Estes' Chief Engineer was able to motivate Pete on many new product and marketing ideas that might not have moved along so fast had DeLorean not been pushing.

McDonald was the prototypical General Motors executive, having come up through the manufacturing division. He had been Director of Manufacturing at Pontiac, moved up to become Director of Manufacturing at Chevrolet, and now had returned to Pontiac as General Manager. During that period he was one of the architects of the new GMAD (General Motors Assembly Division) program.

Shortly after McDonald assumed control, I was summoned to his office. Having been with the agency since 1958, I now lived, breathed, and slept Pontiac. I was enjoying my role as the consummate advertising exponent of the Wide-Track performance era. I hoped that McDonald was going to pick up right where DeLorean had left off. DeLorean had been, in effect, the Advertising and Marketing manager of the Division. So when I was summoned to McDonald's office I thought this might be the start of another great opportunity. While I had never worked with Jim closely, we did know each other. I also hoped that DeLorean might have put in a good word for me.

McDonald was sitting behind his desk when I walked in. The atmosphere in the office was not what I was hoping for, I could feel it. His greeting was not particularly warm. We exchanged a few niceties, and then he started right in by saying, "It's come to my attention that you have had a very special relationship with the previous General Manager. I understand you had an open door. Well, we're going to run the Division a little differently now. We are going to exercise GM management constraints. You will no longer have that open door. You will conduct all of your business directly with the Marketing Department. Your contact will be with the Advertising Manager, and at such time he feels compelled to discuss things with me, I'll be happy to get into them. I want to discourage you from coming directly to me."

McDonald wasn't outright critical of me, but he was saying that DeLorean had veered off the course from normal GM management protocol. By the same token, however, DeLorean had done a fabulous job running Pontiac. The sales records proved it. But in the minds of what I called GM's "blue serge robots" that wasn't important. I hadn't thought that my world at Pontiac was going to remain as good as it was, but I never dreamed it was going to be as bad as McDonald was now describing it.

As a division General Manager, part of McDonald's responsibility was to oversee sales and marketing. The General Manager at that time also made decisions on styling. He didn't necessarily get involved with the basic body shape, but he certainly was required to work with the stylists developing the personalities of his cars. That was one reason John DeLorean invited his top marketing people in to see his new cars very early in their styling development stage.

DeLorean and his team had become big believers in body colored front end styling, introduced on the 1968 GTO. It had already started to show up on the full size car in 1969, which they felt would be a trend. It was a sophisticated new look, especially with the split grille, and made a perfect statement for an avant garde Pontiac.

McDonald didn't like it at all. "If Pontiac was to be a mid-priced or a luxury-priced car, it should have some glitter on the front end," he declared. He ordered us to show all the full-size cars for the remainder of the model year only in profile or in rear end views. At the same time, he directed styling to remove the Endura body color material from the front end of the proposed 1970 full size cars. The 1970 car was a decent looking car with sort of a radiator shell look. However, Pontiac's opportunity to be at the leading edge of a new trend virtually disappeared.

Another post DeLorean move that I fully expected was when Chief Engineer Steve Malone terminated my press cars. The Pontiac Central Office front door had hardly "Hit DeLorean in the ass for the last time," before Malone made sure those damned Wangers press cars were gone. He never did

The 1970 GTO received a newly restyled Endura front end with frenched headlamps and recessed grilles. Many Pontiac enthusiasts consider the 1970 model to be the best looking GTO of all. Along with the successful Ram Air III and IV powertrains, a new 455 cubic inch engine was now available.

understand, and almost immediately, enthusiast press coverage of the 1970 performance Pontiacs literally stopped, and so did sales. I was almost out of the picture by that time, and could only sit by and watch the once proud Wide-Track era begin to spiral into insignificance.

AT THE SAME TIME DELOREAN WAS making his move to Chevrolet, Bunkie Knudsen shocked the industry by moving over to the Ford Motor Company as President. This surprising turn came about because Henry Ford II had grown tired and bored with running his company. He had become interested in politics and was an active supporter of then President Lyndon Johnson. Johnson was seeking re-election, and in exchange for his totally committed support, Ford had been promised the opportunity to serve in Johnson's cabinet. Thus Ford resigned as President, but before leaving he had to choose his successor. Lee Iacocca was General Manager of the Ford Division at the time and appeared to be a shoo-in. Ford, however, apparently didn't like or trust Iacocca and wasn't about to hand the family business over to him.

Knudsen's disappointment after recently losing the Presidency at GM to Ed Cole was common knowledge around town. When Ford offered him the same position, Knudsen resigned from General Motors and accepted the role as President of the Ford Motor Company.

Iacocca's failure to win Henry Ford's support was not unusual. Everybody's got to have a "champion" in the business, and Ford was obviously not Iacocca's champion. In a big company, politics is so important it often overpowers talent and capability. Being in the right place at the right time is a wonderful fantasy, but that's not usually how it happens. You're at the right place at the right time because somebody structured it that way. I really believe that everybody in the business world has got to have a champion, somebody in a position to make things happen for you.

John DeLorean was my champion. He had proven it to me time and time again, and I was totally committed to being a "DeLorean Soldier." I believed in him, and he had shown me equal respect. That's why, when he told me he wanted to take me with him to Chevrolet, he knew I would understand. He was moving up in the Corporation and wanted me to follow. Ernie

A Boy and His Goat

After the infamous Woodward ad "promoting" street racing, and the negative reactions that resulted from it, the corporation really cut us no slack in 1969, giving each of our ads a thorough inspection to make sure Pontiac wasn't subtly "pulling anything." They weren't questioning the creative approach, or much of the factual copy. They were concerned about our showing any aggressive performance or competitive driving.

One of the ads that I proposed lived up to the absolute letter of the edict. In it we showed a bright red, freshly washed GTO convertible sitting in the driveway of a nice middle-class home. Standing next to the GTO was a young man wearing bathing trunks, with a garden hose at his feet and a pail under his right arm. The headline simply said, "A Boy and his Goat." The copy then went on to say that everybody ought to have at least one GTO, and this was his.

We sent the ad downtown to the corporation, and, incredibly, it came back rejected after a couple of days, with a note written to me as account head: "We reject this ad because of the use of the word goat. We have researched this word, and to the best of our knowledge, the goat stands for the butt end of a joke. We cannot allow you to demean your product. Please change the headline."

At first I laughed. I thought it was funny how they could totally miss the point. Then I realized that these people weren't part of our market, so they probably didn't understand the word play. I wrote a reply advising them that the "Goat" nickname had been given to the car by its owners as a term of endearment. This wasn't the first time we had problems making the corporation understand that the name GTO wasn't the only moniker for the car. I backed my letter up with copies of magazine articles and a couple of newspaper stories, all using the term "Goat" as a personal expression of affection for the car, exactly what you spend millions of dollars to try to get across in your advertising.

It didn't take very long for the corporation to reply: "We reject your thinking. As far as we're concerned, the Goat is an unacceptable term to be applied to this car. We cannot allow you to defame the name and the image of your product."

I was livid. I wrote an emotional note to DeLorean stating that we had to make a stand because the people at the corporate level were preventing us from doing good advertising. We had always interpreted the GTO properly in our imaging and our advertising. That was how we had positioned the GTO out in front of the market since 1964. Unless we were

Jones had commented on this at our lunch. Usually, these relationships develop through the friendship of wives, or through a church affiliation, or on the golf course. My relationship with DeLorean, however, was purely professional. It was born from a passion we both had for the car business.

There comes a time in everybody's career when you reach an apex. You find yourself in a situation where you possess a particular capability or knowledge that is timely and much in demand in the marketplace.

For example, if you're in the automobile business, you owe it to yourself to learn as much about the total business as you can. If you're in sales, learn more about marketing, develop an understanding of manufacturing and

permitted to continue to do these kind of creative things, we were going to lose that leadership position. I railed on that, "these people are not qualified to make these decisions," referring to Gale Smith, the Director of Advertising for General Motors. "Consequently, you must now direct yourself to Gale Smith and allow us to have the liberty."

DeLorean passed the memo on to advertising manager John Malone, with a note attached: "John—Jim Wangers is right. Run this ad without corporate approval. JZD." Malone hand-carried the memo to Gale Smith. He let Smith know in no uncertain terms that he had no desire to offend the corporation and allow this advertising to run.

Nothing happened for a few days until I got a call from Ernie Jones, the manager of the agency, who insisted I meet him for lunch over at his country club. With a faint smile on his face he said, "Jim, I'm going to have to let you go. It seems you've offended the Ad Manager of the General Motors Corporation, and he's asked me to get rid of you."

Of course I immediately knew what had happened. I explained everything to Jones, which I had not done up until that time since I didn't feel it was important enough to make a big issue out of with the agency people. Finally Jones said to me, "Well, you know what you did wrong?"

I answered, "I suppose I talked about a client with not quite as much respect as I should have."

"I don't blame you for that," Jones said. "I'll tell you what you did wrong. You put it in writing on a company letterhead. You committed the agency to your opinion without discussing it with us."

"As long as you've learned your lesson," Jones said, "I think I can go back to the corporation and talk them into letting me keep you. But I just hope that you've learned something from this, and under the circumstances, I would suggest that you guys bury that ad."

While I was relieved that I still had a job, I was angry at DeLorean for exposing me, although he exposed himself too, but he wasn't going to get fired over it. I went to DeLorean and let him know how close I came to getting canned and to tell him we had lost the ad. "Well, Wangers," DeLorean replied with a smug smile, "If you weren't always in trouble, I'd think you weren't trying!"

production, and at least try to understand the process of engineering. It's imperative that you educate yourself about all aspects of the business you've chosen. If the doors of opportunity open and you're not ready, you can only blame yourself. There's no formula to predict exactly when that opportunity will appear. In my case, I was just over 40, and I thought I was ready!

When DeLorean told me he was going to withdraw my name as his candidate for the marketing position at Pontiac and to just "sit tight" until he could fit me into Chevrolet's advertising agency I thought I had missed my chance. Again I asked him to reconsider bringing me directly into Chevrolet marketing, reporting directly to him. All he would say was, "Let me see what I can do." I felt that going to Campbell-Ewald was a giant step backward that I didn't need at this time.

"Sitting tight" meant leaving MacManus right after the first of the year in 1969 and getting "lost" for 90 days. About the first week in April, according to DeLorean, I would surface at the Chevrolet ad agency. This way, the Corporation would not think he had "stolen" me from Pontiac. DeLorean called Ernie Jones and explained what he was doing, suggesting that I had expressed a desire to follow him to Chevrolet, and he was making plans to set me up at Campbell-Ewald. He further advised Jones that he was withdrawing my name as a candidate for the Pontiac marketing slot. He didn't tell Jones that he had invited me to go with him to Chevrolet.

Jones didn't want me to leave. Apart from the fact that he respected me for my work, he knew I would not be very popular around Pontiac once DeLorean was gone. "Those guys are going to come out of the walls after you," he said. "They're going to be so anxious to prove they can run that place without DeLorean that they're going to change things, just to change them. That's not a good way to do business, and that's why I want you around the agency. I don't think it will take very long before the new guys at Pontiac will want your help."

What neither Jones or I knew at the time was that DeLorean had already selected someone for the post of Pontiac Marketing Manager. That person was Jim Graham, the guy who had hired me back in 1958, and was a mentor during my learning period. Unfortunately, Jim had some serious disagreements with the management team at the agency and had resigned under strained conditions. He moved to New York, where he enjoyed success in the non-automotive advertising world. Now he was back at Pontiac as a client, and as you might expect, again under "strained conditions." DeLorean had moved fast to fill the position after withdrawing my name. This created a tense relationship between the agency and the Division. I think DeLorean hired Graham almost out of spite. It was really very unfair to the agency.

Right after Graham came aboard, perhaps three months before DeLorean's departure, DeLorean set up a meeting for the three of us. He explained to Graham that I was working on many programs that were not part of the system, like the Royal press cars. He further explained that there was a special budget for this work, which he had approved, and that he would like to see this arrangement continue. Graham agreed that it needed to continue:

"I know Jim, and I'm sure we can work together." For the moment, I felt pretty good about having Jim Graham back in the Pontiac picture.

Just two days later, I was called into Jones' office to talk about a complaint from Jim Graham concerning my rapport with the General Manager, and how this was undermining the system. It was at that moment that I realized my glorious days at Pontiac were numbered—which would be confirmed a few months later by the meeting in McDonald's office (probably the result of Graham's request).

Jones told me we had better take steps to pacify Graham, who was obviously already flexing his muscles. I called DeLorean to tell him about Graham's request. He was unconcerned. "What do you care, you're going to be leaving anyway."

My situation suddenly seemed simpler. Remaining with MacManus, regardless of Ernie Jones' positive attitude, was not going to be acceptable. Jim Graham had made it very clear that Pontiac would be out of bounds for me.

However, things didn't remain that simple. Right after DeLorean took over at Chevrolet I got a call from Larry Shinoda, an old GM styling friend, who had followed Bunkie Knudsen to Ford.

Ford or Chevrolet?

"I want to tell you an interesting story," Larry said, "then you can make a decision for yourself. I was at J. Walter Thompson (Ford's ad agency) yesterday with 'The Man' (a lot of Knudsen's colleagues affectionately called him that). We were talking about the Torino and the Mustang. 'The Man' is pretty upset that we are not getting our share of the youth market."

"He started talking about you," Shinoda continued, "He can't understand why we can't do what you are doing. You've got the whole world thinking that the GTO is the coolest thing out there. Knudsen asked me if I knew you well enough to set up a meeting. I think The Man would really like to have you working for him. If you'd like to follow this up," Shinoda concluded, "I'll make an appointment for you."

The next day Knudsen's secretary called to set up an appointment. Suddenly I was a hot commodity. DeLorean wanted me involved at Chevrolet, Jones wanted me to stay with Pontiac, and now the President of the Ford Motor Company wanted to talk to me.

I met Knudsen at Ford's "Glasshouse" headquarters in Dearborn. After the usual small talk he got right into what he wanted. "Our research shows that young people aren't coming into the Ford showrooms, even though we're winning everywhere on the track." This statement shocked me. It seemed that Bunkie had forgotten the good days at Pontiac and how we made certain we had a showroom full of a good, quick, fun to drive street cars to stand behind any racing.

"We don't need any help with our cars," he bragged. "We know how to make them run. I want you to get us involved with one of those Rock Groups. Get us a song. I want to be on TV in one of those shows where they feature our car, and I still want to know how you got the GTO on all those boxes of breakfast cereal."

He added that he didn't want me to work for the ad agency. Instead, I was to report directly to him, with a five million dollar budget and $100,000 a year salary. He leaned forward in his chair and chose his words carefully. "All I care about is that you get our cars some attention from young people. I have confidence in you, Jim. You and I both know there are cars out there capable of running all over that Pontiac, but you've got the world convinced that the GTO is the only car. I know that takes money, that's why I'm giving you a decent budget (remember, these were 1969 dollars). I'm ready to start right now, I hope you are too."

I sat back, overwhelmed. It sank in that I now had been offered positions with the number one, number two, and number three American carmakers.

"I don't want you running to DeLorean," Knudsen warned. "I figured if there was ever a time to get you, it would be now, since he has gone to Chevrolet, and I don't think you're going to like working for McDonald." Of course Knudsen didn't know that DeLorean had already invited me to follow him to Chevrolet. "I would like you to give me an answer soon," he concluded.

Knudsen was making me a tremendous offer. At the same time I didn't like the idea of working outside the Ford system. I had been through that before. If it wasn't for the great relationship I had developed with John DeLorean, I don't think I would have survived outside the system at Pontiac.

We shook hands., "I appreciate how honest you've been," I said candidly. "One thing I won't do is hold you up. Needless to say, this is a major move for me, and I'll need a little time."

I walked out of his office, but my feet weren't on the ground. I needed advice, but I had no idea where to go. After my real early experience with Burt Durkee at Kaiser-Frazer, my only other mentors were John DeLorean and Ernie Jones, and both of them couldn't be objective in this case. My family lived in Chicago and my father had already passed away.

Despite Knudsen's request, I felt an obligation to tell DeLorean, since he never seemed to take seriously my determined request to work directly for Chevrolet. I thought that by taking Knudsen's offer at Ford, maybe I could solve everything. I could satisfy my ambitions and let DeLorean off the hook. All I had to figure out now was how to get myself excited about a Torino or a Mustang.

So I called DeLorean. I don't think he would have cared if I told him that I decided to stay at Pontiac, but when he learned there was a chance I might be going to Ford, working with Bunkie Knudsen, that was a different story. He said, "Where are you?" I told him I was at my office. "I want to meet you right away, tonight if possible. Don't go anywhere else, and don't talk to anybody about this until I see you."

Frankly I was excited by DeLorean's reaction. He knew that I could stir things up at Ford. Ford and Chevy were always hooked up in a side-by-side sales battle, and at least he thought I might make a difference.

At dinner, John wasted no time in telling me how bad the Ford deal was. He began first criticizing their product, and then said, "They're not going to let you do the kind of things you did for Pontiac."

"Where do I stand at Chevrolet?" I interjected.

"Don't worry," he replied, without seeming too committed to the idea. "I'll get that done." I was now thinking about the comment Ernie Jones had made referring to my professional relationship with DeLorean. The sad truth was that I really wanted to continue working with DeLorean, and it didn't seem like that was going to happen.

I went back to see Jones to bring him up to date. His first comment shocked me. "The only guy in this business I like less than DeLorean is Knudsen." I think Jones had never forgiven Knudsen for what he had done to Milt Coulson, the creative director who had conceived the Wide-Track concept, only to lose his job. "Of your three options," Jones concluded, "naturally I'd like you to stay right here, but if DeLorean says he's going to get you in at Chevrolet, then that's the place for you to go. Starting up with Campbell-Ewald is not a smart move."

Two days later I got a call from David E. Davis. Davis had resigned from *Car and Driver* and, after a few stops, had become the Chevrolet Creative Director at Campbell-Ewald. I had already heard gossip that Davis was particularly pleased about his new role of becoming the "Wangers of Campbell-Ewald," which meant he would have the inside track with DeLorean.

Davis invited me to have lunch, explaining that he wanted to talk to me about something very important. He got right to the point. "I want to sell you on working at Campbell-Ewald." When I asked if he was making the offer at the request of DeLorean, Davis admitted, somewhat embarrassed, that DeLorean had indeed given him that assignment.

I listened as Dave rattled on. He made it sound as if I'd be working for him, which wasn't necessarily a turn off as long as I had the same open door rapport with DeLorean. Davis never let up. He called everyday, urging me to join him. It was obvious DeLorean was really leaning on him.

On one of those calls he invited me to meet with agency President Tom Adams. I knew Adams pretty well during my earlier days at Campbell-Ewald, and found him to be a nice guy. Now he was agency president. What I thought was going to be a routine pep talk turned out to be the opposite.

"I understand John DeLorean is trying to convince you to come to work here," Adams started right in. "I don't want that. I don't want you here, nor do I have room for you. You wouldn't fit into our system anyway."

I was shocked, not only by his words, but by his attitude. I didn't know whether to get up and walk out or to dignify the conversation by continuing with it.

Adams was relentless in putting me down. Instead of stepping up honestly, telling me that he didn't think it was a good idea and trying to work it out professionally, he chose to be rude, almost hostile, hoping to convince me to forget it. Even though he was overdoing it, Adams' attitude pretty much convinced me there was no future there, regardless of what Dave Davis or DeLorean had promised.

I had to tell John about the meeting, even though I laughed at Tom's feigned hostility. "Don't worry about Adams," DeLorean said. "We can handle him. You'll spend most of your time with Davis anyway. As a matter of fact," he went on, as if this had just occurred to him, "I have an assignment for you right now. I want you to get familiar with every one of our 1970 products. I'll make the arrangements, you just go pick the cars up. I want you to give me an appraisal of each car." He wanted me to start working as a consultant, with an office at Campbell-Ewald,. It seemed that by giving me this "off the cuff" assignment, DeLorean was trying to relieve the pressure temporarily, while still holding the door open. Most importantly, he was giving me a reason to turn down Knudsen.

I got another call from Knudsen a couple days later. It was on a snowy Sunday morning inviting me to join him and his wife Florence for brunch at his home. "Iacocca is coming over," Knudsen added, "And I'd like you to meet him. Get here about 11 o'clock. Lee's upset, because I rejected the Maverick announcement advertising (Ford was about to release their new compact, Maverick). "Have you ever met him?" Knudsen asked.

"No," I answered. "But I feel like I know him." I had followed his meteoric rise at Ford over the past several years.

I timed myself to get there right at 11:00. As I drove my 1969 Carousel Red Royal Bobcat Judge into Knudsen's circular driveway, a new '69 Lincoln Continental Mark V followed me in.

Iacocca stepped out of the Lincoln and said, "I guess you're the guy I'm supposed to meet. I'm Lee Iacocca."

"I'm Jim Wangers." I smiled. "Nice to meet you."

Lee complained about having to catch a five o'clock plane for New York to spend time with his ad agency redoing the Maverick announcement advertising. (Out of this re-do effort came one of Ford's finest ad campaigns ever, "Maverick, The Simple Machine.")

"What I don't understand Lee," I said, "Is why you, the General Manager of the division has to go to New York to work with your ad agency. What about your ad guys?" It really was none of my business, but it was a logical question.

"I ran marketing for a while," Iacocca replied. "I know the creatives, and they listen to me. We'll get something back on track very quickly." That was about it. It was not a good time. Iacocca was very preoccupied. After he left for the airport, Knudsen admitted to me that Iacocca was a handful.

Iacocca's cool reception to my presence, plus the problem of working outside the system, plus Ernie Jones' surprising support for DeLorean, all added up to me making my first decision: "pass" on Ford.

I called Knudsen to tell him I wanted to come in.

"I hope you're not planning to tell me no," Knudsen said curtly. "Because if you are, I don't want you to even bother coming in." I told him that's what I had decided.

"What did you do, talk to DeLorean?"

I admitted DeLorean had virtually promised to get me into Chevrolet.

"Wangers, do you value my experience with General Motors?"

"Of course," I said.

"Will you believe me when I tell you there isn't a snowball's chance in hell DeLorean is going to get you that job inside Chevrolet?"

GTO
GM
There are few great moments in life. This is one of them.
There is only one thing more spectacular than owning a GTO. That's driving one. Even if you don't own it.
For a GTO was made to drive. Relentlessly. In fact, the more you drive it, the more eager and responsive it becomes. Like a sleek cat that achieves perfection by being put through a hoop.
A GTO handles itself well because of its 400 cubic inches of powerplant and specially designed suspension. You can order a 255-hp regular-gas version (only with Turbo Hydra-Matic), the standard 335-hp or the 360-hp Quadra-Power 400. All come with the GM safety package which includes folding seat back latches and GM's energy absorbing steering column.
When you drive this driving machine, you will understand the ultimate conceit of our calling it The Great One.
The Great One by Pontiac

From the first 1964 brochure, GTO advertising had always reflected a confident, almost arrogant attitude. This 1967 GTO ad was as close to showing action as we were allowed at the time.

F70 x 14 wide oval rubber is standard. Redlines or thinline whitewalls.
The Great One. Standard safety features include backup lights and a four-way hazard warning flasher.
Reclining passenger seat and head rests front seats cost extra. But why not indulge
The Rally I wheel in the eternal embrace of a wide oval whitewall. Extra-cost.
If you're wondering why we mounted the tach (extra-cost) on the hood, you're excused.
What other cars must feel like as they Great One slide by. Sliding by: the GTO
Our great Rally II wheels. Extra-cost. Wider whitewalls are available, but not on wide oval tires.
If you order the Ram Air option, the scoop becomes an actual good-grief-it's-real! scoop. See below.
Heavy-duty rear axle assembly. For service. Mandatory with 3.90:1 and 4.33:1.
You should try our already stiff suspension before you pay extra for the stiffer shock absorbers we have.
Extra-cost Ram Air option with functional scoop, high output cam, springs. 4.33:1 axle only.
Front wheel disc brakes are extra-cost and with power. The line forms on the right.
Pontiac GTO

Just as we had done for the Super Duty Catalina in 1962, this 1967 two-page color ad showcased our vast array of features, options and accessories for The Great One. This ad glamorized everything from a limited slip differential to an AM/FM/8-track stereo, and is a good example of Pontiac's unique and sophisticated marketing approach.

enormously capable Quadra-Power 400. Stan-
360-hp at 5100 rpm. 438 lb.-ft. at 3600 rpm.

You say you never get tired of looking at The Great One? Neither do we. Let's pause and admire.

The extra-cost custom sports steering wheel. Even though it's not real wood, it still looks sensational.

extra-cost heavy-duty 3-speed comes with a
mounted Hurst shifter at no extra cost.

The Hurst shifter climbing out of an extra-cost console covered with walnut wood grain styling.

The extra-cost Rally Cluster: fuel gauge, battery light, speedo, tach, oil pressure, water temperature.

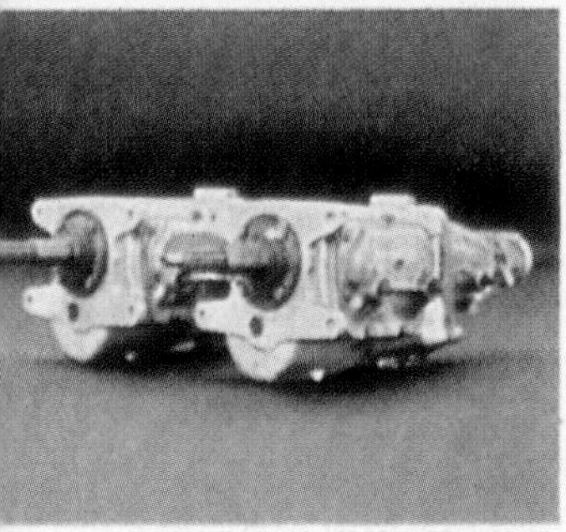

-cost 4-speeds. Wide ratio (2.52, 1.88, 1.46, 1).
e ratio (2.20, 1.64, 1.28, 1). Hurst shifters.

Extra-cost Turbo Hydra-Matic with Hurst quadrant. Right slot is for manual stick shift control.

Our 8-track stereo tape player. It sounds unbelievable even in an open convertible. Extra-cost.

ed Turbo Hydra-Matic. Extra-cost, any engine.
can get a 400 cu. in. 255-hp 2-bbl with it.

Standard safety features include a lane change feature incorporated in direction signal control.

Another standard safety feature is a dual master cylinder brake system with warning light.

Now you know what makes The Great One great.

The infamous Woodward Avenue ad. "Whew!"

You know the rest of the story.

There's only one Great One.
We've been proving it for five years.

As good looking as the 1968 GTO was, its provocative styling gave us some concern when we received negative backlash from traditional GTO owners. They disliked the "puffy and fat" look as compared to the taut, leaner lines of the 1964–67 models. To counter this, we created an ad in which we assembled the four previous year models with the new 1968. As it turned out, our fears were unfounded as 1968 GTO sales registered 87,684 units, second only to the record-setting 96,946 tallied for the 1966 model. Few GTO enthusiasts are aware that the 1964 GTO in this ad was the same famous Royal Bobcat used in the Car and Driver Pontiac vs. Ferrari road test (thanks to our retoucher's talent).

This is a classic example of what happens when you have to schedule advertising long before the product becomes available. Not only did we fail to have The Judge ready when this ad ran, but the prototypes shown in the ad didn't even have the correct stripes or emblems.

After the basic Firebird design was approved by GM, DeLorean added several touches that set it further apart from the Chevrolet Camaro. The major changes were to widen the track, lower the body stance, and add Firestone Wide-Oval tires as standard equipment. These improvements gave even the basic six-cylinder Firebird an aggressive look the Camaro lacked. In spite of a "buckboard" ride caused by the lowered suspension, the Firebird was a huge success its first year. Suspension changes the next year improved the ride.

The red 1964 "Car and Driver" GTO test car and the 1969 RA IV Royal Bobcat were probably the two most famous press cars prepared by Royal. The '64 GTO set off a firestorm of controversy and was instrumental in shaping the GTO legend. The Turquoise and White '69 appeared in 14 different magazine articles, earning respect and recognition for the RA IV engine. (painting by Dana Forrester)

The Firebird Trans Am and GTO Judge were introduced to the press at Riverside, California on December 8, 1968. Both weren't taken seriously by the press at the event. They were actually built as "hypes" to generate excitement and at the same time stimulate sales. While the Judge worked, the Trans Am was a surprising failure. Only 697 were built. (painting by Dana Forrester)

My personal 1969 Grand Prix was the inspiration behind the outstanding 1970 Hurst SSJ limited production Grand Prix. The 1970 SSJ included a 455 cubic inch engine, exclusive custom paint, special wheels and tires, special gold rally wheels, matching Hurst badges and other exclusive Hurst equipment. John DeLorean purposely borrowed the "J" and "SJ" designation from another great American classic, the Duesenberg.

I think the 1969 and 1970 performance brochures were the best we ever produced. The '69 brochure featured a collection of road tests written by the four top automotive magazines, Road & Track, Car and Driver, Hot Rod, and Motor Trend, each testing a different Pontiac performance model. The '70 brochure contained extensive use of technical information and specifications, highlighting the Ram Air IV engine and the GTO's high performance chassis and brakes. The 1970 performance brochure was the last one I would do for Pontiac.

The artist that designed the Judge graphics also painted this personal caricature for me of The Judge parked between the "Establishment" on the right and the "Hippies" on the left. Jim Roche, the Chairman of GM and champion of the Establishment, is giving a Bronx Cheer to a hip John DeLorean (wearing a black turtleneck). A much younger Jim Wangers appears to DeLorean's left, also wearing a turtleneck and beads.

In 1970, Hurst submitted two car concepts to Chrysler. The 300H was accepted, but the "Hurst Golden Charger," to everyone's disappointment, was rejected. The Charger was supposed to come with the 440 engine, and featured candy apple paint accent stripes, matching colored wheels, and a special rear deck spoiler. Although the car was rejected by Chrysler, the candy apple paint idea lived on to see better days, on the "Jim Wangers Chevrolet Milwaukee Classic."

I'm never afraid to borrow a good idea. Our Royal Bobcat emblem had been so hot in the Detroit area that in order to make the Milwaukee Classics stand out from the crowd even more, I copied the design.

The 1972 Monte Carlo Milwaukee Classic. All cars were white with either candy-apple red, tangerine or green painted accents. The car also had special wheels and tires, and a chrome radiator shell. The rear-wheel fender skirts were still available as an option from the factory at that time.

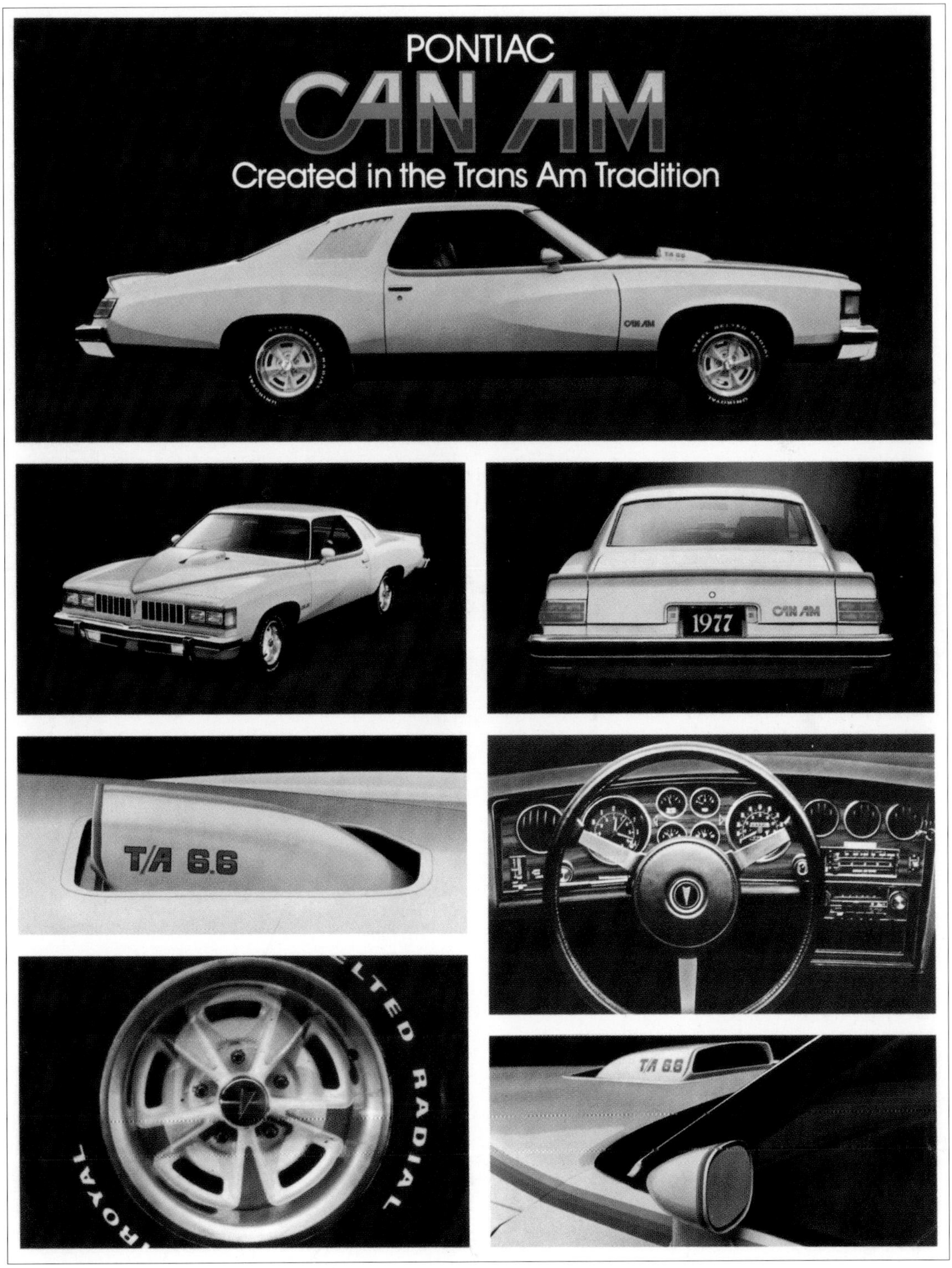

Motortown's second effort for Pontiac in 1977 was the Can Am, a name borrowed from a popular racing series of the time, and a car designed to hype the troubled Le Mans. The car proved to be a huge success when linked through advertising and marketing efforts to the early GTO. Production troubles within Motortown, however, resulted in only a very limited number of cars actually being built.

There's a little GTO in every GT-37.
And you don't have to be over 30 to afford it!
It's Pure Pontiac!
GM

Pontiac tried to burnish the image of the GT-37 by putting it in the same league as the original GTO, but they couldn't hide the fact that it was not at all like the "Goat." The program was short-lived.

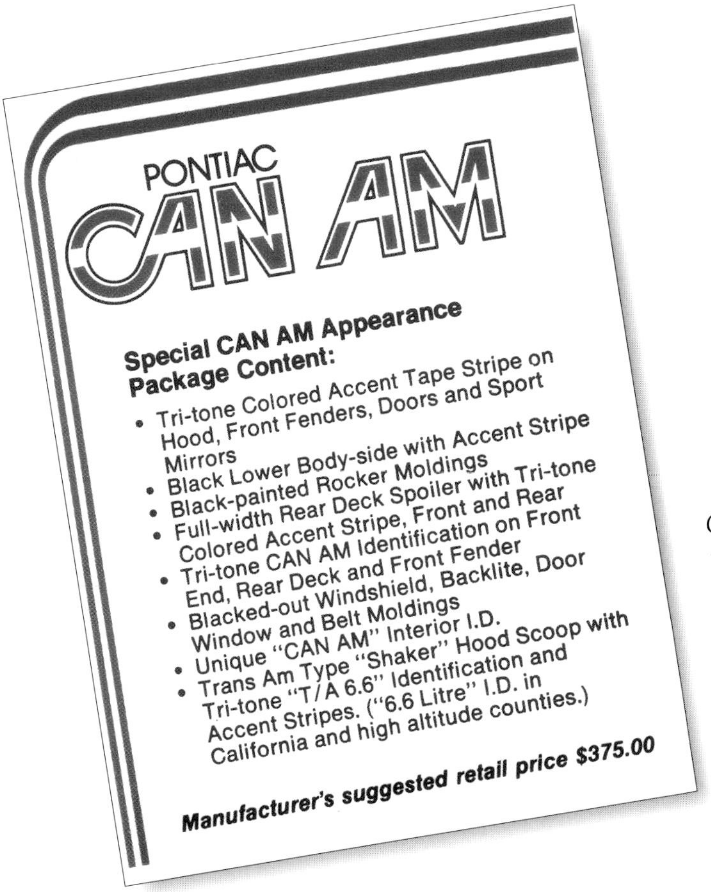

PONTIAC
CAN AM

Special CAN AM Appearance Package Content:

- Tri-tone Colored Accent Tape Stripe on Hood, Front Fenders, Doors and Sport Mirrors
- Black Lower Body-side with Accent Stripe
- Black-painted Rocker Moldings
- Full-width Rear Deck Spoiler with Tri-tone Colored Accent Stripe, Front and Rear
- Tri-tone CAN AM Identification on Front End, Rear Deck and Front Fender
- Blacked-out Windshield, Backlite, Door Window and Belt Moldings
- Unique "CAN AM" Interior I.D.
- Trans Am Type "Shaker" Hood Scoop with Tri-tone "T/A 6.6" Identification and Accent Stripes. ("6.6 Litre" I.D. in California and high altitude counties.)

Manufacturer's suggested retail price $375.00

Can Am window sticker details the various modifications made to the base Le Mans Sport Coupe. Retail price for the appearance package was $375.

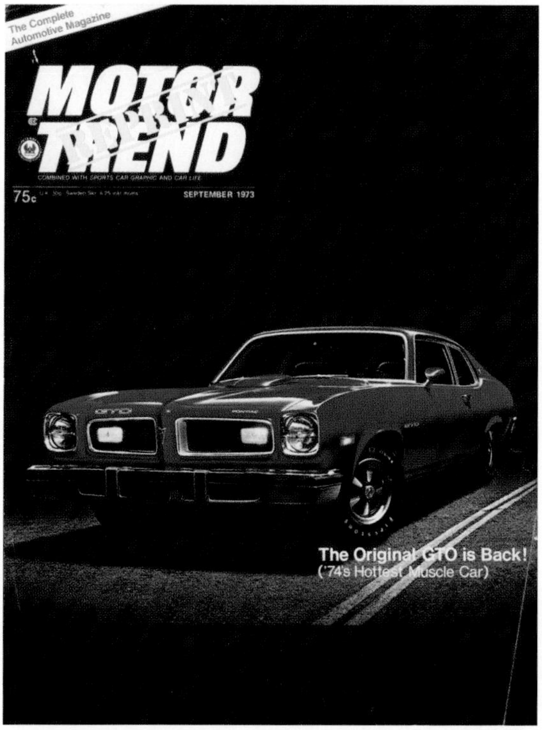

As a brand, the GTO's name had a powerful draw years after the car was introduced. For the 1974 model year Pontiac stuffed a 350 cubic inch engine into a Ventura and called it a GTO. Motor Trend's characterization to the contrary, no matter what, the car was still a 1968 Nova. In 1977, magazines were still comparing new perfomance cars to the GTO's image.

Dodge had the opportunity to put a 2.2 liter engine into their "L" car (Dodge 024 and Plymouth TC3) in 1982, and as an advisor to Kenyon-Eckhardt, Dodge's ad agency at the time, I told them they had a potential "GTO for the 1980s"....a small car with a big engine. So we created a name and a marketing package for the car, now called "Charger 2.2," using one of Dodge's best-known muscle-car nameplates of that era. It sold.

PONTIAC

Every new car dealer likes to see his name on the back of as many cars around town as possible. Others put pressure-sensitive stickers on the trunk. Still others have been known to drill holes in the sheet metal to mount chrome dealer emblems. I was no different. My dealer ID was a brushed, gold-embossed aluminum sticker. They have no collector value today, unlike an original Royal Pontiac license plate frame.

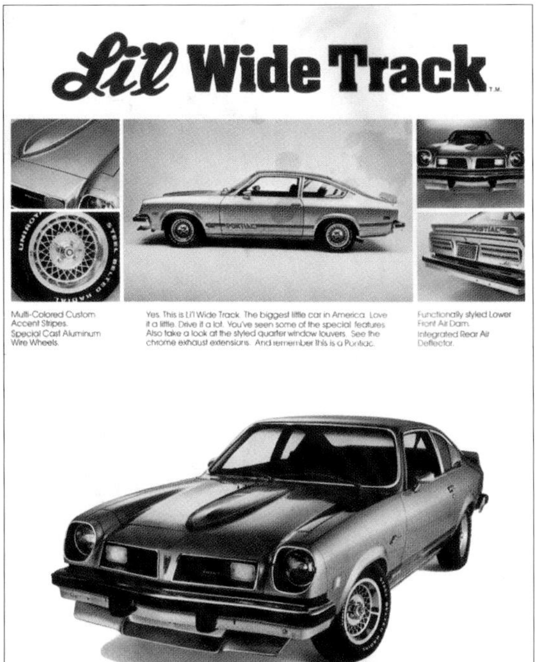
Li'l Wide Track TM
Multi-Colored Custom Accent Stripes.
Special Cast Aluminum Wire Wheels.
Yes. This is Li'l Wide Track. The biggest little car in America. Love it a little. Drive it a lot. You've seen some of the special features. Also take a look at the styled quarter window louvers. See the chrome exhaust extensions. And remember this is a Pontiac.
Functionally styled Lower Front Air Dam.
Integrated Rear Air Deflector.

Pontiac announces the beginning of tomorrow.
The all-new Firebirds are here.

My last advertising efforts for Pontiac centered around the introduction in mid-1970 of the new Firebird. This gatefold ad, which appeared in enthusiast magazines, introduces the new generation Firebird Trans Am and the car's new cousin, the Formula. I disagreed with the concept of the Formula, since it compromised the image of the Trans Am. I always said that the nicest thing you can call a Firebird is "Trans Am." The Formula only cheapened that image. Pontiac unfortunately continues this practice today, selling a Formula model that is less expensive than a similarly-equipped Camaro.

(Above) In a desperate effort to "hype" their slow moving Hornet, AMC created a special sporty hatchback coupe, and called it AMX. Negative backlash to "prostituting" that great name did more damage than good with loyal AMC followers. Sales of the "cosmetic coupe" were at best anemic. (Left) Five years after it first bowed as the Chevrolet Vega, the same car showed up as a Pontiac Astre, or rather a Vega with a split grille. By adding a few cosmetic "bolt-ons," an attractive, muscular looking little hatchback was created. Li'l Wide Track, as the car was called, clearly identified it as a member of the Pontiac family, and did in fact clearly separate it from Chevrolet.

Introducing the Rebel "Machine."
Standing before you is the car you've always wanted.
And, if you like everything about it, except for the paint job, which admittedly looks startling, you can order the car painted in the color of your choice.
You may be wondering why a company like American Motors would paint a car red, white and blue.
And that's what we keep asking ourselves: Why would a company like American Motors paint a car red, white and blue?
But we have nothing to be embarrassed about under the hood, which is all you should be concerned about.
The Machine has a 390 CID engine as standard equipment and develops a horsepower the equivalent of 340 horses all pulling in unison, which is no mean feat.
Next, and this will be particularly impressive to those people who have buried their heads in hot rod magazines since they were old enough to say "zoom . . . zoom . . . lookee it's a car," the Machine has a 4-speed all-synchromesh close-ratio transmission with special Hurst shift linkage and a 3.54:1 standard rear axle ratio (or an optional 3.91:1).
To feed air to your engine, and it will be your engine once you buy the car, we have bolted on a ram-air hood scoop. And in the hood scoop, we mounted a tach that's lighted and registers 8000 rpm's.
Heavy-duty shocks and springs raise the rear end a bit and give the Machine, a raked, just mowed the lawn look.
And our dual exhaust system uses special low back pressure mufflers and larger exhaust pipes.
We will make the description of the rest of the Machine's features mercifully short. Front and rear sway bars, high-back bucket seats, 15 inch tires with raised white letters, mag styled steel wheels, power disc brakes, and racing stripes that glow in the dark.
Incidentally, if you have delusions of entering the Daytona 500 with the Machine, or challenging people at random, the Machine is not that fast. You should know that.
For instance, it is not as fast on the getaway as a 427 Corvette, or a Hemi, but it is faster on the getaway than a Volkswagen, a slow freight train, and your old man's Cadillac.
In short, in order to fully make up your mind about the Machine, you will have to see it in person at your American Motors dealer.
And when you're introduced to it, a simple "How do you do?," "Nice meeting you," or something friendly like "How are your pipes?," will suffice.
Up with The Rebel Machine
For a set of four "Up with the Rebel Machine" decals send 25¢ and your name and address to: Machine Decal Offer, American Motors Sales Corporation, 14250 Plymouth Road, Detroit, Michigan 48232.

Bouncing off the success of their 1969 SC/Rambler, American Motors introduced their follow-up image effort, "The Machine," early in 1970. Originally planned to be released only in a flat black "primer" look, The Machine stumbled when AMC marketers dropped this potentially trend-setting idea. It would have been a first in a market segment where one-of-a-kind "spoof" specialty vehicles had been successful, as proven by the Plymouth Road Runner, The Judge, the Olds Rallye 350, and others. When the car instead was painted as a red-white-and-blue "hippy protester," it seemed only a retread of old ideas, and didn't do well in the marketplace.

Most luxury cars become luxury liners in the corners.
We gave our engineers a tall order. Combine the ride comfort of a luxury car with the precision handling of a sports car. And at the same time, make sure it starts under $20,000."
Their response, the 1995 Nissan Maxima.
All of a sudden, there aren't many luxury cars for anywhere near the price that can stay with it in the corners. And some pretty formidable price tags have tried, including the Acura Legend LS and the BMW 540i.
Our achievement can be attributed to a revolutionary Multi-Link Beam Suspension designed to maximize the handling capabilities of the Maxima's front-wheel drive. Even in the sharpest of turns, it helps keep the angle of the rear tires more perpendicular to the road, which gives the front tires much better steering response.
Car and Driver states, "this Maxima will do grievous injury to several upscale sedans that cost more but aren't as much fun. The Acura Legend comes instantly to mind."
For more information call 1-800-000-0000 or visit your nearest Nissan Dealer.
Arrange to take the new Maxima out for a little test cornering. And experience a whole new sensation. Luxury without seasickness.
The New Nissan Maxima
NISSAN
It's time to expect more from a car.

The 1995 Nissan Maxima featured a new rear suspension design, providing improved cornering and stability. Nissan engaged my firm AMCI to prove the handling of their Maxima in a side-by-side comparison test against two very well recognized luxury sedans. AMCI has conducted this type of comparison testing for just about every carmaker in the industry.

That wasn't what I wanted to hear. "I guess I just don't know what to say," I answered.

"You've already said it," Knudsen said bluntly. "I'm sorry you're making this decision, but at least you were pro enough to call me quickly. Good luck." Knudsen hung up on me.

I had now turned off Ford, with no assurance that DeLorean was going to deliver. Even though I was repelled by the situation at Campbell-Ewald, I agreed to take the temporary consulting assignment. DeLorean was ecstatic. "While you're there, get to know those guys, they'll like you. This might not be as tough as you think."

My decision was made and the pressure was off. I decided to take a little time to myself. But just when I thought the final twist was over and I could start to relax, a voice from my past came calling.

"You're the talk of the town," George Hurst exclaimed. "Every place I go, I get asked the same question. What is Jimmy Wangers going to do?" George Hurst had the painful habit of calling me "Jimmy," but somehow it seemed OK from him. "What's going on?"

"George," I replied, "I'm so screwed up, even I don't know what's going on." I decided to take George into my confidence. Before I even had a chance to tell my story, George popped right in and said, "Put all that stuff aside and come to work with me. I've been looking for a new President to replace me, and I can't think of a better guy. You understand our market, you understand Detroit, everybody who knows you likes you, and probably more important than any of those other reasons is that we're going public. There's really going to be some money around here. I also want to continue doing more of those special cars like the Hurst-Olds projects and I know you like doing those kinds of things."

Maybe George had something, I thought. He started to apply the pressure. "I'll give you some stock, and you'll have the chance to buy some more. You can own a piece of a company you're actually managing. Isn't that everybody's dream?"

The more he talked, the better it sounded. George's enthusiasm and my determined effort to stand up to DeLorean swayed my decision. I felt that if DeLorean wanted me bad enough he would find a way. That was stupid and naive thinking.

As I think back about it, what I really should have done was to set up a consulting arrangement directly with DeLorean at Chevrolet, rather than through the ad agency. But, truthfully, I was scared, scared to strike out alone and start my own business. I had become used to that "warm womb" of security that comes with working for a big company. My whole existence revolved around that weekly paycheck. I was just not ready to become an entrepreneur. I had no experience as a consultant and couldn't believe my talent or my knowledge was marketable. What a costly mistake that turned out to be, as I found out just a few years later.

So I allowed George to convince me. After reaching that decision, I went to DeLorean and told him, hopefully for the last time, "I just don't want to get started with Campbell-Ewald."

"Wangers," responded DeLorean, somewhat impatiently "I'll never understand you. You're going back into the minor leagues." I have never forgotten that remark.

So that's what I did. I bought George Hurst's deal, accepting the role as Director of Marketing. The only thing left to do was get on a plane to Philadelphia to meet the other important Hurst people. A new chapter was opening, and I had no idea what I was getting into.

11

Dealing Myself Out

Reality Hits At Hurst

I HAD KNOWN GEORGE HURST for almost ten years and was still enthralled by him. He had always been committed to building quality products, and his company always did a great marketing job. Virtually every male baby boomer had grown up with a Hurst shifter in their hands. What a great base for new products and new marketing ideas.

I had been personally responsible for much of Hurst's early success, first by introducing him to John DeLorean, and then in convincing Pete Estes to tell the world about Pontiac using Hurst shifters right from the factory. In many ways, Hurst had become a symbol for Pontiac sophistication, and vice versa.

Early in my association with George, he asked me to help him find a young, ambitious assistant. He was about to open a Detroit office and wanted to find just the right person to manage it. He wanted to personally train them. I introduced him to a bright guy named Jack Watson, who had been sort of a Royal Pontiac "groupie." They got along very well, and it wasn't much later that Jack was invited to move to the home office in Warminster, Pennsylvania. Watson fit into the rapidly expanding company very well, later emerging as "The Shifty Doctor," a public relations program that became one of the best in the history of the performance industry. Now, George wanted to pay me back, to end up as his replacement at the company, guiding Hurst to new heights, both within the auto industry and in the consumer marketplace.

I had been invited to stay at George's luxurious home, where I met Lila, his third wife. She was a gracious hostess and immediately made me feel very comfortable after my trip from Detroit. She told me that George had some business to tend to at the office, and that he would arrive later for dinner. Lila and I chatted for a while about nothing in particular, when she suddenly started to share some ugly facts with me. She revealed that George had become a hopeless alcoholic, and that she was doing everything she could to get him into an institution to dry out.

As our conversation deepened, the more frightening it got. The company had apparently soured on George, and the Board of Directors was actively working to squeeze him out. She pleaded with me to join the company to hopefully prevent that from happening. She was a sharp lady, and she loved George. She was dedicated to taking care of him. She also claimed that George's first partner, Bill Campbell, had been forced out already, falsely accused of all kinds of things including embezzlement. Even though he received a six million dollar severance check, Campbell left the company hurt that his lifelong friend George Hurst would allow this to happen. According to Lila, George was "too drunk" to realize what was going on.

Around 11:00 pm after Lila had whipped up a nice dinner, I said, "Honestly, Lila where is George? Is he coming back tonight?" She broke down and revealed that George had come home dead drunk even before I arrived, and had passed out in the bathtub. She couldn't move him, so she had left him there to sleep it off. I offered to help her get him into bed, but she didn't want me to see him in that condition. She assured me he'd be OK in the morning, and sure enough he was, acting as if nothing was wrong.

My first intention was to run away from this as fast as I could. I realized how badly I had been mislead. It was another example of how I let my emotions and my ego overpower my logic. But George, when sober, convinced me that this was just a passing thing and that he had it under control. Lila continued to plead with me to stay, if for no other reason than to help George save his position in the company "After all," she said, "He still does have controlling interest, and he started the damn company. He needs you to help him save it."

This Jekyll and Hyde persona was hard for me to grasp. It was no surprise that George liked to drink. When in Detroit on business he always had a bottle of Jack Daniels in his hotel room. At dinner, regardless of who was present, he'd have maybe four or five drinks, but it never seemed to affect him. George had always been fun loving, he made no bones about that. But he was also a pro. He knew when to quit playing. He was articulate, especially when he was passionate about a product or an idea. But he had fallen victim to the bottle. My exposure to him had only been when he came into Detroit, and that was when he was the dynamic George Hurst I had always known. It was under those circumstances that he had prevailed upon me to join his company.

As we drove to the plant for my first meeting George was his usual self, joking about "last night." But as he introduced me around it was apparent that there was little rapport between George and his top people. The old George Hurst, who had built his company selling floor shifters to Detroit, was tired.

Instead of paying attention to the internal strife developing in his company, George had a new toy. He spent most of his time perfecting his new "Jaws of Life," a device that aided rescuers in extracting injured people trapped in wrecked cars. Nobody else in the company could see the Jaws as a profit making venture, but George, much to his credit, saw it as a contribution to society and was determined to see it through. That was the George Hurst I used to know. Unfortunately, helping the bottom line was particularly important at this time since there were plans underway to take the company public.

I spent the remainder of that week in Philadelphia, returning to Detroit on Friday. The next day Lila checked George into an alcohol rehabilitation clinic.

With George's diminishing control over his company, his plan for me to succeed him seemed unlikely to happen, to say the least. It was obvious from people's reactions in Warminster that they felt I had been forced on them by George, so I quickly dismissed any plan to move to Pennsylvania. The atmosphere in the main office was too hostile, and until—or if—George got back to work, that was not going to change.

In Hurst's Detroit operation, however, the atmosphere was different. I walked in there with the title of Director of Marketing, full of ideas on how to expand their program of building limited production special cars for Detroit. This was an activity that was about to take off.

Some Hurst Specials

The government's new interest in emission controls and safety requirements clearly placed the Feds in the car business. All of the carmakers were suddenly required to spend a disproportionate amount of their engineering man hours meeting these new government standards. There was no talent available to concentrate on projects like sophisticated show cars or much needed marketing hypes. I could see the opportunity for Hurst with its impeccable reputation for quality and performance as being in the ideal position to fill this void.

They were already building the Hurst Olds, and had just sold American Motors the compact SC/Rambler, also known as "The Mailbox," because of its bizarre hood scoop. This car was created in the same philosophy as the Pontiac Judge, which was simply to stuff a big engine (a 390 cubic inch V-8) into a little car (the Rambler American) and dress it up like a circus horse. The SC/Rambler was a huge success, so the folks at AMC wanted a repeat in 1970, this time built off their slow moving intermediate Matador/Rebel series. "The Machine" was aimed almost entirely at the "protest" generation, perhaps even going a little too far. Unlike the SC/Rambler it was a flop.

Most of Hurst's work involved performance oriented cars, such as building the famous Plymouth Hemi Barracuda and Dodge Hemi Dart. They also had a contract from Mr. Norm's Grand Spaulding Dodge, in Chicago, to install the 440 cubic inch engine in a production Dodge Dart. He ordered a couple hundred Darts and had them shipped directly to Hurst, where the 440 cubic inch engines and transmissions were installed.

And of course there was the Hurst Olds. The story of the third Hurst Olds is a sad one. We spent an incredible amount of time preparing a very timely and exciting new car, featuring a new yellow color with matching deep purple and black accents. With increasing pressures from the safety and in-

10. Power disc brakes (front).
11. Rear axle torque links.
12. Handling package (heavy-
luty front sway bar plus heavy-
luty springs and shocks).
13. Heavy-duty cooling
ystem(heavy-duty radiator,
There's more, but you get the idea.
With this car you could make life
miserable for
any GTO,
Roadrunner,
Cobra Jet or
Mach 1.
American Motors'/Hurst
SC/Rambler

Some Hurst Specials

As a Vice President with Hurst, I was there when Hurst built several special promotions cars for various manufacturers. One such was the SC/Rambler, an American coupe called the Rogue, with a 390 cubic inch V-8. It was outfitted with special paint and a bizarre hood scoop known as the "mail box" for obvious reasons. The car was a spoof on the musclecar culture and led to 2500 sales. AMC considered it a huge success.

Hurst's follow-up effort to the SC/Rambler was on the AMC Matador. Called "The Rebel Machine," this 1970 car proved to be a flop. In a sense it was a lot like the 1969 GTO Judge, a hype on the musclecars of the day. Times and tastes were changing faster than we could create cars.

surance folks, as well as fear of rising fuel prices, we proposed using the 350 cubic inch engine package, called the W-31. The car also introduced Oldsmobile's first body colored bumpers. After much review, Oldsmobile decided to go with the car, but not as a Hurst Olds. They wanted to build it in house and label it the Rallye 350. For Hurst, this kind of "thanks, but no thanks" decision was a slap in the face, especially since the car was a huge sales success.

One of the more interesting projects we created was the 1970 Chrysler

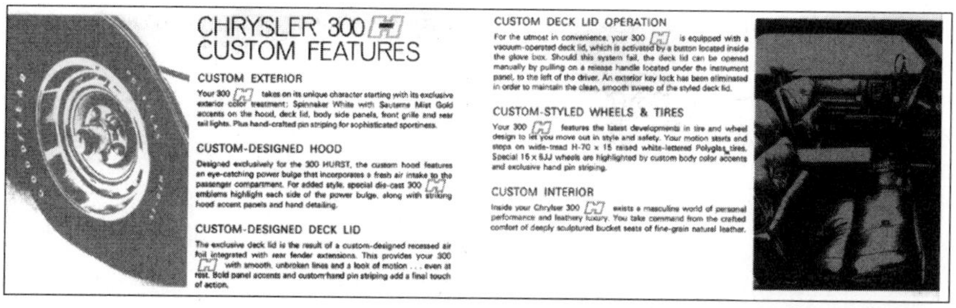

CHRYSLER 300
CUSTOM FEATURES

CUSTOM EXTERIOR

Your 300 takes on its unique character starting with its exclusive exterior color treatment: Spinnaker White with Sauterne Mist Gold accents on the hood, deck lid, body side panels, front grille and rear tail lights. Plus hand-crafted pin striping for sophisticated sportiness.

CUSTOM-DESIGNED HOOD

Designed exclusively for the 300 HURST, the custom hood features an eye-catching power bulge that incorporates a fresh air intake to the passenger compartment. For added style, special die-cast 300 emblems highlight each side of the power bulge, along with striking hood accent panels and hand detailing.

CUSTOM-DESIGNED DECK LID

The exclusive deck lid is the result of a custom-designed recessed air foil integrated with rear fender extensions. This provides your 300 with smooth, unbroken lines and a look of motion . . . even at rest. Bold panel accents and custom hand pin striping add a final touch of action.

CUSTOM DECK LID OPERATION

For the utmost in convenience, your 300 is equipped with a vacuum-operated deck lid, which is activated by a button located inside the glove box. Should this system fail, the deck lid can be opened manually by pulling on a release handle located under the instrument panel, to the left of the driver. An exterior key lock has been eliminated in order to maintain the clean, smooth sweep of the styled deck lid.

CUSTOM-STYLED WHEELS & TIRES

Your 300 features the latest developments in tire and wheel design to let you move out in style and safety. Your motion starts and stops on wide-tread H-70 x 15 raised white-lettered Polyglas tires. Special 15 x 6JJ wheels are highlighted by custom body color accents and exclusive hand pin striping.

CUSTOM INTERIOR

Inside your Chrysler 300 exists a masculine world of personal performance and leathery luxury. You take command from the crafted comfort of deeply sculptured bucket seats of fine-grain natural leather.

The Chrysler 300 series has always stood for elegant power, starting with the original 300 in 1955, which became the 300B in 1956, the C in 1957, and so on. Next in line for lettering was H, and it was natural for Hurst to propose a 300H for 1970. Based on the New Yorker, it came with the biggest engine available in the Chrysler car line (a 440 cubic inch V-8). These pages from an original brochure detail the other special features: a tan and brown leather interior, a beige paint exterior, an integrated spoiler, and an integrated hood scoop. With sales of around 2,500 units, the car successfully continued the 300 nameplate (which Chrysler reintroduced in 1998).

300 H (H for Hurst). The 300, while mostly a stripe and decal package, also featured an interesting hood and rear deck. It was an exceptionally good looking car.

Meanwhile, in Pennsylvania things deteriorated fast. George was very slow to recover, and during the process the company was sold out from under him to the Sunbeam Electric Company, of Chicago. Sunbeam, while a reasonably successful electric appliance company, never understood what they had in Hurst, and proceeded to literally destroy it by doing nothing. Poor George was never again a factor, which in itself was a pity. He did walk away with some significant money, but neither the company nor George would ever be the same.

Even though I was still not sure what I wanted to do, I knew that it was not going to be with Hurst, or I should say with Sunbeam. As I prepared to leave, I reflected back on what a tremendous opportunity this could have been. Actually, Sunbeam was a perfect partner for Hurst. Now they could expand their product line to keep up with the huge maturing youth market.

Imagine the Hurst name, unmatched for quality and durability in the minds of these young males, adorning a new electric shaver, or a hair dryer, or a lawn mower. Unfortunately, it didn't happen, and today Hurst is just another automotive aftermarket supplier, owned by the Mr. Gasket Co.

IT WAS TRULY A LOW POINT IN MY LIFE. It seemed like everything I believed in was collapsing, including my beloved Pontiac. The emergence of Jim McDonald as the top man at Pontiac triggered a new philosophy—or seemingly lack of philosophy—about selling cars. McDonald was not a marketer, nor did he surround himself with marketers. Sales Manager Frank Bridge had retired, replaced by Elmer "Pat" Pettingill, who, while a nice guy, was in many ways a carbon copy of Bridge. He never slowed down long enough to understand that selling a Pontiac was not like selling a Chevrolet. Because the new regime didn't understand or appreciate the *emotional* appeal of a car called Pontiac, they didn't realize the personal involvement these cars commanded from their loyal owners and intended buyers.

The McDonald regime at Pontiac had a new mandate: "The frivolous, fun days of the sixties are over. It's now a serious new world of common sense, conservation, and reappraisal. Our job is not to 'like' cars. Our job is to sell them." Pontiac's brand image as a builder of sophisticated, high performance automobiles was crumbling, in spite of the mid-year 1971 introduction of the absolutely magnificent, low-compression 455 cubic inch H.O. engine. Most customers hadn't heard about the engine because no one at Pontiac wanted to buck the corporation's ban on high performance images, and there were no Royal Bobcats spreading the word around in the car magazines. Talk about a lost opportunity!

One of the big mistakes McDonald made when he first came to Pontiac was to try to sell more cars by reducing prices, and the only way he could reduce prices was to de-content the cars. For example, into the Tempest/Le Mans world came the stripped down T-37 model, and into the GTO world came the decontented GT-37. Both went nowhere, and only served to compromise Pontiac's already sagging image.

As I watched from the sidelines, the serious lack of continuity and communication between advertising, marketing, and sales was becoming apparent. I tried to not let it bother me. After all, it was just business, just another car company. But when I thought about the Herculean effort we had poured into building the tremendous Wide-Track Pontiac image of the sixties, watching it reduced to mediocrity was like looking at the loss of part of me.

Perhaps the most damaging move McDonald made while at Pontiac was to compromise the Bonneville. Not only was Bonneville the best recognized Pontiac and the flagship of the Pontiac line, it was also one of the best consumer-recognized brands in the entire automotive market. All of Pontiac's research proved that Pontiac enjoyed one of the industry's best owner loyalty ratings. After attracting a new buyer into an entry level Tempest or Catalina, Pontiac would hopefully keep them in the family as they worked their way up to the Bonneville. Unfortunately, there was no place to go after the Bonnev-

F. James McDonald (left) assumed the role of Pontiac's General Manager in the post-DeLorean era, early in the 1969 model year. McDonald, who had been manufacturing manager at both Chevrolet and Pontiac, didn't share the enthusiasm for the product as DeLorean did, nor did he ever understand or respect the image of Pontiac. In a confused marketplace, McDonald's approach was to cut content and price on all models. Despite pleas from both inside and outside the Division to retain some emotion, Pontiac ultimately lost its Wide-Track excitement image, leading to a downturn which lasted more than 20 years. Despite his results at Pontiac, McDonald eventually wound up as President of General Motors, serving under infamous Chairman Roger Smith.

illc except into another Bonneville, and that would work maybe once. Certainly Pontiac didn't want these customers going to Olds or Buick just to satisfy their need to step up.

Part of this problem was addressed while I was still working on the Pontiac account. To enhance the Bonneville image, the Brougham option was added. This included more standard equipment, a higher line interior, a vinyl top, and a couple of tasteful emblems. The engine of course was always Pontiac's largest, but not necessarily featuring the highest horsepower. That didn't seem to be important to the upscale Bonneville buyer.

Pontiac desperately needed a new luxury look for the Bonneville. GM had two full-size bodies at that time. They were labelled the B-body and the

Cost Cutting Injures Image

McDonald's determined efforts to lower the price image of Pontiac resulted in the introduction of a new series of Tempest coupes, starting first with the T-37 (T stood for Tempest, 37 was the in-house code for a Hardtop Coupe). The car was supposed to be a poor man's version of a GTO, with a base interior, low-line exterior trim and only modest power from its Pontiac 350 cubic inch V-8. It proved unsuccessful, so Pontiac followed up with the GT-37 with a 400 cubic inch engine and upper-level trim. But this car failed, too, and ultimately Pontiac was not able to produce a substitute for the real GTO. This year (1972) also saw the "great rear spoiler debacle." The neat-looking wing, nicely integrated into the rear deck, was pictured in the new car catalog, in early advertisements, and appeared on several press cars. Due to a supplier problem, the decision was made not to mass-produce the spoiler.

C-body. The B-body was used on the smaller full-size cars, such as the Chevrolet Impala, Pontiac Catalina, Olds 88, and Buick Le Sabre. The longer looking Bonneville was created by simply stretching the wheelbase and rear overhang of the Catalina. The only thing that was bigger on the Bonneville was the trunk space. It was easy for a competitive Olds or Buick dealer to put down the Bonneville by calling it a stretched Catalina, and they were right.

The C-body cars were longer, more luxurious, and had a more formal roof, like the Cadillac DeVille, Olds 98, and Buick Electra 225. All three of these competitive C-body models were vying for the Pontiac Bonneville owner. Pontiac had pleaded with the corporation for years to use the C-body, but to no avail.

One of the last things DeLorean accomplished before moving to Chevrolet was to win approval from the Corporation to use the C-body upper (the greenhouse) on the Bonneville's extended B-body. It was an inexpensive way of providing the Bonneville with a new roof line that was obviously different than the Catalina. Unfortunately, it had to wait for the next new body change, which was scheduled for 1971.

Under McDonald's leadership, the market planners at Pontiac figured "a new roof...a new car...a new name." The Bonneville nameplate, which had been golden with the car-buying public for 12 years, was to be compromised. The fact that the name Bonneville had become so clearly imaged as the very best Pontiac didn't seem to be important. It was to be reduced to a mid-level model.

The new C-body variant was not to be marketed as it was conceived, as "The Mother of all Bonnevilles," but rather to introduce a new higher-line model with a new name. That would have been fine if they needed to replace a mediocre nameplate floundering in failure. But that was not the case with Bonneville. None of McDonald's team had enough Pontiac moxie to realize how destructive this move would prove to be.

Pontiac had already had some experience with this in 1966, when they chose to replace the mid-level Starchief name. Then it was the same car with a new name: the Executive. Pontiac buyers perceived the name Executive as a new model placed above the Bonneville—after all the Executive is the top guy. This confusion, totally of Pontiac's own making, affected early Bonneville sales, even though the Executive was visually several steps below the Bonneville. Pontiac learned a very valuable lesson that later was forgotten: Don't mess with the Bonneville!

Grand Ville Mistake

They introduced their new C-body variation in 1971, this time intended as a step up from the Bonneville. It was called Grand Ville. When traditional Bonneville customers brought their older models in to trade, they were confronted not only with a new name, but also with what looked like a new kind of Pontiac. Gone was the sporty look of the Bonneville, replaced by the formal look of a poor-man's Olds 98 or Buick Electra. First year Bonneville sales were cut in half, and Grand Ville and Bonneville sales combined barely edged out the previous year's total Bonneville volume.

It took real car people to build Pontiac success, and blue serge robots to cripple it. The Grand Ville name was a mistake from the beginning. It never enjoyed total acceptance and was finally dropped after the 1975 model, but not before it had virtually wiped out the sophisticated impact of the name Bonneville. No matter what the top-of-the-line Pontiac looked like, it had to be called Bonneville. It would take Pontiac more than sixteen years to rediscover that.

They continued to punish the nameplate with one misguided, off-target effort after another until 1987, when finally a new car, conceived in the heritage of the great Wide-Track Bonnevilles of the 1960s, appeared in showrooms. Amazingly, the sophisticated and sporty image of those great early cars had survived the many attempts to destroy it. Once again, a great nameplate adorned a worthy car, and that combination has led to continued sales success.

The GTO suffered serious setbacks in the early seventies, due to pressure from the "safety police" and new-found muscle from the Auto Insur-

General Motors cut back engine compression on all their cars in 1971 in order to make the best use of the new low-lead fuels. A compression ratio of no more than 8.5:1, needless to say, affected the performance cars most of all. However, the appearance of the Pontiac 455 H.O. engine had performance that still blew everyone away. Pontiac's engineers used plenty of tricks to build the low-compression engine that ended up powering the second-best performing GTO of all time. The engine made Pontiac the fastest car you could buy out of the showroom in 1971. But because of Pontiac's management at the time, and GM's corporate ban on high performance, the real story of this engine never got out to the public. With the dramatic new functional Ram Air hood scoop, you can bet that if Royal Pontiac had still been around everyone in the world who cared would have known about this car!

ance Companies. But just because compression ratios and horsepower ratings dropped, and the "Goat" got bigger and heavier, it didn't lose all its performance. In fact, record books confirm that a 1971 GTO with the 455 cubic inch H.O. engine was the second fastest GTO ever offered, losing out only to the 1969–70 Ram Air IV cars in a quarter mile comparison. The product was still there thanks to that great engine, but the support was gone. If there was ever a time for the image leader to make a comeback, it was then. Unfortunately, there was no one in Pontiac marketing who thought that way. Instead, they chose to let the car wallow around through 1972, when it returned to being offered as a Le Mans option.

After struggling through declining 1971 and 1972 sales, 1973 really became the pits for the once prince of the line GTO. Pontiac's A-body Tempest/Le Mans had been totally redesigned in 1973, and the car immediately became controversial. Many critics likened it to a Hershey chocolate bar that had been held in a blazing hot summer sun, and had drooped on both ends.

The proposed GTO package was scheduled to introduce another breakthrough approach to a soft nose. The expensive Endura rubber nose was replaced by a new hi-tech flexible plastic material, the forerunner of RIM (Reaction Injection Molded) plastic that is so popular today. Certainly the new 1973 GTO front end was reminiscent of the sensational 1968 car.

By the early 1970s, Europe's leading luxury nameplates were beginning to attract attention in the U.S. market. Both Mercedes-Benz and BMW were bragging about their new "Sport Sedans." In the U.S., it was always thought that a sporty car should have two doors, either a coupe or a convertible. The idea of a sporty sedan was indeed something new. In Europe, where one-car families were more common, the traditional family four-door sedan also had to be the "fun-to-drive" car. Now that good handling, practical four-door sedan, already popular in Europe, was coming to America. The planners at Pontiac recognized this trend, and pushed to be the first American carmaker to offer a "sports sedan." A four-door version of the proposed new GTO was just the ticket, but certainly it should not be called GTO. A four-door GTO? No Way! So to accommodate this new concept the dramatic new front end, which perhaps could have led to the reinvention of the GTO, was taken away.

When Pontiac's new sport sedan bowed as a 1973 model, it was called Grand Am, taking full advantage of the dramatic new front end styling. A matching coupe, also named Grand Am, soon followed, and together they sold over 40,000 units. Interestingly, almost eighty percent of those sales were coupes. Apparently the sport sedan was a little ahead of its time.

The GTO, stripped of just about everything but a hokey air intake system and its great nameplate, was pathetically allowed to crawl over to the side of the road and die. Less than 5,000 were sold. On the serious side, one wonders if this package had been allowed to appear as the GTO, would it have changed Pontiac history?

Another sad story connected to this project was the fate of the fabulous 455 cubic inch Super Duty Engine package. Pontiac engineers felt that the new 1973 A-body car provided a good base for this engine, and recommended it be released in both the Grand Am and the GTO, in addition to the Firebird. One of the popular car magazines, *High Performance Cars,* had the opportunity to drive the GTO engineering prototype, and were so impressed, they named it their "Performance Car of the Year." That award turned out to be an embarrassment, because Pontiac chose not to relcase the engine in either the GTO or the Grand Am, restricting it only to the Firebird—and then making it available very late in the model year.

When Pontiac desperately needed an image leader in the early seventies, the product was there, but the commitment was not. Of course, the unexpected oil crisis in late 1973 put the final nail in the coffin, though Pontiac didn't put up much of a fight.

Instead of embracing the heritage of the great Wide-Track Pontiacs of the sixties, management chose to dump it almost as if they were ashamed to admit that such frivolous, fuel swilling cars ever wore a Pontiac nameplate. They built the same cars, but promoted them with new names and a new ad-

The American car market was seeing the first successful new "Sport Sedan" entries from European companies such as BMW and Mercedes-Benz, so by 1973 Pontiac wanted to be the first American carmaker to exploit this new market. The new soft-nose front end was stolen from the proposed new GTO, to highlight the dramatic styling of the new Grand Am model, released as both a 2- and 4-door (a 4-door GTO seemed totally inappropriate). Early proposals for Grand Am iterations included a Super Duty 455 engine. Lack of management support resulted in that engine never being used in this car. In 1974, Grand Am's semi-sporty personality resulted in its death, another victim of the fuel crisis and a poor Pontiac management decision.

Martin J. Caserio succeeded F. James McDonald as General Manager of Pontiac in 1973. McDonald had since moved to Chevrolet. Caserio came from the GMC truck division, and felt the same way about Pontiac's exciting youth-oriented image as McDonald had: uninspired. Caserio sat on the release of the now-infamous Super Duty 455 cubic inch V-8. It was ready for release in early 1973, but the gutsy days of DeLorean and Estes were gone. This was a controversial engine, Pontiac's ultimate high-performer, and it was kept under wraps by Caserio until late in the 1973 model year.

vertising face, naively expecting the marketplace to accept them as more socially conscious and contemporary. They completely underestimated the intelligent loyalty of Pontiac's many satisfied owners. Pontiac began to suffer a true identity crisis, manufactured in their own conference rooms.

In those dark days of the early seventies, no one could have imagined that less than five years later the Firebird, led by the now highly imaged Trans Am would help spark a significant, though short-lived sales comeback for the Division. When the T/A, as it had come to be called, matured in the marketplace, two very specific features became synonymous with the car, the now famous "Shaker" hood scoop, and the distinctive (if not always tasteful) "Screaming Chicken" decal. It was satisfyingly apparent that the success of this sophisticated "Boy Racer" was a reconfirmation of the GTO all over again. I certainly don't want to suggest that the infamous hood scoop and decal alone made this exciting car; the performance was there to match. It certainly wasn't a paper tiger.

The "Goat" at its worst. After decimating the 1973 GTO by stealing every good feature for the new Grand Am project, Pontiac had the gall to bring this mess to market.

Firebird and Trans Am Still Flourish

Thanks to the devoted persistence of Pontiac Engineering, three exciting performance powerplants were made available for both the Trans Am and Formula models. During this period of low compression, low emission engines, resulting in a downplay of performance in the market, Pontiac stayed in front. Following the 455 H.O. package was the highly controversial "Dream Engine," the revered Super Duty 455. After that came the surprising 400 cubic inch T/A 6.6. During this mid- to late-seventies period, the Pontiac Trans Am and Formula models were considered the fastest American cars you could buy out of any new car showroom.

In late 1972, Jim McDonald, having been General Manager while Pontiac was brought to its knees, was promoted to the top job at Chevrolet, following John DeLorean, who had been moved upstairs to join the GM staff. Martin J. Caserio moved over from the GMC Truck Division to assume leadership of Pontiac. The entire U.S. auto industry had a record breaking sales year in 1973, and Pontiac (and Caserio) got carried right along with it, but for Pontiac it was short lived. There would be three more "down" years before Pontiac rose once again on the back of the Firebird as it grew to become the "darling" of the performance set in the late seventies.

Ironically, the Firebird (and Chevrolet's Camaro) almost met an untimely death. Sales were already floundering in 1972 when the UAW struck GM's Norwood, Ohio plant where all F-cars were assembled. The strike lasted well into the 1973 model year, as literally thousands of Firebirds and Camaros sat frozen in various stages of assembly. Tragically, all would have to be scrapped, since the 1974 model year ushered in a new federal bumper standard, and these cars could not be updated. (The corporate bean counters had studied the future of the F-body and determined that the market

Fantastic Super Duty Ignored

The 455 Super Duty first showed up in late 1973, then reappeared in the new slant-nose 1974 Trans Am and Formula models, only to meet an early death with the advent of tougher emission standards. Needless to say, well-preserved '73 and '74 Firebirds with matching number Super Duty 455 engines are high on any musclecar collector's list. The absolute identification of a true Super Duty is the clearly marked "X" in the middle of its serial number.

showed no signs of growth. Therefore, they recommended that both Camaro and Firebird be dropped at the end of the 1973 model run, rather than incur the cost of engineering a new shock absorbing front bumper assembly.)

Were it not for the hard work of a handful of engineers and product planners, led by Chevrolet's Alex C. Mair and Pontiac's Bill Collins, neither car would have survived. Mair and Collins convinced the Corporation that the F-body cars were more than just musclecars, and deserved another chance. Mair later became General Manager of Pontiac in time to enjoy the fruits of his efforts, as Pontiac's Firebird began its miraculous late seventies sales climb.

The end was near. In an effort to keep the GTO name alive, and right in the middle of the fuel crisis, Pontiac engineers took a Ventura, stuffed a 350 cubic inch Pontiac engine into it, and called it a GTO. Even with the 350 engine (other choices were even smaller), "Shaker" hood scoop, and proper decal i.d., no matter what you did to this car it was still a '68 Nova. GTO aficionados rejected the car outright. Ironically, it was actually a nice little car. To this day, few know that it was a 1974 GTO that captured the Pure Stock title at the NHRA 1974 summer Nationals at Indianapolis. The oil shortage and spiraling gas prices won the war; the GTO expired for good in the summer of 1974.

It is also interesting to note that Chevrolet actually dropped their top of the line Z/28 model in 1975, only to be ordered by an intuitive corporate marketing staff to reinstate it in 1976. "Those guys at Pontiac are going to bury you, and literally run away with that market," they were told, "and that's not good for Chevrolet's long term image."

In 1974, Pontiac decided to bring back still another compromised GTO. The Corporation had forced the X-body (Nova) on Buick, Olds, and Pontiac, and no matter what each Division did with their car, they all ended up looking like a Chevy Nova. In fact, they all ended up with model names that started with the letters that spelled the word N-O-V-A: "N" for the Chevy Nova, "O" for the Oldsmobile Omega, "V" for the Pontiac Ventura, and "A" for the Buick Apollo.

Pontiac took their X-body and tried one more time to recreate the GTO as it had been conceived in 1964, as a lightweight, low-cost, hi-performance car. The Ventura seemed to be just right. Like brewing up a bowl of soup, they searched the pantry shelf for features and items consistent with the image of the early Goat. They grabbed the "Shaker" hood scoop from the Trans Am, the 4-barrel 350 cubic inch engine from the Le Mans, Rally II wheels, trick decal striping, and lastly the treasured nameplate. Actually, the car was not too far off the original 1964 GTO, but this was 1974. In 1964 a 389 cubic inch engine in this size car was a sensation. By 1974 the 350 cubic inch en-

The Fiero: A Missed Opportunity

The Fiero came and went long after my tenure at Pontiac. There's been a lot written about the Fiero. I don't want to discuss the faults that have been broadcast about the car over the years. Instead, I would like to review the Fiero from a marketing viewpoint.

There's no question that when Pontiac introduced the Fiero they had a potential winner, but sales never seemed to match expectations. It didn't help that they made overblown sales projections of 100,000 units per year. The American market for a two-seat car never has and never will support that kind of production. But the real issue was that Pontiac management simply could not get a handle on what they had. I think the problem started when, to get it past GM management, the development team called the Fiero a "commuter car." But it was apparent that Pontiac management planned, once it was in production, to morph the Fiero into a competitive sports car.

That was the wrong way to go and resulted in a marketing debacle. As introduced, the Fiero was a cute little mid-engine car, low slung with good styling that looked sporty, and was easy to drive and own. But by being so hell-bent to change that, Pontiac missed the opportunity of a lifetime. The market was ready to absorb a less sophisticated, dependable little two-place car that was easy on gas and insurance. As far as turning it into a high performance car, Pontiac already had the Trans Am, and they were having a hard time selling it. There was no reason to go racing with the Fiero and develop an entire program around a four-cylinder high output engine. If they had been smart, they would have simply improved the original Fiero into a fun-to-drive, simple, sporty car. Just like the Honda CRX, the Mazda Miata, and the Toyota MR2, all of which soon followed with more success.

gine in this size car made it just another Chevy Nova. The car got good press however, and sold a little more than 7,000 units.

Under the direction of Caserio, Pontiac decided to drop the GTO sixty days before the end of the 1974 model year, while the Grand Am was allowed to survive until the end of the 1975 model year. Both decisions turned out to be tragic mistakes, highlighting the end of an era at Pontiac. Mr. Caserio had certainly left his mark, before turning the division over to Alex Mair in October of 1975. By the middle of the 1975 model year, the country was already beginning to see fuel supplies return to normal, and there was even evidence of new interest in performance. As it would turn out, the youthful Firebird, the high-performance Trans Am, and the sporty Grand Prix would literally carry the division through the remainder of the decade.

In retrospect, none of us realized just how lucky we were during the Wide-Track era. Pontiac had three General Managers in a row who were able to bring their unique talents to the Division precisely when they were needed. Bunkie Knudsen, Pete Estes, and John DeLorean all had one significant thing in common: *they liked cars*. Suddenly, that was gone, and it could not be replaced with one "Experienced General Motors Executive" after another. Managing Pontiac required a "feel" for the car and its market, and it couldn't be learned from a book.

Buying a Pontiac instead of a more sensible Chevrolet or a more conventional Oldsmobile was like the urge to drive fast—it was just more daring and just more fun. Pontiac owners not only liked the way Pontiacs looked, but they liked the way *they* looked in Pontiacs. Once Pontiac lost that charisma, it was downhill fast. Pontiac could never stand up to Chevrolet on a value comparison, nor could it look an Oldsmobile or a Buick in the eye comparing sophisticated luxury. To lead this Division, required an absolute understanding and respect for this.

John DeLorean stood out as "the man," even among these men. DeLorean was the complete car guy, and in my opinion, was the best General Manager Pontiac ever had. I'd even go so far as to say he was the best General Manager any GM Division ever had. He lived Pontiac and his devotion was contagious.

MEANWHILE, THE CLIMATE AT HURST WAS TERRIBLE. I felt I needed a major change in my career, and I began to wonder if it would be fun to be a dealer. I had always been told that being a dealer was the only way to make any real money in the car business. Certainly, I had watched Ace Wilson drain some real profit out of Royal Pontiac.

I had no experience that qualified me to be a dealer, but with my savings and the backing of a few friends, I thought I had enough money to buy a dealership. My first thought was to contact Pontiac, but then I remembered what Pontiac was like with Jim McDonald at the helm, and I wasn't too excited about trying to sell some of their new products. But I did have a good relationship with John Johnson, Pontiac's Detroit Zone Manager, and thought it was worth seeking his advice.

I naively thought that with my overall knowledge of the automobile business, I would make a good dealer—after all, I knew just about everything there was to know about cars and the wholesale/retail system. But the reality was that I had no idea what it meant to be a car dealer, and I learned the hard way. A car dealer is not a car marketer. The only product a dealer has to market is his dealership, not the cars he sells. That's the job of the manufacturer.

I wanted to be in a metropolitan area, and even that was not quite as easy as I thought. I made an appointment to meet Johnson at the Pontiac Zone Office. He first brought up the subject of buying Royal Pontiac. The ironic part was, while I wasn't terribly excited about getting involved again with Pontiac, Royal Pontiac was a different story. It was sort of like going home. I lived in Royal Oak and was pretty well known there. I felt this could be a lot of help in getting established. Of course, you already know that the idea came to an end very early in the discussion stage after Johnson approached Ace Wilson Sr.

Then I turned my interests to Chevrolet. This time, I swallowed my pride and went to see John DeLorean. DeLorean was very gracious and didn't once say, "I told you so." He promised me support in helping me get into a Chevrolet point, although he cautioned me that I must find the exact place myself. He could not help with that, but he did direct me to the Chevrolet Dealer Relations Department. There, I met a great guy named Jerry Molloy, who took me under his wing, helping me to find, purchase, and start up my own Chevy dealership. We became good friends. Over the next four months, under Molloy's direction, I followed up leads in Texas, New York, California, and Wisconsin. I was trying to find a spot in a metro area, not having the moxie yet to appreciate a single-point market.

Chevrolet was particularly interested in expanding their penetration in Madison, Wisconsin. They showed me reams of information confirming strong economic growth in the area and proving the need to establish a second Chevy dealership. I went to Madison to look around. This would be a big program, involving a new site and new construction, all in a new community. I flew into Milwaukee, and on my way out of the city I drove by an old Chevrolet dealership, Garfield Chevrolet, which caught my eye. Although the facility was old, there certainly was plenty of traffic: it hung out over the North/South Freeway, which was a major traffic artery leading to Milwaukee's northern suburbs. But since I was still focussing on the possibilities in Madison, I didn't give it any more thought.

I spent two days in Madison with the Chevrolet people, looking at locations, talking to banks, and even meeting a few community leaders, including the mayor. Everything looked very positive, but as I drove back to Milwaukee, I began to think.

"Are you nuts?" I said to myself. "Here you are, going into a new business that you don't know a damn thing about. You're going to have to acquire real estate, you're going to have to build a new facility, and you're going to end up owing a lot of money to a lot of people." The whole thing suddenly became ludicrous. By the time I got back to Milwaukee, I had talked myself out of going to Madison. When I passed Garfield Chevrolet I now made a mental note to find out more about it. Maybe they would be interested in selling.

Once back in Detroit, I went to see Molloy, informing him of my decision about Madison. He agreed that I was biting off much more than I could chew. I then asked him about Garfield. As it turned out, he had spent time in Milwaukee as an assistant Zone Manager and knew the owner, Ray Foust, personally. Ray was part of an old-line, well respected Milwaukee family who had owned the dealership for decades. While it was nicely established, it was really a small operation, performing way under its potential.

"I can't solicit any dealer resignations or any determinations to sell," Molloy advised, "but as a friend, I will chat with him." A day later, Molloy called, reporting on his talk with Foust. "He might sell," Jerry said, somewhat enthusiastically. "His sons are not interested in the business, and he had already been thinking that maybe it was time to get out."

I immediately went to Milwaukee to meet with Foust. He had thought even more about it, and seemed to be ready to talk. We spent the whole day together, ending up at his home for dinner where I met his wife and family. He wanted to keep the property, and rent it to the new dealership. That certainly made everything a lot easier.

The deal went together and the paperwork was submitted to the Milwaukee Zone Office. All that was needed now was approval from Ralph Farrell, the Zone Manager. Farrell also knew Molloy, who had told him a lot about me, including my relationship with DeLorean. "We should have no trouble," Farrell assured me.

Up to this point, I had not bothered DeLorean, since the deal was progressing without a problem. It was now almost a year since I first began my dealership search, but I had a letter of approval from Chevrolet, along with a letter from the Milwaukee Zone Manager approving me as the purchaser of Garfield Chevrolet. I also had a letter of intent to sell the dealership to me, signed by Ray Foust.

Everything seemed to be on track until the very final stages of the deal, when there was a management switch announced for the Milwaukee Zone Office. Ralph Farrell was promoted out of Milwaukee and replaced by Ralph Sarvis, the son of a former Chevrolet General Sales Manager. The first thing Sarvis did was to put a hold on all dealership changes. Molloy warned me that Zone Managers often used new dealership assignments as payoffs for favors or debts. I was informed very properly by mail that the sale was being held up for more investigation, and that I should not make any plans to proceed until further notice.

An equally frustrated Molloy told me there was nothing he could do. I must give the new Zone Manager thirty days, I was told. Naive as I was, I thought that was reasonable. The thirty days came and went quickly, during which time Sarvis wouldn't return my phone calls. I was beginning to lose patience and respect for the Chevrolet system. Again I looked to Molloy. I was upset, having already laid out a lot of money and time, and I was afraid of losing some of the important people I had already recruited. Out of desperation I asked him to contact Sarvis. Molloy seemed hesitant about getting involved with Sarvis, but he agreed to call.

"Sarvis hasn't made up his mind," Molloy reported. "He feels he has some other candidates that are more qualified." Molloy then confided in me that he didn't like Sarvis, and that it sure looked like he had already selected another candidate. Knowing of my relationship with DeLorean, he counseled, "If I were you, I would pull out all stops."

Having already waited a year, I felt I had nothing to lose at this point. I called DeLorean and asked for an appointment, which he gave me immediately. I told him the whole story. He wrote a few things down and then asked me if I really wanted the dealership. I told him I did, and he responded with a confident smile. "Don't worry, you'll get it."

Two days later the call came from the Milwaukee Zone, not from Sarvis, telling me that my application had been approved. I didn't meet Sarvis until the actual closing and I could tell immediately he didn't like the way things went down. Needless to say, he never warmed up to me.

On September 16th, 1971, Garfield Chevrolet became Jim Wangers Chevrolet. It didn't take long for me to learn how poorly prepared I was to run a dealership. For example, within the first six months I discovered serious employee theft in the parts department. The norm for the retail car business I was told, was to fire the employee immediately, press charges, and make an example of them. I didn't fire anybody. Instead, I allowed them to pay it back out of future compensation. That's the way we would have done it in the ad business. I made that decision at a staff meeting with my six department managers present. Less than six months after that meeting, I had to fire three of those managers for stealing. That's how I learned the business.

One of the things that bothered me most while I was in the retail car business was that I didn't have much time to enjoy cars. I was, however, selling them, and in good numbers. Much more than Chevrolet had expected.

When I moved into Milwaukee, I brought with me a Detroit based ad group named the Patten Agency. Myron (Pat) Patten was the founder and driving force. They serviced only retail car dealers, limiting their clients to one per market. Their humorous campaign, the same in every market, was based around the dealer as a personality, imaging them as sort of a nice person, but a little forgetful, a little selfish, and maybe a bit of a buffoon. It relied almost exclusively on radio as a medium, using outdoor billboards as a compatible support. The theme was simply, "Jim Wangers, What A Great Great Guy," and the jingle went like this:

"Jim Wangers, what a great great guy,
He's sellin' Chevys, and he's got great buys,
On the North-South Freeway at Capitol Drive,
Jim Wangers, what a great great guy.

"Here's that cup of coffee you asked for, Mr. Wangers
Well, thank you Ernie, (Ernie was the company "gopher")
Uh, Mr. Wangers, that was my last dime.
Well, how thoughtless of me Ernie, here, have a sip.

"Jim Wangers, what a great great guy."

That was a typical 30-second commercial, which played frequently in drive time on many radio stations throughout the Milwaukee area.

The reason I am making such a point about this advertising is that it worked. In less than a year I was doing serious volume in new cars, which gave me the opportunity to expand my used car operation. Garfield, before me, had never taken used cars seriously, so this was a new area of activity for the dealership.

The Milwaukee market alone could never generate enough good used cars for every dealer to actively retail, making it necessary to look outside the immediate area. The logical place was Chicago, except that a "Chicago car" had a bad image in Milwaukee. They were usually very easy to pick out because of their dented bumpers (the result of Chicago-style parallel parking). Because of my Detroit connections, I was able to find a steady source of choice used cars from the Detroit area. These better quality cars helped me grow my used car business significantly. While the previous owner had been selling no more than 25 used cars a month, I picked that business up in one year to where we were averaging 80 used cars a month, and growing. Naturally, that helped the new car and truck volume climb, from less than 50 a month to close to 100 a month in the same time frame.

Jim Wangers Chevrolet looked very good, until you looked at the bottom line. I was doing a ton of business, but I wasn't making very much money. I was spending too much to grow too fast. I was over-advertising, which was predictable, but it was paying off in new traffic. But the one thing that I hadn't counted on and kept surprising me was employee theft. After my experience in the parts department, I discovered that my used car manager was taking a "double dip" on all the cars he was bringing in from Detroit. He received a kickback from his wholesaler in Detroit, and then picked up a second "hit" from his detailer in Milwaukee. I bristled when my business manager showed me that I was overpaying by as much as $500 just to get a car on the lot. Of course I had to get rid of him.

These were the kind of problems I was not prepared to handle. I really wasn't interested in management details. I ran Jim Wangers Chevrolet as if I was "Mr. Saturn," about 20 years before anybody ever heard about the Saturn way of doing business. I would not let an unhappy customer go out the door. If a customer couldn't be satisfied, every department had instructions to send them to me. I made myself available, and on many days I spent half of my time solving complaints by "giving away the store," which meant that profitable transactions often turned into losers.

While I wasn't doing a very good job of managing the dealership, I did know how to promote it. One of the better promotions I pulled off was inspired by Elton John's hit record "Crocodile Rock." Early into the song he refers to his "Old Gold Chevy and a place of my own." This record had tremendous appeal, especially to young people, so I decided to create an Old Gold Chevy of my own. At that time, we were having trouble selling our new Vega line, so that's where I directed the promotion.

I thought it was unusual that Chevrolet did not offer the color black on

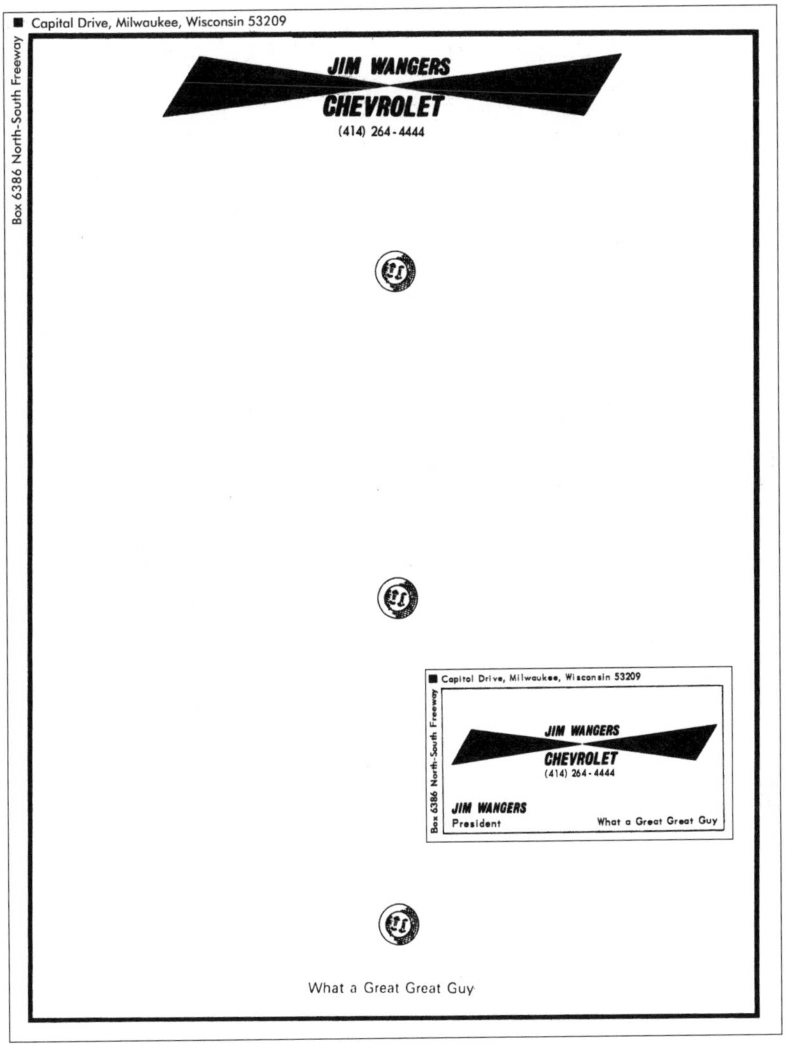

"Jim Wangers—What A Great Great Guy." This was a popular advertising theme at that time for auto dealerships. It was designed for radio use, using music and a corny vaudeville-style joke or two. But it worked! The image was of a stuffed shirt dealer who couldn't turn anyone down and made great, great deals. The dealership letterhead and business card (inset) featured a stylized bow tie and buttons down the middle of the shirt. Of course, the bow tie image had forever been associated with Chevrolet, so it all fit together very nicely.

any Vega. You couldn't get a single black Vega in 1972, even if you were willing to pay extra for it. The only way to get the car painted black was to order 50 of them at once, and then Chevrolet would build them at no extra charge. So I did. Needless to say, none of the other Milwaukee dealers knew about

Jim Wangers Chevrolet version of a Mini-Van, built off a Vega chassis—and a dozen years before Chrysler made the concept viable.

this. I ordered 50 black Vega Coupes and Wagons (no 2-door Sedans) and created my own "Old Gold Chevy." I painted the wheels a bright sparkling gold, added a matching gold accent stripe, and an attractive gold decal emblem. The emblem featured dancing musical notes surrounding the words "The Old Gold Chevy." Since I built 50 cars, the cost of the special items was modest. The Old Gold Chevy was priced less than $75 over a comparably equipped Vega.

Naturally, we cut a radio commercial using the line from the record, "I've got an Old Gold Chevy and a place of my own." We went on to say that the place to find an Old Gold Chevy of your own was at Jim Wangers Chevrolet. Since the car actually referred to in the song was a 1957 Bel Air Hardtop Coupe with the factory anodized grille, I obtained a real one to use in my showroom display.

The day I kicked off the promotion I had all 50 of the Old Gold Chevy Vegas surrounding the dealership. They were inside the showroom, in front on the sidewalk, on the used car lot, and even on the street. When you approached, that's all you saw. We sold them all in just three days, and took enough orders for 50 more. The factory loved me.

I did have some problems from other dealers. Customers would come in to my shop and see the Old Gold Chevy, and then they'd go to another Chevy dealer and not be able to find the same car. Of course the other dealers didn't have one, and so they started immediately to bad mouth the car. They would show the customer the factory book stating black was not offered on the Vega. They suggested to customers that I painted them black in my body shop, and that the paint job wouldn't last long. If the customer came back to me, I'd show them the top line of the price sticker where it

The Milwaukee Classic brought us a tremendous amount of national attention, thanks to our talents in getting media notice. These are the kind of newspaper and magazine articles that give products a lot of credibility in the minds of the consumer, especially those who are performance-oriented. We eventually wanted Jim Wangers Chevrolet to become like Royal Pontiac, specializing in Chevrolet performance products.

The Milwaukee Classic really took the town by storm! As part of an aggressive advertising campaign, we used a combination of heavy radio and outdoor billboards, like this one. We advertised our used cars in the newspapers, but our philosophy was that most car buyers were in their cars, listening to the radio, and passing billboards. So that's where we wanted to be.

read, "Paint: Special Code—no charge." The second 50 moved a little bit slower, but I ultimately got rid of them all.

All in all I considered it a very good promotion. I beat every other dealer in the zone by about a 100 Vegas for that period. I had a lot of fun, it was sort of like the old GeeTO Tiger days back at Royal. I even ordered a few Vega Delivery Wagons and painted the side panels with a trick design, calling them "Mini-Vans." This was a bit of a stretch, but remember, that was more than ten years before Chrysler produced their first vehicle with the same name.

I was so impressed with the Vega program, and the idea of having a special car for the dealership that I decided to create another one. I decided to create a special 1972 Monte Carlo package named the "Milwaukee Classic," which was a salute to the city and my thanks to the wonderful welcome I'd received. That's the way the commercials read: "I am so pleased to be a part of the Milwaukee community, that I have created this special, limited production car, which is going to be a real classic." The package consisted of a white Monte Carlo with handsome paint applications, either candy apple red, candy apple green, or candy apple tangerine. It also had a rather tasteful little radiator shell that I had crafted in a tool shop in Milwaukee.

The Milwaukee Classic

We painted the Milwaukee Classic in our body shop, which was okay when I was building only one or two cars at a time, but when the car caught on (I sold 60) it became a virtual "monster," interrupting the regular body shop routine and resulting in the resignation of my capable Body Shop Manager. Another goof in my long list of personnel mistakes.

Amazingly, in spite of the fact that I made nearly every mistake a new dealer could make, I still made money. The problem was I wasn't making enough money. Between the employees stealing from me, my overspending on advertising, and over indulging in areas that were not productive like the Milwaukee Classic and the other special cars, I was not paying attention to what really paid the bills, which was selling a lot of bread-and-butter Impalas and Chevelles. That nice flurry I had enjoyed out of selling used cars should have been just nothing but pure profit, except it had taken me six months to find out the used car manager was stealing. The problem was that I wasn't tough enough to run a dealership. When I encountered stealing, I tried to help the guilty party rather than firing them outright and pressing charges.

Still, I used a few things I learned from the old days at Royal to help the bottom line. For example, while I never actually sponsored a race car, I always stocked a good supply of Chevy performance parts, and promoted that fact heavily at the local drag strips. In fact, I was the only dealer in the area to show any interest in stocking these parts. We set up a 24-hour parts hotline. No matter what day or time you called, our answering service alerted us and we would get you the part you needed. This service turned out to be a pretty good idea, leading to a high-profit niche in my parts department.

John DeLorean also helped me out. I didn't have any contact with him once I opened the dealership until I went to Detroit for the first showing of the all-new 1973 Monte Carlo. I visited with DeLorean for a few minutes, and sent him a telegram when I got back to Milwaukee, congratulating him

Page 4, Part 2 MILWAUKEE SENTINEL Tuesday, April 18, 1972

WANGERS NEW CHEVROLET DEALER

Auto Man Adds Classic Touch

By RONALD ANZIA

It's not every city which has an automobile named after it. That's a project which had better be good, as the brewers of Old Milwaukee have long been saying.

Jim Wangers is now saying the same thing about his Milwaukee Classic Monte Carlo, a limited production model he is introducing for sale only in Milwaukee and only at his dealership.

"I had to have something that nobody else had," Wangers said Monday in tracing development of the eye catching Classic as the heart of a merchandising effort for his new organization, one which he intends to build around product image.

A 20 year veteran of the auto world but new to the retailing phase of the business, Wangers acquired Garfield Chevrolet, Inc., 4020 N. Green Bay Ave., at the start of March.

The new signs of Jim Wangers Chevrolet, Inc., were going up Monday, concluding a transition period in which the new owner operated under the Garfield name, long familiar here with the leadership of Raymond J. Lorch Sr. and Raymond H. Lorch Jr.

"I've seen this special car concept work," Wangers said in explaining his philosophy of merchandising. "A good, honest product will turn anybody on."

A former drag racer and one of the idea men behind the Pontiac GTO, Wangers isn't looking to sell hundreds of his Classic — he's unsure just what the volume will be — but he is expecting continued production.

As the first in what he hopes will be a long line of specialty cars, the Classic combines improvements in ride and handling with striking good looks.

With the blessing of Chevrolet, Wangers has taken the basic Monte Carlo and added a custom paint scheme, radiator type grille shell, vinyl half top, style chrome wheels, B. F. Goodrich Lifesaver radial tires, Koni shock absorbers, heavy duty rear stabilizer shaft and Classic emblems on wheel centers and panels.

Prominent in the cosmetic appeal of the Milwaukee Classic is a chromed radiator type grille shell. The special auto is a development of Jim Wangers, center, president of Jim Wangers Chevrolet, Inc. With him are Al Rice, left, sales manager, and Dick Jesse, general manager of the new dealership.

—Sentinel Photo by John W. Ahlhauser

In appearance, the Classic stands out. Its prime color is white. The accents are of red, green or tangerine over firemist gold metallic. The irridescent overlays on the hood and along the sides fade away to gold and, depending upon lighting and the position of the viewer, change their visual impact.

Wangers feels the Classic will appeal to buyers in every age bracket and at a price ($4,000 to $5,600) he describes as substantially less than that of the competition at which it is aimed — the Thunderbird, Eldorado, Toronado, Riviera, Grand Prix, even the Mark IV.

Standard Chevrolet engine and equipment options are offered with the Classic, along with an electric sunroof.

And, for the introductory promotion, Wangers has prepared Camaro, Chevelle, Nova, Vega and Corvette versions of the Classic.

The first Classic models were completed in Detroit, then shipped here for sale. Now all of the work is being done at the Milwaukee dealership.

Wangers has been working on the Classic for nearly a year. It's been exposed to the auto enthusiast press and the response, according to Wangers, has been exceptional.

This is Wangers' first dealership. Originally from Chicago, he was supervisor of the Pontiac account during the '60s at MacManus, John & Adams, a suburban Detroit advertising agency. It was in this capacity that he worked with John Z. DeLorean, chief Pontiac engineer, later Pontiac general manager and now Chevrolet general manager.

Most recently, Wangers was with the Patten Co. of Midland, Mich., an agency specializing in retail auto dealer advertising.

He's one who feels the auto manufacturers have overreacted to the pressures of government — "it's unrealistic and unfortunate for the consumer" — and one who believes a large segment of the motoring public remains interested in performance.

The Classic is not a youth's muscle car. It has not been reengineered and the regular Chevrolet warranty holds. Nothing has been done to the engine. Government emission controls forbid that.

"It's just what its name implies — a classic, thoroughly individual automobile with broad based appeal," Wangers said.

Article from the Milwaukee Sentinel announces the special limited edition Monte Carlo called The Milwaukee Classic, available only from Jim Wangers Chevrolet. The newspaper built a story around the new dealership and our special car. I'm in the center of the photo surrounded by Sales Manager Al Rice (L) and General Manager Dick Jesse. Both were from Detroit; Jesse had worked with me at Royal Pontiac.

on the 1973 Monte Carlo and drawing a parallel with the introduction of the incredibly successful 1969 Pontiac Grand Prix. I never got a reply.

When it came time for me to order our new 1973 cars for stock, I instructed my sales manager to put in for an extra supply of Monte Carlos.

Thanks in part to the Milwaukee Classic, I had sold an unusual number of Monte Carlos in 1972, earning me a bigger share for 1973. I knew that the car was going to be a winner, but also knowing that I wasn't one of the Zone Manager's favorite dealers, I really didn't expect much.

As I predicted, we sold right through our initial order of '73 Monte Carlos. We were resigned to taking orders and waiting. One day not much later a car hauler stopped in front of the dealership and began unloading Monte Carlos. We certainly didn't expect that many new cars, but the paperwork confirmed that they belonged to Jim Wangers Chevrolet. The deliveries kept coming, and in the course of a month we received almost all of the Monte Carlos that we had ordered. Mind you, I wasn't complaining. I should have advised the Zone, but since I didn't have a rapport with them I didn't give a damn. All of the cars were correctly floorplanned with GMAC.

This remained a mystery until one day I got a call from DeLorean. All he had to do was ask, "How are you doing?" when a light bulb lit up in my head. I finally realized where the extra Monte Carlos had come from. The conversation was short. DeLorean wished me well, told me to stay in touch, and hung up. He never mentioned the cars, but to this day I am deeply appreciative. We sold every one of those Monte Carlos at a nice profit, which made a sensational start for me in my second year as a dealer.

I Try The Royal Formula

HIGH PERFORMANCE HAD ALWAYS been a very important part of my life, and I didn't want it to stop now that I was a dealer. I started to think about selling some special performance cars again. Despite the effects of Federal controls, interest in performance had begun to pick up, so when I heard from Chevrolet that they were unloading a stock of 450 horsepower, 454 cubic inch high-performance LS-6 engines at a very low price, I bought 25 of them in their crates.

We sold a few engines outright, and I disassembled a few more, selling them for parts. Our already established reputation with the area racers helped us a great deal. The rest I decided to use to create my own "Royal Bobcat" in Milwaukee.

My aim was to convert these ultra-high-compression, manual lash valve engines into good contemporary performance street packages. This meant lowering compression and changing the valve train to a hydraulic lifter arrangement. I made a deal with a small performance shop in the area to do the R&D. I gave them 90 days to put it in a car, drive it on the street, and take it to the track. If it worked, I planned to market it with a new name, the "LS-W" (LS for the 454 engine and W for Wangers). It could fit in any Chevy that had come from the factory with an original big block engine. That included Corvettes, Novas, Chevelles, Camaros, Monte Carlos, Impalas, and Caprices.

Engine testing was done at the Great Lakes Dragway, in suburban Milwaukee with a 1969 Chevelle SS. We finally got it to run in the low 12s at 113 mph. While the LS-W was quick, it was no record holder, but it was a fun car to drive around town.

It turned out to be a very nice installation, but I couldn't sell them in my new cars. The base LS-6 engine had little or no emission equipment compared to what was required in 1973, making them illegal for street use. My LS-W conversion didn't address any of the emissions concerns, so the only way I could sell them was as aftermarket conversions in earlier cars. And after an LS-W engine was installed in my service department, regardless of the year of the car, the only way I would release the car was to have the owner pick it up with a trailer. The owner was also required to sign an affidavit confirming that the car was going to be used in "off-road" activity only, and that there would be no attempt to license it for street use.

The problem was that the boundaries of legality weren't really that clear. This situation came to a head when I sold a new 1973 Nova to a nice couple from Indiana who came all the way just to get an LS-W. After taking delivery of the car they drove it "around the block" and entered the service department as a new service customer. We took out the original Chevy 350 cubic inch engine, along with all its emission equipment, and stuffed in the 454 LS-W package. The owner signed the affidavit and picked up his car with a trailer, as required. I even took photos of the pick up for my files.

They loved the car. I used to hear from them almost weekly, reporting on how good it was running and how many races they were winning. Their enthusiasm lasted about six months, when suddenly I stopped hearing from them. I didn't think about it any more until almost a year later when I got a call from the wife's lawyer. The couple had been divorced, and as part of the settlement the wife ended up with the car. When she took the Nova to register it, naturally it failed to meet Indiana emission requirements. The lawyer told me I had two choices. Either buy back the car, or reinstall the original engine at no cost to his client. Both of these solutions were unacceptable to me. I was fully prepared to fight, considering all the paperwork I had collected, including photos of the car leaving my service department on a trailer. As a solution I offered to convert her car back to the original engine, at a reasonable price, confident that her lawyer would see that I had a strong defense.

I thought that would solve the problem, until I got a visit from the Environmental Protection Agency. It seems the wife's lawyer had reported the case to them, and they had become most interested. They had found a dealer who had violated their laws, and knowingly tampered with emission equipment on a new car. They wanted to make news with my conviction. Even though I had good documented defense material, my attorney advised me that we were going to be set up. The EPA's terms only confirmed this. If we agreed that they could announce the conviction, and with it a fine of $500,000, they would let me settle quietly for $500! All the EPA really wanted was to use Jim Wangers Chevrolet as an example.

The EPA's press release was picked up everywhere, including *The Wall Street Journal, The New York Times, The Christian Science Monitor, Automotive News*, and *Advertising Age*. "Milwaukee Car Dealer Fined for Tampering with Exhaust Emissions," read the headline in *The Milwaukee Journal*, our town's leading newspaper. As a seasoned veteran of the auto industry's PR world, I looked at the bright side of the incident. $500 dollars was a small price to pay for all that press. "Just as long as they spelled my name right," I joked. The Chevrolet Zone manager, Ralph Sarvis was a little more serious, sending me a scathing letter, cautioning me not to let it happen again.

My old friends at *Car and Driver* even got into the act some months later, running a short feature recalling my Royal Bobcat Pontiac press cars. Detailing the EPA incident, they asked in their story "Would you accept a test car from this man?" It was funny, and I got great reactions from many friends all over the country.

Incidently, I reinstalled the original 350 engine in the Nova, complete with all the emission equipment. The Indiana lady picked up half the bill.

In some ways, my experience mirrored the rest of the industry. Automakers were struggling to meet the new Federal Emissions Standards, but current technology proved to be woefully inadequate. Engines were literally choked and strangled, as the engineers leaned down carburetors. Both driveability and performance were seriously compromised, and many owners removed their emission equipment just to make their car run at all, especially in cold weather. Something had to be done.

After a significant amount of research, General Motors introduced a new component. They called it the Catalytic Converter. It enabled them to clean up emissions right in the exhaust system. Used properly, it allowed them to richen the engine again, eliminating hard-starting, and stumbling. The catalytic converter turned out to be so efficient that the U.S. Government mandated that all new cars sold in the United States after 1974 be fitted with the device. GM became the sole supplier to the entire automotive industry. To introduce and promote this rather complicated new device, General Motors planned a massive advertising campaign, awarding the business to my old ad agency, MacManus, John & Adams.

With this windfall in hand, the first thing MJ&A did was to seek out a serious product guy to manage the account. They contacted me to help find that guy. "We need to find a 'Jim Wangers,' and we need him quick. Do you have any suggestions?"

When I told them that the real Jim Wangers was available, and that I would be interested in acting as a consultant, they were surprised. But they had come to me at just the right time. The situation at my dealership was starting to frustrate me. Right after my experience with the EPA, I was informed by the employees in my service department that they were interested in joining a union and wanted me to schedule an election. The Chevrolet Zone office then dropped another bomb, advising me that since I had increased business my facility was inadequate. They wanted me to build a new building, or even move to new location. This was the last straw. I didn't want to spend my life fighting Uncle Sam, a local labor union, and building new buildings for Chevrolet. Whatever magic there had been for me in the retail car business was gone.

In early 1974, less than three years after it opened, Jim Wangers Chevrolet was put up for sale. Once the word got around, I got some serious inquiries. One that really stood out was from a dealer in New Jersey, Danny Zack,

Crime Never Pays

• Jim Wangers, best remembered by the staff of *Car and Driver* for the suspiciously fast (and blatantly non-stock) road-test cars he prepared during his tenure at Pontiac's advertising agency, is now best remembered by the Environmental Protection Agency for the same sort of tricks.

The Justice Department has announced settlement of a suit by the EPA against Jim Wangers Chevrolet in Milwaukee for violation of the section of the Clean Air Act that prohibits dealers from disconnecting or removing emissions control systems. In a consent decree, the dealer agreed to pay a fine of $1200 and to comply with the law for five years.

The EPA charged that the dealership had sold a new 1973 Nova to a buyer from Indiana and then, after the car was driven around the block, replaced the original engine with a 1970 454-cubic inch monster that did not have the emission controls required to meet 1973 standards.

When reached at his office, Wangers admitted to *Car and Driver* that his service department had switched engines but claimed that he had a signed statement from the customer that said the car would be used for off-road competition only. Said an EPA spokesmen: "That's what his lawyers told us too, but you don't usually find a drag-racing car with an AM/FM radio, rear speaker and decor group."

The first sign indicating something was amiss appeared when the customer was unable to register the car in Indiana because it would not pass a state inspection. When his appeal to the dealership for assistance failed, the owner turned to the EPA, which, it turns out, already had an eye on Wangers after reading about his activities in (honest to God) *Super Stock & Drag Illustrated* Magazine.

GENE BUTERA

Would you accept a test car from this man?

Before he became a Chevrolet dealer, Wangers massaged a long series of Pontiac test cars for various automotive magazines including *Car and Driver*. The original GTO (March 1964), which reportedly hit 115 mph in the quarter-mile, was a typical Wangers product. Another memorable Wangers creation was "The Judge" he delivered to us for a comparison of six super cars in the January 1969 issue. Our first hint that something was, well, a little Wangers-ish was when the test car (in supposedly stock form) begain turning in times at New York National Speedway that were quicker than those of the race-prepared GTOs that ran there on weekends. A further examination showed that it—like the recent Chevrolet in Indiana—had an engine from an older car. As a result, we threw it out of the test.

Not being a government agency, *Car and Driver* wasn't in a position to levy a $1200 fine on Wangers for his creativity. We would, however, have gladly settled for a consent decree. *—Patrick Bedard*

This article from Car and Driver humorously deals with a low-point in my career as an automotive dealer. Jim Wangers Chevrolet was fined by the Federal Government for emissions violations, but the payoff was only $500, not $1200 as erroneously reported here.

representing Briggs Chevrolet. They too, were interested in performance, and had learned about me through my experience with the EPA. Zack put a satisfactory offer together. He wisely recognized the equity I had established in the community, and wanted to keep the name Jim Wangers Chevrolet. This was okay with me, although he decided to drop the "Great Great Guy" advertising. Unfortunately, that changed the personality of the dealership. Traffic dropped significantly and a sales drop soon followed.

The union effort in the service department failed, but Chevrolet continued to put pressure on Zack to expand. After only two years he responded by selling to the local Volkswagen Dealer, who had a beautiful new facility close by. He wanted to move Jim Wangers Chevrolet into the same complex, planning a Chevrolet showroom back-to-back with the VW facility, sort of a mini new car mall. Chevrolet balked, objecting to the upstart Volkswagen being so close. Failing to reach an agreement, the new owner simply folded before he ever opened. The Zone office was unable to find another buyer who would either build or move, so the dealership was allowed to die. That was officially the end of the short, sometimes glorious, sometimes troubled history of Jim Wangers Chevrolet.

12

Nothing But Sizzle

Mazda's Image Problems

I RETURNED TO DETROIT AS A VICE PRESIDENT of my old ad agency, MacManus, John & Adams, becoming deeply involved with the catalytic converter. The campaign introducing the converter was designed to educate the new car buyer that this wasn't some magic device stuffed into their exhaust system. It was a significant development, and it was going to be around for a long time. Even the words "catalytic converter" scared people. It was my job to convince them otherwise.

Just as I started to dig into the problem in the summer of 1974, I got a call from a West Coast headhunter asking if I would be interested in interviewing with a major import automaker who was looking for a marketing director. They wouldn't reveal the name of the carmaker, but it wasn't long before a second call came, inviting me to catch a plane to Los Angeles and meet with the people at Mazda.

Mazda was having some serious problems. They had initially built a fine reputation in the U.S. with their revolutionary rotary engine. Their introductory ad campaign had been a huge success, with their slogan, "Most cars go rumpa-rumpa, but Mazda goes hmmmmm." It was well presented, and the public understood. Mazda had literally hit the ground running.

However, trouble started brewing for them when early customers reached 30,000 miles on their rotary engines and discovered that the O-rings involved in oil sealing were wearing out. Replacing these seals was not a major job, but, as often happens, word-of-mouth was that Mazda engines self-destructed at 30,000 miles and had to be completely rebuilt.

Also, while the Rotary engine produced more power, it was significantly less fuel efficient than the other Japanese cars already in the market. Consumers who were comparison shopping Toyota or Datsun were impressed with the instant throttle response of the Mazda, but disappointed with the fuel mileage. To compound Mazda's woes, the EPA released their first (their absolute first) fuel mileage numbers for all cars sold in America. In the subcompact class the Mazda RX-2 was listed alongside the Toyota Corolla and Datsun B-210. Both the Toyota and the Datsun numbers indicated that they were capable of getting better than ten miles per gallon more than the comparable Mazda.

The information hit Mazda like a bombshell. Their marketing team, most specifically the head of the team, Dick Brown, decided to attack the problem head-on. Brown had come to Mazda earlier from Chrysler to head up their U.S. operation. He was one of the first Americans to be given that kind of responsibility from the Japanese.

Brown had done an outstanding job of introducing Mazda in the U.S., and of responding to the O-ring failures by promoting Mazda's offer of complete warranty coverage. For the EPA mileage rating fiasco, Brown and his lieutenants had decided to attack the source of the mileage information by questioning the EPA's integrity. Politically, this was a bad decision, as the newly organized government agency was fighting for its own existence. The last thing they needed was to be challenged by a foreign carmaker who had just entered the market with a strange new engine. The EPA put up a fight and won. Their mileage number for the Mazda RX-2 stuck. Not only did Mazda lose that battle, but they almost lost the war. Sales slumped, and with them went the Mazda image. It was a huge setback for a new company still breaking into the U.S. market.

Mazda's Image Problems

When I flew out to California I found Brown to be a totally delightful guy. He was gutsy and aggressive and I sure liked that. Once my meeting started we spent quite a bit of time talking about my years at Pontiac, working with John DeLorean. Brown was a big fan of DeLorean, and had already talked to him about me.

As it turned out, Brown had a previously scheduled meeting with the EPA on that same day, and had to interrupt my interview to accommodate them. It was to be a two-hour meeting, so Brown gave me an RX-3 Coupe and told me to take a drive down to Irvine in Orange County and look over their new facility. It was a magnificent complex designed to compliment the rotary engine—the administration building was hexagonal. But no one knew that with the dark days coming, Mazda would never occupy the facility.

When I returned from my tour, Brown and I immediately got into the subject of what he wanted from his Marketing Director. I told him my idea of a marketing director's responsibility was to have Advertising, Sales Promotion and Merchandising, Sales Training, and Product Public Relations under his authority.

He said, "I can't give you PR, we've already got a PR department."

"That may be so," I said, "but product PR is different. It's a marketing function." I further explained that these four areas of communication needed to work together, all focussing on a single message, a single purpose, a single direction. The lack of this "single" direction was—and still is today—a huge shortcoming in the competitive world of automotive marketing.

I finally convinced Brown that it would be advantageous to structure the department my way. We talked well into the evening and put a deal together. He made me an offer, and I accepted. As I left his office I was a bit amazed at my own plans: Jim Wangers, the prototypical "American car freak," ready to move to California to work for a Japanese carmaker. What next? I boarded a plane on Saturday with plans to resign from MJ&A Monday morning.

Back in Detroit I found a notice from Western Union posted on my front door that I had received a telegram. It was from Dick Brown, advising me that after I left him Friday night, he had been fired! He no longer had the responsibility or the authority at Mazda to protect our deal. He ended his message suggesting that I had better not resign from my current position. I had already talked myself into moving to California and joining Mazda. By the same token, I was grateful to Dick Brown for communicating so well. He kept me from embarrassing myself at MJ&A.

I was curious by the fast turn of events at Mazda. When I finally did get hold of Dick on Monday, he confided that Mazda's Japanese management were very upset at his decision to go after the EPA. The Japanese felt that Brown had to "go" to signal that they were truly sorry about the incident. He further reported that they were not interested in pursuing a new marketing director, and did not encourage me to pursue the position any further.

As irony would have it, Dick Brown eventually went to work for John DeLorean and his newly founded DeLorean Motor Company. He was hired by John to organize a retail dealer body. He did a good job, and ultimately became DeLorean's first General Sales Manager.

I REMAINED AT MJ&A WORKING ON the GM corporate account through the end of the catalytic converter introduction, which coincided with a major change at Pontiac. Martin Caserio left, to be replaced by Alex Mair, the same GM guy who had saved the Camaro and Firebird just a few years earlier.

Mair had been brought into Pontiac to try to get it back on track. He realized he didn't know very much about Pontiac or its Wide-Track heritage, but he had a 21-year-old son, Steve, who did. As a teenager, Steve had hung around Royal Pontiac, maturing into a serious racer.

"The first thing you want to do Dad, is to get hold of Jim Wangers," Steve Mair told his father. "He's the one guy who can help you get Pontiac stirred up again." So three months after Mair had taken the helm at Pontiac, I was invited to a meeting at his home, set up by son Steve.

This meeting with Mair was the first real contact I had with anyone from Pontiac since returning to MacManus. It went better than I could have imagined. The more I shared my appraisal of Pontiac's current dilemma, and talked specifically about the future, the more intrigued Mair became. To close the meeting, he revealed that he would like me to come to work for him. He wanted to think about just when and how to bring me aboard. I pointed out that Jim Graham was Pontiac's Marketing Manager, and that there was some "baggage" there. Mair didn't think that would be a problem. Graham had demonstrated an uncommon interest in the Shows and Exhib-

Alex Mair became General Manager of Pontiac shortly after I moved back to their advertising agency, MacManus, John & Adams. After selling Jim Wangers Chevrolet, I returned to Detroit and was slated to service the new GM catalytic converter account. When Mair heard I was back in town, he requested a meeting, which led to a consulting assignment.

its department, and seemed to be satisfied just managing that activity.

I didn't hear anything for a while, but apparently Mair finally reached a decision. He called me to his office and announced proudly that he was ready to hire me as Marketing Manager. I pointed out the hurdles, having been through this once before. I told him quite honestly I wasn't sure he could get it done. "The Corporation frowns on bringing people in from the outside," I pointed out.

"Don't worry," Mair replied, almost arrogantly. "I know what to do, and I'll get this handled. I want you, and I'll get it done." I was pleased, but also apprehensive.

Part of my apprehension was due to the knowledge that not everyone at Pontiac was happy to see Mair take over. One of the unhappiest was Sales Manager Jim Vorhes, who had been hired by John DeLorean. DeLorean liked Vorhes, assuring him that he had a solid future at Pontiac. By 1974, he had become General Sales Manager. With Caserio gone, Vorhes believed he was the heir apparent to the throne and resented the selection of Mair from the outside. He seemed to resent every move Mair wanted to make. He should have remembered that the Corporation often did not promote sales-oriented people to the General Manager slots.

Another DeLorean survivor still working at Pontiac was Ben Harrison, in product marketing. Harrison was the planner often credited with the idea of downsizing the 1969 Grand Prix, building it off the intermediate A-body rather than the full-size car. He had precariously survived the McDonald/Caserio days, and when Mair took charge, Harrison got a new lease on life. I had worked closely with Ben in the past and had a lot of respect for his capabilities. He was pleased with the idea of my joining Pontiac again.

I said nothing to the ad agency, it was too premature for that. Unfortunately, word got around anyway that Wangers was talking privately to Pontiac's new General Manager. That caused everybody to be suspicious. I think Vorhes may have spread that word, since Mair had confided in him hoping to gain his support. Vorhes didn't want anyone coming in and counseling Mair on sales or marketing. That was his territory, and he wanted to protect it.

It soon became obvious that I had been right. Mair simply didn't have the "juice" to overcome the resistance. Three weeks later, he let me know. "This just isn't the right time," he said, almost embarrassed.

I had been preparing for this, and had developed another idea. I quickly presented the possibility of working with Mair as a consultant, exactly as I should have done five years before with DeLorean at Chevrolet. The idea appealed to him, and he approved it almost immediately. I would serve as a consultant working with Ben Harrison.

Meanwhile, Jim Vorhes had became a threat to Mair's authority. It was common knowledge around Pontiac that in meeting privately with dealers, Vorhes often openly questioned Mair's capabilities as General Manager, which was not only unprofessional, but unacceptable. It didn't take very long for this to filter back to Mair.

Mair had to make a deal to get rid of Vorhes, which didn't come cheap. A Divisional General Manager cannot simply fire his sales manager. He had to get Corporate approval to have him transferred. Mair approached Pete Estes, who by then was President of GM. Estes agreed to take Vorhes off Mair's hands, but only if he would accept George Spaulding as a replacement. Spaulding had been General Sales Manager of GM's Opel unit in Germany, and was anxious to come back to the states.

Mair complied—and ended up trading one "situation" for another. Just as Jim McDonald had tried to price image Pontiac like Chevrolet, Spaulding, in his new role, wanted to sell Pontiac as more genteel and luxurious, like Oldsmobile. The timing couldn't have been worse. Pontiac was floundering badly, trying to reinvent itself, and the last thing they needed was to become an Oldsmobile.

Spaulding, who I think probably misunderstood Pontiac's image more than any other Pontiac marketing executive, proceeded to wreak havoc on the division. It was Spaulding who was responsible for dropping the full-size car out of the Pontiac line. When Pontiac became the first (and only) GM division to stop building full-size cars, Spaulding honestly believed that "big" cars were never going to be accepted again. "Since Pontiac is the most forward thinking division in the corporation," he said in public statements, "then we should be the first to drop them."

Unfortunately, no one at Pontiac resisted.

When the full-size car market predictably reemerged, Pontiac had to go to Canada and "import" a rebadged Chevrolet Caprice to satisfy its furious dealers. They called it the Pontiac Parisienne, just as it was named in Canada. Fortunately, it worked.

"Smokey And the Bandit"

Movie Star, Take 2

One of the early consulting assignments Alex tossed my way was to evaluate a Hollywood movie opportunity that had been proposed to Pontiac. The comedy action film was called "Smokey and the Bandit."

The project was pitched by an aggressive ex-stunt driver turned producer, named Hal Needham, and was to feature stars like Burt Reynolds and Sally Field. One look at the proposed script revealed that the real star of the film would be a car named "The Bandit." Pontiac was given the first opportunity to participate, and the re-emerging mid-seventies Trans Am was the perfect car.

It was almost as if this opportunity came out of heaven and dropped on Pontiac. I couldn't have been more supportive. I advised Alex to pursue the film aggressively and encourage his people to do whatever was necessary to make it happen. The first energy crisis had eased significantly and the Trans Am was rapidly becoming the industry's highest imaged sporty performance car. The public loved the "Shaker" hood scoop and the "Screaming Chicken" decal.

In 1976, Pontiac had brought another good high performance emission engine to market. The 400 cubic inch powerplant was called the T/A 6.6, out of respect for the Trans Am. It was also available in the Formula model. Coupled with a four-speed manual transmission and a limited slip rear axle, the T/A 6.6 was just about the fastest American production car you could put your hands on at that time. "Smokey and the Bandit" would recast the new Trans Am into a legend.

I have always thought that many of those T/A 6.6 Trans Ams were sold to Baby Boomers who had been too young to own a GTO. The GTO had gone away by the time these "Boomers" came into the marketplace, but now there was another chance, this time it was called Trans Am.

The bottom line is that television and movie tie-ins are generally magnificent opportunities for product exposure, but the cost versus value standard depends on the marketing goal of the individual product, as well as the quality and the popularity of the film.

The original black and gold 1976 Trans Am that ultimately became "The Bandit" one year later.

The other legacy Spaulding left to Pontiac was the decision to eliminate long-recognized nameplates like Catalina, Le Mans, Sunbird, and Tempest. Spaulding stated that there was no more interest in "those sporty hot rod cars." Decades of market planning plus millions of marketing dollars working to establish these legendary model names meant nothing, as they were obliterated by Spaulding who chose to inflict his concept of alphanumeric model numbers on these cars. Perplexed Pontiac dealers were suddenly selling models named T-1000, J-2000, and 6000.

What were Spaulding's reason for these name changes? "They work for Mercedes and BMW, why not for us?" he stated. Spaulding seemed to think of himself as a student of the business, the only problem was his textbooks were, "What Happened Yesterday? "

As far as consumer reaction to this new numbers-for-names game, I heard a funny story about an incident that supposedly took place in New York. A prospect was looking over the new 6000LE model, when he turned to

Some critics called it a Caprice with fender skirts. Pontiac dealers called it The Pontiac Parisienne. The "fill in" full size car sold especially well after management prematurely downsized the Bonneville.

What's in a name? Companies spend years—and many dollars—building a brand name. Unfortunately, only a few survive. Fortunately, Pontiac has had more than their share of winners: Bonneville, 41 years; Grand Prix, 36 years; Firebird, 31 years; Trans Am, 29 years.

the sales person with him and said, "You know, I like this model, but what does the name 'GOOOLE' mean?" Obviously he was interpreting the new alphanumeric name 6000LE to read as a name, just like it had always been.

ABOUT THIS TIME I BEGAN AGAIN to assess myself, and I didn't like what I saw. My career was stalled again and I wasn't having any fun. It had been a difficult time for me ever since John DeLorean left Pontiac. My departure from the agency, the disappointment with Hurst, the unhappy experience of owning a dealership, and the near miss at Mazda were certainly not career highlights. I wasn't marketing product, and that's what my world was all about.

Things got even worse one day when I was summoned downtown to a meeting with our GM corporate client. They were finally becoming worried about what they called "The Japanese Threat." Remember, in the early seventies, whenever we mentioned names like Toyota or Datsun or Mazda, our GM client turned a deaf ear. "That's only in California," Corporate Ad Director Gale Smith would say.

Well, somewhere in their thinking both the "house" and the "lot" fell on them, and they now recognized that the Japanese were a very important competitor in the American car market. To combat this, they wanted to make product comparisons between all the existing GM small cars against the upstarts from Japan. They wanted me to create an ad campaign to prove that the GM family of small cars were longer, lower, wider, had bigger interiors, more headroom, bigger trunk capacity, more horsepower, and finally, were simply better values. This would be the first time GM ever ran comparison advertising that mentioned the competition by name, and the ads proved to be pretty effective. They were all based on published specifications released by the manufacturers themselves

I dutifully put together a series of comparison ads that I later cynically named the "Ashtray Grand Prix" campaign, since it proved that all these GM small cars, while not necessarily better, did indeed have bigger ashtrays. Even though both the agency and the client were happy, I felt I had reached the low point in my marketing career.

Right in the middle of this I got a call from Dave Landrith, an old friend from my Hurst days. "How would you like to build some Pontiacs?" he asked. Landrith had left Hurst and was striking out on his own. He had sold a program to the Detroit area Pontiac Dealers involving the new Pontiac Astre. "They want to do something to separate this 'turkey' from the Chevy Vega. Got any ideas?" he asked. "I sold the program to their local ad agency, and now I have to come up with a car. The first guy I thought of was you."

Pontiac had been handed the Chevy Vega with a split grille. They called it the Astre, and it was exactly the same car the Canadian Pontiac dealers were already selling. Pontiac had a completely different image in Canada than it had in the United States. It was considered a low priced entry level car, and competed directly with Chevrolet. Interestingly enough, they were—and are—successful. It has been that way for a long time. The Astre had the same engine, same transmission choices, same body, same sheet metal, even the same problems as the Vega. The car had been around since 1970, and apart from a front end style change to meet the 1974 bumper standard, it was tired. While the product was appropriate enough for the times, it was certainly not a Pontiac, and Pontiac didn't have the money or the desire to make it into something unique.

I told Landrith I was interested, but I would have to learn to respect the car. Maybe I could come up with an "Old Gold Chevy" again. After all, it was the same old car. So, keeping my "day job," I put some money together with Landrith and formed a new company. We called it Motortown.

Because of both cost and time restrictions (plus government regulations prohibiting certain kinds of modifications), we were not able to touch the Astre's engine or driveline, but we could hang stuff on it. The package itself was a collection of "bolt-ons." From the aftermarket we picked up a spoiler, a front air dam, a window louvre, and a great looking wheel. The only new component that we actually created was a rather elaborate multicolored (red, yellow, maroon) decal stripe package that complemented the silver colored car. All cars would look the same.

The name we came up with was a stroke of genius, if I say so myself. We called it "Li'l Wide Track," which really said Pontiac!

Li'l Wide Track Promotion

The Li'l Wide Track program was a success in Detroit. They took 500 cars the first round and ended up ordering another 500, this time in a choice

After the success of the Li'l Wide Track program, I started a company called Motortown Corporation, which specialized in the design and building of small-volume specialty cars like the Mustang Cobra II, the Pontiac Can Am, Volare Road Runner, and the Aspen R/T. It was the age of the decal GT, where almost all of the "go-fast" improvements were merely stripes and a wheel package.

of colors. Once again I proved to myself the tremendous impact the term "Wide-Track" had on a car called Pontiac.

Eventually the Pontiac marketing folks took notice. They wanted to know why the Astre was doing so well in Detroit. Reluctantly, they allowed Motortown to promote the Li'l Wide Track package to every Pontiac dealer, and we ended up building more than 7,000 during the 1975 and 1976 model years. A small assembly facility, adjacent to GM's massive Lordstown, Ohio plant was set up to handle the volume.

In reality, the best you could say about the car was that it was a Pontiac and not a Chevy. It appealed to young people, got good gas mileage, and was attractively priced. New car buyers were again looking for fun. The same momentum that was pushing the phenomenal growth of Pontiac's Trans Am, which was truly a car of the sixties, was also carrying Li'l Wide Track.

Just about everybody at Pontiac and MJ&A thought it was a bad program and degraded the name Pontiac. It was and did, but it sure helped an otherwise almost unsalable car. At the agency, I stayed in the background whenever the subject was discussed. Nobody yet knew that I was involved with Motortown.

Li'l Wide Track Promotion

The Li'l Wide Track program really got our new company off to a good start. It reaffirmed for me that there was an opportunity for a company like Motortown—as there had been for Hurst five years earlier—to provide a service for the industry's troubled models. Everybody had an "Astre" in their lineup.

Ford, for example, was encountering a similar problem with their downsized Mustang II. When it first appeared in 1974 it was available only with a four-cylinder or a small V-6 engine, which seemed appropriate at the time. But the car, while attractive, had lost all of the macho, performance-oriented muscle of the great fastback Mustangs of the late sixties and early seventies. Ford had abandoned their loyal Mustang owners, and the Mustang II was perceived as nothing more than a "dolled up" Pinto. The sporty fastback version had been virtually ignored, falling to less than 30% of total Mustang sales.

In late summer 1975, Motortown approached Ford with a "hype" for the fastback. We built on the fact that of the great Mustangs of the early glory days, the fastback Shelby Cobras stood out as the most famous—even more specifically the great white-and-blue striped Cobras. So, starting with a solid white Fastback Mustang II Coupe, we proposed adding a hood scoop, a rear deck spoiler with matching front air dam, a nicely integrated rear quarter window louver, and eye catching blue racing stripes. It really turned the "wimpy" looking Mustang II into a sporty coupe—add a set of nicely styled wheels, and the biggest tires available and it was hard not to like the looks of this car.

"We don't have anything like this in our plans," said John Morrisey, Ford Division Marketing Manager, as he contemplated our very well prepared renderings of the proposed car. "Although, I do know that the V-8 engine is scheduled to come back next year. That would sure be a natural for this car, wouldn't it?"

Mustang Cobra II Promotion

Our second successful effort after opening Motortown was bringing the idea for the Cobra II to the Ford Motor Company. We took a fastback Mustang II and re-created the performance image of the earlier Mustang into the new, smaller ("downsized") car. Edsel Ford II personally approved the project and it was highly successful. Maybe too successful. Motortown built more than 27,000 of them, which prompted Ford to break the contract, steal the project the second year, and take it in-house. The car's promotional highlight was Farrah Fawcett using it as her personal driver (her character was "Tiffany") on the very popular TV hit "Charlie's Angels."

"But, here's the problem," he continued. "I love the car, but, I can't do a thing. They don't even let us marketing guys in the front door at styling, let alone present a car idea. But there is one way that might work. There's a young guy working around here who likes cars. He works in product planning, and he's got a little bit of muscle."

The "young guy" turned out to be young Edsel Ford, Chairman Henry Ford II's oldest son. Morrisey told us to leave the renderings and proposal with him, so that he could pass them on to Edsel. "If he likes the idea, and wants to do something with it, he'll take it right to his dad. That's what it's going to take," Morrisey concluded.

We handed everything over, thanked him profusely, and left, thinking that would be the end of it. I doubted Edsel would do anything, and the "not invented here" syndrome was all powerful in Detroit.

At the same time, we were pitching a similar car to Chevrolet to help them with their Monza. We called it "The Mirage," named after a famous Chevy powered race car. It had a real "trick" IMSA look to it, with wide fender flares and a nicely integrated rear deck spoiler. It seemed the Mirage had a better chance of approval at Chevrolet than the Cobra II did at Ford, and we were right. The Mirage got approved before we heard another word from Ford.

It was almost three weeks later when we got a call from John Morrisey. His prediction of the product planning people's reaction was accurate: they didn't even want to see it since they said they had a special Mustang of their own in progress. But he did get to Edsel Ford, and he really liked our renderings. Morrisey reported, "He said you guys have done it right."

Only a guy like young Edsel Ford, who had nothing to lose, could stick his neck out and "buck" the system. He sold the car to his father, and got the funds for us to build a prototype. "Build it as fast as you can," Morrisey said. "We don't care what it will cost. Time is important now."

Ford Finally Gets It Right...Thanks to the 5.0

In the sixties, no company spent more money on building special-purpose race cars than Ford. From NASCAR to Formula 1, Ford dominated racing and won virtually every major event held around the world. But for all their achievements on the track, they were unable to transfer that success to the street. Part of the problem was the product, but even more so was an ineptness in marketing their products properly.

If the sixties were a disappointment for Ford, the late 1980s and the early 1990s have belonged to Ford, thanks to the 5.0 Mustang. They combined all of the elements that were necessary to make the car outstanding, exciting, available and well-priced. It fit the exact mold we had created with our GTO thirty years earlier.

Ford has supported the Mustang's performance thanks to a special parts program made available through special performance dealers. It's Royal Pontiac, Act III. With simple V-8 power in a modestly-priced, good-looking car, marketed to a community that was hungry for performance, Ford hit the target dead on. The car responds well to modifications, and has in effect become the GTO of the '90s. Now, as we go into the millennium, it appears the imports have learned this same trick, especially Honda, Toyota Nissan, BMW, and Mercedes. Each has brought into the market place their versions of high performance personal cars and are working with the next generation of high-tech sophistication.

A fleet of Cobra IIs sits outside Motortown's Dearborn facility waiting to be shipped to dealers across the nation. At one time Motortown had a total of five small satellite plants, from California to Michigan to Wisconsin, working to modify cars as they came off their respective assembly lines.

Our proposal called for Ford to build the original car on their assembly line in Dearborn, Michigan, adding whatever special interior trim they wanted. Then they would ship (or drive) the car to our adjacent Motortown satellite facility, where we would complete the Cobra II conversion, and then ship them back to Ford for final delivery to dealers. After the prototype was accepted by Styling, we received a final "go ahead." The order was to build 5000 cars. All of the costs were based on that quantity.

One of the biggest hurdles we still faced was the Ford Division Sales Promotion Manager. All I could think of was a reprise of Frank Bridge and the GTO. Here was the guy who would be responsible for merchandising the car, saying, "That's not the kind of car we need around here," and predicting that they wouldn't sell 500. He tried very hard to kill it, until he learned that Edsel Ford was behind it, and that the Chairman had approved it.

Although I was still working for the ad agency on the General Motors Corporate Account, and occasionally meeting with Alex Mair at Pontiac, I was seriously thinking of throwing in the towel. This Motortown thing was fun, and it was making money, too.

I made a low-profile trip to the 1976 Ford Dealer Announcement show in Las Vegas. Ford didn't have much new to offer in their 1976 product line. The Granada was still the hot car, and it was unchanged. The Maverick and Pinto were virtually carryover, as was the regular Mustang. Every car offered very little new, except for the neat-looking Cobra II poised on a turntable, hidden behind drapes.

When the dealers finally saw the Cobra II, and learned that it would be available with a V-8 engine, they stood up and applauded for what seemed like ten minutes. Anybody opposed to the car had to change their thinking when they saw that reaction.

The black and gold Cobra II-H was a special mid-year hype recalling the infamous mid-sixties Hertz GT-H promotion. It worked.

Ford Sales Management had been worried that 5,000 would be way too many, but they got 5,000 orders within a week. Once we started shipping cars, more orders showed up almost immediately. By the end of the third month Ford had more than 15,000 sold orders for the car. Motortown was working three shifts around the clock. We ended up building more than 27,000 Cobra IIs for the full model year, duplicating a story that had been written more than ten years earlier with the first Pontiac GTO.

One interesting part of the program was that the car earned its own advertising dollars. The advertising department didn't want to give up any of their regular Mustang budget, so based on a projected volume of 5,000 units, a small fee was collected from every car to buy an announcement ad in the enthusiast magazines. Since the advertising dollars were built into every car, Ford was "forced" to over-advertise the car. Perhaps the best television exposure the car could get occurred when Ford placed it on their hit show "Charlie's Angels," as a personal driver for young starlet Farah Fawcett.

In the middle of the model year we proposed a stunning Black and Gold version of the car, recalling the old Hertz Shelby Mustang GT-H program. Ford liked it, and as a "second shot" it pushed the car to even greater sales records. Demand for the car got so strong that Ford added production in their Milpitas, California plant, asking us to set up a second satellite facility near the plant.

As we neared the end of the 1976 model year we kept hearing rumors that Ford was planning to take the Cobra II program "in house" for 1977. We didn't think much of this since we had signed a two-year contract guaranteeing that Motortown would build every Cobra II during the 1976 and 1977 model years.

The wake-up call over the Ford deal came innocently enough from dealer Bob Ford Ford (no relation) located right in Dearborn. He was mad as hell when he called. He had been a good Cobra II dealer, having sold more than 25 cars, and was very familiar with the product and our quality. "I'm not going to accept this piece of crap you sent me today," he threatened. "I can't believe you guys can't paint stripes any better than this. Every other car I got before from you had perfect stripes."

When he said the word "paint," an alarm went off. We didn't paint the stripes on any of the Cobra IIs. We used only decal stripes, which is why they fit so perfectly. How did this dealer get a Cobra II with painted stripes? The answer was obvious: Motortown had not built the car. The order had been intercepted at Ford and converted to a Cobra II someplace else. We called the dealer back right away, offering to buy the car.

Once we got our hands on the car, we could plainly see the problem. Apparently, Ford had run it through their paint line, practicing for next year. The decal stripes were not easy to apply, and took way too long to install on the assembly line. That meant they would have to paint the stripes, or set up a special sub assembly line. Apparently, their early efforts trying to paint the stripes had not been successful.

Ford did not know of the transaction, but now we owned the evidence. Ford had built a Cobra II, painting the stripes instead of using our decal tape, wantonly violating our contract.

We confronted Ford, but not in an adversarial manner. We were smart enough to know that building that many cars should be done inside a Ford plant, and we were ready to exchange the program for another one in 1977. We had several ideas for special cars we wanted to show Ford. All we wanted was to continue to be a Ford vendor.

Ford finally confirmed they were planning to take the Cobra II program inside for 1977. Supposedly to make up for the loss of our Cobra II business, Ford asked us to submit ideas for a special Granada, a Maverick, a Ranchero, and a Pinto. Then they hit us with the big one. They were considering buying Motortown and setting up a special division within the Ford Motor Company, where they could build all of these limited production cars when they were appropriate.

Motortown had grown into a multimillion dollar company in less than two years. We really didn't know how to respond to Ford. Our company attorney, cautioned us not to get too excited, and not to forget that Ford certainly knew that we had a good potential lawsuit. "This buyout stuff could be a smokescreen," he said.

While our initial goal had not been to build a career business, we now needed to take a realistic look at ourselves. We realized that this was only a temporary period in the auto industry, and once the burdens of fuel mileage goals, emission controls, and safety regulations eased, the manufacturers would again have more time to devote their own talent to their marketing problems and opportunities. The days of the "Decal GT" were numbered.

The Ford buyout did indeed fade away. Our attorney felt we should really start thinking about a lawsuit. Violating their contract and wiping a little entrepreneurial company right out of business could result in some pretty bad press for Ford, especially around Detroit.

We chose instead to believe Ford and listen to their promises. They then awarded us a small contract to build prototypes of three of the four special cars we had submitted. We envisioned this new business to more than make up for the loss of the Cobra II, but there was a catch. In order to award us any new production contracts, they said we must first sign an agreement promising not to sue them for breech of contract on the Cobra II. We were so "pumped" on the idea of building three new Ford cars that Dave and I readily signed the agreement, much to the disgust of our company attorney and some of our board members. (Today, I think that if we had pressed a lawsuit, chances are we would have won. And even though we would have become "persona non grata" forever at Ford—and possibly the entire industry—both Dave Landrith and myself could have retired.)

When we finished building the 1976 Cobra IIs, all Ford business was pulled from us in a flash. As if that wasn't insult enough, they raided our plant, hiring almost half of our staff to help them build the car. Later versions were no longer a Cobra, but just a dressed-up Mustang. They wanted to offer the stripes in several different colors, which in my opinion was a big mistake. As long as the car was going to be called a Cobra, it should be painted in the American racing colors, white and blue, or blue and white. A red and white, or a green and white striped car may have been attractive, but it sure wasn't a Cobra. That kind of thinking ultimately led to the demise of the car, as it never regained its 1976 sales success. It may not have been a great car, some critics say it wasn't even a good car, but it filled a marketing gap in the Ford lineup at the time, and paved the way for a great Mustang future.

Fortunately, all of Motortown's eggs weren't in the blue oval Ford basket. We had developed an excellent relationship with Chrysler, and were already building a couple of cars: the Volare "Road Runner" for Plymouth, and the Aspen "R/T" for Dodge. While they were basically "tape and decal" coupes, they were packaged around Chrysler's 360 cubic inch "big" small block V-8, and did provide some actual performance. They also served to "hype" the Volare and Aspen image. While not as successful as the Mustang Cobra II, they both lasted longer in the marketplace.

Another project we were doing for Dodge was "The Midnight Charger" (a name I never understood). The marketing goal of this package was to build a true luxury sport feel into the struggling Dodge Charger, which after its 1975 redesign had become nothing more than a Chrysler Cordoba look-alike. The Midnight Charger idea actually came from inside Chrysler, but the car took too much time to build on the assembly line, so they farmed the limited production job out to us.

Business remained brisk at Motortown. One of the most provocative cars we created was for the American Motors Corporation. They were looking to build a more sporty personality into their Hornet Hatchback, which was suffering as part of the conservative Concord Sedan/Wagon family. We proposed a package that included a brushed aluminum roof "Targa Band," a dramatic front air dam, a rear deck spoiler, and most importantly, a cherished

One of Motortown's greatest efforts was submitted to American Motors in 1977, based on their new Pacer station wagon. Building on my experience with the earlier Vega Mini-Van, the "SPacer" was ahead of its time (Dodge wouldn't have their own minivan, for another six years). AMC rejected the concept due to their own failing financial situation. Ironically, they would eventually become part of Chrysler.

name from AMC's past: AMX. The car, known as the Hornet AMX, sold only lukewarm in the marketplace, and probably did more damage than good by infuriating anyone who had fond memories of the original AMX.

Not quite as bad as our experience with Ford, but almost as memorable, was an incident at General Motors. Buick was having trouble getting anybody interested in their Skyhawk Coupe, which was really no more than a Chevy Monza without a V-8 engine. They were looking for a special model that might project a more youthful image. They were rebuffed in their attempt to "buy" the Chevy V-8 engine, so their little hatchback coupe remained only marginally powered by their 231 cubic inch V-6 engine. The marketing folks at Buick liked our proposal, and with a few changes issued a go ahead purchase order, authorizing us to build a prototype. The prototype was quickly approved, and we began planning for production.

Not long after, however, we got a call from our seemingly embarrassed marketing contact at Buick asking us to bring the Skyhawk prototype over to their Styling Studio at the GM Tech Center, for another "review." We delivered the car, and helped wheel it into the GM Styling Dome. It quickly be-

In an attempt to hype one of the first small station wagons, Chevrolet's Vega mini-Nomad program was quite successful. Note special window fillers simulating big Nomad styling, and the skid strips on rear tail gate. In 1977, Chevy dealers, particularly in the southwest, sold several thousand of these.

In 1977, Dodge's Charger was closely associated with its cousin, the staid Chrysler Cordoba (Ricardo Montalban and tag line, "Rich, Corinthian leather"). In an attempt to spice up the Charger's image, Motortown came up with the "Midnight Charger." The company built more than 6,000 of these highly-styled coupes.

came apparent that the Buick marketing folks had tried an end run on their own styling staff, or were just plain naive. None of the Buick styling team had ever seen the car.

We retired to a dark corner, virtually out of sight, as several GM styling execs came to look over the car. They included Chuck Jordan, who had just returned from serving in Europe as head of Opel Styling. Jordan was wearing an extremely well tailored and obviously expensive Italian suit, looking every bit the part of a successful styling executive. He examined the car for maybe ten seconds, threw his head back, and let loose with a "two-bit street corner spit," splattering the little Buick's hood. "Don't you guys know that any car bearing a General Motors name should never be shipped to a dealer without our first approving it," he shouted. "Now take this #@%*& thing out of here, and we'll do another car for you." End of story. GM did style another car, which took way too long and was way too complicated and expensive to build. The entire program turned out to be a loser for everybody involved.

ALTHOUGH MOTORTOWN WAS TAKING up much of my extra time and energy, I had managed to keep up with my consulting assignment with Alex Mair, attending the precious few meetings Ben Harrison and I were able to wangle. We threw one good idea after another at Mair, but we could never get anything sold. Every time we put a good concept in front of him, he complained about the realities of trying to fight it through his own organization.

It was tearing me apart to watch the incredible incompetence at Pontiac. What had once been respected as the great, innovative leader in the industry had now become just another hotbed of "me too" mediocrity. Every car in their line, with the exception of the Firebird and the Grand Prix, was

One of the ideas we submitted to Ford, for a car to replace the Cobra II, The "Boss" Pinto could have been a good promotion.

left to twist in the wind of the marketplace, without support. In 1977, for example, the combination of Firebird and Grand Prix (both Coupes) accounted for almost fifty percent of Pontiac's total sales.

We didn't give up on proposals, and turned our attention to the troubled Le Mans. Since its redesign in 1973, sales had fallen more than 60 percent. The time was now for Mair to step up to the Le Mans or face losing it, sales were that bad.

I call cars like the 1973–77 Le Mans a "five-minute car." If you're a good marketer and have a good understanding of why the consumer is buying your car, you should be able to look at a new car and make a decision in five minutes or less if it will be a winner. The 1973 Le Mans was an easy one. You didn't have to be a designer, or a marketer, or an art director, or an engineer to decide that this car was a loser. Four years later the car still had not been improved.

I was particularly impressed with a show car Pontiac had developed in 1976 under the direction of stylist John Schinella, to be part of the U.S Bicentennial celebration. While proposed as a Grand Am, it would also serve as a hype for the entire Le Mans line. It was called the "All-American Grand Am" and was actually considered for production. Schinella, a real Pontiac enthusiast, was also credited with creating the "Screaming Chicken" decal for the Trans Am, and later would play a big role in the design of the Fiero.

A New Promotion For the Le Mans

Unfortunately, the All-American car did not make it into production. That left us still looking for a way to pump excitement into what had now become a dreadfully boring car line. The Le Mans GT was the sole survivor of the good old days, and it had been reduced to no more than a bizarre two-tone paint job, some special decals, and a 400 cubic inch engine. It had not raised an eyebrow in the marketplace.

In the meantime, the Firebird Trans Am was really coming into its own, selling more than 45,000 units in 1976. With that kind of interest in the smaller Firebird package, I thought we could sustain that same interest with

The 1976 "All-American" Grand Am.

an equally exciting Le Mans that had more room and more comfort. I suggested taking the All-American concept a step above the GT and offer a real controversial Le Mans. It was not the time to be conservative.

We borrowed the "Shaker" hood scoop from the Trans Am and bolted in the T/A 6.6 400-cubic-inch engine. We then hooked up the rugged Turbo Hydra-matic transmission. Inside, we "stole" the highly acclaimed Grand Prix instrument panel, modeled the rear deck spoiler as it had been proposed on the All-American car, and created a wild decal striping package. We dug up a name from the sixties. We called it the Judge, and recommended that the first cars all be painted Carousel Red (right off the 1969 car). Our concept was simple, build a Trans Am with some room in it, and throw in a little bit of the GTO.

The biggest surprise was that Alex Mair actually liked the car—everything but the name and the color, that is. "I think we may have a winner here," he said. "We need to show everybody that this consulting thing is working." (This car was probably the tenth good idea we had put in front of him.) Our program called for the car to be built as a Le Mans Sport Coupe at Pontiac, with the Grand Prix instrument panel, the T/A 6.6 engine, and the special Turbo Hydra-matic transmission. The cars would then be trucked (seven at a time) to the Motortown facility in Troy, Michigan, about 15 miles from Pontiac. Motortown would then finish the car by cutting a hole in the hood to accommodate the scoop, fit the integrated rear deck spoiler, and attach the sophisticated die-cut decal striping. The finished cars would then return to the Pontiac marshalling yard for shipment to the dealer.

Presenting the car to Pontiac management was a tough act. Bill Hoglund was the Division Comptroller and he couldn't see why they had to ship cars "halfway around the world" to get them built. He added further that he didn't see how Pontiac could make any money on these cars. I don't think he could see past the numbers to the image value of the whole program, and that it might just get buyers thinking positively about a pretty cold car called Le Mans.

Mair listened intently to both Hoglund and Sales Manager Jim Vorhes, finally succumbing to their objections, which were mostly to the operation of the program, not to the car itself. Vorhes would probably have objected to any idea brought in by Mair. As a matter of fact, I think both Hoglund and Vorhes kind of liked the car, except for the color and the name.

It looked like another good idea headed down the drain as Mair refused to overrule his staff, that is, until he got into a discussion about the car with his son Steve, who had a better feel for Pontiac than did his dad. A couple of days later, Alex came back to Ben Harrison and myself, wanting to take another look at the car. We all agreed on a replacement color, white, which offended nobody and would nicely accept the red, yellow and orange striping. Ben Harrison then came up with an absolutely perfect new name, "Can Am," which was not only more contemporary but also fit nicely into the Pontiac family.

Can Ams sit outside the Motortown plant, waiting to be picked up for shipment to Pontiac dealers.

In his next management presentation Alex Mair was a "tiger," overcoming every objection and forcing both Hoglund and Vorhes to go along with the program. The Can Am project was approved, and Motortown was awarded a contract to build 2,500 cars. Pontiac stylist John Schinella became very supportive of the car because it was so similar to his special Bicentennial Grand Am show car.

The Motortown facility in Troy was tooled up, special personnel was hired, tooling contracts were awarded, and the program was ready to go. One very difficult procedure that had to be addressed, was the cutting of the hole in the hood to accept the "Shaker" scoop.

The program got off to a good start shortly after the introduction of the new 1977 models. The early cars sold very well, and the interested dealers quickly reordered. Vorhes went on a his annual winter dealer tour with a team of sales execs, visiting every zone. He was greeted with enthusiastic reports on the Can Am as the dealers were asking for more cars. Vorhes returned with potential orders for more than 5,000 cars.

We set up the Pontiac Can Am program with experience we had learned from the Ford Cobra II effort. We built the advertising dollars into the price of the car, enabling us to prepare good showroom literature and an ad for the enthusiast magazines. The first Can Am ad was a real winner, although it violated the rule GM had set down almost ten years earlier. The headline read, "Remember the Goat?", and made a very timely, yet very subtle suggestion that the new Pontiac Can Am was a GTO all over again. We also got some very good reports in the car magazines as we had set up two very special Royal Bobcat-type press cars. The Royal formula still worked. The Can Am was proving exactly what Pontiac needed to re-establish the Le Mans brand.

Alex Mair was so pleased that he directed Motortown to build a prototype for the proposed 1978 Can Am. The 1978 Le Mans introduced a signif-

I was very pleased with the Can Am. Better yet, it was proving everything I had said about what Pontiac needed for the Le Mans; it injected excitement and image back into the brand.

icant engine downsizing program, with Pontiac's new 301 cubic inch V-8 replacing both the 400 and the 350 V-8s. Frankly, the 1978 Can Am looked even better than the 1977 model.

As for myself, it was time to make a change. I was working in conflict of interest by owning the company that was building the Can Am for Pontiac. I officially resigned from MJ&A, making a special effort to explain to Alex Mair personally about the conflict of interest. Alex was pleased that I avoided an "incident," and I really think he was sorry to see me leave.

Advertising Should Chase the Product

It's interesting that even in victory with the Can Am I turned out to be a loser. I picked up a new adversary in Bill Hoglund, who felt he had been put down. Hoglund returned to manage the division in 1980, and in early 1981 he organized the famous Ann Arbor Image Conference. This certainly was a much needed step in the right direction, which hopefully would have linked the floundering division to its great 1960s Wide-Track heritage. I was specifically "uninvited" by Hoglund, and I could only watch from the sidelines when out of the conference came the new advertising theme, "We Build Excitement." Pushing that phrase for the entire 1982 Pontiac line revealed almost a contempt for both the customer and the need to sell a truly sophisticated product. Putting it simpler, all through the 1960s Wide-Track era, Pontiac advertising was constantly struggling to keep up with the product; the cars were great and the customer knew that before we told them. When "We Build Excitement" was introduced, the performance of the product was poor; it was "chasing" the advertising and didn't catch up 'til several years later. Advertising with unrealistic claims results in more customers laughing at you than laughing with you. Unfortunately I was never able to restore communications with Bill Hoglund, who really had many good ideas for Pontiac, but could never seem to implement them.

Motortown was now planning on a 5,000-unit build program, and everything seemed to be going great, until disaster struck. We had already built more than 1,100 cars when we discovered that the rear deck spoiler tooling had cracked. Even worse, it could not be replaced quickly, as we were told it would take 90 days. This meant an immediate interruption in production. Dealer orders had been increasing steadily so Pontiac decided to build ahead. Thus, there were almost 1,000 special white Le Mans Sport Coupes waiting to be shipped to Motortown. Our storage lot was already completely filled, so these cars sat at the factory. As you can imagine, storing almost 1,000 white cars in one place becomes somewhat of a spectacle. Every time management looked out of their office window on this virtual "sea" of white cars, they got more concerned.

We made an alternative proposal, suggesting that Pontiac ship the completed cars without rear-deck spoilers. We would then send the spoiler to the dealers with instructions to complete the simple installation. Pontiac rejected that idea.

There was another agenda working that I didn't pick up on right away. Word was out to the public that the 1978 Grand Prix was going to be downsized, so it seemed that everybody wanted the last of the "big ones." Pontiac was on their way to selling more than 285,000 1977 Grand Prixs, by far the most successful Grand Prix in history. Since the Can Am used the Grand Prix instrument panel, every Can Am built meant one less Grand Prix. This was certainly another good reason to cancel the Can Am program.

The Grand Prix instrument panel that we "stole" for use in the Can Am. Sales success of the Grand Prix eventually put pressure on our supply—and was "instrumental" in Pontiac killing the Can Am project.

The 1977 model was the most successful Grand Prix in history, selling more than 285,000 units.

Less than a week after the spoiler tool cracked, Pontiac pulled the plug. The Le Mans Sport Coupes already built as a part of the program were shipped to the dealer, minus the Can Am features that would have been added at Motortown. My breakthrough Can Am program, hopefully destined to start the Le Mans back on track, had overnight become "Wangers' Folly."

Motortown was acquired by Evans Automotive, who went on to produce several specialty cars. The Pontiac Grand Prix SSJ in 1978 tried to help Pontiac recapture some of the elegance and glamour of their original Grand Prix. Then in 1981, the Grand Prix was lengthened and the styled roof and Targa band concepts worked even better. Sales success in various areas around the country reflected that the public liked these cars and the image they portrayed.

The abrupt cancellation of the Can Am contract really hit hard at Motortown, and led to the decision to sell the company. In early 1978 Motortown Corporation was sold to a large Detroit automotive conglomerate named Evans Industries, who immediately folded it into their Evans Automotive Division.

In many ways, Motortown had been doomed to eventual failure. Our main competitors of the time, American Sunroof Company (sunroofs) and Cars and Concepts (T-tops and sunroofs) were more engineering oriented. They actually altered the chassis or body as necessary. Motortown was basically marketing oriented and would build anything in a limited production quantity as long as it was a bolt-on concept. Over the next few years, the kinds of modifications that ASC and C&C did would become very important to the limited production specialty car business, especially in the development of such models as the Chrysler LeBaron and the Ford Mustang convertibles.

The Can Am debacle leading to the loss of Motortown was hard to swallow. I could have succumbed, but instead I learned from it—a lesson I had to be "hit over the head" with a few times before I took full notice: I should stay out of areas where I have no expertise (like playing dealer, or rear deck spoiler tooling) and concentrate on what I do best, marketing cars.

13

The Consultant

Specials Yet Again

279

EVANS WAS A HUGE CORPORATION, selling everything from parts to service work. One of their subsidiaries was a customizing division specializing in the manufacture of vinyl top packages.

The popularity of vinyl tops and the introduction of GM's full size C-cars like the Cadillac DeVille, the Buick Park Avenue, and the Olds 98 could not have come at a better time. The C-cars had been converted to front wheel drive and had some unusual styling cues. GM's designers didn't seem to know what to do with the greenhouse on these cars. I saw an opportunity for somebody to come in with a vinyl top to improve the look of those cars by changing the configuration of the greenhouse, for example making a four-window out of a six-window sedan. This was all accomplished by using a fiberglass cap that fit over the roof. The cap would then be covered with vinyl.

Evans asked me to sign on with them as a consultant, so I finally took the big step. I formed a firm called Jim Wangers and Associates and went out to drum up business. Surprisingly, I found that because of my reputation and my experience, a little bit of effort went a long way, and it wasn't difficult to find consulting jobs. Evans was very aggressive, going after just about every car make out there.

Another contract I locked up was with Young and Rubicam, the ad agency for Lincoln-Mercury. L-M was trying, unsuccessfully, to market their Capri side-by-side with the very successful new 1979 Mustang. This was the same old Mercury marketing problem: there was nothing really to build image apart from the different nameplate. To generate some excitement in the Capri line I suggested a special model called the Black Cat, which was basically a black car with gold trim. The proposal was approved, the car was on the assembly line and was headed for the marketplace when at the 11th hour they changed the name. Mercury was afraid of the racial overtones and the possibility that they could be criticized for direct purpose marketing at a minority group. The name was changed to Black Magic.

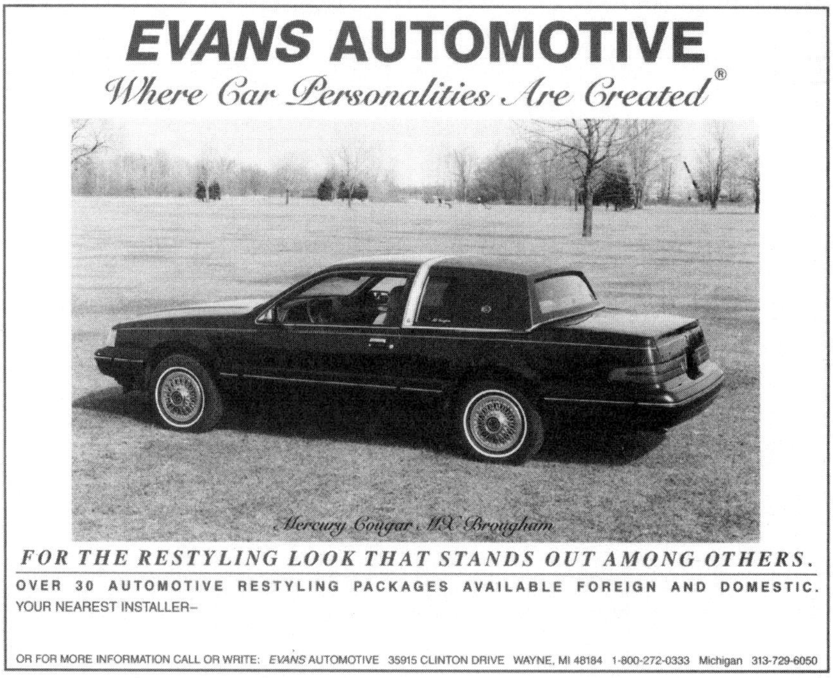

Working With Evans

One of the successful efforts created while consulting with Evans Automotive was this Mercury Cougar MX Brougham, which almost made a different model out of a regular Cougar, simply by adding a vinyl-covered roof cap.

I also took an assignment with Kenyon-Eckhardt, the "new" Chrysler Corporation's new ad agency. While at Ford, Lee Iacocca had befriended K&E's management team who had the Lincoln-Mercury account. When Iacocca came aboard at Chrysler, one of the first things he did was convince K&E to cancel their Lincoln-Mercury contract and take over the entire Chrysler account. While Iacocca brought many of his lieutenants with him from Ford, one particular executive arrived at Chrysler even before him. Hal Sperlich had been a brilliant product man at Ford, and he had a vision for a front-wheel drive "minivan." Henry Ford II wasn't interested in front-wheel drive for his new midsize cars, which were debuting in 1978. This was the platform on which Sperlich wanted to build his minivan. He and Henry Ford II got into a heated discussion about the merits of the project, and Sperlich lost both the project and his job.

Iacocca suggested to John Riccardo, then head of Chrysler, that he take Sperlich aboard. When Sperlich arrived at Chrysler, he discovered the front-wheel drive "K-car" chassis (already on the books, long before Iacocca would tout it as the "savior" of Chrysler) and realized that he now had the platform for his minivan. When Iacocca arrived at Chrysler, he approved the funding to bring the minivan to market. Sperlich's home run pumped millions of dollars into Chrysler's empty coffers and helped bring the company back.

Even before Iacocca released the K-car, the Riccardo administration was building two front drive cars, the Dodge Omni and the Plymouth Horizon. At first, only Plymouth, as the entry level division, was to get the car. But the Dodge dealers screamed so loudly that they shouldn't be cut out of that market that Chrysler went with two versions. Both cars were exactly the same, the only difference being their emblems. They packaged both cars around a Volkswagen drive train. The Omni and the Horizon, though not a resounding success, were the first domestic FWD cars sold in the U.S. market.

The Omni/Horizon program represented a blending of images. Plymouth, up until that time, was still the low priced entry from Chrysler. Dodge had the image of being a step-up statement. These cars were marketed in different Divisional structures; the guys with the blue signs were selling Chryslers and Plymouths and the guys with the red signs were selling Dodge cars and trucks. Both versions started out as four-door models. From the four doors they brought out the nicely styled little coupes. The Omni 2-door was

The Plymouth/Dodge Positioning Mistake

The positioning of the Plymouth nameplate as no more than a Dodge "me-too" lookalike was a serious marketing blunder. Consider the lack of distinction among the models, apart from their names: Volare/ Aspen, Omni/ Horizon, Reliant/ Aires, Sundance/ Shadow, Voyager/ Caravan, and Neon/ Neon, where they didn't even bother to find a separate name. Plymouth was repositioned to compete side-by-side with Dodge, rather than as the compatible entry-level sister, enabling Dodge to assume the logical role of the "step-up" model.

By no longer offering Plymouth as the corporation's low-price statement, Chrysler withdrew from that highly competitive domestic segment, leaving it to be dominated by Ford and Chevrolet. The Plymouth nameplate had always been highly accepted as a viable alternative to low priced Fords and Chevrolets, which was exactly as it was intended by Corporate founder Walter P. Chrysler. In fact, the term "Big Three" first applied to these low-priced nameplates—Ford, Chevrolet, and Plymouth—before becoming the accepted nickname for their Corporate parents.

After the exclusive entry-level image of Plymouth was destroyed, it was a natural follow-up that the market became more confused about the Dodge nameplate. Was Dodge still a bigger and better Plymouth, or was it now simply an alternative that you bought from the guys with the "red signs," rather than the guys with the "blue signs"? The consumer didn't know, and more significantly, didn't care. Somehow, comparing an entry level Ford, Chevy and Dodge didn't sound right, and with new contenders like Saturn, Toyota and Honda in the picture, it became even more confusing.

In order to have a successful mid-price step-up statement, you must first make a strong, entry-level low-price statement. With the repositioning of Plymouth and Dodge, Chrysler was without that dramatic one-two punch.

called the O-24, the Horizon package was the TC-3. My contact at K&E was John Morrisey, with whom I had worked selling the Cobra II to Ford. Morrisey had been lured away from Ford to run the Chrysler account for K&E. Out of our discussions it became apparent that it would be better if I was structured as a consultant. So along with my work with Evans Automotive on vinyl tops, I was given what amounted to a full-time consulting assignment with K&E. I resigned my position with Young and Rubicam because of the obvious conflict of interest. Working with Evans didn't seem to bother anybody. As Jim Wangers and Associates, I put together the idea of developing the Charger 2.2 package. The single overhead cam 2.2 liter engine had been developed for the K-car. I suggested they take the 2.2 engine, which was already scheduled for the lightweight Dodge 024, and design a package that would create a special model. I wanted to include some visuals like an air scoop, a window louvre, and a spoiler, along with some ID striping. With the 2.2 engine and the four-speed manual transmission, the car was a pretty good performer. I suggested it be named the "Charger 2.2," to tie it to the Dodge heritage.

I showed the idea to K&E. They liked it very much and decided to make it their project, and prepared a presentation for Lee Iacocca. The loudest objections came, surprisingly, from Sperlich. I couldn't understand why he was cool to the project, since this was the kind of product marketing he liked. It was so obviously a car that would sell well and was inexpensive to build.

What I would find out later was that Sperlich was overseeing the development of the new turbocharged Chrysler Laser and Dodge Daytona which were to be released in 1983. The back and rear quarter window design on his new Laser and Daytona were embarrassingly similar to the look we had created with the Charger 2.2.

Another factor that compromised the Charger 2.2 was the reemergence of Carroll Shelby. Iacocca had lured his old friend away from Ford and brought him in to be a performance consultant. He would create the 1983 Shelby Charger, which meant the Charger 2.2 ended up as a one-year model. Had the Charger 2.2 followed up with a turbo in 1983, I think it would have been even more successful. The new Shelby had a lot more features and boasted a higher price. I think Chrysler hurt themselves by destroying the momentum they started with the Charger 2.2.

Putting together the Charger 2.2 program for Chrysler and Evans was a huge boost for me professionally. I received credit for the project (which in itself was significant) and helped reinforce my position in the industry, which was something I really needed after the collapse of Motortown.

I wasn't finished with the Charger 2.2 yet, however. It was the only form of competition Chrysler had against the Ford Mustang and the Chevrolet Camaro. While it's hard to imagine the 2.2 liter 4-cylinder Charger as a competitor to these two musclecars, the Charger had one thing going for it. It didn't attract the wrath of insurance companies the way the two more powerful pony cars did. I had a plan.

The Charger 2.2 ad that resulted from the tests against such competition as the Mustang GT and Camaro Z/28.

First Comparative Testing

Under the name of Jim Wangers & Associates, I employed the United States Auto Club (USAC) to do a CVA (Competitive Vehicle Analysis). We got a Mustang, a Camaro, and a Charger 2.2 and rented the Orange County Raceway to do some testing. We found an interesting thing. From a standing start, the Charger 2.2 would out accelerate both cars to 50 mph. For 0–60 mph, no matter how hard we tried we couldn't get the Charger to stay out in front of the other cars, but we could always get a clear-cut win to 50 mph.

I had the times certified by USAC, then the agency's art department designed some ads touting that the Charger 2.2 could beat the Camaro and the Mustang. What was a little tricky about the ads was that the number 5 and the number 6 in the typeface we used were not quite distinctive. They actually showed 0–*50* mph, however, if you read it fast it looked like 0–*60*.

The comparison test developed into a pretty good ad campaign. It was unheard of, a four-cylinder car beating these sporty cars. But the 2.2 was much lighter, had front wheel drive and "grabbed traction." The campaign was so good and so well read that Chrysler got a letter from the Department of Transportation thanking them for recognizing the new 55-mph national speed limit and promoting fun driving with a safety-oriented message!

After the comparison testing, something interesting happened in my relationship with K&E. There was a lot of pre-planning going on towards the introduction of the new Chrysler Laser and Dodge Daytona sport coupes. During a regular press conference, Iacocca stated that the Chrysler Corporation was going to bring to market two of the best performing sport coupes on the U.S. market. It didn't take the press long to challenge Iacocca on his statement. These cars were going to have to be pretty damn quick to beat

The First Front-Wheel Drive Shoe

I always loved tie-ins, and put together another good one with Kinney shoes and the Charger 2.2. We dreamed up a promotion with a shoe they were calling "Chargers," referring to them as "a first front wheel drive shoe." A series of illustrations and diagrams (which never got into an ad, unfortunately) showed that when you walk, you in effect propel yourself forward off the balls of your feet, which is, they claimed, "front wheel drive." They had come up with a front wheel drive shoe which had some reinforcement built into the sole. It could have been a real nice "spoofy" program. The problem, unfortunately, was that Dodge backed out on some of their earlier commitments and the program sputtered to an end.

Camaros and Mustangs. Because the statement had been made by the Chairman of the Board, K&E decided they'd better find out if it was true. And if it was true, then they had better plan to do some serious promoting. In a sense, this was the beginning of the first truly planned aggressive comparison advertising. The Charger 2.2 had been almost tongue in cheek, but it had been so effective that the creative types at the ad agency were anxious to do more performance comparison advertising using the new Daytona and Laser.

This created the obvious need for real testing, much the same as we had done for the Charger. It was then that K&E's comptroller came to me and said, "You know, I think that there's an opportunity here for you to make more money and at the same time, relieve some of our overhead." K&E suggested that I resign as a consultant, terminating my consulting relationship that I had established as Jim Wangers and Associates, then start a new company to buy this testing.

The scenario was that I would hire my own people and bill K&E, not only for my services but also for the expenses incurred in conducting the outside testing. And when we got involved in large projects, they wanted it to be treated as if they were actually buying the project.

That is how Automotive Marketing Consultants, Inc. (AMCI) was born. I was finally going into business for myself, or to be honest about it, I was being forced to go into business. I simply rolled over the company that had been functioning as Jim Wangers and Associates and it became AMCI.

The first employee I hired into AMCI was Al Carpenter, who had helped me a great deal in developing our testing procedures. I had first met Al when he was doing PR work for George Hurst. In fact, one of his early assignments was managing "Miss Hurst Shifter," the very beautiful Miss Linda Vaughn. I had already established a good working relationship with USAC and the National Hot Rod Association (NHRA), both having participated in certification testing on the Dodge Charger 2.2 program.

It was right about this time that a major change was announced in the Chrysler advertising program. The Dodge dealers were upset that only one creative ad agency was handling the entire Chrysler Corporate product line, and insisted that the Dodge Division be allowed to have its own advertising agency. To pacify these important dealers, Chrysler management split the account, returning Dodge to BBDO, the agency that had the account before Iacocca put the entire corporation in K&E's hands. They were awarded both the Dodge car and truck business. Now that Dodge advertising was being handled by a competitive agency, the advertising direction changed. The original "prove Iacocca right" program would now only involve the Chrysler Laser, as the Dodge Daytona creative went off in another direction.

We were able to prove that the Chrysler Laser Turbo did out-perform both the Chevrolet Camaro Z/28 and the Ford Mustang GT. In fact, the Laser even beat the vaunted Porsche 944 in some of the comparisons. The ads were believable and helped launch the new sporty Laser quite successfully, getting it off to a better start than the Dodge Daytona, even though Dodge had a little more defined performance image.

One of the reasons we succeeded was that we "stacked the deck" to some degree. When we selected the Camaro, we made sure it came with the standard 305 cubic inch, low compression V-8 engine, fitted with a regular 4-barrel Quadrajet carburetor. You only got real performance from the Camaro if you ordered the optional Cross-Fire injection engine. If you walked into a Chrysler dealer and ordered a Laser with a turbocharger, you didn't select the turbocharger as an option, you ordered a model called the Chrysler Turbo Laser. We did the same thing with the Mustang GT, selecting the base model with its 2-barrel carbureted 302 cubic inch V-8 engine.

The turbocharged front-wheel drive Chrysler, even though it was only a 4-cylinder, could beat both the Camaro and the Mustang, this time legitimately to sixty mph. The copywriters had to be very sure that every ad stated clearly that all cars were equipped with their "standard" engines.

Chevrolet was understandably upset when they saw the ads. Chrysler's legal department responded quickly and confidently by making the certified USAC test results available. Chevrolet backed down, recognizing that the test was a legitimate comparison of "standard" engines. I'm sure there were a few grumblings around the corporation for offering the Z/28 with such a "wimp" of a standard engine.

AMCI then helped introduce another new Chrysler, the LeBaron GT-S, a high performance five-door sport sedan, powered by the same turbocharged powerplant that had performed so well in the Laser. The Chrysler GT-S held its own against the more sophisticated BMW 528E and Mercedes 190E sport sedans, resulting in a memorable TV commercial where the BMW, in a braking comparison with the faster stopping Chrysler, almost ran off the flight deck of an aircraft carrier.

Shortly after I completed those two comparison programs for Chrysler, I got a call from Campbell-Ewald, the Chevy ad agency. They wanted to talk about a program they were putting together for the 1985 Corvette. When the all-new Corvette had been introduced in 1984, Chevrolet bragged, somewhat recklessly, that it was "The best new sports car on the planet." It didn't take long for the enthusiast press to start poking holes in the Corvette armor. The car had been tardy getting to the marketplace and didn't even offer a manual transmission until late in the 1984 model year. The sportier tuned-port injection engine was held back until 1985, the standard suspension was barely adequate, and the optional Z51 sport suspension rode so hard it could shake your dental fillings loose. The Corvette did perform well in competition, but it was unacceptable as a street package.

Chevrolet was taking a lot of "heat" for their sophomoric advertising puffery. Every one of the car magazines began conducting comparison tests of their own, picking specifically on the automatic transmission, softly suspended Corvette. As you might expect, the car showed up poorly in almost every one of those comparisons. The negative press was quickly tarnishing an otherwise great effort from Chevrolet.

By 1985, the car was retuned from bumper to bumper. Chevrolet was ready to make a major reinvention statement for the Corvette. They wanted to take on all of the self-styled critics and prove once and for all that the new Corvette was indeed a world class sportscar. The team at Campbell-Ewald came to AMCI, impressed with what we had done for the Chrysler Laser. "You beat up on our Camaro Z/28 pretty badly, especially at a time when we didn't need it," they chided. "We were vulnerable, as we are now with our Corvette. We need help, and we need it fast."

We felt that nothing should be held back, so we decided to prove that the new 1985 Corvette could stand up in a performance and handling comparison against great cars like the Lamborghini Countach, the Ferrari 308 GTSI, the Lotus Turbo Esprit, and both the Porsche 928 and 944.

The test program lasted 90 days, and the Corvette performed surprising-

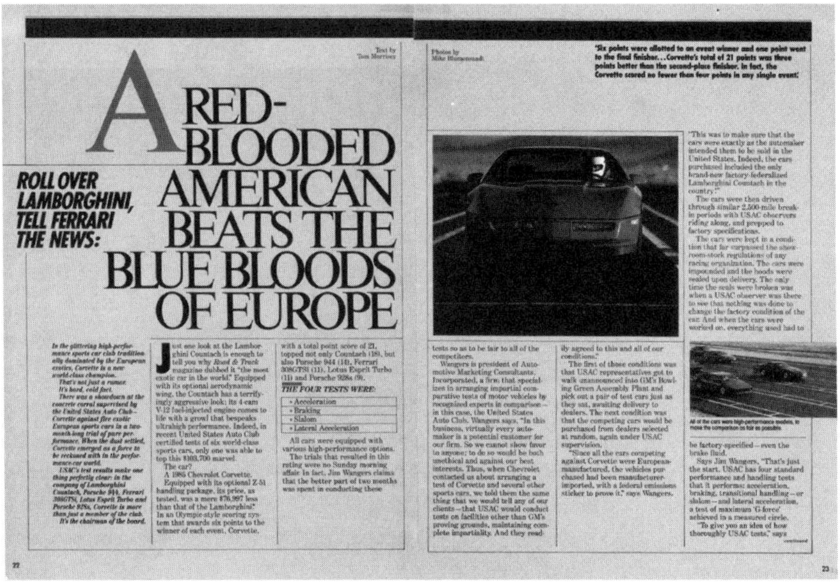

ROLL OVER LAMBORGHINI, TELL FERRARI THE NEWS:

A RED-BLOODED AMERICAN BEATS THE BLUE BLOODS OF EUROPE

In the glittering high-performance sports car club traditionally dominated by the European exotics, Corvette is a new world-class champion.

That's not just a rumor. It's hard, cold fact.

There was a showdown at the concrete corral supervised by the United States Auto Club—Corvette against five exotic European sports cars in a two-month-long trial of pure performance. When the dust settled, Corvette emerged as a force to be reckoned with in the performance-car world.

USAC's test results make one thing perfectly clear: in the company of Lamborghini Countach, Porsche 944, Ferrari 308GTSi, Lotus Esprit Turbo and Porsche 928s, Corvette is more than just a member of the club. It's the chairman of the board.

Just one look at the Lamborghini Countach is enough to tell you why *Road & Track* magazine dubbed it "the most exotic car in the world." Equipped with its optional aerodynamic wing, the Countach has a terrifyingly aggressive look; its 4-cam V-12 fuel-injected engine comes to life with a growl that bespeaks ultrahigh performance. Indeed, in recent United States Auto Club certified tests of six world-class sports cars, only one was able to top this $103,700 marvel.

The car?

A 1985 Chevrolet Corvette.

Equipped with its optional Z-51 handling package, its price, as tested, was a mere $76,997 less than that of the Lamborghini." In an Olympic-style scoring system that awards six points to the winner of each event, Corvette, with a total point score of 21, topped not only Countach (18), but also Porsche 944 (14), Ferrari 308GTSI (11), Lotus Esprit Turbo (11) and Porsche 928s (9).

THE FOUR TESTS WERE:

- Acceleration
- Braking
- Slalom
- Lateral Acceleration

All cars were equipped with various high-performance options.

The trials that resulted in this rating were no Sunday morning affair. In fact, Jim Wangers claims that the better part of two months was spent in conducting these tests so as to be fair to all of the competitors.

Wangers is president of Automotive Marketing Consultants, Incorporated, a firm that specializes in arranging impartial comparative tests of motor vehicles by recognized experts in comparison—in this case, the United States Auto Club. Wangers says, "In this business, virtually every automaker is a potential customer for our firm. So we cannot show favor to anyone; to do so would be both unethical and against our best interests. Thus, when Chevrolet contacted us about arranging a test of Corvette and several other sports cars, we told them the same thing that we would tell any of our clients—that USAC would conduct tests on facilities other than GM's proving grounds, maintaining complete impartiality. And they readily agreed to this and all of our conditions."

The first of those conditions was that USAC representatives got to walk unannounced into GM's Bowling Green Assembly Plant and pick out a pair of test cars just as they sat, awaiting delivery to dealers. The next condition was that the competing cars would be purchased from dealers selected at random, again under USAC supervision.

"Since all the cars competing against Corvette were European-manufactured, the vehicles purchased had been manufacturer-imported, with a federal emissions sticker to prove it," says Wangers.

"Six points were allotted to an event winner and one point went to the final finisher...Corvette's total of 21 points was three points better than the second-place finisher. In fact, the Corvette scored no fewer than four points in any single event."

"This was to make sure that the cars were exactly as the automaker intended them to be sold in the United States. Indeed, the cars purchased included the only brand-new factory-federalized Lamborghini Countach in the country."

The cars were then driven through similar 2,500-mile break-in periods with USAC observers riding along, and prepped to factory specifications.

The cars were kept in a condition that far surpassed the showroom-stock regulations of any racing organization. The cars were impounded and the hoods were sealed upon delivery. The only time the seals were broken was when a USAC observer was there to see that nothing was done to change the factory condition of the car. And when the cars were worked on, everything used had to be factory-specified—even the brake fluid.

Says Jim Wangers, "That's just the start. USAC has four standard performance and handling tests that it performs: acceleration, braking, transitional handling—or slalom—and lateral acceleration, a test of maximum 'G-force' achieved in a measured circle.

"To give you an idea of how thoroughly USAC tests," says

The story of Chevrolet's Corvette comparison against a Ferrari, Lamborghini, Porsche, and Lotus.

Product Comparison Testing: It Wasn't Always

One of the things that frustrated me by during the "glory days" of the sixties was the inability to make any head-to-head performance comparisons in advertising. We struggled with this all through the most competitive horsepower race in American auto industry history. Every advertiser, not just the automakers, were forbidden to mention a competing product by name in their advertising, which gave birth to the meaningless term "Brand X." This rule was policed by the Federal Trade Commission (FTC).

Then came the late seventies, when the soft drink wars were heating up. The bottlers wanted to do some aggressive "taste test" campaigns, which naturally called for head-to-head brand name comparisons, so they petitioned the FTC for relief, and won.

Once this hard-and-fast rule had been overturned, I immediately saw it as the breakthrough I had been waiting for. My new company, AMCI, along with the United States Auto Club, won approval from the FTC to allow all automakers the right to use head-to-head comparisons in their advertising. The conditions under which the testing was to be performed, which we submitted as part of our petition, are still in use today. Such things as vehicle acquisition, break-in methods, weather and track surface monitoring, and even driver techniques are but a few of the procedures that must be a part of every test. Today, head-to-head performance testing plays an important role in automotive marketing. I'm sure glad I got there first.

ly well. It got beat in some tests, but it won many others. In their advertising, Chevrolet wisely showed their defeats as well as their wins, which added a level of believability and credibility to the entire program. Certainly, these side-by-side comparisons did a marvelous job of restating the Corvette in a world of competitive sportscars.

By now, AMCI had become a well recognized vendor in the Detroit automotive community for conducting certified comparison testing. We broke new ground in developing techniques and procedures necessary to perform these highly critical tests, using state-of-the-art electronic non-contact sensor equipment, manned by highly competent personnel.

After the Corvette comparison campaign, I formed a marketing alliance with USAC, representing them as their exclusive marketing arm. For example, whenever they received an inquiry for a test program, they turned it over to AMCI, and whenever AMCI was called in to perform a test, we always invited USAC to certify. This exclusive marketing alliance resulted in a surge of activity and growth.

All of the industry's legal departments developed a trust and confidence in AMCI testing integrity. At the same time, the network television people responsible for screening proposed commercials were pleased when they saw an AMCI Certification Report accompany a comparison test ad.

Since its early days, AMCI has earned a good reputation, not only for intensive state-of-the-art comparison testing, but also for its ability to do a Competitive Vehicle Evaluation program, advising a client how their vehicle stands up to its competition.

The concept of product comparisons in sales training was not new, although by the eighties it had deteriorated to a textbook kind of banal analysis, based on published public data. In many ways, it was exactly like what I had done for General Motors way back in 1975 for what I called "The Ashtray Grand Prix," and it was still just that. It reached the absurd point where everybody lined up their "ashtrays" for a big comparison. Whoever had the deepest ashtray or the widest ashtray or the easiest to operate ashtray had the best comparison story to tell. Using that same logic, the manufacturer would then say, "Because I've got the best ashtray, I obviously have the best car."

In addition to using that logic in their consumer advertising, many of the carmakers used it to train their retail sales personnel, many times insulting them, certainly boring them. Equipping a new breed of educated sales consultants with both informative and meaningful dynamic product information, and doing it in an entertaining way, was the format for good sales training. Selling to a much more educated and informed consumer, who wants to know more about performance, handling, driving experience and safety characteristics, is not an easy task. These consultants needed to have driven and been trained not only on their product, but on all the competitive products in their segment.

This kind of training and driving experience will reveal that their product is not always the best in its class. It may not have the quickest acceleration, or the smoothest ride, it may not stop as well as some of its competitors, or it may even be noisier. But, in order to be an effective sale consultant, they must know this. They must not only be aware of the competitive realities of their car, but they must then be taught how to sell against that deficiency, especially when their customer brings it up. Presenting a larger, easier to operate "ashtray" no longer prepares a sales consultant to greet the "new" consumer.

In expanding AMCI's staff, I added a couple of "young lions," who not only liked cars, but also understood the new generation of automotive consumer. My nephew, Gordon Wangers, west coast marketer David Stokols, and experienced automotive test driver Gary Thomason, brought to AMCI a new dimension, enabling us to take full advantage of our familiarity with just about every automotive product offered for sale in the U.S. marketplace. Today, these guys run the company and I'm just having fun.

As the guy who once was afraid to break out of that "warm womb" of big company security, I can only look back at the gamble of going into business for myself and see the tremendous luck and help I have had in growing AMCI. In my "glory days" of the sixties, when I used to think about what I would do when it came time to retire, never in my wildest dreams did I think that I would one day be awash in all kinds of exciting cars as part of AMCI's comparison testing and product evaluation process.

Me retire? Are you nuts?

14

Why the Tiger Roared: Sellin' Cars Isn't Like Selling Toothpaste

IN THE AUTO INDUSTRY TODAY, conventional wisdom states that selling cars is no different from selling dishwasher detergent. The accepted business plan is that establishing a brand, and managing that brand, is the same, whatever the product. Brand management is not a new approach to automotive marketing. Long before brand management came into fashion, there were visionaries in Detroit—John DeLorean was one, Bunkie Knudsen another—who understood the importance of establishing a brand image for a car line. The difference between then and now, however, is that in the sixties we were trying to establish *Divisional* advertising themes. The different Divisions within GM, Ford, and Chrysler were all imaged apart from each other.

The best all-time example of brand imaging is the theme line "Wide-Track," used by the Pontiac Division. Starting with an all-new car in 1959, the term was first introduced as "Wide-Track" wheels, which ultimately grew to become Wide-Track Pontiac. Every communication we did, whether an ad, promotional poster, or catalog, we always referred to the car as the Wide-Track Pontiac.

These theme lines were built around product features. The track width was something you could actually see in a Wide-Track Pontiac. As the cars grew more exciting with increased performance and cutting-edge styling, the Wide-Track Pontiac theme began to stand for more than just a feature, it became a signature for the entire Division.

Once we gave a car line an image, we built on that image with each new model as it was added to the line. Today, that's called brand imaging, but the approach is different. In today's structure, each model within a product line has its own brand manager, who develops an imaging strategy totally separate from other products in the Division. This new approach was introduced to the Detroit community by GM, and has been picked up in varying adaptations by Ford and Chrysler, as well as Toyota and Nissan. GM aggressively pursued their brand marketing concept by hiring experienced marketing people from outside the automotive community, many of them with a history of packaged goods experience. They have embraced the packaged goods marketing practice of selling several similar products under different brand names.

In that situation, the concept of individual product brand management is a must. They certainly don't want to brag that there are several brands of Proctor and Gamble toothpaste, or many different breakfast cereals all marketed by Kellogg's, or all kinds of soft drinks bottled by Coca-Cola. Each of these packaged products is sold as an exclusive brand, and not aggressively connected to the corporate parent. Promoted and packaged individually, they sit side-by-side on the same shelf, looking as different as possible from their sibling brands. For packaged goods like toothpaste and breakfast cereal, the science of brand management has been well proven.

The point of imaging each brand is to make them appear to be independent products. When you are exposed to a communication from a toothpaste manufacturer, whether it be an advertising coupon, TV commercial, or magazine ad, the package is clearly identified. The manufacturer hopes that the very color of the package will excite positive thoughts about the taste, or about the health benefits of a special ingredient, that is so much a part of that particular brand. The next time you are in the supermarket, staring at the toothpaste shelf, consider how those communications may have prompted you to make an impulse purchase, spending $2 or $3. That positive image popped into your head, struck a bell of familiarity, and resulted in a decision to select that particular brand that time.

Take the example of soap marketer Tide. They are convinced, and have significant research to prove, that the color of their box, whether seen on TV, or in a magazine, or even on the side of a race car, is a key part of the public's making the choice to take Tide off the shelf.

This works for selling toothpaste, breakfast cereal, or soft drinks, but does it work for automobiles? Frankly, I don't think so.

Certainly you don't make an impulse decision to acquire an automobile. You may have an impulse to look at a different manufacturer's cars as a result of some sort of advertising communication, but the final decision to purchase is another matter. Consider that you already own a specific brand, or that your neighbor is boasting about his recent choice, or that your mechanic says Yes to your choice while your favorite car magazine says No. Choosing a new car is certainly not an impulse.

All of this builds to a specific point. The current thinking among GM's brand marketing people is to build brand image into each individual model. Again, consider Pontiac. In 1997, the redesigned Grand Prix was introduced as the Widetrack Grand Prix, with the copy line "Wider Is Better." This successful effort thrust the great Wide-Track Pontiac brand image back into the marketplace from which it had been absent for 25 years, yet it was still so strong that it was enthusiastically accepted, almost as if it had never gone away. And yet, I could hardly believe that Pontiac's next new car introductions, specifically the Firebird, Grand Am, and Bonneville, would not be marketed under the WideTrack banner.

This is a serious marketing mistake. You can't isolate each car line in a Divisional family and build a strong image for each model, especially when the divisional image is so strong, as is the Widetrack label. As powerful as the name Bonneville or Grand Prix or Trans Am are in the marketplace, they don't have the same impact as the name Wide-Track Pontiac.

The intermingling of brand and product image at Pontiac in the sixties went beyond advertising and promotion. It also included styling. Consumers knew immediately that they were looking at a Pontiac, whether a sporty Firebird, luxury Bonneville, or common-sense Le Mans, thanks to a distinctive grille and aggressive styling. They were all part of the family of Wide-Track Pontiacs, which had come to mean sophistication, performance, excitement, safety, handling, and comfort. We didn't call it brand marketing or brand imaging (there were no brand managers to report to), nor did we attempt to make a science out of it. We were surrounded by people who understood and liked cars.

In those days the Division was run by passionate men with a genuine savvy for what the market wanted. They came from the car business. I can tell you that nobody better than Pontiac is in a position to re-invent that experience today. More than packaged goods, the automobile is an ever-changing, dynamic product. While features may change, every new car will still require sophisticated marketing to separate one car from the rest of the pack. Even though the product changes, nothing changes in communication.

Take some final examples. Throughout the fifties and sixties, Oldsmobile had well established their "Rocket" theme. It was always assumed that every Olds had a Rocket engine. In 1977, Olds sales were far above projections, and production of the standard 350 Rocket V-8 fell short. To keep customers satisfied, they arranged to buy V-8 engines from Chevrolet, but still put the same Rocket 88 decal on the air cleaner. Even they didn't appreciate the power of their own rocket image. When it was discovered that it wasn't a real Rocket V-8, all hell broke loose. Even though the substitute-engine cars were satisfying to drive, they weren't legitimate Olds Rockets. The result was a class action lawsuit and extreme embarrassment for both Oldsmobile and GM. The public didn't forget, but Oldsmobile did, and are still trying to find a new theme to re-image the Division.

Or Cadillac, whose image through the sixties was accepted as the "Standard of the World," which was another way of saying, "We are the best." Of course, this was before competition from the luxury imports became a factor. Cadillac had to drop the line, because there was no way they could prove they were the "standard of the world." Cadillac, too, is searching to find another appropriate theme.

Finally, there is the problem of a brand image being too strong. That's the dilemma that recently plagued Volkswagen in the U.S. When they first came to this country, the Beetle was their only product, and it quickly became known as the Volkswagen. When the highly imaged vehicle became a success, that success belonged to a car named Volkswagen, not to a model called the Beetle or Bug. When the Beetle fell from favor in the marketplace, both the Beetle product and the Volkswagen nameplate suffered. It was difficult for VW to market another vehicle. When the public heard the name Volkswagen, they immediately thought only of the Beetle, and their like or dislike of that car. The first Beetle replacement, the Rabbit, encountered stiff sales resistance. It was not a Beetle, nor did it match the perceived image of a car called Volkswagen. It took VW almost two decades to wipe out the memory of the Beetle and re-establish sales success with a replacement product. Today, it is almost ironic that VW is marketing a New Beetle by making specific reference to the original. It will be a tough job to ensure that the image of the old Beetle does not overpower their newly successful Volkswagen image.

Regardless of how many decades have gone by, no matter how the culture evolves, no matter how sophisticated the medium becomes, one thing is irrevocably true: the names Pontiac and Wide-Track share an intimacy that can't be cancelled. For an automobile, the Widetrack Pontiac is perhaps the most powerful and successful brand image ever created.

Afterword: Preserving The Legend

IN THE SUMMER OF 1980, I WAS INVITED by the Pontiac Oakland Club International to be a guest speaker at their convention, in Gettysburg, Pennsylvania. Having never been to one of these events, I really didn't know what to expect. It was the first time I had any interaction with this new generation of Pontiac collectors and I found it to be a perfectly delightful experience. I was so pleased that I was able to tell them something new about their car that they had not known before.

It was hard to believe that just six short years after the Pontiac GTO expired in the marketplace I was attending an event where enthusiastic collectors were showing off the famous car. In the car business, when a model is eliminated, you forget about it, replacing it with another model, hoping the public will forget about it too. That's the business I had always been in. I hadn't really become aware of the enormous grassroots growth of the restoration hobby.

Preservation of the Pontiac GTO and its legacy really started in the mid-seventies, as budding hobbyists began to "freshen up" their first generation (1964–67) cars. All they had for inspiration and guidance was the Antique Automobile Club of America (AACA) and the already flourishing Chevrolet Corvette restoration hobby. Both of these groups looked down upon the GTO enthusiast as a blue-collar, knuckle-busting amateur who didn't have the faintest idea what restoration was all about. Even more, they didn't have a car worth restoring. To them, the GTO (and most other musclecars of the sixties) were nothing more than "used cars."

Nonetheless, persevering GTO owners continued to seek out and restore these early models. They were actually quite affordable in those days, thanks in part to the nagging fuel crisis and the perception that these cars were gas guzzlers (which they were). They had also hit the bottom of their depreciation cycle. There were quite a few original owners who had babied

GTOs take to the famous track at a GTOAA national meet in Indianapolis, Indiana.

their Goats from the first day These cream puffs became a very important part of the hobby as they gave inspiration and encouragement to the new group of collectors.

It didn't take long for the GTO hobby to catch on. Restoration books, appearing in the early eighties, catapulted the idea of restoring a GTO to nearly equal that of the Corvette. The restorers were either totally dedicated to originality or to just adding the factory options that turned their GTO into the way they would have ordered it new. An original "Royal Bobcat" emblem for example, was worn with great pride.

The first of the modern Pontiac owners clubs, The Pontiac Oakland Club International (POCI) was established in 1972 to preserve all Pontiac cars and their history. GTO owners became a significant part of their membership. A new club, dedicated solely to the GTO, The GTO Association of America(GTOAA), was established in 1979 and it, too, enjoyed rapid growth. GTO restoration continued to get more sophisticated as a set of judging standards developed by the upstart GTOAA raised the level of restoration quality to a point where it surpassed every other musclecar club in the country.

While most American carmakers were only casual about their heritage, Pontiac had always demonstrated a genuine concern about their great cars of the past. Part of that concern was apparent in 1989 when, thanks to the efforts of Jim Mattison, a longtime GM employee and a real Pontiac enthusiast, arrangements were made to establish the Pontiac Historical Services. Completely independent from parent Pontiac, PHS can document the authenticity of all Pontiac cars built since 1961. Once supplied with a vehicle identification number (VIN), this information is matched to a Dealer Invoice and the vehicles's "Billing History," sheet. These two documents confirm the legitimacy of both the car and the options installed when it was built. Jim Mattison and his Pontiac Historical Services have saved many Pontiac collectors from investing large sums of money into bogus cars.

There are three specific Pontiacs that are most often misrepresented. The entire 1964–65 GTO production was built as a Le Mans with the GTO option, therefore requiring the Dealer Invoice or "Billing History" sheet to verify that the car was actually built as a legitimate GTO. Converting a same-year Le Mans may look the part, but it sure ain't a legit Goat, and therefore is worth a lot less money. The second most potential phony is a 1969–71 Judge optioned car. All of them (Hardtops and Convertibles) were built as regular GTOs with the Judge option. The VIN would show it only as a GTO, but the Dealer Invoice or Billing History documents will verify the car as having been built with the Judge option. The third most common Pontiac fakes involve the first three years of the Firebird. All Firebird V-8 cars carry the same VIN identification. Again, only the Dealer Invoice or Billing History will identify that the car was built as either a base Firebird V8, a Firebird H.O., or as a Firebird 400, for example.

Preventing "Fake" Cars

Mattison, who is officially referred to as a Pontiac Historian and Advisor, reports that as these precious Pontiacs get older, they get harder to find and are more prone to be faked. "I'll estimate that better than 50% of the Judge requests we get now are not legitimate, and close to 75% of the 1964 and 1965 GTOs we check are bogus," he said matter-of-factly. "This business is not always fun. One of the toughest jobs I ever had was to tell a guy who had inquired about his 1969 Judge Convertible that the VIN he sent us clearly proved that the car was indeed built as a Judge...Hardtop!"

The incredible increase in value of these sixties musclecars began to attract investors looking for quick money. After the temporary collapse of the stock market in 1987, many of these investors who were not knowledgeable car enthusiasts left the market in search of more tangible investments. Collector cars of all kinds became a fad, with big money changing hands for Ferraris, Lamborghinis, Porsches, and other exotic nameplates. American musclecars were part of this dizzying spiral. Exotic, hard-to-find cars like L88 Corvettes, LS6 Chevelles, or Plymouth Hemi Road Runners, as well as specialty cars like Yenko Camaros and Royal Bobcat Pontiacs commanded ridiculous money. Pontiac's 1971 Judge convertible, a car they couldn't give away in 1971 with only 17 having been built, became a collector's dream. For a while, these cars were the talk of the investment world. Of course, they weren't worth the prices that were paid, but it was a true indication of how inflated the market had become.

Just like any inflated market, it had to tumble. Less than two years after the stock market crash in 1987 the bottom dropped out of the collector car market. Many investors suddenly found themselves owning cars worth half the price they had paid for them. When the dust cleared, one thing remained, the hobbyist. The very people who had built the GTO (and musclecar) hobby as a labor of love were still there. They were ready to continue preserving the legend, not only as a financial investment, but as an emotional investment in a great automotive legacy.

If there was a benefit from the surge of investor interest in American musclecars, it was the explosive growth of the restoration industry, including companies responsible for reproduction parts. The availability of these parts has guaranteed the serious restorer that there will be a supply of correct parts for years to come, allowing these collector cars to be more than just museum pieces. You should drive and enjoy these cars, just as their original owners did when they were new.

Involvement with these restored cars has created a new culture and a new social life, as new owners found they had a lot in common. They enjoyed each other's company as they went on cruises, took tours, and even attended national conventions. Many local clubs devote a great deal of time and energy raising funds for a variety of charitable causes. Since that first trip to Gettysburg in 1980, I've been lucky enough to have been invited to speak all over the world, in the U.S., Mexico, Canada, Australia, and even Europe. Everywhere I go, I find people intensely devoted to the hobby and to their cars.

The attraction of these old cars also includes an interest in old ads, catalogs, posters, or other dealership paraphernalia. Any trivia involving the Tiger is exceptionally valuable, as is memorabilia about Royal Pontiac or other participants in the great Super Duty days. Original copies of old 45 rpm

Even in Australia there's Pontiac fever. This car was converted to right-hand drive—for a cost—immediately after it was unloaded from the ship. Getting caught on the road in Australia with a left-hand drive car results in an unbelievably high fine, maybe even a prison sentence.

A GTO club meet brings out the best of Pontiac's famed four-wheeled legacy.

records of "GTO," or "GeeTO Tiger," or even "Wide Trackin'" are particularly appealing. The 1964 hit "GTO" has even recently been re-released.

One thing that always overwhelmed me is the quality of restoration I see at every show. Row after row of magnificent Pontiac cars proudly stand at attention, dressed and polished just as they were thirty or forty years ago as new cars. These treasures are indeed playing their part in "preserving the legend."

Today, the hobby is much bigger than just the appreciation of sheet metal. It is now a cultural experience, where every member enjoys the fantasy of reliving the "Good Ol' Days." Everyone has a story to tell about the time they got into it with a Road Runner or an SS 396 down Main Street, or the first time they were out alone with a girlfriend in lover's lane. All of the neat things that were part of Americana during the sixties come to life at these gatherings.

As a matter of fact, I have one memory that I often relive myself, of an experience that taught me a lesson I will never forget. It happened early in my travels. I was at the famous "Straits Area Antique Auto Show," in St. Ignace, Michigan, where I had been invited to be a guest speaker. While touring the show I was attracted to a row of especially beautiful Pontiacs. The proud owners recognized me, and graciously invited me to join their group. After a warm exchange of greetings, they began firing questions at me, which I frankly love. As the exchange became more relaxed and intimate, I too relaxed, stepping back to rest against a car. The pleasant conversation went on for another ten minutes or so, when we all agreed "we had to go," and began to drift apart. After many handshakes, and even an autograph or two, I overheard the owner of the absolutely flawless dark blue 1967 GTO Convertible that I had been comfortably resting against say, "I wonder how much a genuine Jim Wangers assprint will improve the value of my car?" If that's not preserving the legend, I don't know what is.

My personalized Michigan license plate adorns one of my all-time favorite cars, a 1965 post Coupe.

Index

Art Credits

N.W. Ayer: insert p. 1

Leo Burnett Co.: 171

Car and Driver: 106, 251; insert p. 10 (bottom)

CECO Publishing Co.: 286

Chevrolet (Campbell-Ewald advertising): 20, 23, 29,

Chiat-Day/Nissan: insert p. 32

Chrysler Corporation: 32, 185 (top), 225, 270 (bottom), 283; insert p. 29 (bottom)

Dodge (Grant Advertising): 34

Ford Motor Co.: 263, 266

MPC Models: 172, 173

Petersen Publishing Co.: 129

Plymouth (N.W. Ayer & Co.): 35

Pontiac (DMB&B): ii, 64, 79 (bottom), 85, 94, 99, 100, 102, 109, 118, 119, 121, 124, 126 (bottom), 127, 138, 156, 160, 161, 166, 175, 176, 180, 187 (top), 189, 192, 194, 195, 197, 198, 202, 204; insert p. 2, 5–7, 9, 12 (bottom), 14, 17–22, 25 (top), 28 (top), 30 (top)

Pontiac P.R.: 41, 51, 52, 53, 54, 69, 89, 93, 111, 126 (top), 132, 137 (top), 145 (left), 147 (top), 150, 162, 163, 165, 167, 179, 185 (bottom), 186, 200, 205, 211, 227, 230, 232, 233, 235 (bottom), 236, 237, 256, 258, 259, 272; insert p. 23 (top)

Eric Schiffer: 101, 123

J. Walter Thompson: 147 (bottom)

Jim Wangers Collection: iii, 2, 3, 4, 6, 17, 21, 44, 61, 68, 73, 76, 77, 79 (top), 82 (courtesy Harry Wesch), 84, 90, 108, 120, 130, 133, 134 (courtesy Mellville Shoe Corp.), 137 (bottom), 140, 142, 143 (courtesy John Kosmala), 145 (right), 146 (courtesy Dick Nesbitt), 148, 152, 191, 199, 235 (top, courtesy *High Performance Cars*), 243, 244, 245, 247, 261, 265, 269, 270 (top), 271, 274, 275, 280, 296, 298; insert p. 3 (bottom), 4, 8, 10 (top), 11 (courtesy *Pontiac Enthusiast*), 12 (top), 13, 15, 16, 24, 25 (bottom), 26–27, 28 (bottom), 30 (bottom)

Wells, Rich & Green: 224; insert p. 32 (top)

Paul Zazarine Collection: 47, 98, 139, 151, 153, 177, 187 (bottom), 190, 196, 228, 234, 294, 297; insert p. 11

About The Authors

Jim Wangers is that rare combination of automotive enthusiast and automobile executive who was in the industry at the right place and the right time. After stints at Kaiser-Frazer, Chevrolet and Chrysler, Wangers joined Pontiac's advertising agency in 1958, just as Pontiac's new and aggressive management was turning over the division's staid image in place of youthful performance. His intimate knowledge of what excited performance enthusiasts allowed Wangers to transmit their passion to the managers and engineers at Pontiac, who in turn developed products like the legendary GTO, Catalina 2+2, Firebird 400, and The Judge.

In the early 1970s Wangers left Pontiac and struck out on his own, opening a Chevrolet store in Milwaukee. He soon discovered retail was not for him, and he returned to Detroit to became a highly respected consultant for Chrysler, Ford and GM. He established Automotive Marketing Consultants, Inc. in 1981.Now living in California, Wangers travels thousands of miles every year to attend shows and races while constantly adding to his collection of Wide-Track Pontiacs.

Ever since he was a child, **Paul Zazarine** has been in love with cars. In school, when other kids dreamed of being jet pilots or firemen, Zazarine wanted to road test cars for *Motor Trend*. For over 20 years, Zazarine has been restoring and writing about musclecars. His books include *How To Restore Your Musclecar, GTO Buyer's Guide*, and *1964–1967 GTO History and GTO Restoration Guide*, which won a Moto Award for the Best Automotive Technical Book of 1985. From 1985 to 1988 he edited *Musclecar Review* magazine until being tapped to relaunch and edit *Corvette Fever* magazine. He also launched *Mopar Muscle* magazine in 1988.

As editor of *Corvette Fever*, Zazarine was involved in a number of hobby activities. Most important to him was serving for five years as a member of the board of directors of the National Corvette Museum, and being part of the team that saw the museum dream become reality on Labor Day 1994. Today Zazarine works as a writer/editor from his home in Florida, where he lives with his wife Liz and their two Corvette roadsters.

Dana Forrester painting series: 14" x 22" personally signed and numbered prints available from Jim Wangers. For more information call (800) GTO-1964.